OUR BELOVED FRIEND

Our Beloved Friend

The Life and Writings of Anne Emlen Mifflin

Gary B. Nash and Emily M. Teipe

THE PENNSYLVANIA STATE UNIVERSITY PRESS
UNIVERSITY PARK, PENNSYLVANIA

Library of Congress Cataloging-in-Publication Data

Names: Nash, Gary B., author. | Teipe, Emily M., author. | Mifflin, Ann Emlen, author.
Title: Our beloved friend : the life and writings of Anne Emlen Mifflin / Gary B. Nash and Emily M. Teipe.
Description: University Park, Pennsylvania : The Pennsylvania State University Press, [2022] | Includes bibliographical references and index.
Summary: "A biography of the elite Philadelphia Quaker and early reformer Anne Emlen Mifflin, along with her annotated collected writings and selected correspondence"— Provided by publisher.
Identifiers: LCCN 2022032449 | ISBN 9780271093888 (hardback) | ISBN 9780271093895 (paper)
Subjects: LCSH: Mifflin, Ann Emlen. | Quaker women—Pennsylvania—Philadelphia—Biography. | Society of Friends—Clergy—Biography. | Society of Friends—Pennsylvania—Philadelphia—History—18th century. | Society of Friends—Pennsylvania—Philadelphia—History—19th century. | LCGFT: Biographies.
Classification: LCC BX7795.M47 N37 2022 | DDC 289.6092 [B]—dc23/eng/20220810
LC record available at https://lccn.loc.gov/2022032449

Copyright © 2022 Gary B. Nash and Emily M. Teipe
All rights reserved
Printed in the United States of America
Published by The Pennsylvania State University Press,
University Park, PA 16802–1003

The Pennsylvania State University Press is a member of the Association of University Presses.

It is the policy of The Pennsylvania State University Press to use acid-free paper. Publications on uncoated stock satisfy the minimum requirements of American National Standard for Information Sciences—Permanence of Paper for Printed Library Material, ANSI Z39.48–1992.

CONTENTS

Foreword | vi
CORDELIA FRANCES BIDDLE
Acknowledgments | ix
List of Abbreviations | xiii
Editorial Apparatus | xv

Introduction | 1

Part 1: A Quaker Life

1   The Early Years, 1755–1778 | 17
2   A Season of Trials, 1778–1788 | 43
3   Faith in Action, 1788–1798 | 66
4   A Widow's Ministry in the New Nation, 1798–1804 | 87
5   Serving the Church Militant, 1805–1816 | 114
    Epilogue | 132

Part 2: Writings and Testimonies

6   My Religious Progress | 141
7   Radical Pacifism | 186
8   Antislavery | 194
9   Our Native Brethren | 200

Part 3: Correspondence

10 Letters Among Friends, 1776–1799 | 229
11 Letters to Family and Friends, 1800–1813 | 269

Image Gallery | 309
Appendix | 320
Bibliography | 322
Biographical Note: Gary B. Nash, 1933–2021 | 339
CYNTHIA SHELTON

Index | 341

FOREWORD

Gary B. Nash and Emily M. Teipe's *Our Beloved Friend: The Life and Writings of Anne Emlen Mifflin* shines a welcome light on a woman intricately involved in colonial America's quest for independence. A member of the Society of Friends, Anne Emlen Mifflin followed a long tradition of female ministers active in a religious community that upheld gender parity. Her righteous indignation over the cruelties of slavery, and her pleas for abolition, which were met by platitudes or opposition, further distanced her from the patriarchy of the Revolutionary War era and the emergent leadership of a new statehood. She needed (and had) an indomitable spirit in order not to react in anger.

As a descendant of the Biddle family (originally Byddyl) that fled England to escape persecution as Quakers, I view Anne as an intellectual heir to the early firebrands like Esther Biddle (variously spelled Hester or Ester, d. 1697), who traveled widely throughout her native England, as well as Europe and the Caribbean, preaching a steadfast belief in the Friends' understanding of God's desire for earthly justice and peace. The majority of the colonial Biddles became Anglicans and eventually Episcopalians when the Episcopal Church formally separated with the Church of England over the issue of giving fealty to Britain's monarch. In Philadelphia, the Quaker Emlens and Episcopalian Biddles were neighbors intent on forging a new nation. Given how polarized twenty-first-century America has become, contemplating the members of one faith supporting another—which was true also of interactions with Philadelphia's Jewish community—brings a welcome sense of relief. Nash and Teipe's work manifests faith at its zenith laboring mightily for the common good.

The authors are uniquely qualified to document their subject's life, as well as the turbulent era in which Mifflin dwelt. Gary Nash has focused on colonial and revolutionary America. A professor of history, Emily Teipe's prior works have centered on the American Revolution and the role of women in American history. As a writing partnership, Nash and Teipe provide vital context and bring humanity to their subject. Their comprehensive use of Mifflin's correspondence, journals, and essays paints a compelling portrait of a woman wrestling with her sense of call to divine service. A member of Philadelphia's educated elite, she lived on Chestnut Street, across from the Pennsylvania State

House. There, surrounded by the family's increasing wealth, she could have followed her mother's and her mother's acquaintances' example of cleaving to hearth and home. Instead, she began examining her soul, penning the private and illuminating "Account of My Religious Progress," a challenging (and often withering critical) essay titled "The Payment of War Taxes for Military Purposes," as well as reports of her missions to Iroquoia and Upper Canada. She was staunch in her Quaker conviction that all persons are created equal. Those deliberations make for immersive and absorbing reading. How much simpler would her life have been if she had ignored the necessity of cleaving to the disciplined center of her faith as a Quaker?

Anne Emlen Mifflin's writings invite the reader into the heart and psyche of a driven woman on a quest to challenge the status quo of racial injustice. Throughout, her abhorrence of slavery as a demonic practice is clear, as is her conviction that any thoughtful person (whether religious or irreligious) should labor toward its abolishment. She would make a fine role model for a current generation of social activists who would empathize with her personal decisions regarding familial relationships, namely how to maintain her mission despite leaving behind her two young sons. Her impassioned ministry and far-ranging travels came at great emotional cost.

Having published a biography of Saint Katharine Drexel (*Saint Katharine: The Life of Katharine Drexel*, 2014), I note similarities between the faith journeys of Anne Mifflin and Katharine Drexel. Both grew up in affluence; both felt impelled to walk in God's path of justice and mercy; both experienced dark nights of the soul; both kept private journals weighing their sense of call; both struggled with family members who failed to understand their fervor, or for whom the example of abnegation created an emotional chasm; both fought strenuously against an entrenched system of racism. However, Katharine had no biological children. She was never forced to choose, as Anne was, between maternal love and vocation. The two women, however, embraced causes that were politically unpopular: in Mifflin's case the necessity of freeing all enslaved Americans; in Drexel's providing black Americans with an education. Both women were equally driven to improve the lives of indigenous peoples who were suffering cruelly under the dominance of whites.

How could she not have grieved over her sons' abdication of the faith that was central to her being? What were her methods of coping with disappointments that might have felt crushing to other parents? The fact that three of her brothers were dismissed from the Society of Friends in 1778 and 1779, and that two were slave owners, must have grieved her at a period in her life when the bonds of kinship were vital. Anne did not separate love and support from transgressing family members, nor could she overlook her mother's lapse of faith during the currency debate. Those frayed family relationships must have wounded her. If so, she accepted the burdens of grief. Her invincible spirit remained intact and vibrant.

Understanding Anne Emlen Mifflin's life's quest within the context of the tumultuous era in which she lived permits macro and micro views within *Our Beloved Friend: The Life and Writings of Anne Emlen Mifflin*: revolutionary fervor, the molding of a new government, the abiding question of slavery, and the rights of tribal peoples. Gary Nash and Emily Teipe's narrative both balances and arcs that of a single person acting out of private conviction within a corporate and often hostile maelstrom.

—Cordelia Frances Biddle

ACKNOWLEDGMENTS

The co-authors had never met until Sharon V. Salinger, professor emerita at University of California, Irvine, recommended Emily for a research project. Over lunch at the Henry E. Huntington Library in San Marino, California, we discussed publishing some of Anne Emlen Mifflin's letters. Emily then raised the possibility of writing a biography of Anne, a Philadelphia Quaker and second wife of Warner Mifflin, who had been the subject of Gary's 2017 book *Warner Mifflin: Unflinching Quaker Abolitionist.* There was an astounding mass of crumbling commonplace books and correspondence from the hand of the gifted, reform-minded woman; but as Gary noted, to unravel the life and writings of this ignored and complex figure, he would need for his co-author a female historian who lived in the light of the Society of Friends and had lived a vibrant life as mother and wife. Thus began our collaboration. To Sharon Salinger we are deeply indebted for bringing us together, her former student and her former mentor.

This study of Anne Emlen Mifflin's life, her travels, and her writing led us on a paper trail twisting through many archives and libraries. All debts rightfully begin with the generations of the Emlen family who preserved Anne's copybooks and letters for many decades before depositing them at the Historical Society of Pennsylvania (HSP) in Philadelphia in the 1940s. Tenth-generation Emlens live today in Philadelphia and its suburbs, still treasuring the role their ancestors played in building the City of Brotherly Love.

Like all historians, especially in the wrenching pandemic year of 2020–21, we would have been lost in the woods without the help of archivists, librarians, and research assistants who have been indispensable in collecting, maintaining, and making available archival and printed materials; their resourcefulness and faith in the patrons of their institutions has been truly remarkable. At HSP, Sarah Heim in the Manuscript Division responded to every request regarding the Emlen Family Papers and related collections. At UCLA, where one could no longer roam the stacks and check out books and journals, we had thousands of digitized books accessible to our personal computers. Complementing this, the University of California libraries had contracted with HathiTrust to make available online thousands of esoteric printed materials, particularly relating to religion, that the collaborative repository has digitized in recent years. Working from the opposite side of the country, we were fortunate to have Kevin Johnson, a graduate student at Rutgers University–Camden, serve as our research assistant, paging and scanning the Emlen Family Papers and other collections at HSP. Kevin's many hours spent sending us hundreds of pages of Anne's letters and writings was indispensable to this project.

Next in importance to the cache of Emlen Family Papers at HSP were the manuscript collections of Quaker materials at Haverford College's Quaker Collection and Swarthmore College's Friends Historical Library. At Swarthmore Pat O'Donnell, ever obliging, steered us to letters and documents we would otherwise never have found, and Jordan Landes, curator at Swarthmore's Friends Historical Library, assisted so well in finding just the right documents. Sarah Horowitz, curator of rare books and head of Quaker and special collections at Haverford College's Lutnick Library, was exceedingly helpful during a period when the Friends Collection had to be warehoused while the library was under renovation (rendering the collections largely inaccessible for two years).

Other archivists, curators, librarians, and fellow scholars deserve praise for their help, bridging the miles between Southern California and the East Coast. Jim Green, longtime librarian at the Library Company of Philadelphia and one of the profession's luminous experts on early American printed materials, was most helpful. Billy G. Smith, professor of history at Montana State University, assisted ably by Paul Sivitz, has recorded, processed, and mapped data on the population of Philadelphia in the late eighteenth century that allowed us to identify by occupation, wealth, and residence Anne's neighbors, her extended Emlen family, and scores of people to whom she referred in her writings. This compilation, which has no parallel for any other city of the early republic, allows the historian to look through both ends of a telescope, to view Philadelphia as a whole and also to track its residents block by block and street by street.

Pat Spero, librarian of the American Philosophical Society, had the minutes and documents of the Philadelphia Yearly Meeting's Indian Committee generously digitized and emailed to us. Jennifer Abbott at the Maryland State Archives, Mike Lear at the Franklin and Marshall College Library, Ed Richi at the Delaware Historical Society, and Phoebe Bean at the Rhode Island Historical Society all kindly responded to our inquiries. Anne Mellor and Helen Deutsch, literary scholars at UCLA, helped with matters related to Anne Emlen's poetic relationship with member of Congress Thomas Burke, as did David Fairer from Leeds University. Thanks also to Norman "Ned"

Donoghue and Ken Milano for tracking down the crumbling will of Anne Emlen Mifflin's grandfather buried in the City Archives of Philadelphia. Librarians Lauren Reiter and Eric Charles Novotny at Penn State University offered vital assistance as well on research requests.

At the Philadelphia Contributionship, the longest tenured insurance company in the United States, archivist Carol Smith located the interior and exterior descriptions of the Emlen ancestral home on Chestnut Street. At UCLA's Charles E. Young Research Library, Tula Orum and other research assistants spent many hours tracking down newspaper notices that can now be retrieved in the digital age. All these friends of history held the rusty keys we needed to open caches of treasure to bring back to living memory *Our Beloved Friend*, Anne Emlen Mifflin.

Out in the world of faceless and nameless individuals, going back three centuries, a legion of people belonging to the Society of Friends dutifully recorded the records that made it possible to track Anne Emlen Mifflin's life on virtually a month-by-month basis. There may be no other religious group in the modern world that has kept meeting records more fully, and it is remarkable that a great percentage of them have survived fire, flood, and inattention. The many hundreds of volumes of Quaker records in their original form are lodged at Haverford and Swarthmore College libraries, where curators have provided excellent online guides to them.

Because of the COVID-19 shutdown, we could not camp out at Haverford or Swarthmore, so we drew on the extraordinary work of the Church of the Latter-Day Saints, whose members have microfilmed a major portion of Quaker meeting records. Their affiliate, Ancestry (http://www.ancestry.com), became our silent friend, providing us online access to the painstakingly preserved Quaker data. The magnitude of this enterprise can be appreciated by viewing the record books that came under the umbrella of the Philadelphia Yearly Meeting. They vary from burial records to membership lists, minutes of preparative, monthly, quarterly, and yearly meetings minutes of the Meeting for Sufferings and the Meeting of Elders and Ministers, to correspondence with the London Yearly Meeting to listings, meeting by meeting, and more than one hundred handwritten folio volumes that pertain to Anne Emlen Mifflin. Although the Mormon Church and the Ancestry web service were primarily interested in copying and preserving these materials for genealogical research, in the process they have amassed a database that has enriched research capacity for an entire community of scholars while also putting libraries of all sizes and characters essentially on the same plane.

Early on we were fortunate to have Emma Lapsansky-Werner of Haverford College, Sharon Salinger of University of California, Irvine, Jean R. Soderlund of Lehigh University, as well as Mike McDowell, an independent scholar, read the manuscript and provide insightful commentary that has improved the overall results and flushed out errors. Cordelia Biddle, Philadelphia novelist and biographer, read a later version of the manuscript and offered observations on Anne's life and character. Ned Donoghue, author of a forthcoming book on Quakers who were exiled to Virginia during the American Revolution, read chapter 2 and shared his research on revolutionary Philadelphia. Esteemed Friend, professor emeritus, and recorded minister Lloyd Lee Wilson, whom Emily first met at the Rich Square Monthly Meeting in Woodland, North Carolina, kindly shared his extensive knowledge of Quaker history and spirituality.

We cast a wide net searching for illustrations and images for the book. Dr. Carol Soltis of the Philadelphia Museum of Art lent us her expertise to find and identify the portrait of Mary Emlen Beveridge. The following archivists gave us their valuable assistance in securing illustrations: Charles Griefenstein at the American Philosophical Society and Bruce Laverty at the Athenaeum, both in Philadelphia; Mark Procknik at the New Bedford Whaling Museum; Megan Crayndon of the Maryland State Archives; Mary Brooks of Westtown School, West Chester, Pennsylvania; and Eleanor Gillers at the New-York Historical Society.

We appreciate the support of our editors Kathryn Yahner and Laura Reed-Morrison of Penn State University Press, the external reviewers, our indexer Enid Zafran, and cartographer Erin Greb, who provided two elegant maps. Many thanks as well to our exceptional copyeditor Nicholas Taylor, who did such an excellent job of fine-tuning the manuscript.

In the five years devoted to this book, tethered to our personal computers, we researched, wrote, exchanged ideas, and edited many drafts, all in email cyberspace. We worked without financial research support except for a small grant from UCLA's Academic Senate Research Fund. For this financial assistance we are grateful.

We are especially indebted to those helping hands on the front lines. Thanks to Gary's grandson Nicholas Johnson for installing, and maintaining, his new computer, and to my son William Teipe for his expertise, tireless patience, and invaluable help with the finer points of formatting and for troubleshooting when things went awry.

ABBREVIATIONS

Note: Unless otherwise designated, Friends meeting minutes or ephemera are drawn from the Ancestry archive available at http://www.ancestry.com.

ACS	American Colonization Society
ALS	Autograph letter signed
BYM	Baltimore Yearly Meeting
C-P-W	Cox-Parrish-Wharton Papers, Historical Society of Pennsylvania, Philadelphia
DCMMM	Duck Creek Monthly Meeting Minutes, transcription, Historical Society of Pennsylvania, Philadelphia
DPA	Delaware Public Archives, Dover
EFP	Emlen Family Papers, Historical Society of Pennsylvania, Philadelphia
Emlen Diary	Diary of Anne Emlen, Emlen Family Papers, box 1, Historical Society of Pennsylvania, Philadelphia
FHLSC	Friends Historical Library, Swarthmore College, Swarthmore, Pennsylvania
HSP	Historical Society of Pennsylvania, Philadelphia
IC	Indian Committee
LC	Library of Congress, Washington, DC
MMM	Murderkill (and all name variants) Monthly Meeting
MMMMM	Murderkill (and all name variants) Monthly Meeting Men's Minutes
MMMWM	Murderkill (and all name variants) Monthly Meeting Women's Minutes
MRP	Anne Emlen Mifflin, "My Religious Progress"
NGMMMM	New Garden Monthly Meeting Men's Minutes
NGMMWM	New Garden Monthly Meeting Women's Minutes
PAS	Pennsylvania Abolition Society
PMM	Philadelphia Monthly Meeting

PMMM	Philadelphia Monthly Meeting Minutes
PMMMM	Philadelphia Men's Monthly Meeting Minutes
PQM	Philadelphia Quarterly Meeting
PWMM	Philadelphia Women's Monthly Meeting
PWMMM	Philadelphia Women's Monthly Meeting Minutes
PYM	Philadelphia Yearly Meeting
PYMM	Philadelphia Yearly Meeting Minutes
QCHC	Quaker and Special Collections, Haverford College, Haverford, Pennsylvania
SQM	Southern Quarterly Meeting
WQM	Western Quarterly Meeting

EDITORIAL APPARATUS

Parts 2 and 3 of this book gather in one place the bulk of this remarkable Quaker woman's outgoing correspondence and the memorials, her spiritual autobiography, some of her poetry, and unpublished meditations on a variety of topics that filled several commonplace books. None this material has ever been published. In making selections, the editors have focused on documents that best illuminate Anne Mifflin's antislavery activism, her travels to Iroquoia to work with Seneca and Oneida women, and her efforts to strengthen the discipline of the Society of Friends, especially in remote areas to which they had migrated after the American Revolution. A few letters of a personal nature address her family's private life. Unfortunately, only a few letters addressed to Mifflin have survived. Most of these appear herein. Some letters judged of limited interest have not been included.

The editors offer modernized transcriptions of the writings of Anne Mifflin that flowed from her pen. These transcriptions substitute twenty-first-century American spellings and punctuation for Mifflin's eighteenth- and early nineteenth-century flow-of-consciousness forms while replacing most archaic words with their contemporary American counterparts. Any underlining or strikethroughs in the reproductions of Mifflin's writing reflects the original manuscripts.

The editors have tried to retain the style and flavor of Mifflin's writing while providing texts intelligible to today's readers. Thus, for example, in keeping with her writing style and the early Quaker tradition of plain speech, they have retained the pronouns *thee*, *thou*, and *thine* (or *thy*) rather than modernizing to *you* and *you*. Mifflin rarely used periods or question marks. More commonly she inserted a dash, comma, or semicolon in places where today we would end a sentence; then she continued her thought. By modern standards her sentences are long and difficult to follow. Therefore, the editors have elected to break up some sentences and to impose modern punctuation, the exceptions being cases where her usages emphasize her meaning or are easily comprehensible. As with her sentences, Mifflin's paragraphs are sometimes unwieldy; therefore, the editors have added, and sometimes removed, paragraph breaks.

In the interest of readability, the editors have introduced several other textual modifications. The word "Friend," with its first letter capitalized, signifies a Quaker; the same word, with first letter in lowercase, a non-Quaker. Fully spelled-out words replace most contractions and abbreviations, and datelines appear at the top of each document, no matter their position in the original. Mifflin wrote dates in the Quaker style, with numbered months and days in place of month-day names of pagan origin. The editors have preserved this style, while supplementing it with square-bracketed standard American forms. Square brackets serve several other purposes. They indicate words that are uncertain due to the illegibility of a manuscript, whether the uncertainty arises from Mifflin's hand or damage to a document. They signal other editorial insertions as well: words that add missing parts of speech or provide clarity. The editors have also chosen to ignore an author's deletions in a manuscript unless they contain significant material, in which case that material is provided in an endnote. Additionally, they have added, without comment, marginal notations obviously meant by the author for insertion at specific points. Where such notation clearly represents an afterthought, the editors have rendered it as a postscript or post postscript. The word "and" replaces the ampersand, and "per," the symbol ℔. All biblical citations refer to the King James Version unless otherwise noted.

In handling proper names and Mifflin's other forms of address, the editors have introduced a number of regularizations. Whenever a document includes a previously unmentioned person, they have supplied an identifying endnote. The index also indicates places of first appearance. In cases where the editors have been unable to identify an individual, they have noted that fact. Where Mifflin misspelled a name, the correct spelling follows in square brackets. And finally, where the editors have judged that another hand may have written a document signed "Anne Mifflin," they have noted that judgment.

INTRODUCTION

By January 1780, Anne Emlen had reached her limit. Putting pen to paper, she poured out her frustration in her journal: "Since my indisposition, I have been impressed with an apprehension of duty in leaving my dear Mother's house until she can see her way to forsake the use of Congress currency and the support thereof in the payment of taxes. Oh! that I may be able to endure the change should not a resignation of the will be accepted for the deed."[1]

Anne Emlen, also known as Nancy (1755–1815), was the twenty-five-year-old daughter of one of the wealthiest Quaker families in Philadelphia.[2] Single and living with her mother at the Emlens' Chestnut Street home, across the street from the Pennsylvania State House where the Continental Congress was conducting the War for Independence, she found herself in the throes of a dilemma—how to find her religious identity and, just as important, how to determine her life's work. This personal battle conducted during the American Revolutionary War gave special poignancy to the decision to leave home because of her recently widowed mother's tendering of Continental currency. It was a difficult decision, one that not only jeopardized Anne's reputation, even among likeminded Quakers, but also put at risk the assets bequeathed by her wealthy father. Anne believed that if she used "tainted" Continental currency stained with the blood of fallen soldiers, she would dishonor the Quakers' bedrock principle of pacifism. Resolute in her service to the Prince of Peace, she would not compromise on this issue as had many beleaguered Friends including her own mother. Quakers such as Anne who held firm to their pacifist and neutral convictions found themselves in a perilous position during the war.

ANNE EMLEN'S MISSION

Considering Anne's family, particularly her brothers and sisters, the Emlen siblings were no gauge of the family's dedication to the faith. Truth be told, Anne and her brother James were the only ones of the eight Emlen children who exercised significant devotion or service to the meeting. By her late teenage years, Anne had entered her stage of convincement[3] and strived to live day-to-day as a devout member of the Society of Friends. With this deepening of faith, she took on the ascetic customs of Quakerism, adopting wholeheartedly plain speech and dress, denouncing all frivolities, and adding the midweek meeting for worship to her regular First Day attendance. Holding to the doctrine of the Inward Light that all believers—every man, woman, and child—sought that which is of God in everyone, she engaged in the busy work and worship of the Philadelphia circle of Friends.

Nourished from budding youth on the belief that in the Divine light there is neither male nor female, Anne inhabited a small community where (compared to non-Quakers) Friends' widening of gender boundaries was exceptional. This was evident in female Friends' access to education, approval to teach, to counsel, and to work autonomously within their own women's meeting, and for those female friends called to ministry the freedom to travel, to preach, and to prophesy. However, lest we paint them as radical mavericks, let us remember they had gained this liberty under the protective mantle of male leadership who approved their comings and goings, recorded their ministry, and authorized a sound education for their daughters. Within this setting, Quaker females behaved within the bounds of female propriety, sensibility, and decorum.[4] As Sarah Crabtree states, "Although female public Friends ventured far beyond the roles traditionally proscribed for women of that era, the way both they and their audiences interpreted their successes and shortcomings demonstrated the finite limits of these possibilities."[5]

During this period of spiritual awakening, Anne scoured religious treatises to determine her life's purpose; she began writing page after page of ruminations and reflections on religion in several commonplace books that have lain virtually undisturbed for nearly two and a half centuries. These commonplace books, along with others, comprise a small stack easily lifted from two archival boxes at the Historical Society of Pennsylvania (HSP). From these green boxes scholars can also gently extract dozens of brittle, yellowed letters written to Mother Emlen from the faraway places Anne traveled in the cause of strengthening the ties that bound Quaker faith communities. One can read her poetry and, of great importance, the two spiritual autobiographies in her commonplace books that trace her emergence, amid great anguish, to become an esteemed minister of the Society of Friends. Providentially, 130 years after her death, an Emlen descendant gifted HSP the writings that had flowed from her pen. Today, in a sorry state of deterioration, they flake away at the edges when handled or lifted from the storage boxes.

But in the summer of 1777, as Anne finished a freshly journaled pocket-sized commonplace book, she questioned if there was any purpose or value at all in writing down her musings:

> I must now put one question to myself; of what use is it thus to note down the actual actions of that time which can never again be recalled? Recollection furnished me with an excellent one, that of looking back to see if to any purpose these days have past; though like most undertakings this was entered on with a design superior to its execution. And as I wish not to fatigue myself with too great a length of uninteresting particulars; I will wind up with the first resolution to turn every succeeding Day to some good account, either of improving my mind or manners. Heaven crown my wishes and endow me with Divine certitude.[6]

Consequently, but fortunately, much of what we know about Anne and her life's work can be reconstructed from her own writing in journals and letters, supplemented by correspondence from her contemporaries and the copious records of Quaker meetings. In her lifetime, the accounts of Quaker ministers, generally published years after their death, made for popular reading when circulated among Friends. Like those of many Quaker ministers, Anne adopted the Friends' genre of spiritual autobiographies to express her inner struggles, including engaging details of her journeys and informing us on the state of particular meetings.[7] Anne's journaling provided her a unique space to carry on a dialogue with God, sharing concerns best expressed privately, in what Cinthia Gannet frames an "uncensored free space."[8] However, until now, Anne's journals have only served the original purpose that she intended—"for the perusal of my children."[9] Piecing together these rich sources provides a vivid account of this young Quaker woman's religious transformation and how she became in time a fearless warrior in the "Lamb's War," emulating her Quaker ancestors' crusade waged in the seventeenth century.

While trying to determine her specific calling, Anne was often sidetracked by fending off persistent suitors and believed well into her late twenties that she was not intended to be a wife and mother. However, after a delayed, tremulous approach to marriage, she finally wed at age thirty-three.

It is passing strange that Anne Emlen, who married Delaware's Warner Mifflin (1745–1798), a passionate abolitionist, has remained lost to American history for these last two centuries since her death, especially when we consider the bold expeditions that carried her thousands of miles to preach the good news to Friends in Canada, New England, the mid-Atlantic region, the South, and new communities in the trans-Appalachian West. In every sense a trailblazer, she was the first white woman to visit Genesinguhta on Seneca land, where she met and spoke face to face with Chief Cornplanter and his half brother, the venerable prophet Handsome Lake. On these grueling trips to minister, encourage, and organize relief to native people, Anne tallied up staggering mileage, often on horseback. In an era when the life expectancy of a female was forty-one years, Anne continued trekking into the wilderness at the age of fifty-eight.

Throughout her life Anne was just as much the restless, curious intellectual as she was a devoted minister. She became one of the most determined, reform-minded, activist women of her generation, and her labors established a number of "historical firsts." Her mission? To make a sinful nation contrite and to raise awareness that a watchful God would not allow a people dedicated to inalienable universal freedom and Christianity to go unpunished if they continued their iniquitous practice of owning slaves and waging abusive assaults on native people.

Foreshadowing the Free Produce Movement of the 1830s, she urged Quakers to boycott indigo-dyed material. In this way she hoped to end the exploitation and untimely death of slaves whose lives were severely shortened by exposure to toxic reagents used in the brutal processing of the indigo plant.

In 1795, traveling to Annapolis to petition the Maryland State Assembly for the "speedy abolition of the inhuman commerce in slaves," she became the first woman, along with her sister-in-faith Mary Berry, to present a memorial to a legislative body. Thus, Anne Mifflin and Mary Berry prefigure by some thirty years the succeeding generation of male and female abolitionists; yet history has not provided them so much as a "byline." Indeed, her overall accomplishments, contributions, visionary scope, and work as an early social activist foreshadowed the reform fever that would grip thousands of Americans in the antebellum period.

Decades before the formation of women's antislavery societies in the 1830s, Anne was the first woman to speak out with a plan for a state-subsidized, voluntary return of free African Americans to their ancestral home in Africa. She took this case, or tried to, all the way to the mountain plantation of the Sage of Monticello.

All the while, Anne played a role in launching Westtown School, which operates to this day in Chester County, Pennsylvania. She served on innumerable Friends committees; worked for the Female Society for the Relief and Employment of the Poor, the Society for the Free Instruction of African Females, the Society for the Free Instruction of Females of Color, and the Aimwell School in Philadelphia assisting the daughters of poor families; and attended all of the Friends' requisite gathered meetings in Kent County, Delaware, and in Philadelphia to women's monthly meetings in both states to the Western and Quarterly Meetings, the Half-Year Meeting for Elders and Ministers in Philadelphia, the Philadelphia Monthly Meeting for Sufferings, and the famed Philadelphia Yearly Meeting. Among her many services, Anne also performed the Quakers' due diligence by calling on the sick, assisting the poor and the dying, and reviewing notices of intention to marry that were required of all Friends' prospective marriage partners. Considering all her achievements that have not been previously acknowledged, Anne Emlen Mifflin bears the authenticity of a premiere female Quaker activist of her generation.

QUAKERS: THE SOCIETY OF FRIENDS

Anne was raised, educated, and nourished within the cocoon of American Quakerism at its vital center in eighteenth-century Philadelphia. She matured under the stewardship of renowned Quaker elders and served in a religious society emerging as an offshoot of the Protestant Reformation. Within their first century of development, Friends fended off attacks from other Christians by drawing strength from active participation in a common religious experience that made them all "Children of the Light." Adversaries of Friends, such as the Puritans, had scorned Quakers as "the choke weed of Christianity," and English philosopher Thomas Hobbes scoffed at the Quakers' demolition of class distinctions, where "every boy or wench thought he spoke with God Almighty."[10] Nonetheless, fired by an egalitarian ethos, the Friends had stripped their liturgy to bare silence, deleted the sacraments and the priestly tradition, and removed religious statuary and all other trappings of a formal "high" church. Indeed, Friends managed to simplify their worship and purify their Christian sect even more than the Puritans had purified Puritanism.

Quakers held the view that salaried clergy delivering sermons from a carved pulpit were nothing but "a hireling ministry." In plain functional meetinghouses, lacking a pulpit, organ, choir, or communion table, silent meditation took up most of the service, broken only when a Friend, man or woman, so moved by the Spirit spoke spontaneously. Sometimes a Public Friend or minister might present a prepared address or speak extemporaneously. From their founding in mid-seventeenth-century England, Friends trusted that an uncluttered simplicity of belief and modest manner of worship would return believers to the purer days of first-century Christianity.

That same ideal of simplicity governed speech and dress. Founder George Fox had told his followers that "ye that dwell in the light and walk in the light, use plainness of speech and plain words." Thus, the singular and familiar "thee" and "thou" replaced the plural and deferentially formal "you," in effect, a form of social leveling. Likewise, refusing "hat honor," doffing one's cap at the approach of a social superior, was intended to reject a customary form of deference. In dress, plain clothing signified a distaste for apparel advertising one's wealth or social classification. Hence, the woman's dove gray or dull brown gown, plain shawl and bonnet, and avoidance of lace and silver buckles and buttons, and the man's drab coat and broad-brimmed black hat, all followed the dictates of Pennsylvania's Quaker founder William Penn: "If thou art clean and warm it is sufficient; for more doth but rob the poor." For Friends, everyone was equal in God's sight. Such a commitment to equality, like water flowing downhill, led naturally to the Quaker concern for social justice.[11]

Though from the beginning Friends had disdained a salaried clergy, they put great stock in identifying those men and women, some as young as sixteen, who exhibited extraordinary spiritual gifts. This recognition would be no less critical to Anne's success. She was free to pursue a religious vocation, encouraged, groomed, and supported to do so because of the "superior privilege" that Friends, *but no other church*, granted to women. George Fox had taken unprecedented steps to authorize devout Quaker women to teach, prophesy, and travel as religious missionaries. He also insisted women participate in church governance, form their own meetings, keep records, manage funds, oversee the care of women, children, and the poor, approve or disapprove proposed marriages, preach the word of the God, and serve as counselors in their local areas.[12] Such a pious candidate was Anne Emlen Mifflin. Designated a minister in her early thirties and charged with advising youth and backsliding adults, she visited families in neighboring or regional meetings and steered many Friends along the true path.[13]

As a "Public Friend" whose "gift" of inspired speaking was acknowledged by local meetings for worship, Anne and other disciples like her endured extraordinary deprivations, often sojourning thousands of miles on foot or on horseback. Regarded as vital to the spiritual sustenance of Friends, Quaker ministers served "almost the same function as the circulation of the blood in the animal organism," as Quaker historian Frederick Tolles has put it, "giving Friends at the remotest extremities of the Atlantic world a sense of belonging to a single body."[14] On her own prolonged ministerial travels on horseback, Anne was always accompanied by another Quaker female and usually by one or more male Public Friends.[15] Traveling alone was dangerous for any woman, but for female Friends, this gave justification for those wary of Quakers to believe the worst about them.[16] Quakers for the most part prudently avoided the perils of travel by going in a group and partaking of Friends' hospitality along the way.

THE QUAKER MEETING

While the Quakers were not strictly hierarchical, they were highly organized. When founder George Fox set up the tier of meetings that still function today, he stressed the need for Friends to keep procedural records such as meeting minutes, epistles, correspondence, condemnation of certain members' behavior, and certificates of removal and admission that permitted members relocating to another area to establish themselves in a new meeting or to admit a sojourning or preaching member to other meetings. Clerks wrote memorials to honor deceased Quakers, noted the approval or disapproval of a couple's intent to marry, issued travel certificates for Public Friends, and recorded various other items of interest to the members.

Among the numerous meetings held, Anne attended many in order to bolster herself spiritually for the life to come. "To be in this world but not of it" meant that a devout Quaker prepared for the afterlife by treating every moment as if it were their last.[17] In the gathering for First Day worship—the silent, unprogrammed meeting[18]—Friends were expected to enter with serious intent and expectation of experiencing the Divine presence. Meetings sometimes started with a query or question in the form of self-examination, followed by silent meditation.[19] Anne's spiritual mother, Susanna Lightfoot, revered as "a powerful minister of the word," expressed grave concerns about the behavior of the younger members at meeting for worship. "When I have sat down in our meetings and cast my eye over the people," she exclaimed, "how have I been grieved to see the haughtiness of the young men and the folly of the young women looking one upon another as if there was nothing to do; coming to meetings just to see and be seen."[20]

By the time Anne attended meetings in the later eighteenth century, membership consisted of elders, ministers, overseers, and members at large. Elders were men and women who advised members and guided those serving the ministry. Overseers, the backbone of the meeting, were indispensable and selected from the most substantial members to act as financial trustees of the meetinghouse proper, to supervise funds, and to arbitrate disputes among members. This core group of ministers, elders, and overseers provided leadership and monitored all the members.

As wealthy as the Emlens were, they filed into meeting and took the next available seats just like everyone else. Quakers did not reserve or buy pews, a custom in other English churches that led to the visible rank ordering of their congregations. Moreover, Friends' seating order, with men and women apart in separate areas, and ministers and elders taking an elevated place in the gallery, was a less hierarchical arrangement than it sounds. As Mary Maples Dunn pointed out, the architecture displayed the equality and authority members were giving to women. Friends did not erect churches but instead built domestic meetinghouses in "which women acquired their own space." In the meetinghouse, a partition was customary to divide a space equally into two rooms—one for men's meeting, the other for the women's—or they could remove the screen to accommodate a large, unified meeting for everyone.[21]

Anne's Philadelphia meeting[22] would have required a preparatory meeting to clear up any minor problems before the monthly meeting, to report any violations of discipline, and to see to general maintenance of the meetinghouse. Monthly meetings comprising all the local meetings in and around the city took on most of the work of the Society of Friends and any member in good standing could attend. In meeting deliberations, decisions were never made by vote or majority rule. In an effort to reach consensus, following discussion it was up to the clerk to discern a "sense of the meeting"—that is, the will of the group. The monthly meeting controlled funds and donations to charity, supervised Friends' schools, disciplined any member guilty of a moral offense, reported all proceedings and recommendations to the quarterly meeting, and upon the consent of the Women's Meeting approved or disapproved an impending marriage.

Monthly meetings within the county of Philadelphia sent representatives to the quarterly meeting, which functioned as a halfway meeting between the monthly and the yearly meetings for the purpose of handling any problem that the local meeting could not solve. At quarterly meetings, correspondence from the yearly meeting was read and special quarterly meetings could be formed for ministers and elders to facilitate their work within their own congregations.

Capping this hierarchy of meetings in Philadelphia was the Philadelphia Yearly Meeting, made up of thirty-five monthly meetings within Pennsylvania, New Jersey, Delaware, and northern Maryland. PYM issued advice for the guidance of monthly and quarterly meetings, and its decisions were binding on all quarterly and monthly meetings within its jurisdiction. Yearly meetings, such as PYM and London Yearly Meeting, maintained close communication with each other and, by conducting regular visitations, created a uniform standard of faith and practice.[23] In her journals and correspondence, Anne made frequent reference to participating in these meetings as an esteemed minister and member in good standing.

WOMEN AND RELIGION IN EARLY PHILADELPHIA

In recent years, women of colonial and revolutionary Philadelphia have attracted more attention and provide context for the study of the life of Anne Emlen Mifflin. Karin Wulf's *Not All Wives* delves deeply into the many facets of single women's lives. Sarah Fatherly's *Gentlewomen and Learned Ladies* enlightens us on the educational, literary, and legal dimensions of Quaker City women before and during the revolution. Bruce Dorsey's *Reforming Men and Women* explores the organizational reform activities of women (and men) in the antebellum decades. Susan Klepp's *Revolutionary Conceptions* has set the standard for early demographic history, while Sarah Knott's *Sensibility and the American Revolution* examines the self-understanding, or "sensibility," of (mostly) Philadelphia upper-echelon women and men. Susan Branson's *Those Fiery, Frenchified Dames* traces the political thought of elite Philadelphia women in the decades following the American Revolution.

A handful of biographies and diaries of mostly upper-class Philadelphia women have also expanded our knowledge of the social, economic, and cultural lives of Philadelphia womenfolk and their families. Among them are Anne Ousterhout's *The Most Learned Woman in America*, about Elisabeth Graeme

Fergusson; David Maxey's *A Portrait of Elizabeth Willing Powel*; *Milcah Martha Moore's Book*, edited by Catherine La Courreye Blecki and Karin Wulf; *The Diary of Hannah Callender Sansom*, edited by Susan Klepp and Karin Wulf; Marla R. Miller's *Betsy Ross and the Making of America*; Owen S. Ireland's *Sentiments of a British-American Woman*, about Esther Deberdt; the much celebrated three-volume *Diary of Elizabeth Drinker*, edited by Elaine Crane Forman; and Richard Godbeer's *World of Trouble*, about the famous Drinker family. These carefully crafted studies add to what we know about women's births, marriages, deaths, burials, sicknesses (and their remedies), as well as their doctors, family relationships, social networks, household furnishings, diets, consumption patterns, servants, and churchgoing.

Almost a half century ago, Mary Maples Dunn tried to break the stained-glass ceiling, so to speak, in calling for studies of women's roles as religious prophets, leaders, and shapers of individual congregations.[24] Her plea has largely been unfulfilled so far as it treats Philadelphia-area women, though Jean Soderlund answered the bell a decade later with an important essay on Quaker women's far-reaching authority within the Society of Friends.[25]

More satisfying are studies of Protestant women's spiritual autobiographies. Long ago, Howard Brinton pointed toward the plethora of seventeenth- and eighteenth-century journals by Quaker women who traveled widely on both sides of the Atlantic in their "Gospel Labors," as their odysseys were often titled.[26] Widely read, mostly by Friends, as a source of inspiration and instruction, such journals lost currency as Quakers themselves became a smaller and smaller part of the religious landscape.

Charting a new course, the outstanding scholars Mary Beth Norton and Linda Kerber combed archives for evidence of how the origins, conduct, and outcomes of the revolution were affected by women's involvement.[27] This had not been imagined by previous generations of students or the reading of history by the public in general. For women's part in the American Revolution, they knew little more than patriotic icons such as Molly Pitcher, Betsy Ross, and Abigail Adams.

As women have flooded into the history profession, an impressive output of studies has emerged treating the role of women entering the public arena in the antebellum decades where supposedly the real action occurred. Thus, women abolitionists, suffragists, prison reformers, and temperance advocates began to receive their due.[28] More recently, with the outpouring of women's history and literature, feminist literary critics have broadened our appreciation by extending the limitations of long-forgotten journals and autobiographies.[29]

This surge of scholarship indicates that there is much fertile soil to be tilled, casting women as agents of change in the colonial, revolutionary, and early republic period. Of note, for example, Rufus Jones's earlier characterization of the middle period (late seventeenth and early eighteenth century) of Friends' history as a withdrawn, quietist era has been deflated by scholars such as Sarah Crabtree, who studying the itinerant female ministry has redrawn the era as a transformative phase energized largely by a wave of pious female prophecy and ministry in England and America.[30] Having ourselves benefited from this amplified research on Quaker women and in keeping with the Friends' penchant for spiritual biography, we bring to light Anne Emlen Mifflin, a study we hope will add to the history of women who ventured "outside the meetinghouse."

ANNE EMLEN MIFFLIN: HER LIFE AND WRITINGS

Anne's life stands in sharp contrast to the Philadelphia-area women about whom we have learned so much in recent decades. This raises the question: Why has this most significant female Quaker activist of her generation, what the French call *une femme engagée*, been overlooked and remained a cypher? This is baffling considering her unprecedented activism, untiring moral energy, busy pen, and agile mind, which produced a compendious body of writings. We present this first detailed biography of Anne Emlen Mifflin primarily in the interests of scholarship and research but also with care to conserve the fragile documents she left behind. We have transcribed and incorporated selected works from among Anne's journals, letters, and accounts.

Part 1 of *Our Beloved Friend* provides a biography of this extraordinary Quaker woman whose life began as the Seven Years' War erupted and ended as the War of 1812 drew to a close. This premiere biography of Anne Emlen Mifflin, while introducing an important historical figure to the public, endeavors to portray the difficult waters she navigated balancing her commitment for Truth's sake alongside the responsibilities of a devoted daughter, mother, and stepmother. Ever zealous to answer the Divine call, she fought self-doubt and the nagging fear that she might not carry out God's will. While fulfilling her ministry to the Society of Friends and to the nation at large provided unmeasured joy, her life was also yoked with pain, disappointment, and emotional distress, sufferings that remained her unwelcomed companions.

Part 2 contains a variety of Anne Emlen Mifflin's writings composed over forty years. Included are a passionate and deeply self-searching "Account of My Religious Progress,"[31] a bluntly controversial essay on "the payment of taxes appropriated for military purposes," a groundbreaking epistle addressed to the New Garden Monthly Meeting encouraging Friends to boycott textiles dyed with indigo, an antislavery petition to the Maryland Legislature, and two engaging firsthand accounts of Anne's mission to Iroquoia and Upper Canada. All these essays and accounts, bathed in the passion and deep thinking she brought from pen to paper, are annotated.

Part 3 is composed of selected correspondence Anne wrote to or received from distinguished people in her circle. Among some seventy letters and other writings recovered from a variety of archives, thirty-two have been chosen, comprising correspondence with both Quaker and non-Quaker personages, such as a biting letter to Thomas Burke, North Carolina delegate to the Continental Congress; a letter challenging John Dickinson, the "Penman of the American Revolution"; tender poems to her two newborn sons; several letters to John Parrish, Philadelphia's leading activist after Anthony Benezet; a letter to Moses Brown, New England's leading Quaker reformer; another to Paul Cuffe, a Bedford Afro-Pequot ship's captain and merchant; others to her mother, reporting on religious visitations from the outer boundaries of Quaker settlement; as well as unpublished letters to the press concerning the legacy of Warner Mifflin, her deceased husband.[32] Also among them is a moving letter to her nine- and seven-year-old sons recounting the life of their deceased father. A few letters from the widely traveled and eminent John Pemberton are included. All these letters are annotated.

NOTES

1. Anne Emlen Mifflin, "My Religious Progress," January 1780 (hereafter cited as MRP), below.

2. Anne's given name was Anna, but into her teens she was called Nancy, a popular eighteenth-century nickname. Throughout this work, we mainly refer to her as Anne; to denote her maiden status, Anne Emlen; and to signify that period of her life as wife and widow, Anne Mifflin.

3. *Convincement*, a Quaker term, indicates when an individual from another religious tradition becomes a Friend; it is not the same as *conversion*, which Friends regard as a lifelong process. See Brinton, *Friends for 300 Years*, 7. What Anne experienced in her late teens was a deepening of faith, a sense of her transgressions, and a firm resolve to live a more authentic Christian life.

4. Crabtree, "In the Light and on the Road," 129.

5. Ibid., 131.

6. Diary of Anne Emlen, August 19, 1777, box 1, Emlen Family Papers, HSP (hereafter cited as Emlen Diary). Anne did not title the diary, which consists of her journal keeping in several commonplace books dating from May 1777 to June 1787 with a time gap between September 1784 and March 1787.

7. Anne's description of her spiritual struggle and renunciation of frivolities was a common motif in seventeenth- and eighteenth-century Friends journals. Howard Brinton in *Friends for 300 Years* (206–8) explains how John Woolman, Job Scott, and the like wrote of denouncement of worldly pleasures when assuming a call to ministry.

8. Friends' journal writing established by the founders served as wisdom and spiritual literature for the faithful. J. William Frost in *Quaker Family* (30–33) maintains these journals reveal the personal nature of Quaker journalists' ministries. Cinthia Gannett in *Gender and the Journal* (48) found that eighteenth-century Quaker women's journals provided a "linguistic free space for uncensored expression."

9. MRP, below. Michele Lise Tarter in "Reading a Quaker's Book" (186) notes that unpublished journals gave "Quakers a place to write as they were inspired free of surveillance or censure." In this regard, Anne who neither intended nor foresaw her writing would be published was unconcerned about censorship; her writing was for her eyes only or exceptionally for her children to read.

10. Quoted in Tolles, *Quakers and the Atlantic Culture*, 21.

11. Fox is quoted in ibid., 77; Penn is quoted in Jones, *Faith and Practice of the Quakers*, 77. For more on plainness, see Lapsansky, "Plainness and Simplicity."

12. See Fox, "Woman Learning in Silence." See also Larson, *Daughters of Light*, 32, on how women's authoritative status in the church evolved and encouraged literacy for both the male and female laity; and Bacon, *Mothers of Feminism*, on how the unique, innovative role Quaker women played in the Society of Friends prepared them for leadership on a larger scale in early nineteenth-century social reform.

13. Ironically, Quaker ministers and elders took on the color of a spiritual elite, though as their name implied, most elders were mature in years.

14. Tolles, *Quakers and Atlantic Culture*, 25. Tolles described the itinerating ministry as "the bloodstream of the transatlantic Society of Friends" (29).

15. Michener, *Retrospect of Early Quakerism*, 169. In *Daughters of Light* (chap. 2), Rebecca Larson explains that female Quaker ministers' appointments to serve were exceptional and distinct from every other Christian body in the world.

16. Kathleen Brown in *Goodwives, Nasty Wenches, and Anxious Patriarchs* (274) emphasizes the danger for female travelers of sexual assault, especially when stopping over at inns or taverns.

17. Frost, *Quaker Family*, 41.

18. One conducted in silence with no liturgy but individuals, so moved, might pray, speak, or read from scripture.

19. In 1743, when the Philadelphia Yearly Meeting (PYM) adopted systematized queries, "this meeting directs that the following queries may be read in the several Monthly and Preparative Meetings within the verge of this meeting, at least once in each quarter of the year." Michener, *Retrospect of Early Quakerism*, 255.

20. *Account of* [. . .] *Susanna Lightfoot*, 12.

21. Dunn, "Saints and Sisters," 600.

22. The Emlens had attended the Great Meetinghouse, at Second and High Streets, which was built in 1695 and demolished in 1811. Later, Anne attended the Arch Street

Meetinghouse. The Arch Street main meeting room, completed in 1804, measures 3,000 square feet and can hold 250 people and an additional 100 in the gallery. See the Arch Street Meetinghouse website, http://www.historicasmh.org.

23. The number of meetings changed during Anne's lifetime; after 1790 the northern Maryland Meetings included the Eastern Shore of Maryland Meetings. See Frost, *Quaker Family*, 3–5. Frederick Tolles in *Meeting House and Counting House* (ix) notes that "Quaker thinking on most subjects varied little from place to place so that the ideas of English and American Friends down at least to the Revolution can be regarded as practically interchangeable."

24. See Dunn, "Saints and Sisters." Dunn's contribution was recognized in a special issue of *Early American Studies*, vol. 17 (2019), on "Women and Religion in the Early Americas."

25. Soderlund, "Women's Authority in Pennsylvania and New Jersey Quaker Meetings."

26. Brinton, *Quaker Journals*. In *"Wilt Thou Go on an Errand"?* editor Margaret Hope Bacon disinters the journals of three early Quaker female ministers.

27. Norton, *British Americans*; Kerber, *Women of the Republic*.

28. In *Quakers and Slavery* Jean Soderlund presents Quaker women in the revolutionary era who led the cause of cleansing the new nation from the cancer of slavery. Margaret Haviland in "Beyond Women's Sphere" shows how young and unmarried Quaker women crossed gender boundaries to found organizations that succored the non-Quaker poor and downtrodden. Janet Lindman's "Beyond the Meetinghouse" highlights three women from different denominations and regions active in reform. Bruce Dorsey in *Reforming Men and Women* (11) notes the encounter of one of Anne Emlen Mifflin's friends, who warned that a young Quaker woman helping others not of her faith and not needy risked "slander and calumnies."

29. See Jelinek, *Women's Autobiography*, especially the chapter "Quest for Community"; the essay by Van Vlack and essays by Keller in Keller and Keller, *Encyclopedia of Women and Religion*, vol. 1; and Brekus, *Religious History of American Women*. In "'To Have a Gradual Weaning,'" Janet Lindman explores the relationship between spirituality and the physical emotional life of female Friends in early America with a particular interest of those in the ministry. Amanda Herbert's "Companions in Preaching and Suffering" explores itinerant Quaker women in the wider scope of the Atlantic field of ministry.

30. See Jones, *Dynamic Faith*, 57; and Crabtree, *Holy Nation*.

31. In chapter 6, where indicated, some passages have been omitted from this account due to space considerations.

32. Space considerations have obliged us to exclude about forty other incoming and outgoing letters. See the appendix for a list of letters, commonplace books, and other documents in the Emlen Family Papers (hereafter cited as EFP) at HSP or conserved at other repositories that have not been included here.

Part 1
A Quaker Life

Chapter 1

THE EARLY YEARS, 1755–1778

Nothing in Anne Emlen Mifflin's background suggests that she would become the premier female Quaker activist of her generation. Born in Philadelphia on April 30, 1755, at a time when the American colonies were embroiled in the Seven Years' War, she was the sixth of eight children parented by brewery master, merchant, and extensive landowner George Emlen (1718–1776) and Anne Reckless Emlen (1720–1816). Little could her parents imagine that she, among their brood, the inconspicuous sixth, would lead an extraordinary life of spiritual commitment and service to the Society of Friends and gain a historic reputation as an activist and a reformer to the entire republic.

Anne's journey through childhood and adolescence coincided with an unusually turbulent period of colonial American history, marked by the Seven Years' War and then the fracturing of relations between the colonies and their parent country in the War for Independence. For Friends living in eastern Pennsylvania, the center of American Quakerdom, the escalating imperial crisis in the early 1770s put them to the severest test they had faced since their arrival on the shores of the Delaware River a century before. Like all other Quaker families, the Emlens were at a crossroads, for hard choices had to be made and bedrock principles reconsidered as the colonies considered separating themselves from England. Reaching the age of twenty when royal troops faced Massachusetts militiamen at Concord and Lexington, Anne found herself making her own decisions on matters of political and religious allegiance that young women, whether Quaker or otherwise, had rarely been required to face.

Examining her family background reveals much about how Anne entered the Philadelphia scene as a fourth-generation member of the Emlens in the City of Brotherly Love. As it happened, the Emlens figured among the most distinguished families of the Society of Friends, with their name and accomplishments understood to be part of Philadelphia's growth and sophistication as the colonies' largest city.

Anne's ancestors ascertained that a certain George Emlen (ca. 1657–1710), born in Somerset County, England, crossed the Atlantic as an orphaned young man who had displeased his guardian aunt by "embracing the principles of truth . . . or turning Friend," as two of his sons wrote in "Some Account of the Life & Death of George Emlen."[1] As he crossed the Atlantic, bound for new opportunities in America and a friendlier Quaker environment, Anne's great-grandfather carried little of value save the family coat of arms with the inscribed advice *honestum praetulit utili* (preferring the honest to the agreeable). Modeling these words, it seems, was his passport to success.

Shortly after arrival, in 1685, Emlen made the kind of marriage that placed him on the path to success. His bride, Eleanor Allen, was the daughter of Nathaniel Allen, one of William Penn's most trusted friends and one of three commissioners sent by the colony's founder with orders to lay out the city of Philadelphia.

Emlen's good fortune in marriage was abruptly shattered by two tragedies: the sudden death of his wife a few days after giving birth to their third child and the death of their three children. Yet, in 1693, when the tax assessor recorded the names of the several hundred householders in the primitive Delaware River village, Emlen was charged with taxable possessions that placed him in the top quarter of those assessed.[2] A year later, George Emlen married Hannah Garrett, a young Quaker woman whose immigrant parents had settled in Chester County when the colony was still in its infancy.

Emlen's success as a scrupulously honest and devoted Quaker was little short of astounding. Taking hold as a brewer and retailer of cider, beer, and wine, he quickly established himself as the proprietor at the sign of the Three Tuns Tavern on Chestnut Street near the Delaware River waterfront. We get a sense of his success as a tavern keeper from his teeming clientele, roughly estimated by the one hundred sets of pewter tableware used at the tavern and listed in the inventory of his worldly possessions after his death in 1710. The year before, the city's tax assessor pegged him in the top twentieth of wealthy

Philadelphians.³ As the first in his family to settle in Pennsylvania, George embodied the Quaker economic ethic that brought extraordinary business success to many Friends in Philadelphia's infancy.⁴

Eager to honor the accomplishments of their father, two of his sons, Joshua and Samuel, Anne's great uncles, described his death on Christmas Day in 1710 and how many Philadelphians followed the casket to the Quaker burying ground. He "hath left a good name behind him," his sons wrote, "as he lived, so he died, a meek pious peaceable Christian." Sensitive to the tarnish that might be affixed to the occupation of tavern keeper, his sons took pains to record that their father was "very careful to avoid the allowance of the least degree of that excess too prevalent in the generality of houses of that sort of later days, which renders the occupation far less respectable than it otherwise would be."⁵

The weighty patriarch of the Emlen family was also a contemplative, bookish man possessing fifty books, the largest library in Pennsylvania inventoried up to 1711, which included five Bibles; William Penn's *Address to Protestants upon the present conjuncture* (1679), an appeal for liberty of conscience and the cleansing of a morally dissolute society; *The Way to Health* by an English physician; other religious books; and forty-four "small ould bound bookes."⁶ This became the core of the Emlens' literary inheritance passed down through four generations in due course to Anne and her brother James.

Anne's great-grandfather had sunk roots deep into William Penn's "greene country town," fulfilled every immigrant's dream of establishing a successful business, staked a claim to book loving and civic responsibility, and passed on to his widow and children a plenteous estate. By all appearances, the immigrant George Emlen kept faith with the credo of the first lowly Quakers in England who had carried across the Atlantic their belief in an Inward Light and the virtue of a soul-saving life of hard work, sobriety, and dutiful veneration to a watchful God.

The first of George Emlen's children, George Emlen II (1695–1754), Anne's grandfather, was only beginning to learn the art of brewing beer and managing the Three Tuns Tavern when his father died in 1710. Anne would never meet her grandfather, who died the year before her birth. But she certainly knew how he expanded the Emlen brewery handsomely and how, in 1730, at age thirty-five, he had been elected a member of the Common Council, the governing body of the city. She would also have learned that in 1731 he was counted among the charter members of the Library Company of Philadelphia— promoted by its founder, Benjamin Franklin, as the first North American subscription library. George Emlen II seems not to have contributed any of his father's numerous books to the Library Company, but his charter membership testified to his desire to contribute to the civic and cultural life of the city. Like his father, according to brothers Joshua and Caleb he was reckoned "a man of very good repute for sobriety, diligence, industry, and care." The account continued that George Emlen II, after his father's death, became head of the family and "a tender father to his [seven] brothers and sisters."[7]

Building on the brewhouse and tavern he inherited, George Emlen II made numerous land purchases in and outside the city, beginning in 1729 and continuing for many years. The most important was a large lot with a three-story brick house on the north side of Chestnut Street, directly across from the colony's State House (later to be called Independence Hall). He purchased the residence in 1729 from one of the city's premier house carpenters, aptly named Joshua Carpenter. Erected on a still unpaved street, this fine example of Georgian-style architecture stood on what was then the western extremity of the city. Beyond it, looking toward the Schuylkill River, was pastureland for cattle and horses. The Chestnut Street house, situated amid an eclectic mix of private homes, businesses, tradesmen's quarters, and pastoral land, would become Anne's birthplace.[8]

By the 1740s, signs of the family's growing fortune materialized in all manner of ways. Silver began to replace pewter on the Emlens' dining table while gold buttons adorned their daughter's dresses. Servants waited table and harnessed stable horses for carriage rides to the countryside, where the Emlen properties accrued.[9] Thus, the Emlens followed many successful Philadelphia Friends who had left behind the simplicity of England's Quaker founders. Proud of their achievements, they were glad to trade asceticism for the comforts brought by business success. Among those amenities was the labor of indentured servants and enslaved Africans. Woven into the fabric of the swelling port city, bound laborers were to be found toiling in the homes of the city's wealthiest citizens and even those of middling wealth.[10]

The affluent life embraced by Anne's grandfather was perhaps tempered in the Emlen household by the spirituality and meekness of the woman he married. Grandmother Mary Heath Emlen (1692–1777), the daughter of Robert and Susanna Heath, immigrants from Staffordshire, England, had reached Pennsylvania around 1701 when she was nine. Her marriage at age twenty-four in 1716 was the beginning of a long membership in the Philadelphia Women's Monthly Meeting. By 1728, the meeting recognized her as a minister with special gifts in lifting her voice. For many years, while raising three children, she carried her message to Quaker meetings throughout Pennsylvania and New Jersey and northward to New York and New England. Such was the intensity of her religiosity that she was recognized in the published *Memorials Concerning Deceased Friends* (1786), remembered for "her ministry [that] was lively and delivered in much innocence and brokenness of spirit," a woman much admired for "Christian candor and plain dealing."[11]

A PHILADELPHIA CHILDHOOD

Grandmother Mary became an everyday presence in Anne's early life. How much her grandmother's plain dealing and brokenness of spirit affected Anne in her early years is an open question. Certainly it was considerable, for Anne filled her diary with tender comments while attending her grandmother in the last few weeks of her life, as she was "struggling between life and death in great affliction." Anne vowed, "To copy her shall be my care; to be like her my great aim."[12]

While Anne greatly admired the "piety, temperance, frugality, and industry" of her grandmother, Mary Heath Emlen was somewhat overshadowed by Anne's father, George Emlen III (1718–1776), the first-born in the third generation of Emlens. He too continued the brewery business while adding to the family fortune as an importing merchant and rentier. If one account of George's marriage to Anne Reckless (1720–1816) in 1740 is trustworthy, the couple's appetite for luxurious living had swept aside the ethos of their ancestors. In this description of their wedding, the party rode white horses with the ladies decked out in white waists and red skirts made of silk.[13]

If the account of this immodest display was exaggerated, it is indisputable that George Emlen III was among those Philadelphians who began building country homes north and west of the city at midcentury in displays of gentility, leisure, and extravagant household furnishings.[14] Other possessions, including a profusion of four-wheeled, horse-drawn coaches, suggest a pronounced change from simplicity to sumptuousness, from moral certitude to moral laxness.[15]

Rising to contest this amassing of Friends' wealth and their deviation from the core belief that serving and worshipping God was the mark of a true Christian stood members pushing for a dramatic reformation of Quaker life. In Philadelphia, the foremost apostle of this reform, Anthony Benezet, blended pleas for a return to Quaker fundamentals alongside a forceful campaign to cleanse the Society of Friends from the evil of slave keeping.[16] It was this reform movement, with its fervent proponents and outspoken opponents, that dominated the proceedings of the PYM and all its constituent parts just as Anne was pondering her place and purpose in Philadelphia Quaker society.

Growing up in affluence in Philadelphia, within the web of Quaker families interconnected by marriage and affection, Anne Emlen was nurtured in a family with mixed attitudes toward both worldly gains and spiritual losses. Grandmother Mary, who lived until 1777, was sixty-three years old when Anne was born. Anne's mother, Anne Sr., was much involved in the women's meeting of the Great Meetinghouse on High Street and no doubt dutifully raised her brood of eight—born at regular intervals between 1742 and 1757—in the Quaker faith. In navigating childhood with seven siblings, all but one of them her elders, Anne Jr. learned the give and take of living in a large family.

The capacious three-story brick house, standing almost in the shadow of the State House, was a short walk from the venerable Friends meetinghouse at Second and High Streets and from the public markets on High Street. With 157 feet of frontage on Chestnut Street and a depth of 178 feet, the property was even larger than the Robert Morris home, a block away, where President and Mrs. Washington, with a retinue of indentured servants and slaves, would take up residence in 1790.[17]

The Emlens' home, built with generous proportions, included a piazza ten by fourteen feet, an old-fashioned sitting room and kitchen measuring eighteen by thirty-four feet, both two stories high, with wainscoted walls and a large mantel above the kitchen fireplace. Throughout all three stories the floors were laid in wide-planked yellow pine. The house was sturdily constructed, with exceptional craftsmanship such as double architraves round the doors, single architraves over the windows, and paneled chimney breasts above the fireplaces on each floor. The second floor, made up of two large rooms, featured a large folding door between the two. The leaded glass windows had exterior shutters in both the front and the back of the structure. Climbing to the third floor, one could see that same care to detail with plastered walls, spacious closets, and four plain, ridged, dormer windows. A trap door opened to the roof, and winding stairs led from the lower story all the way to the garret. It is easy to imagine the youthful Anne with book or writing materials in hand scurrying up those steps to reach some private little nook on the upper floor or in the attic where she could read or write without interruption, occasionally peering out the window from her lofty position at the passersby and carriages moving on busy Chestnut Street.

From that vantage point, at the vital center of Philadelphia, curious Anne might enjoy watching town dignitaries and colonial legislators passing in and out of the State House.[18]

By midcentury a burst of growth on land west of High, Chestnut, and Walnut Streets rapidly filled in with new houses and shops, sending the city's population soaring to about nineteen thousand by 1760. The Emlens' Chestnut Street property, in the words of Anna Coxey Toogood, "came to be a busy center for blacksmiths, coach makers, and modest businesses like shoemakers and hairdressers."[19] On any given morning's walk, young Anne could meet a variety of close neighbors: widows Christiana Edward and Ann Queen; innkeepers William Hassell and James Garvin; coach maker Israel Bringhurst; and a clutch of glaziers, mariners, wagon masters, grocers, tobacconists, fishmongers, upholsterers, laborers, and mighty merchants such as Robert Morris and Joseph Shippen. A short stroll would have taken her a block past the bustling, upscale boardinghouse of Mary House, where Madison, Jefferson, and other delegates to the Continental Congress would be lodged. On some occasions she must have stopped to purchase sweet cakes from the free African American women who vended their delicacies on Chestnut Street.[20]

While the Emlen siblings lived in great comfort within the uppermost tier of Philadelphia Quakers, only one—Anne's younger brother James—showed any interest in religion or reform, either within or outside the Society of Friends. Although Anthony Benezet, the saintly leader of the Quaker early abolitionist movement, lived just a few blocks east of them at 115 Chestnut Street and worshiped at the same meetinghouse, the Emlens stayed aloof from the groundbreaking Quaker abolitionist movement that in 1758, under the auspices of the PYM, forbade the importation or purchase of slaves. After almost two decades of debate, finally in 1774 the PYM called on Quaker slave owners immediately and unconditionally to free their adult slaves and release children of slaves at maturity (eighteen years for girls and twenty-one for boys). Anne's parents themselves owned several household slaves, but nothing is known about them, even whether they obtained their freedom. Three of Anne's siblings owned slaves after marrying, as did many of their neighbors in Middle Ward.[21] As Anne reached twenty, she surely was aware that most of Philadelphia's numerous Quaker slave owners had complied to free their slaves but hundreds of non-Quakers, owning more than a thousand slaves, remained unmoved by the Friends' appeal to conscience.[22] Two of Anne's brothers, George and Caleb, both merchants, were among the last Philadelphia Friends to liberate their slaves.[23]

Although the efforts of the antislavery Quakers did not engage the interest of Anne's family, some of her siblings felt the sting and zeal of reformers determined to renew the Society of Friends' discipline, which had grown lax during the years when the Emlen family was making its mark on Philadelphia society. Of particular concern was the absence of some members from weekly meetings for worship and the disregard by others of the rule that Friends only marry Friends.[24] This return to a rigorous enforcement of the venerable Friends' discipline had started shortly after Anne's birth in 1755.[25]

The Emlen family had experienced harsher disciplinary action in 1769 when Anne, then fourteen, saw her older sister Mary (1746–1820) marry the Scot immigrant merchant David Beveridge (ca. 1730–1812). The newlyweds were disowned by the Philadelphia Monthly Meeting (PMM)—Mary, for marrying "in a manner contrary to the good order established in the Society," and David, for using "unsavory language, fathering an illegitimate child," comporting himself "in his dress and address deviating from the known testimony of Friends," and for "being married to another woman."[26] Despite the disownment from meeting, the couple continued to live—at least part of the time—in the Chestnut Street house, where in 1773 Charles Willson Peale captured their likenesses in oil, another infringement contrary to Friends' belief since having one's portrait made was a worldly, self-indulgent display of wealth.[27] But true to Quaker toleration within those families where a member had been disowned, Mary and David continued to be prayed for, supported, and loved, although in this case Anne's parents' toleration must have been stretched to the limits. The Beveridges remained a daily presence in the Emlen house, serving as a profane example and perhaps influencing adolescent Anne to mix with gay young friends who danced, wrote poetry, rode on jaunts into the countryside, and dressed as smartly as their parents would allow.[28]

COMING OF AGE

Anne never disclosed much about her adolescence even to her diary; however, her older sister and brother-in-law, through their affluence and stylish social life, may have encouraged her to live well, marry well, and indulge life's pleasures. What would become her defining physical and spiritual characteristics could hardly have been foreseen in her teen years when she had to grapple with the sudden loss of her father and her esteemed Grandmother Mary. She also had to confront the personal and social embarrassment of family scandals and the fear and anxiety of an approaching war in Philadelphia.

While navigating these issues, Anne "experienced the benefit of school education."[29] Although specific details are unknown, one historian claims she attended Anthony Benezet's Girls School for at least part of her early years. Walking only a block east on Chestnut Street, she joined the daughters of the city's wealthiest families, both Quaker and non-Quaker, to study Latin and French, history and geography, mathematics, and other staples of classical studies.[30] Later, Anne likely attended the school established in the home shared by Rebecca Jones (1739–1817) and Hannah Catherall (1736–1806), located in Drinker's Alley. Under the tutelage of these two unmarried women, both Quaker ministers, Anne developed an appetite for poetry. Catherall and Jones not only assigned poetry readings but also encouraged their female pupils to write their own—a talent Anne developed, as we will see, in her twenties and thirties.[31]

Rebecca Jones's approach to learning esteemed the Quaker "religiously guarded education" that aimed to protect the "innocence of children from worldly influences," and while Jones prioritized literacy as well as domestic skills for girls, there is no evidence she intended to structure different expectations for male and female children. Nonetheless, her own standing as a teacher and public minister served as an erudite model to encourage female students if she sensed they had a religious calling. It is likely Friend Jones would have observed the sensibility and intelligence of young Anne Emlen and lavished attention on her.[32]

Anne's highly literate letters reflect training in a curriculum imported from eighteenth-century England, where "ornamental studies" centered on teaching young ladies genteel skills such as needlework, dancing, French, and painting to prepare them for a life of man pleasing. Anne's education also typified the best schools, which stressed a meatier program of history, literature, moral philosophy classics, and the foundations of Enlightenment-driven natural history, astronomy, botany, and biology.[33] The study of literature, natural history, and sciences fed her natural curiosity, and instruction under accomplished Quaker educators provided unique female role models in an otherwise male-dominated urban culture.

It bears emphasis that Anne grew up nurtured on the exceptional Quaker testimony of equality, expressed in the belief that all are endowed with the Inward Light by their creator—that there is that of God in everyone. In eighteenth-century America, no other Christian denomination held such a doctrine—not only that all men were created equal, but that both male and female were equal in God's sight, that there was no inferior or superior nor classification of rank. These advanced Quaker principles and the exposure to female leadership in the Friends' ministry at an early age surely impressed her deeply in those formative years.

By her own account, Anne enjoyed a close relationship with her father. Raised in favorable circumstances, he had added to the family fortune as a dry goods merchant and proprietor of inherited properties. To these he added an extraordinary bundle of properties stretching from Southwark and Moyamensing on the southern border of the city and into the Northern Liberties and beyond. Arriving in 1767, the tax assessor listed seventy-two rent-bearing properties and assessed Emlen for £800 in property taxes, putting him in the top 1 percent of the city's taxpayers. By 1774 the number of his properties had grown to eighty-eight and his taxable estate to more than £1,000.[34] The number of taxpayers in Philadelphia whose assessed estate exceeded that of George Emlen could be counted on one hand.

Reaching his fifties, Anne's immensely wealthy father partially withdrew from the bustle of the counting house to spend more time at the Emlen country seat in Whitemarsh, a few miles west of Philadelphia. Like scores of Quakers, as well as Anglicans, Presbyterians, and those of other denominations, he did not shun riding in his carriage to and from the city, displaying the family's commercial success and upward mobility. His deliberate retreat into a contemplative life left him time to ponder the work of German mystics, some of whom had landed on the shores of the Delaware. When James Allen, wealthy son of the colony's chief justice, stopped by the Emlen house in 1773, he found Anne's father reading the work of Jacob Boehm, the sixteenth-century shoemaker-philosopher whose prolific output included speculations that human nature was a compound of sulfur, mercury, and salt. Worried about Boehm's mysticism and visions, more traditional Christians condemned him; but radical Protestant immigrants—Mennonites, Schwenkfelders, Moravians, and Dunkers from Germany—carried his Neoplatonist ideas over to colonial Pennsylvania with the key idea that people of diverse linguistic and ethnic backgrounds would mingle together to forge a spiritually unified society.[35]

In January 1776 Anne's father died of apoplexy a few days before Thomas Paine's *Common Sense* came off the press. In mourning, Anne likely found comfort among brothers and sisters who shared her loss. Two months after his passing, in a letter to dear friend Hannah Pemberton, she explained that his death had made "a deep impression on a mind, not long since depress'd with grief" and she felt "deprived of many happy hours of instructive entertainment," which she had passed with her father in his favorite study and how "supremely blest" she had been spending time with him. His "natural bent" for reading, study, and a more private life had shown Anne the satisfaction to be gleaned from a contemplative retirement, where his readings in mysticism seem to have left an imprint on his impressionable daughter.[36] Two years later, consulting some of his writings, Anne remarked that "he was a far more religious man than many imagined."[37]

Within two weeks of her father's death, Anne would learn that he willed her a fortune of £1,500 and left her mother an immense fortune with bonds, mortgages, and notes alone topping £10,000.[38] The Chestnut Street house was bequeathed to her mother, and Anne Jr. would reside there for the next thirteen years. Her father's death would prove a crucial change in Anne's life. Anchored in the affection and faith of the Society of Friends, Anne began to fortify her religious devotions by attending, along with First Day services, the weekday meeting for worship. In addition to reading deeply in scripture, Quaker treatises, prescriptive literature, and, more lightly, the verses of English poets such as Addison, Dryden, and Pope, she also admired the poetry of writing spinsters Hannah Griffitts and Susanna Wright, who may have inspired her own composing of poetry.[39] Anne also took delight in exchanging poems with Hannah Pemberton and other young Quaker women in what appears to have been an informal literary circle.

THE CHURN OF REVOLUTION

By the time Anne reached age twenty on April 30, 1775, colonists had remonstrated, demonstrated, rioted, and boycotted for more than a decade to seek a rollback of harsh parliamentary measures that most believed undermined their rights as freeborn Englishmen and -women. The Continental Congress, composed of delegates of property-owning adult white males, had been meeting in Philadelphia across the street from the Emlen house since May.[40] But a point of no return was at hand and only last-minute efforts to reconcile the rebelling Patriots could quench the flames of a revolution already burning.

No sources disclose how the Emlens reacted to this looming crisis; the carefully kept records of the monthly, quarterly, and yearly Quaker meetings do not indicate if Anne's father was active in Philadelphia Friends' leadership;

neither were Anne's older brothers listed as active in the meeting; indeed, several of her relatives considered leaving the Society of Friends in order to take their part in what would soon be acclaimed the "glorious cause." Nevertheless, as the war clouds gathered, Anne grappled with the sudden loss of her father, the recent passing of Grandmother Mary, the personal and social embarrassment of family scandals, and the fear and anxiety of what was coming to Philadelphia.

It was clear to Friends that the American Revolution would go hard for them, especially those in the mid-Atlantic region. Already characterized as people protecting their self-interest under a cloak of religiosity, Quaker leaders of the Philadelphia Yearly Meeting, convening in January 1776, endeavored to clarify their position. Just two weeks after the death of Anne's father, the Philadelphia Meeting for Sufferings issued a stunning declaration of faith that advised Friends to "guard against every attempt to alter or subvert that dependence and connection" with the English government under which the colonies had flourished. Affirming that warning, the yearly meeting held that "the setting up and putting down [of] kings and governments" was "God's peculiar prerogative, for causes best known to himself."[41]

However, this declaration, intended to hold Friends to their "Ancient Testimony," instead instigated rebellious colonists to ridicule and abuse Friends. After a decade of petitioning and remonstrating, Patriots were plunging into all-out war; moreover, to be lectured about how they were entitled to protest English policies if done peacefully, but were wrong to challenge royal and parliamentary authority, was infuriating for both moderate and radical colonists.

A prevalent opinion held that Friends' religious principles aligned with loyalty to the English government. But as Jane Calvert has argued, their loyalty was not to George III but "to their core theological principles and to their own uniquely Quaker Constitution in Pennsylvania," which, in addition to other features, emphatically protected religious liberty.[42] Beyond argument, the principle at the heart of that constitutionally protected religious liberty was pacifism—the forswearing of violence in any form. Whether Quakers were passive Loyalists or passive Patriots—the latter far outnumbering the former—the protection of their religious liberty required that they give support to *neither* side. Strict neutrality was the Friends' rule.

Neutrality, however intolerable to Patriots, was tantamount to withholding consent from the state revolutionary government and the Continental Congress. That alone compromised the legitimacy of the revolution. Such "disaffection," as it was commonly called, came to be seen as more dangerous than unvarnished loyalism, for the self-declared Loyalist could easily be rooted out, whereas the peaceful Quaker, withholding consent, was more difficult to deal with and impossible to coerce into active support of a revolution whose goals were being pursued violently.[43]

Living at the center of the fast-moving events, Anne must have despaired when the Second Continental Congress, which had first convened across the street from her home on May 10, 1775, began issuing paper money in late June to finance a Continental Army. Friends had to decide whether to use the paper currency for monetary exchange. Like all Quakers, the Emlens were surely appalled when the radical Committee of Observation and Inspection targeted prominent Friends, including Emlen cousins who refused to accept Continental bills of credit. In February 1776, the committee condemned Quakers John Drinker, Thomas Fisher, and Samuel Fisher as "enemies of their country" and ordered them to shut up their businesses and conduct no further trade in the city.[44] When this order came just weeks after her husband's death, Anne Emlen Sr., like many Friends frightened over the possibility of hostile confrontation, yielded to the Philadelphia revolutionary authorities. Though Mother Emlen chose not to follow her kin's example, Anne Jr. agonized for months over this contentious matter.

When Thomas Paine scorched the Friends in the third edition of *Common Sense* in April 1776, contradicting the yearly meeting's claim that the Quakers were apolitical, devout Friends reacted by adopting a siege mentality. In a disheartening move, some Quaker men in Philadelphia splintered off to establish the Free Quakers and thus abandon the pacifist principle as they took up arms against the British.[45] The Declaration of Independence, proclaimed in July 1776, accelerated this flight from the Society of Friends.

Walking the precarious line of neutrality and pacifism, refusing to swear allegiance to a revolutionary government, Anne's Friends in the faith could hope for a quick end to the war and console themselves that although this trial by fire would purge the weak among them, it would result in a smaller, more honorable Society of Friends.[46] With war raging up and down the Eastern Seaboard, Anne's own search for answers quickened. When South Carolina's Edward Rutledge stood in the State House in October 1776 and demanded the hanging of Quakers who balked at accepting Continental currency, she had another ugly reminder of the price that Quakers might have to pay for standing by their religious principles.[47] A new militia law passed in early 1777 further bespoke the mounting hostility to Friends. Whereas the previous militia law permitted conscientious objectors to provide a substitute instead of shouldering arms themselves, the new law disallowed substitutions and imposed heavy fines on nonparticipants.[48] As a single woman Anne was not required to pay taxes or swear allegiance to the revolutionary government and the penalties levied on tax and test oath protesters did not affect her directly, but she could be in serious trouble if she refused to use Continental currency. This predicament would occupy her thoughts as spring yielded to summer in 1777.

POETRY AND POLITICS

In June 1777, following Washington's retreat from New York City, Philadelphia's hectic war preparations, and the frantic proceedings of the Continental Congress, Anne indulged in a brief diversion from the chaos—a lyrical and coy exchange of poems with the dashing thirty-two-year-old Thomas Burke, the ebullient Irish-born doctor and lawyer who had arrived in the city in March 1777 as a North Carolina delegate to the Continental Congress.[49] Echoing the sixteenth-century English poet Edmund Spenser, he was "Collin" and she was "Chloe." Anne was a Quaker in good standing though far from devout; Burke was anything but religious. Collin serenaded Chloe with pastoral couplets, to which she responded in rhyme. To Chloe:

> You ask me, fair Chloe, to strike the gay Lyre,
>   Once more to attempt the soft Strain.
> Alas! Long neglected has slept ev'ry Wire,
>   And I strive to attune them in vain.
> The Time is no more when a Virgin's bright Eyes
>   And sweet Smiles could gay Transport impart;
> No more from fair Bloom those Emotions arise
>   Which once so enchanted my Heart.

Chloe replied:

> Sly Reynard espied a Crow light on a Spray
>   With a Prize that he wish'd to possess;
> Complimenting to gain it, he judg'd the best Way
>   And thus did the weak one address:

> "Thou Goddess of Melody, prithee bestow
>   One Lay to divert it true Friend,"
> By Vanity blinded, the ignorant Crow
>   With her Discord the Aether did rend.

The harsh realities of the bloody War for Independence would pit Anne's Quaker pacifism against this Irish-born colonist's defense that violence was required to repel a hated English occupying force. Pondering an American push for independence and worried about how pacifist Friends could weather the storm besetting them, Chloe pleaded with Collin:

> Come, Collin, acknowledge this Doctrine is right,
>   The Test of true Patience and Worth,
> That 'tis highly unlawful for Christians to fight
>   Or the Shiloh was ne'er upon Earth.[50]

Collin agreed in theory, though by this time it was rumored that a massive British and Hessian army was gathering to attack Philadelphia in a knock-out blow to end any American pretensions of independence.

> With thine will he join his benevolent Pray'r
>   That Warriors their Rage may forego,
> That Love universal and Virtue may share
>   O'er Man all Dominion below.[51]

Collin and Chloe's friendship began to unravel three months later when the British surged northward from the head of Chesapeake Bay to engage Washington's army at Brandywine Creek. Vacating his congressional seat, Collin dashed off to join a North Carolina regiment at the fierce, blood-drenched Battle of Brandywine. He left for Chloe a twenty-one-stanza poem, "Ruthless War," which he hoped might persuade her that gaining liberty required violence:

> Collin, too, feels his injur'd Country's Woe;
>   He deeply mourns the Wound at which she bleeds,
> To his fair Friend would give at least to know
>   From Force, not Choice, we join the deathful Deeds.

> Ambition proud and Avarice severe
> > Invade our Land across th' Atlantic Main.
> Not ours the Crime that lifts the pointed Spear
> > Amidst his Fields to pierce the peaceful Swain.[52]

But Anne's fascination with Burke was waning. That they held starkly different values and beliefs became abundantly clear when hundreds of wounded American soldiers were carried into the city for treatment and rest. She sent off a lengthy letter to him two days after the Battle of Brandywine (September 11, 1777), a conflict that cleared the way for the British forces under General William Howe to storm Philadelphia. Asserting her pacifism and the guiding principle of humility, she scolded Burke for his belief that the wealthy, by their lavish lifestyles, deserved praise for employing the poor. "Remember, Collin," she chided, "those who are placed in conspicuous stations owe the duty of a right example to that multitude, which is ever looking up for imitation, to the manners of its superiors."[53] Hoping to hold onto her friendship, Burke sent another poem that addressed "his compliments to Miss Emlin [and] begs her to accept of the enclosed apology for his not obeying her commands."[54]

OCCUPIED PHILADELPHIA

Two weeks before this incident with Burke, Anne and her family had been reminded just how dangerous and uncertain it was to maintain neutrality as the British approached Philadelphia. On August 31, the Continental Congress had fingered forty-one men they deemed "inimical to the cause of American liberty" and recommended their detention. Included were Caleb Emlen, Anne's brother, and Samuel Emlen Jr., her father's cousin. An arresting committee, finding a sick Samuel Emlen confined to his bed, broke into his desk searching for incriminating papers "of a public nature." Samuel was given parole, while Caleb Emlen, once confronted, "took the oath as required by law and was therefore discharged."[55] If this was not frightening enough, Anne and her family trembled when Pennsylvania's Supreme Executive Council charged twenty other men, seventeen of them Quakers, as persons also "inimical to the cause of America." Denied the opportunity to defend themselves, not even informed of the charges against them, the accused were to be exiled to the Virginia frontier. Several of the Quaker men were related to the Emlens; others were close friends. Forced from the Masonic lodge where they had been imprisoned, they were manhandled by soldiers from the Philadelphia militia "into the Waggons by force" and "drove off surrounded by guards and a mob," wrote Anne's cousin, Sarah Logan Fisher.[56] As the militia made its way westward through the streets in a pouring rain to the falls of the Schuylkill River, it likely passed the State House on Chestnut Street, in plain view of the Emlens, who surely watched in dismay.

Ten days later, on September 26, the British Army, under General Lord Charles Cornwallis, triumphantly rode into Philadelphia. Continental Congress delegates had already fled to Lancaster, and half or more of the thirty thousand Philadelphia residents had decamped to New Jersey or to counties west of the city. But Anne and her family stayed put. There, on a windy, cold morning, they watched Cornwallis and Hessian Lieutenant-General Wilhelm Knyphausen lead the Crown forces into the city with fifes trilling and drums beating out "God Save the King." Riding alongside the soldiers was Joseph Galloway, friend and relation of the Emlens, former speaker of the Pennsylvania legislature, delegate to the First Continental Congress, and, by the onset of the war, a hard-bitten Loyalist. Not a shot was fired as three thousand troops paraded through the city and stopped at the State House, across from the Emlen home. Sarah Logan Fisher described the motley spectacle and marveled how "baggage wagons, Hessian women, horses, cows, goats, and asses brought up the rear."[57]

One British officer claimed that the massive, red-coated army entered the city "amidst the acclamation of some thousands of the inhabitants, mostly women and children." A Hessian officer observed that "the inhabitants, who are said to still number 10,000, came to meet us and showed in various ways their pleasure at our arrival."[58] With Philadelphia a war zone under military occupation, how could the twenty-two-year-old Anne and her family withstand the British takeover of the city? Were the Emlens in that cheering crowd? It is unlikely, for they were never charged with loyalism, and their house was never targeted by Patriots; thus they were more fortunate than other Quakers who were repeatedly harassed and whose homes were assaulted over perceived support for the British.

In some respect, Anne and her family must have welcomed the British occupation, though it would have been imprudent to say so. Once in control of the city, the British strictly banned the use of Continental paper currency and declared the specie and paper money issued previously by the prerevolutionary Pennsylvania government to be the only legitimate medium of exchange.[59] Thus, Quaker families and other Loyalists no longer had to deal with the wrath of the Committee of Observation and Inspection for refusing to traffic in Continental currency. Of benefit to many, including Anne's family, war taxes were held in abeyance since Pennsylvania's revolutionary government no longer held sway in the city. For nine months, no Patriot tax collector would arrive to harvest assessed taxes, no sheriff would come to 179 Chestnut Street to garnish an equivalent amount in household furnishings or to confiscate other moveable property from the Emlens.

In this unusual circumstance the PYM convened to consider their position only a few days after the British seized the city. Customarily as many as a thousand Friends from New Jersey, Delaware, Maryland, and the Philadelphia hinterland would have joined hundreds of Philadelphia Friends for their annual gathering; however, this time only the most intrepid members would attempt to pass through the British picket lines surrounding the city. George Churchman, one of Chester County's foremost Quaker ministers, confided to his diary, "Even in times of outward commotions and blood shedding" true Friends could "not shrink from upright endeavors to hold our yearly meeting as a public testimony of an unshaken zeal for the cause of righteousness, even where difficulties abound."[60] Warner Mifflin, who would a decade later become Anne's husband, was among those brave Friends who attended, believing they could not disappoint the Almighty by avoiding the war-scarred city.

Almost certainly Mother Emlen, Anne, and her siblings attended the yearly meeting, convened on September 30, as did nearly every other Friend still in the city. One of the meeting's main tasks was to draft a peace testimony to be presented by a delegation of Friends to the commanding generals of the contending armies. The epistle, as Friends called such a remonstrance, begged both armies to halt the violence and follow "the peaceable Doctrines of Christ to seek the Good of all." The delegation also made the firm denial that Quakers' refusal to bear arms on behalf of American independence was by no means equivalent to betraying the "glorious cause." They argued in the epistle that this was not so. Friends' opposition to war and the shedding of blood affirmed their peace testimony but did not make them traitors.

On October 3, the yearly meeting appointed a six-member delegation, which included Warner Mifflin, to deliver their epistle to Generals Howe and Washington. News reached the city the next day that General Washington and his officers, eager to avenge the defeat at Brandywine and the humiliation of the British uncontested occupation of Philadelphia, had gambled with a bold but injudicious plan to attack the large contingent of Howe's troops encamped at Germantown, just west of the city.

On the morning of October 4, the Emlens and other residents surely heard the cannon fire booming through the fog. Then the fateful word came about the mounting casualties and the retreat northward of Washington's forces after their futile assaults on the British lines. Nonetheless, the next day, adjourning their yearly meeting but not yet knowing fully the outcome of the battle, Friends sent the mounted peace delegation on its way. A week later the delegates arrived back in the city, reporting that both Howe and Washington had listened to the epistle and allowed the delegation to pass on unharmed. "We believe the Lord's Hand was in it," they reported, "guarding us from improper compliances and bringing us through this weighty service, though it was a time of humbling baptism."[61]

Not knowing how long the British army would occupy their city, the Emlens were fearful of widespread attacks on neutrality-seeking Quakers. Fortunately, no British officers demanded quarters in their spacious house.[62] Yet it was a time not only for the Emlens but for all Quakers to pray that "the Lord's Hand" would protect them.

If this war was a test for beleaguered Friends, broadly hated by the Patriots for their refusal to pay war taxes or to sign oaths of allegiance to the revolutionary government, it was also a time to reexamine religious and political commitments. Anne, like so many others from the topmost stratum of Philadelphia society, had been disturbed by the radicalization of Philadelphia politics as fervent Patriots commanded the streets and created a state constitution that left conservatives such as John Adams aghast that adult males without property should have the vote. Keeping her opinions in a commonplace book, Anne asked, "How shall I impose a silence upon myself, when the subject is so very interesting . . . and what every member of the community is more or less concerned in?"[63] She did not have to look far, for within view of her own home, British officers paraded in and out of the State House, where many of them were quartered.

Faced with this reality, Anne took solace in her writing, filling copybook after copybook with extensive "Notes on the Bible"; 120 pages of details from Samuel Bownas's *Account of the Life, Travel, and Christian Experiences of the Work of the Ministry of Samuel Bownas*; a long and moody "Account of My Religious Progress"; and an oversized commonplace book titled "Notes on Quaker Doctrine" with abstracts of minutes and advices from the London

Yearly Meeting organized by topics—among them Education, Mourning Habits, the Poor, Slaves, Sufferings, Plainness, and Youth.

In another twelve-page expostulation, "Some Notes on the Payment of Taxes Appropriated for Military Purposes,"[64] Anne ransacked world history to detail the savage wars that had slaughtered or subjugated innocent peoples. Because it especially provoked her indignation, she recorded how the British in Africa used their military power "to enable the heathen in conjunction with professed Christians to make war with and make merchandize of their brethren." So also did she consider the long history of European-Indian violence in America, where "the Indians [have] been instigated to acts of evil and murder [of] Christians," and how "Christians scalping Indians have stained the earth with human blood for a miserable share in the spoil of a plundered world."[65]

Along with hours spent reading, taking notes, and pondering ideas on religion and politics, Anne also carried on daily domestic duties, walking Philadelphia's occupied streets to visit friends, attend meeting twice a week, and shop for the family's foodstuffs. Yet routine was anything but normal. During the first two months of British occupation, Patriot forces blockaded Delaware River traffic, obstructing the king's ships necessary to supply the city and the British Army. By encircling the city with the Continental Army and Pennsylvania militia, General Washington created a stranglehold, preventing farmers willing to vend their produce to either the British or the remaining Americans. "Money will not procure the necessaries of life," wrote Sarah Fisher, "for as the English have neither command of the river nor the country, provisions cannot be brought in."[66] Though Anne never mentioned it in her commonplace books, the Emlen family, like the entire civilian population, faced subsistence shortages or worse until the British opened the river on November 15, 1777. The poor who in the best of times tottered on the brink of catastrophe were in a "dreadful situation for the lack of provisions and firewood," reported Christopher Marshall, a former Friend. Even the daughter of the Frederick Muhlenberg reported that her family was "now living on potatoes and bread."[67]

During the city's subsistence crisis, Washington's attempts to besiege occupied Philadelphia could also be felt at the Emlens' spacious country home in Whitemarsh. Inherited by her older brother, the pleasant refuge had been used by Anne, her parents, siblings, and friends as a retreat from the clutter, noise, and boisterousness of the city; however, its peace and rusticity was interrupted when Washington appropriated it as his headquarters for a month beginning in early November.⁶⁸ Thankfully the country house was spared destruction during the Battle of Whitemarsh, launched by the British on December 5. As the shattered American troops withdrew two days later, trudging in torn, ragged condition to reach winter encampment at Valley Forge, they had stripped the Emlen property of fences, which the soldiers used for firewood, impelling Anne's brother George to request compensation from the American commander in chief.⁶⁹ Quakers might abstain from war, but they could not prevent armies from encroaching on their homes.

Six months later, the British strategic retreat from Philadelphia on June 18, 1778, was cause for a noisy Patriot celebration. But as we will see in chapter 2, for Anne and her Quaker Friends the blessing was mixed. They worried about the revenge Patriots might take on disaffected Quakers when they returned to the city. Would Mother Emlen resume paying war taxes that the state revolutionary government would surely impose? And what would happen once Continental currency circulated again? Would Quaker pacifists be targeted if they refused to tender the rebel money?

In a last insult to injury, the retreating British officers led the Philadelphia Tories in a spring frolic a month before their departure. Like most Friends, Anne was appalled by their lavish *Meschianza* (Italian for medley)—a gala festivity to honor General William Howe as he withdrew and turned over command of the city to General Henry Clinton. Taking ostentation, indulgence, and debauchery to new heights, on May 18 officers paraded through the city's Northern Liberties to the Delaware docks in commandeered coaches, stepped onto boats and galleys rowed by the officers' slaves, and drifted down the river with bands blaring. With adoring young Philadelphia women from Loyalist families at their sides, they reached the riverside home of their ally, the merchant Joseph Wharton, on the southern boundary of the city.

To initiate the eighteen-hour extravaganza, British officers costumed as medieval knights and their ladies masqueraded as Turkish maids. A mock medieval chivalric tournament—Knights of the Blended Rose battled Knights of the Burning Mountain—was fought to a draw. As darkness fell on the scene, some four hundred guests sat in splendor to applaud fireworks and dancing, as select women balanced on their heads turbans festooned with jewels and feathers. With midnight approaching, twenty-four slaves, dressed in Turkish outfits as symbols of subordination and aristocratic privilege, served a lavish banquet followed by carousing and dancing that kept many of the celebrants from their beds until almost dawn.⁷⁰

Anne's friends saw in the *Meschianza* a stark example of British disdain for everything that Quaker simplicity honored. Expressing her disgust in poetic form, Hannah Griffitts's scratched verses in her commonplace book described

> A shameful scene of dissipation
> The death of sense and reputation
> A deep degeneracy of nature
> A Frolick for the lash of Satire
> A feast of grandeur fit for Kings
> Formed of the following empty things
> Ribbons and gewgaws, tints and tinsel
> To glow beneath the Historic Pencil.[71]

Elizabeth Drinker, whose husband and the other Winchester exiles had returned to Philadelphia only days before, lashed out at the gaudy display, writing, "How insensible do these people appear while our land is so greatly desolated and death and more destruction has overtaken and impends over so many."[72]

There was no peaceful interval or respite for colonists between the British departure and the return of the Continental Congress. The revolutionary regime returned to Philadelphia as quickly as they had left and the Pennsylvania state government was reinstated immediately as well. Consequently, Philadelphia Quakers such as Anne Emlen had every reason to expect renewed assaults from the revolutionary government because of Friends' refusal to support the ongoing violence between two warring armies. Like so many in her faith community, Anne found herself at cross-purposes. Neutrality had not spared them from the conflict; rather, it subjected them to hostility from all sides. As Anne weathered the external battle, she also contended with her own soul searching—how to determine her own identity and life's purpose.

In this tenuous state of things, Anne and her mother busied themselves assisting some of their longtime friends such as non-Quaker Grace Growden Galloway, who had remained in Philadelphia after her Loyalist husband left with the British Army. With the return of revolutionary forces, Loyalists again were targeted and risked incarceration, having their properties confiscated, or worse. Though the retreat of the enemy's forces meant that Philadelphia was no longer the cockpit of war, for Anne Emlen a sea of troubles had only just begun, with more challenges awaiting her.

NOTES

1. "Some Account of the Life & Death of George Emlen, as given in Writing by his Sons Joshua & Samuel Emlen, late of this City, Philadelphia," transcript by Wistar, Morris Wistar Wood Collection, 1716–1942, Quaker and Special Collections, Haverford College, Haverford, Pennsylvania (hereafter cited as QCHC).

2. See "First Tax List for Philadelphia County."

3. Emlen's inventory, described in Thompson, *Rum, Punch, and Revolution*, 30, is transcribed in Philadelphia Wills and Inventories, no. 90, Genealogical Society of Pennsylvania Collections, HSP. For Emlen's wealth in the year before his death, see Parker, "Rich and Poor in Philadelphia," where the tax list is enumerated.

4. The ethic of the Society of Friends in constructing a thriving economy in early Pennsylvania is surveyed in Tolles, *Meeting House and Counting House*.

5. "Some Account of the Life & Death of George Emlen," QCHC.

6. Wolf, *Book Culture of an American City*, 23; Horle et al., *Lawmaking and Legislators in Pennsylvania*, 1:705, 820.

7. "Some Account of [. . .] George Emlen."

8. Toogood, *Historic Resource Study*, 1–2, 6–8.

9. While most prospering Quakers were acquiring enslaved Africans, George Emlen II relied mostly on indentured servants.

10. The acquisition of unfree laborers, who composed about one-third of the city's workforce by midcentury, is traced in Salinger, *"To Serve Well and Faithfully"*; and Nash, "Slaves and Slaveowners in Colonial Philadelphia."

11. *Memorials Concerning Deceased Friends*, n.p. The Quaker term "broken in spirit" describes devout obedience to the Holy Spirit. It does not imply brokenness or weakness. Abbot, *To Be Broken and Tender*; Burnell, *Broken for Life*.

12. Emlen Diary, May 16, 1777. Mary Heath Emlen died on June 1 and was buried two days later, her body ravaged apparently by cancer.

13. Frank Willing Leach, "Old Philadelphia Families: Emlen," *Philadelphia North American*, October 25, 1908.

14. Reinberger and McLean, *Philadelphia Country House*; Lindsey and Dunn, *Worldly Goods*.

15. For the increase in carriage owners by 1772, see Oaks, "Big Wheels in Philadelphia." Whereas many wealthy Friends owned enclosed, four-wheel carriages, the Emlens owned the less pretentious "post-chaise" chariot.

16. In the copious literature on the rise of Quaker worldliness and reform, of particular importance is Jack Marietta, *Reformation of American Quakerism*. More recent works portray the lives of Anthony Benezet and John Woolman, two exemplars of asceticism, humanitarianism, and spirituality: Maurice Jackson, *Anthony Benezet*; Slaughter, *Beautiful Heart of John Woolman*; and Plank, *John Woolman's Path to the Peaceable Kingdom*.

17. The Emlen property included a blacksmith shop and brewery established by Anne's grandfather. Assessed in 1787 at £1,200, it was one of the most valuable properties in the city. For more on the Emlen plot, see Toogood, *Historic Resource Study*, 6–9, 59–60.

18. A detailed survey of the stately Emlen residence was recorded in 1819 for the Philadelphia Contributionship for the Insurance of Houses from Loss by Fire. Although the inspection of the home occurred four years after Anne's passing, the surveyor's descriptions of more permanent architectural details indicate the home had retained the original structural elements since Anne's childhood. The description of the home's exterior and interior

reflect the Georgian neoclassical style. Despite the home's architectural grandeur, the surveyor emphasized its plainness in keeping with Quaker standards. Emlen House, Insurance Survey S03898, Philadelphia Contributionship Digital Archives, http://www.1752.com.

19. Toogood, *Historic Resource Study*, x.

20. Ibid., xi, 6n33.

21. Anne's father was assessed for two slaves in 1767 and for one in 1774. Since only slaves between the age of fifteen and fifty were assessed, the Emlen household may have included others. In Middle Ward, where the Emlens lived, more than one-fifth of the householders owned slaves, numbering eighty-seven in total; certainly, chattel bondage was within Anne's view in the city daily.

22. See Nash and Soderlund, *Freedom by Degrees*; data in chapter 3 shows how the gradual manumission of slaves was correlated with religion, occupation, and city versus rural residence. None of the Emlen family joined the Pennsylvania Abolition Society, established in 1775 when Anne was twenty.

23. Ibid., 64, 144.

24. Women's monthly meetings were charged with monitoring the marriage process and determining a couple's "clearness" to marry.

25. Marietta, *Reformation of American Quakerism*, 61–67.

26. Philadelphia Monthly Meeting Minutes, 1765–1771, November 25, 1768, February 24, June 27, July 28, October 27, November 26, 1769 (hereafter cited as PMMM). Beveridge had been accepted into the PMM after arriving in Philadelphia in 1750. PMMM, 1750–1756, January 31, 1751. Throughout this book, unless otherwise designated, Friends meeting minutes or ephemera are drawn from the Ancestry archive available at http://www.ancestry.com.

27. Charles Coleman Sellers's description of Peale's portraits of Mary Emlen Beveridge (1746–1820) and husband David Beveridge, in *Portraits and Miniatures by Charles Willson Peale* (31–32, 288), notes that if Peale captured David Beveridge's mien—"the face is obstinate and willful, the wide, straight mouth full of fun and caught in the very act of uttering a joke"—then one is all the more taken by the tolerance of Anne's parents for their son-in-law. A century after Peale painted the couple Charlotte Adams gave a lively account in "The Belles of Old Philadelphia," labeling Mary Emlen Beveridge "the sweetest bit of millinery that ever waited for the spirit to move!" in her "crisp, fresh, charming costume in which the latest Paris mode is cunningly adapted to Philadelphia Quaker notions of simplicity. It was doubtless, very expensive simplicity" (37–38).

28. A glimpse of Anne's pastoral visits to the Beveridge home (known as Echo) can be seen in a watercolor of "Echo" rendered in 1792 by James Peller Malcolm and shown in Snyder, *City of Independence*, fig. 97. William Birch's watercolor of an idyllic garden scene at Echo is shown in Cooperman, *Country Seats*, 53.

29. Emlen Diary, April 19, 1770.

30. Brookes, *Friend Anthony Benezet*, 42, 48. Brookes notes that Benezet taught at the Girls School almost continuously from 1757 to 1782. Howard Brinton in "Quaker Contribution to Higher Education" locates the Girls School at Chestnut and Fourth Streets.

31. For the Jones-Catherall school, see Wulf, *Not All Wives*, 47–48, 111–12.

32. Bouldin, "'Days of Thy Youth,'" 209–11.

33. Friends saw value in educating their children beyond the religious motive. Tolles, *Meeting House and Counting House*, 149; Fatherly, *Gentlewomen and Learned Ladies*, chap. 3

34. Both the 1767 tax assessor's list in the Van Pelt Library, University of Pennsylvania, Philadelphia, and the 1774 list in the Pennsylvania Archives, Harrisburg, are available on GenealogyBank, https://www.genealogybank.com.

35. Allen, "Diary of James Allen," 179–80. Allen promised Emlen a copy of the Dunker leader Peter Millar's *Dissertation on Man's Fall*. For spiritual visionaries in early Pennsylvania, see Erben, *Harmony of the Spirits*.

36. Anne Emlen to Hannah Pemberton, March 6, 1776, vol. 28, fol. 177, Pemberton Papers, HSP.

37. Emlen Diary, June 29, 1777.

38. The badly decayed will is in the vault of the Register of Wills office in Philadelphia. More about its contents are presented in chapter 2. The inventory is accessible at Pennsylvania Wills and Probate Records, 1683–1993, Ancestry, http://www.ancestry.com.

39. Nancy (Anne) Emlen to Hannah Pemberton, March 6 and May 18, 1776, vol. 28, fol. 177, and vol. 29, fol. 54, Pemberton Papers, HSP; "Clarissa" [Sally Pemberton] to "Belinda" [Nancy (Anne) Emlen], Incoming Correspondence, Wharton Family Papers, HSP. Most of Griffitts's poems are in Blecki and Wulf, *Milcah Martha Moore's Book*.

40. The First Continental Congress met at Carpenter's Hall from September 5 to October 26, 1774. The Second Continental Congress convened at the Pennsylvania State House on May 10, 1775, after Anne's twentieth birthday.

41. *The Ancient Testimony and Principles of the People Called Quakers Renewed with Respect to the King and Government*, signed on January 20, 1776, was printed in hundreds of copies and in the *Public Ledger* on January 27, 1776.

42. Calvert, "Thomas Paine, Quakerism, and the Limits of Religious Liberty," 606.

43. For more on this, see Sullivan, *Disaffected*, chap. 1.

44. Ibid., 132. Already hated for his *Observations on the Late Popular Measures*, John Drinker, brother of Henry Drinker, was a prominent leader of the PYM. The charges had no legal basis but were effective. The *Pennsylvania Journal* reported the action on February 7, 1776.

45. In *The Relation of the Quakers to the American Revolution* (291n15), Arthur Mekeel found that the PMM disowned thirty-six members for joining the Free Quakers.

46. Marietta, *Reformation of American Quakerism*, 221, 226–27. Sydney V. James in "Impact of the American Revolution" writes that while purifying their Society, Quakers developed a heightened sense of their identity as a people who however small must become the conscience of the nation. For more on the Friends' neutrality position and their detractors, see Sharpless, *Quakers in the Revolution*; Mekeel, *Relation of Quakers to the American Revolution*; Marietta, *Reformation of American Quakerism*; Bauman, *For the Reputation of Truth*; and Brock, *Pacifism in the United States*, chap. 8.

47. Cited in Godbeer, *World of Trouble*, 133. Like Rutledge, many members of the Continental Congress regarded rejection of the paper money as an act of treason.

48. In the view of recent Drinker family biographer Richard Godbeer, this "redefined pacifists as delinquents and traitors" (ibid., 136–37).

49. Burke (1744–1783) emigrated from Ireland around 1760 and in 1771 moved to Hillsborough, North Carolina, where he reconciled the acquisition of slaves with his protests to British tyranny. Elected to the Continental Congress in December 1776, six months later he joined the North Carolina regiment that was badly bloodied at the Battle of Brandywine. Elected governor of the Tarheel state in June 1781, he died at age thirty-eight in December 1783. Burke had been writing poems celebrating colonial resistance to English trade policies

since the 1760s. See Walser, *Poems of Governor Thomas Burke*. Burke's biographer claims his volatile temperament was the cause of challenges to duel and unending squabbles in Congress. See Watterson, *Thomas Burke*.

50. Anne inscribed these verses in her diary on May 26, 1777. She noted other instances of receiving letters or verses from Burke on May 28, June 11 and 26, and July 3. See Emlen Diary.

51. The poems of Collin and Chloe (forty-five stanzas in all) appear in Walser, *Poems of Thomas Burke*, 41–46. The verses were published in *Gentleman's Magazine* in April and May 1778.

52. Walser, *Poems of Thomas Burke*, 47–49.

53. Nancy (Anne) Emlen to Thomas Burke, September 13, 1777, Thomas Burke Papers, box PC55.1, State Archives of North Carolina, Raleigh.

54. Quoted in Walser, *Poems of Thomas Burke*, 66.

55. [Gilpin], *Exiles in Virginia*, 72, 265.

56. Fisher, "Diary of Trifling Occurrences," 447; [Gilpin], *Exiles in Virginia*, 131–33.

57. Fisher, "Diary of Trifling Occurrences," 450.

58. Both quotations are from McGuire, *Philadelphia Campaign*, 19.

59. For the difficulties in maintaining the integrity of colonial paper money during the British occupation, see Sullivan, *Disaffected*, 147–52.

60. Quoted in Nash, *Warner Mifflin*, 60. The next two paragraphs are drawn from this book (61–66). In chapter 2 of *The Philadelphia Campaign*, Thomas McGuire presents the Battle of Germantown and the retreat of Washington's contingents to their encampment at Pennypack Mills.

61. Report to the PYM, quoted in Nash, *Warner Mifflin*, 66.

62. While some British officers demanded quarters in the homes of Quakers, most availed themselves of the hundreds of houses left empty by fleeing families. See Sullivan, *Disaffected*, 145–46, 165–68; and, for an account of "unwanted guests" quartered in the Drinker house, Godbeer, *World of Troubles*, 156–65.

63. "On Politicks," box 1, EFP. Anne was far from alone in stepping into the political realm. For more on genteel Philadelphia women exhibiting political consciousness and joining the revolutionary fray, see Fatherly, *Gentlewomen and Learned Ladies*, chap. 6.

64. For full text of this essay, see chapter 7, below.

65. Ibid.

66. Fisher, "Diary of Trifling Occurrences," 454. Fisher further related that "not a barrel of flour to be bought at any price . . . scarcely any meat in market, nor [a] pound of butter or an egg at any price."

67. Marshall and Muhlenberg's daughter are both quoted in Sullivan, *Disaffected*, 152.

68. The antebellum historian Benson J. Lossing in *Pictorial Field-Book of the Revolution* (2:320–21) described the Emlen country house as "a sort of baronial hall in size and character, where its wealthy owner dispensed hospitality to all who came under its roof."

69. George Emlen to George Washington, November 20, 1778, and Washington to Emlen, December 13, 1778, in Lengel, *Papers of George Washington*, 18:400–401, also available in George Washington Papers, Library of Congress, Washington, DC (hereafter cited as LC), via Founders Online, https://founders.archives.gov.

70. For the fullest account of the *Meschianza*, see Shields and Teute, "Meschianza."

71. The full poem is in Blecki and Wulf, *Milcah Martha Moore's Book*, 32.

72. Crane, *Diary of Elizabeth Drinker*, 1:306 (May 18, 1778).

Chapter 2

A SEASON OF TRIALS, 1778–1788

The British retreat from Philadelphia brought no relief for the Emlens or others who had remained in the war-torn city. The challenge during the summer of 1778 was to adjust and adapt to living under another military force—the Patriot revolutionary government. Treading carefully with a badly fractured economy, Philadelphians sought survival by persevering from day to day. For Anne Emlen, at age twenty-three, her inward conflict focused on her personal travail to discern how best to serve God. Such a pursuit was not unusual, for it had been experienced by scores of young Quaker women for more than a century on both sides of the Atlantic.

However, Anne's search for answers had to be conducted in the maelstrom of revolution, within a community where Friends disaffected from the Patriot cause were regarded as pariahs. This further complicated her questing of how a true Friend should deal with the contentious matter of paying war taxes with the paper currency that the Continental Congress had issued to finance the war. This contention between her religious principles and the currency dilemma brought Anne many months of relentless self-examination from which she would not secure peace of mind until the War for Independence ended.

Of marriageable age, Anne faced a series of proposals with apprehension. "My mind was tried from time to time," she wrote in her commonplace book, "with various exercises and scruples and with different presentations of marriage, which in some instances caused me searchings of heart or deep inquiries to know the mind of truth; for as it is a weighty thing to propose, so is it a weighty thing to decide, where the objects appear worthy."[1] Her quandary, it seems, was not whether a suitor appeared a good prospect—after all, in her own right she had secure wealth and held an elite social position—but rather how it rested with her own spiritual searching on how best to serve. The crux of the matter was whether she could be an effective instrument for God *and* a dutiful wife; or should she devote herself entirely to religious service as a single woman? In either case, Anne reflected that she was "not near enough the kingdom through obedience and purity of soul."[2] As this chapter explains, these tossings of mind, as she called them, would unsettle her for some time as she tried to work out how best to fulfill her life's purpose.[3] In the midst of this spiritual ruminating she would turn down a number of worthy suitors, but eventually find one whose pious devotion and deep-set integrity were as redoubtable as her own.

QUAKERS AND THE WAR

After the Continental Congress returned to Philadelphia on the heels of the British evacuation in June 1778, Anne's distress at the world around her reached a critical point. A cloud of revenge hovered over the city as returning radical revolutionaries saw "the weakening of British power as an opportunity to punish, neutralize, or cast out" those who had withheld unalloyed support from the "Glorious Cause."[4] For those who had refused to take the Patriots' oath—to renounce the king and pledge allegiance to Pennsylvania's revolutionary government, which most Friends regarded as illegitimate—a revived and fortified Test Act caused deep concern.[5] By doubling taxes on dissenters and threatening imprisonment, banishment, and even death, the Test Act of 1778 also imposed especially punitive fines on those in trade, education, law, and medicine.[6] Although the thirst for revenge did not touch Anne personally, it did affect many of her neighbors and Friends.[7]

During the summer of 1778, once the anger and bitterness of radical Patriot Philadelphians subsided, it gave way to state authorities generally refusing to carry out the program of retribution allowed by the law. Indeed, the cry for republican simplicity as an antidote to the dissipation of an occupying army's fondness for theater, cockfighting, horse racing, and extravagant parties earned some sympathy for Friends; after all, Quakers were exemplars, at least in theory, of a more plain and restrained mode of living. Notwithstanding the Pennsylvania legislature's retreat from a vengeful state policy to further harass neutrality-bound Friends for refusing to take the oath of allegiance, the retribution against outright Loyalists invoked both sorrow and sympathy from Anne and her family.

A few months after the British departure, under the horrified gaze of Philadelphia Friends, two Quaker males were hanged for treason.[8] Both Abraham Carlisle, a carpenter, and John Roberts, a wealthy miller living outside the city, had been indicted for high treason. Charged only a few days after the British had decamped, they were soon convicted of assisting the British Army during its occupation of the city. They had hoped for clemency (which in fact had been recommended by both the indicting grand jury and convicting petit jury), but the hundreds of petitions filed in their favor failed. It is understandable that Anne and her family may not have wanted to witness two condemned Friends walking behind a horse-drawn cart bearing their own coffins as it proceeded from the Old Gaol along Market Street to Center Square (at the site of today's City Hall), where they were hanged on November 4, 1778. But the next day, when Carlisle was to be buried, Anne was likely among the thousands who followed Carlisle's coffin to the Friends Burying Ground a few blocks from the Emlen house.[9]

Anne never mentioned the doleful scene in her commonplace books, perhaps fearful given that two Friends had been executed and sensible that some things were just too difficult to write about. But Anne and her mother would have certainly agreed with diarist Elizabeth Drinker that it was "an awful solemn day." But mother and daughter likely numbered among the "many sympathizing Friends" who did their best to console the families of the convicted men.[10] The executions were a heartrending reminder of the perils that Friends or anyone suffered, living under the revolutionary war zone in that volatile city. Several months later, while on her way back to Philadelphia, Anne lodged at the home of John Roberts's widow and offered spiritual comfort to her. Noting the visit, Anne interjected in her diary, "May her flock of offspring come out refined by their sufferings."[11]

In another instance, Anne and her mother risked much in their support for outspoken Grace Growden Galloway, whose husband Joseph Galloway was the most detested Philadelphia Loyalist of all. Unavoidably, Anne witnessed a family trauma as it played out close by at the Market Street home of the Galloways. Benjamin Franklin's former close friend and political ally, the haughty Galloway was broadly hated for serving as police commissioner of Philadelphia during the British occupation. It was only a matter of official paperwork before Pennsylvania's revolutionary government attained the Galloway properties and confiscated the mansion at Sixth and Market Streets, only a few blocks from the Emlen residence.[12]

Anne and others were mindful of how Grace Galloway had hurled insults at Patriots; how she refused in her own words to "acknowledge their authority as I was an English woman and could not be a traitor" to the king; how she wrote pathetic letters to her departed husband and daughter after they left the city with the British in June 1778; how she nursed her emotional wounds as her health rapidly declined; how she tried to fight in the courts for the properties she had inherited from her father; and how she suffered spells of deep depression. "I am fled from as a pestilence," a besieged Grace confided to her diary. However, those avoiding her did not include Mother Emlen, Anne, or her future husband. After Captain Charles Willson Peale forcibly removed Grace from her confiscated house on August 20, 1778, Anne and Mother Emlen visited the stricken woman at the home where she lodged temporarily with a friend over the next few years.[13] Thus Anne Sr. and Jr. risked the umbrage of Philadelphia Patriots for living up to the name *Friends*.

The fateful months in 1778–79 accented Anne's growing faith commitment even though more practical matters disrupted her spiritual musings. Like every other Philadelphia market shopper, she found it impossible to ignore the steep decline in the value of Continental currency as soon as it was reinstated as legal tender following the British withdrawal. Congress watched in despair as the price of household commodities spiraled upward. Everyone could see how this inflicted the most hardship on those who could least bear up under the runaway inflation. Many war-savvy merchants and financiers engaged in currency speculation, forestalling, monopolizing, and price gouging. One citizen decried that Philadelphia matched the dissipation found in London and Paris; another lamented the city's "avaricious bustle" amid "the dirty struggle" for riches and noted how "monopoly and extortion" ruled the day.[14] The French minister observed how "every Lady and Gentleman were endeavoring to outdo the other in splendor and show."[15] Members of the Continental Congress were as much to blame, exposed in the press and in handbills scattered about the city describing how they reveled at unseemly balls, feasts, and dancing assemblies while other Philadelphians suffered the casualties of war.[16]

Given the Friends' precarious position, it was not advisable that Anne speak out over the collapse of civic morality in letters to city newspapers; instead she vented her disillusionment and anger at Thomas Burke, her former poetic correspondent. In March 1779, she confided privately in her commonplace book how she prayed to God for "prudence, divine prudence, which may prove a stay to my mind and a bridle to my tongue." With no immediate answer to her prayer, she went after her literary foil again, blistering Burke with an eight-page letter laying bare her anguish at what she was seeing in the streets of Philadelphia.[17]

The anger that Anne directed at Burke may have been triggered partly by her disgust at the vulgar display of arrogance and self-indulgence at the recent *Meschianza*. What she witnessed daily in the insatiable appetite for material goods, pursuit of wartime profits, and distress among the lower orders of Philadelphians struggling for their daily bread likely added to the intensity in her letter. Burke had argued that the war profiteers in fattening their purses and burnishing their lifestyle should be *complimented* for providing work for the poor. His bold statement that importing "luxuries are necessary to employ the . . . laboring poor" left Anne indignant. "Then stop the channels of luxury by limiting trade to the necessaries of life," she proposed; "in feeding a vanity and excess . . . destructive to true peace . . . must finally ruin hundreds who now dance the giddy whirl of thoughtless dissipation, if the prevailing extravagance continues."[18]

Giving no quarter, Anne cited the early Quakers' stance against acquisitiveness and ostentation, and taking it a step further asked, "Is money deemed the riches of a nation? . . . Yet money is but a nominal good, in reality a great evil; and heartily should I rejoice if it were banished [from] society as its most subtle and insinuating foe." Where, she asked, did silver and gold come from after all but the "unwholesome mines," where enslaved Africans lived out their short and miserable lives?[19] Here she channeled the argument of John Woolman and Anthony Benezet that slavery was rooted in avarice and an obsession with luxurious living.[20] Half of society "are bond servants to the others," Anne continued, "who are daily resting in the means which the unremitted labor of those furnishes unbridled passions whom chance or avarice has placed beneath them." Anne aroused some regional pride to counter Burke's southern allegiance, asserting that here, in the midst of a revolution, where "we of the North" were supposed "to raise a more exalted standard of righteousness than has hitherto been erected," it was "high time . . . for some valiants to arise, animated with the genuine spirit of liberty, who shall plead the cause of truth and equity, point the defects in government, and generously seek to restore the original rights of mankind." Ending her letter, she declared that their friendship was broken. Striking a conciliatory pose, Burke excused himself for his earlier remarks that had offended her but held his ground that his arguments were only such that "I must derive from reason and experience."

A Season of Trials, 1778–1788

Still, he understood that it was time to withdraw since he could not "deem myself worthy to *approach your purity.*"[21]

Revealing herself as an enemy of slavery and an advocate of universal freedom, Anne sided partially with radical Philadelphians who, as she put these words on paper, were publishing newspaper articles that scourged "such a frequency of public entertainments and dissipation" when "numbers of our fellow citizens are suffering every hardship, naked, without house or home, and destitute of the necessaries of life for the subsistence of themselves and their little ones."[22]

Given these excesses, Anne told Burke that if sumptuary laws were passed to put a ceiling on anyone's riches, there would be "no motive for the pursuit of needless wealth." Stopping the growing inequality "might serve to avert a thousand acts of tyranny now experienced towards the poor." Though she was frightened by what she called the "licentious pursuit of liberty," ironically Anne, a wealthy property owner, echoed the proposal of the radical architects of Pennsylvania's 1776 constitution to limit private ownership of large tracts of land, arguing that "an enormous proportion of property vested in a few individuals is dangerous to their rights and destructive of the common happiness of mankind."[23] Though this attempt to pass a so-called agrarian law to prevent the maldistribution of wealth never made it into the state's constitution, it went to the heart of Anne's argument with her former friend. Having stated her case and pitching indignation at Burke, Anne confided to her close friend Hannah Pemberton that she desired never to see or talk with him again.[24]

THE QUESTION OF CONTINENTAL CURRENCY

In trying to hold fast to her Quaker beliefs, Anne's most torturous decision involved the use of Continental paper currency. For some time, she had worried about trading in the money regarded by the most devout Friends as complicit in the violence between the American Patriots and the British imperial war machine. At the same time, since the issue divided Friends sharply, the PYM left the decision to each individual's conscience, and likewise the matter of paying war taxes. The Emlen household was one of many in which family members squabbled over these issues. Anne's mother was willing to comply in using Continental currency and paying war taxes, while Anne was not. By mid-1778, once Continental currency had been restored, mother and daughter were so sharply split on the matter that Anne wondered if she should leave home entirely and seek shelter elsewhere.

Precipitating this tension at 179 Chestnut Street was a visit on May 19, 1778, from Martha Harris, a prophesizing minister of the North Wales Meeting located northwest of Philadelphia. Striding into the meetinghouse at Second and High Streets, "in a singular path as did some of the prophets of old" with "ashes on her head as a token of mourning," Martha warned "with an awful countenance" that God "was about to scorch Jerusalem as with lighted candles" because "of the wrong things among us, one principle of which as a burden to her soul was Friends circulating the Continental paper currency, the great sinew of war."[25] She "said there was but one step between Friends and death, and in 30 days they would be tried." As Anne recounted in her commonplace book, "It struck my mind that in 30 days the English would leave the city, and, if so, I would receive it as a sign that I must as an individual desist from the use of that [Continental] currency, made as the great engine of war, or it would be [the] spiritual death to me."[26] When the British did leave the city just under five weeks later, the die was nearly cast for Anne.

Deeply moved by Martha Harris's testimony, Anne expressed herself openly on the tangled issue of Continental currency despite the dangers involved. This raised concern among her closest female friends in Philadelphia. Cousin Sally Fisher acknowledged that her "coz" faced some difficulties. "At meeting in the afternoon," she wrote, "Dear Cousin Nancy [Anne] Emlen appeared in a few words in prayer. Oh may she be divinely directed and preserved steady."[27] On another occasion, Sally expressed empathy for Anne, who was suffering the cruelty of others: "[I] felt a pity and sympathy that I cannot express for my dear Coz Nancy [Anne]. How afflicting must it be for her who endeavors daily to wait and diligently to seek for renewed strength to be the companion of such light, vain, unthinking company whose [illegible] behavior must be a constant cause of sorrow and exercise to her mind."[28]

Strengthening Anne's resolve to leave the city was the troubling behavior of her older brothers. Not only were the colonies in revolt, but members of the Emlen clan were rebelling as well. George, Joseph, and Caleb Emlen were dismissed from the Society of Friends for numerous infractions of Quaker ethical standards during 1778 and 1779. Earlier, George and Caleb, both merchants, had been repeatedly warned to liberate their slaves until they finally relented in 1779.[29] But in the meantime, a darker shadow was cast on the Emlen household. Despite the efforts of his monthly meeting to work with him to modify his sinful behavior, Caleb's spotty attendance at meeting and his use of intemperate language brought him disownment in late 1778.[30] Then George, the oldest sibling, was disowned a year later for using "unsavory language," paying military fines, and swearing an oath supporting the revolutionary government. When elders tried to advise George to mend his ways, he declared that he did not desire "to be considered as a member among us."[31] Compounding the sorrow of Mother Emlen, son Joseph was disowned for excessive tavern going, drunkenness, and adultery late in the same year.[32] With the Emlen household unsettled by three sibling disownments, Anne confided in the account of her religious progress, "My mind hath been clothed with sorrow under a sense of the great deficiency in a spirit of sound discipline in many families. And the erroneous conduct and benighted mind of a brother has affected me with fearful apprehensions lest he should be forever lost. Oh! Thou who canst turn the heart of man as a man turns his water course in the field, I pray thee to turn his captivity. Comfort my tender Mother amidst all her exercises and enable her to steer along consistent with thy righteous will in deed and word."[33] Although Mother Emlen's voice is silent in all of this, her youngest daughter's disagreement over currency, taxes, and talk of leaving home must have deeply saddened her.

Anne was presented a way forward when she visited the Western Quarterly Meeting in March 1779. Hearing of Anne's distress regarding the Continental paper currency question and the criticism leveled at her, a graying Quaker couple—Thomas Lightfoot, an elder,[34] and his wife Susanna, a Public Friend—invited Anne to make a retreat from the city "that was providentially timely" to take shelter at their home in Pikeland, some thirty miles west of Philadelphia.[35] "My sympathizing friend, Thomas Lightfoot, brought his carriage when he came to the Meeting for Sufferings," Anne recounted, "and took me to their peaceful habitation."[36] "Since my indisposition," she continued, "I have been impressed with an apprehension of duty in leaving my dear Mother's house until she can see her way to forsake the use of Congress currency and the support thereof in the payment of taxes. I see no other way for true peace; what is before me I know not but [I] must rely solely on thy divine sufficiency, Gracious Creator, who hath hitherto sustained me and knoweth how to deliver safely out of, as well as lead into Jordan."[37]

Coincident to her painful separation from family, Anne received another marriage proposal and reflected later that it was fortunate she had left the city or the frequent conversation with the suitor might have "put me in the power of a man not enough, I fear influenced by best wisdom." She turned him down in a decisive letter but in no sense regarded the situation lightly. A few months later she expressed relief that she was still favored with his friendship as she "had some fears [he] would take umbrage at my rejection of his overtures."[38]

Taking refuge with the Lightfoots was by no means a reclusive retreat. In May 1779, Thomas and Susanna invited Anne to accompany them to a general meeting of Eastern Shore Friends, and to visit numerous gatherings of Friends, partaking of fellowship, food, and stopping along the way in the customary Quaker manner.[39] Reaching Kent County on May 7, they lodged at the home of "an endearing well-concerned couple," Warner and Elizabeth Mifflin. Then leaving the Mifflin's Chestnut Grove plantation, they crossed the peninsula, arriving at Third Haven to lodge at Joseph Berry's, where Anne's cousin Samuel Emlen greeted her with the biblical salutation "The righteous shall hold on his way and men of clean hands wax stronger and stronger."[40] Anne likely accepted this salutation as blessed assurance that she was on the right path, writing that this greeting was "repeated to my comfort among the Ministers and Elders where I was invited and introduced." In what was surely a critical turning point in her young life, she was asked at some meetings to speak on diverse matters and to give spiritual counsel to young people in attendance. Although no meeting had formally recognized Anne as a minister or Public Friend, she was certainly being encouraged to conduct herself as one, which raised her hope of achieving such an office. "It is a great thing," she told her diary, "to speak in the name of the most high."[41]

On May 1, 1779, at Third Haven General Meeting, Anne received another emotional boost when she dined at the Tent House, where a number of Friends from the Western Shore were quartered.[42] Throughout this journey Anne had complained of insomnia and a heaviness and travail of soul; upon entering the Tent House, however, her morale was lifted when sensing the apostolic spirit and witnessing the pleasing sight of Friends assembled there.[43] At this gathering, Anne was invited to attend the select meeting "but fear of never being worthy led me to decline; tho' not insensible of the advantage to be reaped from such a privilege."[44]

The opportunity to stay with the Lightfoots in Pikeland and the benefit of their stewardship seemed providential, and even more their serving as Anne's spiritual parents. Susanna Lightfoot, already suffering what would be her last illness, became a matchless spiritual mother to Anne.[45] They related well to each other as Anne attested early on: "Dear Susanna Lightfoot becomes more and more my endeared and faithful friend."[46] Despite her weakening condition, Susanna's active ministry and her wisdom served Anne as an exemplary model.

Susanna was revered for her "weighty conversation" and as a "living and powerful minister of the word," one of "solid and grave deportment," and remarkable for bearing up with steady waiting on the Lord in her afflictions.[47] In their travels through Chester County and down the Eastern Shore, the Lightfoots brought Anne into contact with many influential Friends and occasions to speak and exercise her faith.

Casting her net beyond the circle of Philadelphia Friends, Anne often encountered the unexpected. She lodged, on one sojourn to Haverford preparative meeting, with a widow she assumed was like-minded on not paying taxes but discovered "it was not so and if I had attended to my inward feelings more than outward information [I] might have steered clear of a breach of my testimony against partaking with those who do not wash their hands from the stains of the world."[48] Anne preached to many along the way, such as a tavern keeper on the excesses of his intemperate trade (but explaining to her diary that they had stopped there only out of necessity to feed the horses).[49] At the house of Friend John Morgan, who faced disownment for compliance with martial requisitioning, she stayed all night laying before him "the danger of offending Heaven." On a journey to Catawissa, she ministered to the wives of Job Hughes and Moses Roberts, men imprisoned on suspicion of being Loyalists, and she returned later to rejoice with Hughes and Roberts on their release from jail and reunion with their families.[50] Stopping to worship with Friends both near and distant, visiting the sick, consoling the dying and their families, or comforting mothers in childbirth, Anne's lamblike service was reinforcing the idea that she had a genuine calling.

On the road traveled with the Lightfoots in Chester County, Anne logged many miles of service as a novitiate, but her path was also pitted with periods of depression, anguish, sleeplessness, and alarming dreams as she searched for signs from the Divine that she had gifts and talents the church might use. For months, she agonized whether she was fit to speak before men,[51] but the sense of inadequacy and scrupulous self-examination that kept her awake many nights was not an uncommon reaction for one so prompted to follow the Master's bidding.[52]

Six months after the uplifting experience at the West River Tent House, Anne confided to her diary how her mind was under "such discouragement" that she feared "I was like to be a dwarf in Israel."[53] Two months later, she believed "the hand of the most High is upon me in a diseased state, sent I believe in love," and in March 1780 she wrote that "bodily disposition is shook over me as a load" such that she pleaded with the "Lord, that powerful God of mercy . . . to stop the current of my affliction." In May 1780, promising "obedience and purity of soul," she entreated and yielded: "Thee, Oh! Blessed, that thou wouldst make of me, what thou wouldst have me be."[54]

It was a period of testing as to whether she was fit for a place in the legion of God's Truth seekers. Her determined opposition to the use of Continental paper currency continued to follow her like a dark cloud after moving to Chester County. But no matter how difficult, she never wavered, knowing it was the right decision:

> As the Almighty appears as in thick darkness, so hath he been pleased to approach my soul in his blessed manifestations. For after a season of wading exercise . . . I was relieved in a manifestation of duty to forbear partaking of what was purchased with Continental currency, which being accompanied with the evidence of sweet peace. As the Lord's people are a willing people in the day of his power, my whole will became melted down into resignation provided I might be favored with further confirmations of this being a required duty, which appears needful as the putting into execution this scruple will be attended with a cross and difficulty.[55]

Again, she reiterated in her private journaling that she felt "centered in humble resignation to endeavor for the maintenance of a faithful testimony against the currency . . . though to the loss of much outward substance which I have apprehensions may be the case. Yet [I] would rather encounter the danger of this trial than forfeit that sweet serenity which covers my mind whilst writing this."[56]

That peace that passes all understanding that Anne so fervently desired began to inhabit her mind by the spring of 1781. Over many seasons Susanna Lightfoot had nurtured her with prayer, sound advice, and cautions such as "it was no crime to be tempted but to yield to the temptation was the evil" and other maxims she preserved to review in years to come.[57] To her commonplace book she confided she was risking "this world's friendship" and also "many conveniences and pleasant accommodations of life"; but all she wanted was "Oh! Father of mercies to fill me with the peace of thy kingdom, which will make the most sparing diet and mean attire wholly reconcilable." For "what can be more joyous or supply the want of any external comfort than basking as in the sunshine of thy favor or being embosomed in thy heavenly love and life." Having passed the test of fidelity and a small victory in refusing to use Continental currency, she was ready to enlist in the church militant. A month later, she wrote, "My time passeth sweetly on, much in the love of God which may be maintained I trust through vigilance."[58] Moving forward, she accepted that she was genuinely chosen to enter the ministry. This became all the more evident after attending a Methodist service in Chester County, where she bristled when a young woman was denied the right to speak. "Male and female are declared to be one in Christ," she wrote in her commonplace book.[59]

Though the bold move to leave her mother's home and live with the Lightfoots in Chester County strengthened Anne spiritually, it also brought sharp criticism. One female friend found her adamant position on Continental currency "extraordinary," believing "she carries the matter too far."[60] Some avoided her socially; others were reluctant to visit. Friend Anna "Peggy" Rawle preserved in her diary how she and other young friends had visited Anne in Chester County, though they were concerned "now she had taken a religious turn. I always thought her a very fine woman and do still, though the length she carries her scruples seem more likely to make people despair."[61]

Trying the patience of her peers was one thing, but ignoring the advice of John Pemberton, eighteen years her senior and a revered elder and traveling minister, was another matter. Pemberton firmly counseled her "to return to thy mother's home to avoid any censure which an uncharitable world may cast out." Sounding like a stern uncle, he urged her to "calmly resign to the voice of pure wisdom."[62] But whose "pure wisdom" exactly? If he was trying "to preserve me from the shafts of calumny," Anne replied, the gentle Pemberton was wasting his time. She was fully prepared to bear "a winter season of reproach," insisting, "it is not in mine own will but in the Cross thereto that I have submitted, to become as a mark to shoot." She concluded, "I must endeavor to stand my ground, knowing in the depth of some painful experience on what ground and foundation I do stand on."[63]

FINDING HER RELIGIOUS ROLE

In order to gain sanction for the move to Chester County, in August 1781 Anne requested a certificate of good standing from her Philadelphia meeting in order to join the Concord Monthly Meeting in Concordville, a few miles from the Lightfoot home. But this was a hurdle she could not surmount. If she would not yield to her mother, her friends, or the much-respected John Pemberton, how could she convince the committee appointed to her case to deal with her request? Thus, she was obliged to bow before the committee of women and "rest it [the request] for the present."[64] When she appealed to her meeting again, maintaining that this was what she believed God intended for her, the committee of senior women opposed the move, compelling Anne to kneel before their judgment and accept that this "was not the proper time for her removal."[65] Although she submitted to the committee's decision, she remained in Chester County but probably made occasional visits to Philadelphia.

The refusal of the women's meeting provided Anne a lesson in patience and submission. Quietly placing this setback aside, she turned again to prayer and meditation, which pardoned her for a time from her latest suitor, the much-respected Jacob Lindley, a Chester County Public Friend and frequent delegate to the PYM.[66] "The subject of marriage," she wrote, "sought an opportunity with me that we might look over some past circumstances. We both concluded if we had kept near the guide ourselves and not leaned so much to the council of others, perhaps it might have been. But the right time was over and we parted good friends," though Anne observed her suitor was "exercised to trembling" when he tried to speak of it. Having not yet recovered and still holding affection for her, he would make one last unsuccessful effort to win her hand the following year.[67]

With an American victory over the British secured in October 1781 and independence and peace nearly assured, Anne moved back to her mother's Philadelphia home.[68] Because of her controversial, strict adherence to pacifism, she had not yet been appointed a Public Friend by the Philadelphia meeting, and this caused her to ponder: Was she an empty vessel that God would never fill? Could she be a conduit for the Holy Spirit? In a long letter to John Pemberton in 1785, she poured out her desire "to preserve my integrity (*if favored to have any*) Godward, that no erroneous influence whatever may ever cause my feet to slide from the beaten path of Christ's Companions." Anne feared she had compromised her standing within the community but insisted she would stay the course as a welcome "way of self-denial or abasement of self."[69] Breathing the language of the Lamb's War of seventeenth-century English Quakers,[70] she was determined "to join the already enlisted Troops, the Captains, Generals, and Commanders-in-chief of the heavenly Militia, whose king and awful ruler and commissioner is the Majesty on high."[71] It was merely a matter of awaiting the call.

A SPINSTER'S LIFE?

Marking her thirtieth birthday, April 30, 1785, Anne mused in her commonplace book, "This day having arrived at 30 years of age, I suppose commences that period of time wherein I may be styled what is called an Old Maid. May I through divine grace be so favored to conduct in my future path as to furnish one evidence to different ranks, that it is not marriage or celibacy [that] gives merit or demerit to a person but a life ordered in the fear of the Lord and seeking his glory. I cannot fully account for the respectful mode of speaking sometimes used respecting persons advancing in a single state. It is not founded in reason, neither in our holy religion."[72] But if she was to be one of "Christ's Companions," how could she measure out her life as a spinster? She had crossed the threshold into a new decade, and before too long her views on the single state would be dramatically altered.

Entering her thirties, Anne, like all Friends, was enmeshed in a joint effort to redefine what her role would be in the peacetime community. Quakers had suffered greatly during the revolution, partaking in Christ's "cup of affliction" but standing fast to their pacifist principles while living in the love and convincing authority of gospel truth. Even so, with the war concluded, peace would bring its own problems. North of Philadelphia, the Falls Monthly Meeting, responding to PYM advices, warned of the growing worldliness of its members, observing their absence from meeting and the negligence of Quaker parents to "unguarded youth and others." This behavior showed a disturbing deviation from Friends' Christian testimony.[73]

In postwar Philadelphia, the issue of backsliding members revealed another problem—the sale and excessive use of strong drink. From Chester County too, where Anne had sheltered for many months during the war, came doleful reports of widespread excessive use of spirituous liquors.[74] Having lived as outsiders and suspects during the war, a few Friends yearned for some reengagement in worldly political affairs.[75] But "the leading trait of post-revolutionary reform spirit," writes Sydney James, "was its increased devotion to simplicity" or plain living, which meant avoidance of ostentation such as extravagant hair styles, fashionable dress, or lavish entertainments.[76]

Anne needed no reminder of Friends' simplicity, for she had already vested herself in Quaker plain style, wearing only drab-colored clothing and shunning all "gay society" in order to purge herself of worldliness. Finding her at the home of Elizabeth and Henry Drinker, Ann Warder, wife of an English merchant visiting the city, grimaced that Anne "wore today a dark snuff colored tabareen, but looked old and so awkward made that if her person was not so agreeable it would be disgusting—I mean the dress."⁷⁷ Anne's painstaking notes on Samuel Bownas's Quaker treatise *A Description of the Qualifications Necessary to a Gospel Minister* (1750) betokened her search for spiritual authorization as she tried to purify herself for the work ahead.⁷⁸ Anne was taking on the life of an ascetic, attracting notice for the depth of her spirituality and severe simplicity, along with signs of that special gift from God that was preparing her for the role of public minister.⁷⁹ In June 1785, she wrote with satisfaction about a "seasonable doctrine" that a visiting Friend delivered before the Women's Monthly Meeting. Noting the "superior privilege we [women] enjoyed to others of the nations" who blocked women from "any service they might be in the church militant," he encouraged women to improve "our gifts" and "come more to that live coal which cleanses and fits for service believing the Lord would fit and prepare some . . . to a faithful discharge of duty."⁸⁰

Her spiritual devotion and dedication were not lost on the passionate, debonair reformer Jacques-Pierre Brissot de Warville, one of the remarkable Frenchmen who came to Philadelphia in the postrevolutionary period. He had arrived from Paris in August 1788 to represent a French consortium eager to speculate in the American revolutionary debt and western lands. But unofficially he came to nourish his antislavery commitment by making connections with Philadelphia-area Friends. A few years before his own conversion to abolitionism, Brissot had been inspired by the American Quakers, whom he regarded as models of Enlightenment humanitarianism. In France, he had cofounded the Société des Amis des Noirs (Society of Friends of the Blacks).⁸¹ "One of the purposes of the journey I made to America," Brissot wrote in his memoir, "was to serve the cause of the blacks and to spread the branches of the Society I had just instituted in Paris."⁸²

While in the city, Brissot paid a visit to Anne at the request of Warner Mifflin, who was courting her at the time. Brissot recounted how "Miss Ameland," the once frivolous, beautiful young Quaker girl who "loved the world, wrote poems, composed music, and danced," had turned her life inside out despite jesting from her friends. She "renounced all these amusements to embrace the life of an anchorite in the very midst of society. . . . What sweetness! What modesty! And at the same time, what a pleasant conversationalist."⁸³ Brissot could see that despite her assuming the habits of an ascetic, Anne Emlen had lost none of her sparkle and charm. Brissot's appraisal came at a time when Anne's quickening involvement in the Philadelphia Women's Monthly Meeting was finally earning her recognition. Just a year before she had been appointed at age thirty-two to transcribe the minutes of the women's meeting into the minute book. Then in 1788 she accepted an assignment to join eight other women to unite with members of the men's meeting to visit black Philadelphia families "to promote their moral and religious welfare."[84] This was an appointment of special importance, aligning the women's meeting with the work of the Pennsylvania Abolition Society that had been reorganized a few months before with revitalized plans to aid the burgeoning free black community.[85] Also, such work went forward just as Richard Allen and Absalom Jones were emerging as founders of the city's first black churches and the Free African Society, which modeled the Quaker practice of sending visiting committees to inspect the conduct of city dwellers.[86]

DECIDING TO MARRY

An appointment to the stewardship committee for visiting free black families may have warmed Anne to the avid interest that Warner Mifflin, then forty-one, was paying her. The Kent County, Delaware, Friend was a highly regarded elder well-known in Philadelphia for his dedicated antislavery activities, for freeing his own slaves, and for convincing his father to free nearly one hundred more. Anne would also have heard of Mifflin's role after the Battle of Germantown in 1777, where he and other Friends beseeched the warring armies to turn their swords into ploughshares, and his service as a delegate in the Friends' mission to Princeton six years later to press the abolitionist cause before the Continental Congress. Widowed in June 1786, within a few months he was overwhelmed in trying to raise his five children as their sole parent. Mifflin saw in Anne an attractive consort to raise his children, to run the household when he was away on his incessant missions, and to stand with him as a deeply pious helpmate mutually committed to benevolent reform both inside and outside the Society of Friends. Warner had known Anne since her several years of living with the Lightfoots in Chester County, for she had dined and lodged at Warner's Kent County home during her two cross-peninsula journeys to attend the Maryland general meetings in 1779 and 1781.

The courtship was far from easy for Anne, who by this time had established herself as a single, independent woman active in the meeting, determined to remain unmarried. In her "Account of My Religious Progress" she traced the course of her resistance—and his persistence—stating "How far this may be founded on the Rock, I know not." For Warner, it was an uphill struggle requiring his characteristic persistence. Anne had initially refused his proposal and twice asked that the matter be dropped, but he prevailed as she noted that he "became professed with a belief that I was to become his companion."[87] By mid-1788, Warner's friends were suggesting other possible wives. He desperately needed what his friend Henry Drinker bluntly termed "a housekeeper to superintend his family concerns and discharge a parental duty to his children during his absence from them."[88]

Nonetheless, just when his pursuit seemed a lost cause, on July 26 Warner did the unthinkable: without Anne's consent, he sought approval from his meeting to marry her and bolstered his request with a letter from his father, Daniel, assuring that Warner had "clearness to marry."[89] The meeting held up their decision for another month, during which time the prospective groom pleaded his case with success, marked by Anne's joining him at the Philadelphia Women's meeting twice on August 29 and September 26, 1788, for their final approval.[90]

Though still haunted that she was making an unwise step, Anne acceded. "This day [10th mo. 1788] is the expected time of my second espousals, not unto God as formerly, but unto one of his devoted servants. May the connection be a happy one, but if the gloom that has overspread my mind at this season with plenteous tears flowing from mine eyes, like the gloom of the day perhaps denotes but a solidity and if any peculiar trials before me and disconsolate time for me throughout this marriage."[91] Her brooding on the forthcoming nuptials had apparently been more than prewedding jitters. Some who knew that Warner Mifflin fathered five children (the oldest eighteen) believed his mission-driven penchant for extended trips away from home made him an unsuitable husband for Anne; moreover, friends further disapproved Anne leaving Philadelphia for such an unhealthy part of the country.[92] Nevertheless, they were married on October 9, 1788, at the High Street meetinghouse. Anne said her vows clad as plainly and colorlessly as possible: the dress, bonnet, shawl, and cloak were all of "brown Holland linen," recounted one attendant. Only her cap was white, "made of fine linen perfectly plain and tied with white linen tape under the chin." For this observer, Anne's glowing countenance still shone through: "Under this peculiar garb," wrote Elizabeth Brookes, daughter of one of the founders of the Quaker Sandy Spring meeting north of present-day Washington, DC, "the beauty for which she had been conspicuous was not impaired." Staying after the newlyweds left the meetinghouse, "her fashionable friends" were united in thinking that "she had done all in her power to disfigure her beautiful face and person, but to no purpose."[93] James Pemberton,

Mifflin's friend and mentor, reported that after more than a week in Philadelphia, "Mr. Mifflin, with his prize, set off . . . for his habitation in Kent" after a marriage found "less reconcilable" by many friends who had come to value Anne's "improving in experience and usefulness."[94] Looking back some years later, Philadelphia merchant Thomas Cope described the scene succinctly: "The once celebrated beauty and poet, Nancy Emlen, [was] now the plain and pious Ann[e] Mifflin."[95]

What had convinced Anne to take such an about-face and accept Warner's proposal? Had Warner finally convinced her to say yes by promising that their union could enhance her spiritual calling? He certainly had the wherewithal to make such a bargain. Anne admired Warner as a formidable laborer in the Lord's vineyard and respected his esteemed piety.[96] Perhaps she anticipated that as her husband he could advise her spiritually on how to seek a ministry of her own. Nonetheless, for the time being, Anne simply noted, "Now A. Emlen but no longer is after this day. May the change be at best for my soul's good, though outward trials of rather a sore nature should be my portion, now as hereafter. Amen."[97] Having taken this momentous step, a very different life at Warner Mifflin's Chestnut Grove plantation, in Kent County, Delaware, awaited her.

NOTES

1. MRP, below.
2. Ibid.
3. Anne's "tossings of mind" are expressed by a similar sensation in Quaker biographies of those struggling to find their spiritual path. Note Sarah Crabtree's description "In the Light and on the Road" (131) of the young Patience Brayton as she began her "spiritual captivity."
4. Sullivan, *Disaffected*, 200.
5. Based on Christ's admonition to "swear not at all" (Matthew 5:34), Quakers refused to swear an oath on the principle it "set up a double standard of truth, one in the courtroom and one outside it, carrying the implication that untruth would be uttered in the absence of an oath." Quoted in Brinton, *Friends for 300 Years*, 141. Brinton posits that no testimony resulted in more suffering for Friends than the refusal to take an oath (140–41).
6. Brinton, *Friends for 300 Years*, 201–5; Ousterhout, *State Divided*, 191–92.
7. Friends such as Samuel Rowland Fisher, husband of one of Anne's cousins, continued to be persecuted as late as March 1779; arrested on charges of consorting with the British, he was found guilty, imprisoned for two years, and required to forfeit half his estate. Ousterhout, "Controlling the Opposition," 23. For Fisher's account of his trial and imprisonment, see Fisher, "Journal of Samuel Rowland Fisher."

8. For a full account of the treason trials and executions, see Maxey, "Treason on Trial"; and Lawson, "Revolutionary American Jury."

9. Elizabeth Drinker and four of her children attended, and she noted it was "a remarkable large funeral." Crane, *Diary of Elizabeth Drinker*, 1:334 (November 5, 1778). For an estimate of four thousand in the procession, see Larson, "Revolutionary American Jury," 1496.

10. Crane, *Diary of Elizabeth Drinker*, 1:333 (November 4, 1778). Friends were cautious about making public statements about the hangings; the Philadelphia Meeting for Sufferings maintained silence for a number of years, which was best explained "as the most prudent course to follow as long as other Friends were still exposed to retaliatory measures." Maxey, "Treason on Trial," 105.

11. Emlen Diary, May 23, 1779.

12. An accessible account of the travail of the Galloway family, and especially Grace Growden Galloway, is provided in Evans, *Weathering the Storm*, 185–244. For the confiscation of Loyalist property in Pennsylvania, see Ousterhout, "Pennsylvania Land Confiscations."

13. Galloway, "Diary of Grace Growden Galloway," 141. Brokenhearted at the departure of her daughter and angry to the end with the husband who verbally abused her and manipulated her dowry inheritance, Grace Galloway died in April 1782. Anne Emlen, one of the last to visit her, also attended the funeral. Deborah Morris to Elizabeth Galloway, May 29, 1782, Galloway Papers, LC. For more on Anne's quiet bond of allegiance to the Galloway family, see her letter to John Pemberton, January 15, 1785, below.

14. George Clymer to Susanna Wright, February 15, 1779, quoted in Rosswurm, *Arms, Country, and Class*, 170.

15. Quoted in Miller, *Triumph of Freedom*, 474. The first French minister appointed to the United States, Conrad Alexandre Gérard de Rayneval, staged weekly lavish balls and entertainments in his ornately decorated house.

16. Gérard declared in 1778 that "the spirit of mercantile cupidity forms perhaps one of the distinctive characteristics of Americans." Quoted in Miller, *Triumph of Freedom*, 477.

17. Anne Emlen to Thomas Burke, March 3, 1779, ser. 4, box 14, fol. 152, Cox-Parrish-Wharton Papers, HSP (hereafter cited as C-P-W). Anne was responding to a February 9, 1779, letter from Burke, available in Smith, *Letters of Delegates to Congress*, 12:36. In her diary Anne acknowledged on May 28 having received some verses from Collin (Thomas Burke). The long delay in answering him was likely due to attending Grandmother Mary Heath Emlen in her final weeks of illness. Emlen Diary, May 16–June 1.

18. See the full text of Anne's letter to Burke in chapter 10, below.

19. Friends regarded avarice as a sin, as described in Penn's *No cross, no crown* as "an epidemical and a raging distemper in the world, attended with all the mischiefs that can make men miserable in themselves and in society." Likewise, PYM epistles focused on this year after year; see Tolles, *Meeting House and Counting House*, 80–84.

20. Eighteenth-century reformers Woolman and Benezet believed that Friends' economic success sapped the Quaker doctrine of equalitarianism, which required shunning an accumulation of great wealth, and they followed the lead of the scorned Benjamin Lay, as shown by Marcus Rediker in *The Fearless Benjamin Lay*, 59–60.

21. Thomas Burke to Anne Emlen, March 10, 1770, box 2, EFP, Burke's emphasis.

22. [Anne Emlen], "Philanthropos," *Pennsylvania Packet*, January 21, 1779, quoted in Rosswurm, *Arms, Country, and Class*, 170.

23. *Proceedings Relative to Calling the Conventions of 1776 and 1790*, 52, quoted in Rosswurm, *Arms, Country, and Class*, 104.

24. Anne Emlen to Hannah Pemberton, March 8, 1779, vol. 28, fol. 180, Pemberton Papers, HSP.

25. Elizabeth Drinker noted that Harris visited the Pine Street meetinghouse and the Great Meetinghouse where the Emlens worshiped on May 19, 1778, a day after the *Meschianza* and then went on the next day to the Bank Street meetinghouse. Crane, *Diary of Elizabeth Drinker*, 1:306–7 (May 20–21, 1778). The quoted passages are from MRP, below.

26. MRP, below. Martha Harris returned to Philadelphia on September 6, warning Friends again that "a very trying time was nearly at hand," and appeared at the September yearly meeting, the largest "ever known here," as Elizabeth Drinker noted in her diary. Crane, *Diary of Elizabeth Drinker*, 1:325 (September 6, 1778); 1:329 (October 1, 1778).

27. Sarah Logan Fisher Diary, n.d., vol. 6, HSP. Sally's meaning is either that while attending Friends at the meeting for worship she prayed for Anne or that Anne herself attended and offered up a short prayer. In either case, Sally held Anne in the light, praying she might receive divine guidance and strength.

28. Ibid., December 3, 1778, vol. 6, HSP.

29. Nash and Soderlund, *Freedom by Degrees*, 144.

30. Caleb Emlen (1744–1797), Anne's older brother, was disowned by the PYM in 1778 for using "loose and profane language" and neglecting attendance at meetings. Philadelphia Men's Monthly Meeting Minutes (1777–1781), July 31, November 23, 1778 (hereafter cited as PMMMM). Caleb had been previously sanctioned by his meeting for purchasing a slave in 1773. PMMMM (1771–1777), August 27, 1773, July 29, 1774. His wife, Mary Warder Emlen (1747–1811), maintained good standing with the Philadelphia Women's Monthly Meeting (hereafter cited as PWMM) and therefore exemplifies how fractured religious allegiances did not necessarily disrupt a marriage or a family.

31. PMMMM (1777–1781), September 24, October 29, December 31, 1779.

32. PMMMM (1777–1781), November 26, December 31, 1779, March 31, 1780.

33. MRP, March 1782, below. Anne probably referred to the disownment of her brother Joseph, the third of three Emlen brothers sanctioned by the PMM in 1779–80. The Society of Friends acted in disciplinary measures with unusual probity and objectivity for a religious group at this time. Even though George and other siblings behaved brazenly, the Friends meeting cast no aspersions on the rest of the family, nor did the Emlen family do so toward errant members.

34. Thomas Lightfoot (1728–1793) was the son of Irish immigrant Samuel Lightfoot, who had served as deputy surveyor during the land settlement between Maryland and Pennsylvania and mapped out much of Lancaster and Chester counties. Thomas likewise worked as a land surveyor. He served as a prominent Quaker elder of the Goshen Monthly Meeting and became a delegate to the PYM. In 1760, he married Susanna Hatton (1719–1781), a widowed Irish Quaker minister. After their marriage, Susanna continued her ministry in America by joining Uwchlan Meeting in 1763. Four years after Susanna's death in 1781, witnessed by Anne, Thomas became a Public Friend and married Rachel Hunt. See Lightfoot Manuscripts, 1737–ca. 1948, RG5/184, Friends Historical Library, Swarthmore College, Swarthmore, Pennsylvania (hereafter cited as FHLSC). After the recent loss of her father and the death of her revered grandmother Mary Heath Emlen just two years prior, Anne welcomed the paternal protection of Thomas and the spiritual guidance of Susanna.

35. Emlen Diary, June 20, 1779.

36. MRP, below. Lightfoot recounted that "I returned home on the 28th instant [March 1779], bringing with me my beloved young friend Nancy Emlen." Rutherford, *Quaker Women Passing*, 13. The Lightfoots had just attended the Meeting for Sufferings in Philadelphia when they visited the Drinker household. Crane, *Diary of Elizabeth Drinker*, 1:341 (March 28, 1779).

37. MRP, below.

38. Emlen Diary, June 20, 1779.

39. Third Haven General Meeting, Talbot County, Maryland. Anne's account of this sojourn with the Lightfoots begins in her diary notation on May 2, 1779, from New Garden, Chester County. See Emlen Diary.

40. Job 17:9 states that the righteous may be confident that nothing can hinder those who abide in the perfect will of God.

41. Emlen Diary, May 8, 1779.

42. At this time, the Maryland General Meeting gathered every six months, alternating between West River in Anne Arundel County (on the Western Shore) and Third Haven in Talbot County (on the Eastern Shore). By 1700, to accommodate increased attendance, Friends had built a wood framed canvas structure and pitched tents in the surrounding fields along what came to be called Tent House Creek. The West River Meeting continued until 1785, when it merged with Maryland monthly and yearly meetings that met in Baltimore. National Register of Historic Places, "Quaker Sites in the West River Meeting, a Quaker Community in South Anne Arundel County, Maryland, ca. 1650–1785," May 1, 2008, https://mht.maryland.gov/secure/medusa/PDF/NR_PDFs/NR-MPS-12.pdf.

43. Emlen Diary, May 11, 1779.

44. Anne recognized the weightiness of this invitation. The ministers and elders of select meetings were responsible to cultivate younger members who showed promise in the "growth and purity" of the ministry; in Anne's generation, select meetings were taking on more of the monthly meetings' role as a disciplinary body. James, *People Among Peoples*, 14–15.

45. See chapter 6, note 54, below, on the intensification of Susanna's illness.

46. Emlen Diary, May 3, 1779.

47. "The Testimony of Uwchlan Monthly Meeting concerning our Beloved friend Susanna Lightfoot," Philadelphia Yearly Meeting Minutes (1686–1850) (hereafter cited as PYMM).

48. Emlen Diary, May 1781.

49. Ibid., September 1781.

50. Ibid., June 1781.

51. For the challenges and hardships that female Quaker traveling ministers endured, see Larson, *Daughters of Light*; and Crabtree, *Holy Nation*.

52. Jewish and Christian tradition abound with examples of reluctant prophets, ministers, and saints such as Moses, Gideon, Jeremiah, Saint Paul, and George Fox, who, when called to God's service, doubted their ability to serve.

53. A reference to Leviticus 21:19–21, which defines hunchbacks or dwarves as unclean and not suitable for the priesthood. Anne likely uses this imagery to express how dejected and unworthy she felt.

54. Emlen Diary, November 1779, January 1780, March 1780.

55. MRP, Nov. 1779, below.

56. MRP, May 1780, below.

57. Emlen Diary, April 19, 1779.

58. MRP, April 1781, May 2, 1781, below.

59. MRP, May 26, 1781, below.

60. Sarah Logan Fisher Diary, March 23, 1781, vol. 10, and Anna "Peggy" Rawle Diary, March 1, 1781, HSP, both quoted in Norton, *Liberty's Daughters*, 128.

61. Anna Rawle Diary, March 1, 1781, HSP; the quote is from a transcription of her diary.

62. John Pemberton to Anne Emlen, June 6, 1781, vol. 35, fol. 143, Pemberton Papers, HSP.

63. Anne Emlen to John Pemberton, June 12, 1781, vol. 35, fol. 144, Pemberton Papers, HSP.

64. Philadelphia Women's Monthly Meeting Minutes (1781–1792), August 31, October 4, 1781 (hereafter cited as PWMMM). Anne Emlen lived with the Lightfoots while waiting for her removal certificate.

65. PWMMM (1781–1792), February 22, March 29, 1782. The committee was composed of Sarah Harrison, Elizabeth Rodgers, and Margaret Haines, senior figures of the meeting.

66. Her distant cousins noted this as did Anne herself. Sally Fisher (Kent County) to cousin Sally Fisher (Philadelphia), spring 1781, in Sweeney, "Norris-Fisher Correspondence," 221; Anne Emlen to Sally Fisher, June 12, 1781, box 9, fol. 7, Corbitt, Higgins, Spruance Papers, Delaware Historical Society, Wilmington.

67. MRP, September 1783, below.

68. The exact time of Anne's return cannot be determined. She may have gone back to Philadelphia for the yearly meeting in 1780 and 1781; on December 1, 1782, she wrote from Philadelphia to John Pemberton, indicating that she was back in the city (box 10, fol. 51, C-P-W). The minutes of the PWMM have no notations until 1787 that Anne was active in the business meeting, though she almost certainly attended First Day meetings at the Great Meetinghouse.

69. Anne Emlen to John Pemberton, January 15, 1785, vol. 42, fol. 162, Pemberton Papers, HSP.

70. A metaphor of Christ as sacrificial lamb waging war against Satan in Revelations 17:14: "These will make war with the Lamb and the Lamb shall overcome them, for he is Lord of Lords and King of Kings, those with him are called chosen, faithful." The Quaker founders, viewing history as an ongoing struggle with evil, adopted the ensign of the Lamb's War and enlisted in the cause to fight spiritually, peacefully, and sacrificially if need be. Naylor, *Lamb's War*.

71. Anne Emlen to John Pemberton, January 15, 1785, vol. 42, fol. 162, Pemberton Papers, HSP.

72. MRP, April 30, 1785, below. For the lives and attitudes of single women, see Wulf, *Not All Wives*; and Chambers-Schiller, *Liberty, a Better Husband*. Still single at age thirty, Anne was in good company. By 1786 nearly 25 percent of Quaker women remained single. Wells, "Family Size and Fertility Control," quoted in Tarter, "Written from the Body of Sisterhood," 86.

73. James, *People Among Peoples*, 268–71, esp. 270.

74. Report from Chester QM in PYMM (1780–1798), October 1, 1784. The strong language of the report pointed to "the corrupting and debasing and ruinous effects consequent on the importation and retailing large quantities of distilled spirits whereby the intemperance of them [Friends] is greatly aided and encouraged to the impoverishment of many, distempering the constitution and understanding of many more, and increasing all manner of vice and dissolution throughout the land."

75. In an April 1784 letter to Nantucket Friend William Rotch, James Pemberton had warned that Friends should shun all participation in electoral politics and put "no

confidence . . . in the friendship of the men of this world or of those who are actuated by its unstable spirit." Quoted in Bauman, *For the Reputation of Truth*, 175.

76. James, *People Among Peoples*, 271.

77. Warder, "Diary of Ann Warder," 445–47.

78. Anne Emlen, "Extracts from Samuel Bownas Council [Counsel] to the Ministers and Elders," box 1, EFP.

79. Bruce Dorsey in *Reforming Men and Women* (39–49) explains the role of divinely inspired young unmarried Quaker women in the Philadelphia area.

80. MRP, June 28, 1785, below.

81. For the broader context of French visitors and émigrés to Philadelphia, see Furstenberg, *When the United States Spoke French*.

82. Quoted in Rossignol, "Jacques-Pierre Brissot," 146. In close contact with London Quaker abolitionists such as Thomas Clarkson and Granville Sharp, Brissot had joined the Society for Effecting the Abolition of the Slave Trade in 1787, after its founding in London (ibid., 141).

83. Brissot de Warville, *New Travels in the United States*, 166–67. An anchorite is a devout individual choosing extreme seclusion for religious purposes.

84. PWMMM (1781–1792), December 28, 1787, March 28, 1788. The minutes recorded that the delegation visited forty-five black families. Such visits continued the work initiated in 1781 when the Philadelphia Quarterly Meeting (hereafter cited as PQM) established a Committee to Inquire into the Conditions of Freed Slaves. The efforts of Philadelphia Friends in support of the free black community is detailed in James, *People Among Peoples*, 290–92.

85. Nash, *Forging Freedom*, 90–94, 103–6.

86. Ibid., 98–101, 109–25.

87. MRP, December 1786.

88. Henry Drinker to James Thornton, July 26, 1788, Richard Cadbury Collection, QCHC.

89. Duck Creek Monthly Meeting Minutes (1705–1830), July 26, 1788, transcription, HSP (hereafter cited as DCMMM).

90. MRP, October 1788. The PMM Record of Certificates (1779–1822) shows that the meeting had approved the union on August 23, when it recorded that Warner was an elder "in unity of orderly life and conversation" (61). Warner and Anne's appearance at PWMM on September 26 was the final requirement for the couple's clearness to marry. PWMMM (1781–1792), August 29, September 26, October 31, 1788.

91. MRP, October 1788, below.

92. Warder, "Diary of Ann Warder," 62. Kent County's flat plains were seasonally disease-ridden, taking a fearful toll especially on young children.

93. The marriage vows between Anne and Warner and the Elizabeth Brookes account are in box 1, fol. 24, Mifflin Family Papers, Special Collections, Franklin and Marshall College Library, Lancaster, Pennsylvania.

94. James Pemberton to John Thornton, October 21, 1788, Richard Cadbury Collection, QCHC.

95. Harrison, *Philadelphia Merchant*, 105–6.

96. Anne witnessed Warner give testimony on several occasions, such as at the Third Haven general meeting. Emlen Diary, May 17, 1779.

97. MRP, October 1788, below.

Chapter 3

FAITH IN ACTION, 1788–1798

After Anne, the reluctant bride, moved to Warner's Chestnut Grove plantation she immediately became stepmother to his five children, the youngest not yet four years old. It portended an overwhelming beginning to married life, but in reality the significant household staff, perhaps several of them black women freed by Mifflin in 1775, would shoulder much of the burden, leaving Anne free to pursue her religious work. Considering that before their marriage Anne knew of Warner's reputation and zeal in the cause of abolitionism, she must have greatly admired his dedication and savored the possibility of sharing in that ministry. One can imagine also that she was elated at the chance to leave Philadelphia for a fresh start at the Murderkill meeting.

This chapter traces the arc of Anne's Quakerly commitment upward over the decade of marriage, even as sad events and the decline of her husband's health pulled her life downward. From the young woman filled with self-doubt in her early twenties she would emerge after marriage into an important leader of her monthly meeting even while bearing her own children and playing stepmother to her husband's.

MOTHERHOOD AND THE MURDERKILL WOMEN'S MEETING

Notwithstanding Anne's misgivings over taking the big step of marriage and the earlier years of longing yet questioning how to be of service to Quakerism, her prayer—"I pray thee in and through the inexhaustible riches of thy goodness to make known unto me and lead me safely in the way thou wouldst have me to walk"—had been answered in great measure.[1] As soon as Anne arrived at her husband's home, opportunities came flooding in, beginning with immersion in the work of the Murderkill Women's Monthly Meeting.[2] Not only did the Murderkill women gladly accept her removal certificate from the PWMM in January 1789,[3] but they also recognized her talents and dedication and began appointing her to important committees.[4] Anne's devotion to her faith was finally being rewarded. By November 1789, Murderkill Friends chose her as one of four women to attend the recently formed Southern Quarterly Meeting (SQM).[5] Ironically, the married state Anne had so dreaded brought improvement and promoted her religious service. From this point forward, her meeting counted her as one of its most valuable members.[6]

Anne's service to her meeting had to be balanced with considerable responsibilities at home. Hardly a month after settling in Kent County, she watched her husband saddle up to resume his incessant lobbying of state legislatures on the issue of slavery. This time he was headed for Annapolis, Maryland, where he hoped to persuade the legislature to repeal the law blocking the manumission of slaves and another regarding the treatment of mulatto children.[7]

As soon as he returned in December 1788, Warner anticipated another journey, hoping that the Philadelphia Meeting for Elders and Ministers would approve his request for traveling to London to meet with Friends there.[8] For more than two years, Warner had been trying to get approval for travel to confer with "meetings for discipline" so as "to build up Israel" and to urge the London Yearly Meeting to involve themselves more vigorously in the growing transatlantic antislavery crusade. Though he had secured endorsements from the Duck Creek Monthly Meeting and the Western Quarterly Meeting (WQM), he had been unable to convince Quaker leaders in Philadelphia, who were concerned that leaving his young motherless children behind was imprudent. The fact that Philadelphia Friends expressed concern for the wellbeing of the Mifflin family must have given Anne some consolation, and she was likely relieved as well when Warner's traveling certificate to cross the Atlantic was delayed in months-long deliberations by the Philadelphia approving body.[9]

Nevertheless, Anne's ease at having Warner home, where he could be with her and help parent his five children, did not last for long. She was seven months into her first pregnancy in February 1790 when Warner bade her farewell again. His plan was to join ten Quaker leaders, mostly from Philadelphia, in a campaign to persuade the first federal Congress meeting in New

York to stop the nefarious slave trade, set the nation on the path to gradually abolish slavery, and take steps to ameliorate the conditions under which some seven hundred thousand enslaved black people toiled. Taking on such a weighty mission, he could not assure her how long it might take or when he might return to the family.

In the first sustained lobbying effort in American history, Warner Mifflin emerged as the consummate advocate alongside other distinguished men in the Quaker delegation. Unfortunately, letters between Anne and Warner have not survived and she did not confide the matter in her commonplace books on how it stood at Chestnut Grove as the Friends' lobbying effort ran its course. But almost certainly Anne followed the debates in Congress that were widely reported in Philadelphia and New York newspapers. In them, she could read the debates over the petitions of the Philadelphia and New York yearly meetings where members pleaded for the cessation of the slave trade or raised fiery arguments on another petition sent from the Pennsylvania Abolition Society and signed by its president, the failing Benjamin Franklin; this one took a more radical stance in calling for Congress to consider "all justifiable endeavors to loosen the bands of slavery" and "countenance the restoration of liberty to those unhappy men, who alone, in this land of freedom, are degraded into perpetual bondage."[10]

Once the Quaker delegation had presented its petitions before the Senate and the House of Representatives, southern Congressmen unleashed a torrent of attacks, particularly targeting Mifflin as a seditious meddler. Word soon spread that seven of the eleven Friends were heading home on February 16 but Warner was not among them. Even as Anne reached the eighth month of her pregnancy, he remained in New York to buttonhole members of a congressional committee charged with considering the Quaker petitions. He also helped flood the Congress with antislavery pamphlets, then waited for days while the legislators took up other business, after which he stayed in New York still longer to obtain an audience with President George Washington. Finally, the matter reached a climax on March 23, when the House committee report was tabled. The only satisfaction the Quaker delegation could take was that the report was allowed to rest in the House journals and that the newspaper coverage had kept the slavery issue alive in the public's mind.[11]

Two days later, on March 25, 1790, a weary Warner Mifflin, leaving headaches, winter colds, and stinging attacks behind, departed New York. The anguish his wife suffered during the six-week absence can only be imagined. Perhaps she accepted it as another test of her strength and commitment. Whatever the case, he arrived in time for the birth of their first child, a son whom they named Samuel Emlen Mifflin after Anne's brother, cousin, and uncle.

Without a word in her commonplace book about her long travail, Anne wrote only a set of prayer-like verses to express her religious devotion and signify how keenly she understood the precariousness of life for the newborn:

> Thanks be to my Sov'reign Lord
> For mercies thou hast sent
> Who with the blessings there affords
> Adds that of sweet content.
> The boy thou'st given to my arms
> My offring is to thee
> Oh! Keep him spotless from all harms
> In sweet simplicity.
> Preserve him midst each dang'rous ill
> That oft encounter youth
> And thro[ugh] thy Grace his bosom fill
> With righteousness and truth
> That he a pattern forth may shine
> Of wisdom and of love
> Where in assemblage may combine
> The serpent and the dove
> That Solomon's superior choice
> And Samuel's purity
> May raise with usefulness his voice
> And with his life agree
> Thus to thy Throne of heav'nly grace
> I bring my infant son
> As Abram and Elkinah's Wife
> In faithfulness hath done
> And in like faith which they professed
> As ancient records tell
> A name is giv'n in which I rest
> And call him Samuel[12]

Anne's involvement in Quaker activities was hardly interrupted by pregnancy, childbirth, or childcare. But Warner's prolonged absences, leaving her with the responsibility of managing Chestnut Grove, must have caused anxiety and perhaps even lingering regrets about her decision to marry. Yet, four months after the birth of Samuel, leaving the breastfeeding to a milk nurse, Anne set out on the road to Third Haven as a delegate from the MMM to the SQM.[13] Again, even before Samuel had learned to walk, Anne exercised a preference for a religious vocation over domesticity. Sallying forth in ministerial duties for more than a month with Friend Philena Lay (authorized by the MMM), they visited members of the Nottingham and New Garden monthly meetings and families of other Friends within the compass of the SQM.[14]

During this trip, observing the showy apparel of the Quaker women wearing indigo-dyed clothing, Anne and Philena grappled with a weighty issue, if only at the local level. While Quakers had recovered from their pariah status during the revolution and begun to prosper again on their fertile Chester County farms, Mifflin and Lay chafed at seeing Friends straying from the simple life by indulging in new consumer goods. Shortly after their sojourn through Chester County, they wrote a chilling epistle calling on the conscience of the New Garden meeting to examine their members' actions and questioned how Friends could uphold the testimony of simplicity, which called to mind the fundamental beliefs of Quakerism formulated at its inception in the mid-seventeenth century.[15]

In the epistle's most emphatic passage, the women ministers prodded New Garden members, pointing out that in acquiring apparel dyed deeply blue, prospering Friends had blood on their hands. Did Anne and Philena know that on the South Carolina and Georgia plantations indigo cultivation had become a cash crop second only to rice? Whether or not they had knowledge of this, they did know that to produce this intense dye, enslaved workers had to throw the indigo plants into boiling vats, which emitted "poisonous exhalations" that brought "hundreds and thousands of poor slaves to an untimely end."[16] Their wish was to make it clear that Friends were complicit in the production of indigo at the cost of human suffering and loss of life. By focusing on the business of fabricating "lavish and unnecessary" articles of clothing, they tapped into the movement in England to boycott sugar, thereby strengthening the argument that this slave-produced, wildly popular consumer item was saturated with the blood of enslaved Africans.[17] Here, on the western side of the Atlantic, a thirty-six-year-old mother of one and a forty-four-year-old widowed mother of four were among the first to fertilize the seeds of what would become the Free Produce Movement in America in the early nineteenth century.[18]

In late winter of 1791, Anne was recognized as a minister and hastened to serve as a delegate to the Meeting of Ministers and Elders in Philadelphia.[19] If this was her first trip back to Philadelphia since her marriage three years before, it was one of happy reunion with family and Friends intermingled with poignant memories of times past.

Anne's second pregnancy did little to impede her religious duties. In February 1792, close to delivery of their second child, she accepted an appointment to join three other MMM women and some in the men's meeting in "visiting Black People for their spiritual and temporal good."[20] This was consonant with the commitment that Kent County Quakers had made during the revolutionary years when they acknowledged responsibility for providing "restitution"—what today we call "reparations"—to their manumitted slaves so that the newly liberated might go into the chilly world with the means to succeed as free farmers or artisans. A month later, welcoming her second son, Anne composed verses by Lemuel's cradle expressing her relief and gratitude for a successful birth:

> The unequal'd mirror of thy Word
> Oh! Lord My heart reveres
> Which doth true wisdom ere afford
> Surpassing length of years
> The perils of a lying-in
> Are many, great, and sore
> Thou has preserv'd from wreck therein
> And I'll thy name adore.
> Thy word was giv'n, a son was sent
> Preserve him if thy will
> With thy pure mind to be content
> Thy precepts to fulfill
> Instruct him in thy royal law
> Make him in love therewith
> That he may move in holy awe
> And dread offence to give
> Thus if his life continued is
> Retain him in thy fear
> That his first fruits he may thee give
> And to thy Throne draw near

Yet, if for time, but a short space
His life be lent to me / Oh! May I through thy calming Grace
To thee resigned be.
Thou knowest how to portion out,
The bitter and the sweet,
And in each turn we need not doubt,
But mercy we shall greet.
As names significant were giv'n
By ancient Israel
Not without cause I'll do so ev'n
And name him Lemuel.[21]

EXTENDING HER MINISTRY

As dedicated to strengthening the bonds of Quaker unity as her husband, Anne left Chestnut Grove frequently over the next few years. Only six months after Lemuel's birth, she traveled with Warner, a delegate from SQM to the PYM, in September 1792 on a 180-mile round trip that must have taxed her slight frame, even as they traveled the King's Highway northward with their horse-drawn chair. Anne returned to Philadelphia for the Half-Year Meeting for Elders and Ministers in March 1793, one of five women appointed from her quarterly meeting.[22] By this time, she shared Warner's satisfaction that his tract, *A Serious Expostulation with the Members of the House of Representatives of the United States*, had been published in the nation's capital. Anne no doubt agreed with Warner that the authors of the Declaration of Independence had never "intended a part of the human race to hold an absolute property in, and unbounded power over others" and that "the great principle (of government) is and ever will remain in force that men are by nature free."[23]

But Anne had her own calling and work to take on. In January 1793, when Lemuel was only ten months old, she stood before her meeting to express how "her mind [was] engaged" to accompany Philena Lay to visit Friends' meetings in neighboring Sussex County. Visiting Cool Springs and Three Runs preparative meetings with traveling certificate in hand, she spent several weeks in the summer of 1793 in an effort to extend her ministry.[24] Left behind were her two sons and the stepchildren, this time under the care of their father.

Anne's numerous religious visitations suggest she found little satisfaction in the role of stepmother, housekeeper, and Chestnut Grove manager; furthermore, given Warner's household staff, Anne's domestic exertions were not necessary. Her duty to the church militant outranked wifely or motherly duties, and the women of her monthly meeting found no fault with this.[25] In January 1794, they appointed her clerk of the Murderkill Women's Monthly Meeting. This was a sure indication of her growing repute, for the station of clerk made her essentially the spiritual leader of a hundred families or more. In May 1794, again with her beloved Philena Lay, she journeyed for a number of weeks to monthly meetings in Pennsylvania and New Jersey, where she could provide inspiration and counsel to those "who live[d] remote" from established meetings.[26]

Anne's third pregnancy also did nothing to keep her at Chestnut Grove. In December, never road-weary it seemed, though six months pregnant, she made the forty-five-mile trip to the SQM at Easton, Maryland.[27] Such a cross-peninsula journey on primitive roads would hardly have been recommended by today's prenatal protocols. Again, prioritizing the ministry dictated such an action.

Come March 1795, in her fortieth year, Anne delivered her third child, a girl. She and Warner named her Mary Ann, the namesake of revered Grandmother Mary and steadfast Mother Emlen. Attending the cradle for five anxious months, they sorrowed as the sickly infant languished, probably from the autumnal fevers that were the bane of Kent County life. Death was no stranger to Chestnut Grove—four of Warner's nine children by his first marriage had died there in infancy—but lowering baby Mary Ann into the grave at the Murderkill meetinghouse burial ground in August must have been heartrending in the extreme.[28] This was the last child Anne would bear. Mary Ann's death suggests that Anne's midlife pregnancy and her strenuous travel on horseback well into her last trimester could have set the course for this loss. It is understandable, then, that frail Mary Ann survived but a few months.[29]

ADDRESSING THE MARYLAND LEGISLATURE

A few months after Mary Ann's death, Anne resumed her duties as Public Friend, this time proposing to take her ministry to Annapolis to address the Maryland legislature on the odious trafficking of fellow humans.[30] For several years Anne's husband, with members of the SQM and the Meeting for Sufferings in Philadelphia, had lobbied Annapolis to put a stop to the shipment of slaves to the South that was tearing apart slave families.[31]

When her monthly meeting endorsed the trip, it came as a blessed respite. What better outlet for her grief, after losing her infant daughter, than to go on an errand of mercy? Her welcome partner on this mission, Mary Berry (1731–1806), was a highly respected minister from Third Haven Monthly Meeting across the Delmarva Peninsula in Talbot County, Maryland. Described in her meeting's minutes as "our beloved and ancient Friend," Mary had made innumerable trips "in Truth's service" throughout Delaware, Maryland, Virginia, and North Carolina since the late 1770s.[32] Now, at age sixty-four, she joined Anne in becoming the first women on either side of the Atlantic to write and present an appeal on the issue of slavery to a state legislative body. Not only were they stepping onto the public stage; they were also entering the political arena, a place where women were generally scorned for breaching a customary gender boundary. Thus, Anne and Mary predated by many decades the emergence of those nineteenth-century female abolitionists highlighted in our history books as trailblazers in the antislavery cause who addressed male audiences.[33]

In their two-week trip to Annapolis, accompanied by Warner Mifflin and four other male Maryland Quaker abolitionists, Anne and Mary made good use of their time, conducting two public meetings in the Maryland State House and another at the adjacent Methodist meetinghouse "appointed principally for the blacks."[34] Anne, more reserved in her public testimonies, may have yielded to Mary, who was described by a fellow Quaker minister as "lift[ing] up her voice like one of the sweetest singers of Israel" and "as much set on things from above as anyone I ever saw without exception, and she shines accordingly."[35]

Momentously, on December 5, 1795, the clerk of the legislature read the remarkable address from these two women, which focused on how the internal slave trade was tearing slave families apart as masters sent what they regarded as *surplus*—that is, enslaved people—to labor in the burgeoning cotton fields of the Deep South.[36] Frequently, this separated husbands from wives, and parents from children. They had heard and seen with their own eyes how the heartlessness of slavery had "enfeebled mothers through oppressive toil, and [how she and the] helpless child [were] torn from each other's embraces, with other separations of the nearest connections in life." Such cries from fractured families had surely "pierced the very Court of Heaven from whence a decree may issue from him who ever remains to be the refuge for the oppressed."[37]

Despite "some violent opposers," by a vote of forty-seven to twenty-one the petitions were sent to a committee for consideration—a sign itself that efforts on behalf of enslaved Marylanders at least caught the attention of state legislators. The issue was held over until the next year when the lawmakers would stiffen penalties against importing slaves and clear the way for the voluntary manumission of slaves who were not more than forty-five years of age.[38] Recalling the petition to the Maryland Assembly some nine years later, Anne would take the view that although it had not succeeded, "yet it discharged our duty and they at best paid so much respect to our petitions as to read it before our brethren." Just the same, Anne thought the assembly had read the petition "perhaps from its novelty."[39]

PARTNERING WITH WARNER

Trying to balance family responsibilities with service as a Public Friend put Anne through one test after another. At Chestnut Grove, she had to contend with Warner's recurrent illnesses and, by the mid-1790s, his failing health. Though a man of sturdy frame, at age forty-five health problems continued to afflict him. One politician who knew Warner well described him as "a great fellow near seven feet high." As early as October 1791, Warner had reported a return of his "very weak situation," and he sensed "that my days may not be many more."[40]

Life at Chestnut Grove placed demands on Anne in a never-ending cycle of joy, death, and grief. The wedding of Warner's oldest child, Elizabeth, at the Murderkill meetinghouse in July 1792 made the family gathering all the more rewarding because the groom, Clayton Cowgill, was the eldest son of Warner's friend, John Cowgill, a Quaker stalwart mobbed during the revolution for refusing to traffic in Continental currency. Warner "found it a great thing to give up to the parting with a child" and could not help thinking about "what would I do then if I was a Negro and had a daughter carried from me to Carolina."[41]

In 1794, Warner and Anne made the decision that the third daughter, fifteen-year-old Susanna, should be apprenticed in housekeeping to a Chester County Quaker family. The marriage of twenty-one-year-old daughter Ann had followed in mid-1795, then the death of the infant Mary Ann, and finally, on the last day of the year, Warner's seventy-three-year-old father died at the old family homestead in Accomack County on Virginia's Eastern Shore. Such was the pace of life at Chestnut Grove.[42]

During these years the steady flow of slaves seeking freedom never ceased. In 1790, Warner had professed, "I am much burdened, for the poor blacks are running to me in droves from Maryland—men, women and children," that they "get out of the way of being sold into Georgia and South Carolina. Thinking I can do something for them, they fly to me." His letters to Philadelphia friends were speckled with such comments as the 1790s unfolded. In 1794, nine slaves fled their Virginia masters to make "their way to Warner Mifflin and thence to Philadelphia." Returning from Philadelphia with Anne later that year, he wrote, "I have had no less than five negroes, day and night, and sometimes as many as eleven for a night, most fleeing Maryland." In 1795, returning from Annapolis with Anne, he reported, "I have now two men standing waiting for advice that have just escaped from the Chesapeake from the Carolina raiders. I . . . have not been without one or more almost every day since my return . . . I am loaded thereby almost as much as I can stand under."[43]

As the wife of a man who had framed his life around service to what he called "my African brethren," Anne also bore the burden of Warner's calling as a living magnet for Eastern Shore slaves terrified of being sold south to South Carolina and Georgia. Perhaps out of caution, she made no mention in her commonplace book that road-weary black refugees seeking freedom on their way north found their way to Chestnut Grove and necessarily involved her. Anne shared both Warner's anxiety and stress. Doubtless she pitied the slaves of the Upper South whose families were being sundered by the pitiless internal slave trade, and she also knew the risk Warner was taking. Often summoned to court by slave holders, he was able to fend off these suits, probably for lack of criminal evidence. Nonetheless the peril and threat was always there that her husband might be convicted and imprisoned, leaving her alone to parent the flock of children, to oversee his household, and to tend to the plantation.

As the eighteenth century drew to a close, Anne's partnership with Warner yielded some happier results as well. Her calm demeanor hitched to reformist leanings came into play in 1795–96 when the PYM made an unprecedented decision to overturn the long-standing ban on full membership for black worshipers. For years, though agreeing that God had made of one blood "all nations of men," most Friends argued that "unrestricted admission" to the Society of Friends would entitle black members "to the privilege of intermarriage." To this they were strongly opposed.

Years earlier, in 1783, Anne had reported that "mountains of opposition [were] . . . leveled" against a mixed-race woman (half-white, three-eighths Indian, and one-eighth black) who had raised the membership question and saw her request turned down after her application was referred to the PYM.[44] Eleven years later, another mulatto Quaker worshiper who had applied for membership met a similar fate. Clerk of the meeting James Pemberton reported that the fear of interracial marriage was still held by the majority of Friends.[45] But the issue of membership for black Quakers would not die. With Anne and Warner in attendance, the PYM in 1795 again took up the thorny discussion after Cynthia Miers, a Rahway, New Jersey, mulatto worshipper, pressed her case. Joseph Drinker, a cooper of modest means, lacking the leadership credentials of his brothers John and Henry, had submitted passionate testimony. "If Christ died for all," he asked, "how could Friends escape charges of hypocrisy for denying full membership to dark-skinned people?" In countering the time-worn Quaker argument that black, would-be Quakers should "fold by themselves . . . that there should be onefold for black sheep and another fold for white sheep," Drinker asked his fellow worshipers to examine their hearts to "see if pride is not the bottom [of] these prejudices so that some are ready to say [to] these poor despised blacks, standoff, I am more holy than thou art."[46]

Unable to agree on the mulatto worshiper's petition, the yearly meeting sent the matter to a committee of worthies for consideration. Among those eager to testify were Anne and Mary Pusey Mifflin, the widow of Warner's father, Daniel, who had died just nine months before.[47] Anne was agreeable to offer her support, having participated in the biracial worship at the Murderkill meetinghouse, along with the Mifflin family. This practice contrasted with that in Philadelphia, where black Quakers gathered at the Bank meetinghouse apart from their white counterparts, who met at the Pine Street and High Street meetinghouses.[48]

After attendees at the 1796 yearly meeting reached the final decision, John Hunt from New Jersey called it "a heart-tendering time, even to tears. . . . I never seen more love, nearness and sweetness before amongst Friends." Hunt noted that the decision to admit the mulatto woman to membership was agreed by mutual unity and that from this moment forward, "monthly meetings should be at liberty to receive all such where they were convinced of their sincerity without distinction of nation or color."[49] Considering that her efforts had resulted in admitting a person of color to the formerly all-white meeting, Anne certainly deserved some of the credit for this historic decision.

One year after the wall of color bias tumbled down, Anne again showed her mettle as a key facilitator in the acceptance by the Society of Friends of the Quaker-like Nicholites (or New Quakers as they styled themselves), who had established pockets of worshipers in Delaware, Maryland, and North Carolina.[50] The Nicholites, like the Quakers, relied on the inward urgings of conscience rather than external authority. Like the Quakers, they were pacifists, refused to swear oaths, practiced more gender equality than other churches, rejected all hierarchical religious practices, purged themselves of slave holding, eschewed dancing and music, and emphasized plain living and self-denial even to the extent of refusing to grow flowers in their gardens or to allow them in their houses.[51]

In the fall of 1797, eighty Nicholites had appealed for membership to a preparative meeting overseen by the Third Haven Monthly Meeting on Maryland's Eastern Shore. The SQM appointed Anne and Warner, along with two of his married daughters, a son-in-law, and other relatives, to call on the Nicholite families "in order to feel after their growth and standing in the Truth."[52]

THE WAVERING CANDLE

By this time, Anne could see that her husband was failing, and his determination to attend the upcoming PYM in September must have worried her. From Warner's perspective, he reasoned that his presence at PYM was needed and Divinely appointed. Congress was taking up the petitions of four free black men who had been liberated in North Carolina by their Quaker masters but fled to Philadelphia to avoid re-enslavement under a vicious Carolina law. Warner believed he had to answer the Master's call and be there.[53] Moreover, earlier in the year, Warner had published *The Defence of Warner Mifflin Against Aspersions cast on him on Account of his Endeavors To promote Righteousness, Mercy, and Peace*, a pamphlet he hoped would keep the antislavery issue alive and trouble the consciences of Congressmen who wanted the matter buried.

Saying farewell once again to Warner as he left Chestnut Grove to go to Philadelphia must have left Anne beside herself, for the city had once again become a charnel house. Yellow fever gripped the city with nearly the same force it had in the 1793 epidemic. When Warner arrived in September of 1797 for the yearly meeting, Philadelphia was already hollowed out, but he trusted that a merciful God would spare him. Back in Kent County, Anne watched and waited while fifty-two of their Philadelphia Friends died before the fever abated in mid-October, by which time a weakened Warner managed to return safely to Chestnut Grove.

Answering her inner promptings, Anne worked as much as her husband to give a dutiful service to the Quaker church militant. In early 1798, she requested a certificate to sojourn with Mary Berry to Barbados to share her spirituality with the dwindling Friends' population on the island, where enslaved Africans vastly outnumbered the white planters.[54] Anne's intention to make this trip while her husband's grip on life was loosening is almost incomprehensible. Had he urged her to go, despite his deteriorating condition? Or had she like Warner received a call from above that she felt must be answered? It may have been an act of Providence that Anne and Mary had to postpone their trip because the Caribbean region was aboil with wartime conflict between England and France. Meanwhile, the never-idle Anne, with her meeting's approval, visited Friends' families within the Chester Monthly Meeting in March.[55] But the alarming decline in Warner's health signaled to Anne that her immediate duty was to nurse her stricken husband, who lifted his pen barely enough to write, "I have a great bodily weakness, a cough continues, and my breast is disordered . . . and I have as great a debility of mind as of body."[56] Warner allowed that "I have a very swelled face from violent pain in my teeth."[57] Despite the summer heat and humidity descending on Delaware, Warner and Anne—based on their positive findings from the previous visitations to the Nicholites—ventured back to the Eastern Shore to finalize arrangements for easing the Nicholites into the Quaker fold.[58]

In early July, with Anne beside him, Warner embarked on what would be his last journey. He wrote in a loving letter to his children at Chestnut Grove that he was "preparing for the final farewell to all things here below" as he and Anne made their way to visit daughter Susanna in Chester County. Saying that he was "very weak" with his "breast considerably affected," he reminded his children "what a comfort it must be to a parent passing away to have a hope of their children preparing to do their day's work consistent with the mind of their Maker."[59]

In July of 1798, the nation's capital was already in the grasp of another ferocious yellow fever epidemic: Congress decamped in mid-July; President John Adams retreated to Quincy, Massachusetts; and by early August more than three quarters of the city's population had left, scattering in every direction.[60] For Anne, the shadow of widowhood was imminent. Warner was in a feeble state. Knowing how inadvisable it was to make their annual pilgrimage to Philadelphia, nonetheless she must have reluctantly agreed to go with him.

A few days before they left home, Warner tried to draft his will, conscious that this was required by the Friends' discipline for those facing their end. "Expecting in a few days to set off to attend our yearly meeting in Philadelphia," he wrote, "that city being at this time visited with an epidemic disorder of which great numbers dye, by accounts received, and great part of the inhabitants in consequence thereof have left the city," he was setting down his last will and testament. "It feels awful to undertake this journey," he spelled out in the first paragraph, "but believing it my duty to proceed therein, having nothing in view but to be found in the discharge thereof to Him who gave me being, and whom I have faith to believe can preserve me even amidst the raging pestilence, if he is so pleased to do, however I desire to be resigned to his holy will therein."[61]

Reaching the city, Anne and Warner found handbills plastered to tavern doors and lampposts with these ominous warnings: "REFLECT BEFORE IT IS TOO LATE . . . WHY DO YOU PREFER FAMINE, SICKNESS, AND DEATH TO HEALTH AND PLENTY . . . GO BEFORE IT IS TOO LATE."[62] They soon heard that one hundred Philadelphians a day were contracting the fever, with half as many ending up in death carts and transported for burial.

In better times, usually one thousand or more Friends attended the yearly meeting, but on this visit only Anne, Warner, and some sixty or so Quakers arrived. Undeterred by the frightening handbills and the death scenes, some of that small remnant who had survived the previous epidemic of 1793 believed that even though they had acquired immunity, an ever-watchful God was testing them. The scene was so appalling that after gathering for the first meeting on September 24, 1798, the intrepid Friends relented, decided to adjourn, flee the city, and not reconvene until January 1799.

While most Friends headed home, Anne and Warner stayed in the city to aid stricken Friends. At his lodgings, with death staring him in the face, Warner lifted his pen to compose the last letter he would ever write. Addressing President John Adams, he poured out years of accumulated sorrow at the oppression of black Americans and the sinfulness of white Americans who had turned their backs on the nation's founding principles: "What would the president do, as a man who had stood in the vanguard of the Age of Enlightenment, a constitution writer, a signer of the Declaration of Independence, a minister to England and America after the revolution?" "Do thy duty [and] discharge thyself," Mifflin pleaded. If lacking constitutional power, did Adams not have moral capital to draw upon? "Would to God," Warner chided, "our President might be animated . . . to call the consideration of our legislature to the grievous . . . oppression of our fellow-man, the Blacks in this land."[63]

After a few days, Anne and Warner also yielded and left ghostlike Philadelphia. Weakened by years of poor health, Warner carried the dreaded pathogen back to Chestnut Grove. At home, attended by Anne and ravaged by yellow fever, he passed away on October 16, 1798. Compounding Anne's loss, the fever had already claimed her cousin Samuel Emlen and her younger brother James. Dying shortly after returning to his Chester County home from the yearly meeting, James Emlen had also believed "himself bound in duty to attend with the friends at the usual time and place, and this was the third time he had attended under such circumstances."[64] James Emlen's passing left six children orphaned.

On the day after Warner's death, October 17, 1798, following funeral services, four African American men bore Mifflin's casket from a hearse to the Murderkill burial ground at Magnolia, Delaware.[65] It was fitting that the family chose these men to bear Warner to his final rest. The names of the pallbearers are lost to history, but it is likely that at least one of them was among the enslaved black people liberated by Mifflin a quarter century before. Grieving at the graveside with Anne were the Mifflin children, there to see their father buried just five days short of his fifty-third birthday: twenty-one-year-old Warner Jr., nineteen-year-old Susanna, fourteen-year-old Sarah, eight-year-old Samuel, and six-year-old Lemuel. Forbidden to attend were the many slaves of Thomas Rodney, younger brother of Caesar Rodney, a signer of the Declaration of Independence and a pillar of Dover Christ Church. If local slaves were quarantined for fear that the germ of freedom would spread, free black people thronged fearlessly to the funeral to honor their friend and liberator.

Nathaniel Luff, a Quaker physician from Dover attending the service, described how Warner's widow "delivered some tender and interesting expressions of his respecting the black people . . . he having been much concerned for their welfare in his illness." Mifflin, the doctor noted, "departed quietly and in resignation to the Divine will." In a final salute, Luff confided to his journal that Mifflin had been one of the Quakers "who hesitated not to venture their lives in that sickly place [Philadelphia] under a sense of their religious duty to their annual appointments [as a delegate to the PYM]."[66] Later, putting grief behind her, Anne collected her thoughts to preserve for sons Samuel and Lemuel their father's final moments:

I was his steady nurse with your [half] brother Warner [Jr.] and [half] sister Susan. Not very long before his departure, married with loss of sleep, grief, and attendance. I retired to another room to see if I could be sustained by a few moments rest but sleep was far from me and when about to return I received a message that he wished to see me; I went; and with a look filled with tenderness, he said he loved to have me by him. A most affectionate embrace took place. . . . Not long after, with much composure, though with some evident increase in pain (as he had laid in much quietness and without much apparent suffering for the greater part of his sickness) the solemn moment took place.

Anne recounted Warner's last moments, especially his worries about his young children, and how, "after repeated looks of inexpressible concern on my account, [he] desired me not to grieve for him."[67] Having at his bedside witnessed his suffering and the "agonies at seeing him die," how could Anne not grieve? In the autumn of 1798, with due respect given and tender remembrances made, Anne Emlen Mifflin entered widowhood.

NOTES

1. MRP, December 1786, below.
2. Murderkill, derived from the seventeenth-century Dutch meaning literally "hidden river," was (and still is) spelled variously as either Motherkiln, Motherkill, or Murtherkill.
3. The Murderkill Monthly Meeting (MMM) was carved out of the Duck Creek Monthly Meeting, which met for the first time only three weeks after Anne and Warner's wedding in Philadelphia. Murderkill Monthly Meeting Women's Minutes (1788–1845), January 10, 1789 (hereafter cited as MMMWM).
4. Anne was soon appointed to a committee to strengthen the education of the youth. MMMWM (1788–1845), March 9, April 11, 1789. Jean Soderlund has discussed how the economic status of women and their freedom from household work increased the likelihood of appointment to important committees. Soderlund, "Women's Authority in Pennsylvania and New Jersey Quaker Meetings," 722–49, especially 730–34.
5. The SQM met alternatively at the Third Haven meetinghouse in Easton, Maryland, and the Little Creek meetinghouse in Kent County, Delaware.
6. Also delegated to attend the SQM were Philena Lay from Sussex County and Mary Pusey Husband Mifflin, the third wife of Warner Mifflin's father, who had just joined the MMM with her four children. On January 9, 1790, Anne was appointed with four other women to unite with men to visit Friends' families to fortify their faith. MMMWM (1788–1845), November 7, 1789, January 9, 1790.

7. The lobbying trip to Annapolis is recounted in Nash, *Warner Mifflin*, 159; and Mifflin's letters to John Parrish and James Pemberton, November 29, 1788, and December 29, 1788, in Nash and McDowell, *Writings of Warner Mifflin*, 322 and 325.

8. See Nash, *Warner Mifflin*, 147–49.

9. Ibid., 150–51.

10. For more on her husband's lengthy lobbying effort in New York City, see ibid., 160–74.

11. For another account of the Quaker lobbying effort, see Di Giacomantonio, "For the Gratification of a Volunteering Society."

12. MRP, May 1790, below. Perhaps adjusting to marriage, becoming the parent of five stepchildren, and moving from the bustle of Philadelphia to rural Kent County left Anne little time for entries in her journals for the next nineteen months, other than the one plaintive entry on the eve of her marriage. Even so she did celebrate the birth of her two sons with rhymed prayers of thanksgiving. See MRP, April 13, 1792, where Anne inserted loose pages on which she wrote these poems, which accounts for the pagination being out of sync.

13. MMMWM (1788–1845), August 7, 1790, and February 12, 1791. The SQM had been carved out of the WQM in 1789.

14. Ibid., June 11, 1791; MMMM (1788–1830), June 11, November 15, 1791; New Garden Monthly Meeting Men's Minutes (1790–1802), August 6, October 8, 1791 (hereafter cited as NGMMMM); New Garden Monthly Meeting Women's Minutes (1785–1804), September 2, 1791 (hereafter cited as NGMMWM). Orphaned at a young age, Philena Moss (1747–1797) grew up in Accomack County, Virginia, at Pharsalia, the slave-based plantation of Daniel Mifflin. In 1768, after marrying Baptist (his name) Lay (1736–1793), a Sussex County farmer, she became a mainstay at Cold Spring meeting in Lewes. Philena Lay's devotional life is recounted in "Testimony of Murtherkill Monthly Meeting Concerning Philena Lay" in *Memorials Concerning Deceased Friends*, 72–75.

15. "To Friends of the Monthly Meeting of New Garden," New Garden Monthly Meeting, Miscellaneous Manuscript Collection, FHLSC. A copy of the epistle was signed by the authors "Philena Lay, Ann Mifflin, Philadelphia 1st day of the month 1791." For the postwar resumption of consumerism, see Carson, Hoffman, and Albert, *Of Consuming Interest*.

16. It is unclear how Anne and Philena acquired the knowledge of the brutal indigo production in South Carolina and Georgia, where it had undergone spectacular development beginning in the 1740s.

17. Holcomb, *Moral Commerce*. Holcomb's treatment of the war against sugar, triggered by William Fox's anonymous *An Address to the People of Great Britain on the Utility of Refraining from the Use of West India Sugar and Rum*, does not treat the incipient boycott of indigo sparked by Warner Mifflin and Benjamin Lay.

18. British abolitionists, the majority of them Quakers, broached the idea of an international boycott of products made by slave labor in the 1780s after forming the Society for Effecting the Abolition of the Slave Trade. In 1791, William Fox's *Address to the People of Great Britain* urged a boycott of slave-produced sugar. This galvanized the movement on both sides of the Atlantic. Nearly four hundred thousand Britons supported the boycott as an effective nonviolent protest of the exploitation of slave labor. Holcomb, *Moral Commerce*, 42–44.

19. PYM, Ministers and Elders, Miscellaneous Manuscripts, 1785–1795, accessed at Ancestry, http://www.ancestry.com, as PYMM (1781–1795), frame 438.

20. MMMWM (1788–1845), February 14, 1792.

21. In the MRP Anne notes, "Written 12 days after the birth of my son Lemuel born 3 Mo:23rd."

22. PYMM (1774–1798), September 22, 1792, March 23, 1793.

23. In *A Serious Expostulation*, while answering charges hurled against him by southern members of Congress, Mifflin tried to reach a national audience in order to keep the antislavery crusade alive. Calling slavery a "national iniquity" and a "national guilt," he told the House members that "[I] plead the cause of injured innocence" and "open my mouth for my oppressed brethren, who cannot open theirs for themselves." For more on *A Serious Expostulation*, see Nash, *Warner Mifflin*, 185–88.

24. MMMWM (1788–1845), January 15, 1793. Several weeks later, the SQM chose not to appoint Anne as a representative to the impending yearly meeting in Philadelphia, presumably not wanting to send the mother of two infant boys to the city where the yellow fever epidemic was scourging the population. Warner attended the meeting, one of only 60 of the 140 delegates appointed by their local or regional meetings. Some 400 Friends succumbed to the grisly disease, including the wife of Anne's younger brother James. For an incisive account of the epidemic, see Smith, *Ship of Death*.

25. For those married women with a Divine calling, Friends held that the wife was "more the Lord's than her Husband's." Larson, *Daughters of Light*, 143. Meetings supported the service of a minister over the demands of a spouse and authorized women endowed with the gift of gospel ministry to make religious travels while their husbands remained at home. Ibid., 144. With regard to Warner and Anne, there were instances where neither remained at home.

26. MMMWM (1788–1845), January 14, May 14, 1794; Murderkill Monthly Meeting Men's Minutes (1788–1830), May 13, July 15, 1794 (hereafter cited as MMMMM).

27. MMMWM (1788–1845), December 14, 1794.

28. No extant letter from either Warner or Anne mentions Mary Ann's brief life or her death. Anne's journals ended with her prayer to Lemuel, so historians are deprived of her innermost thoughts after 1792. In a similar example, Sarah Crabtree's "In the Light and on the Road" (134n15) notes regarding the death of the Quaker minister Patience Brayton's two young children that they were barely mentioned in her journal, a practice Crabtree claims was not uncommon among women in colonial America.

29. In *Good Wives* (140–41), Laurel Thatcher Ulrich notes that travel for pregnant women in the seventeenth and eighteenth century was most favorable in the second trimester. In her ten-year marriage to Warner, Anne bore three children; unless a miscarriage or stillborn went unrecorded, she conceived no more after the death of Mary Ann in 1795. It cannot be determined if Anne practiced any form of family limitation after the loss of Mary Ann. Robert Wells's "Family Size and Fertility Control" shows that Quaker families had on average 5.7 children. Anne's marriage at age thirty-three and widowhood ten years later yielded a shorter child birthing period, and Warner's frequent absences from home would further explain the lower-than-average birth rate.

30. In visiting the MMM in the autumn of 1794, Mary Berry and Anne likely planned to present a memorial opposing the trafficking of slaves. Berry, "Memoir of Mary Berry," 115. Mary received traveling certificates to visit the MMM and to journey to Annapolis. Third Haven Monthly Meeting Men's Minutes (1771–1797), July 17, December 11, 1794. Anne and Mary almost certainly conferred while attending the SQM in mid-December 1794 since the quarterly meeting was pressing the Meeting for Sufferings in Philadelphia

to endorse the draft of their memorial. Anne did not request a traveling certificate to Annapolis from her meeting until the following November, probably because she had been pregnant with her third child. MMMWM (1788–1845), November 15, 1795; MMMMM (1788–1830), November 10, 1795.

31. For more on the Friends' antislavery efforts in Maryland, see Nash, *Warner Mifflin*, 180, 196–97, 202–3.

32. Carroll, *Quakerism on the Eastern Shore*, 88–89, 135–36, 155–56; Berry, "Memoir of Mary Berry." Mary and her husband James Berry, one of Talbot County's earliest manumitters, led the liberation of slaves on the west-facing bayside of Maryland.

33. Elisabeth Heyrick (1769–1831), an English philanthropist, is noted as the first woman on either side of the Atlantic to take a firm stance against slavery in the 1820s, whereas in the United States historians have singled out Quaker activist Lucretia Mott (1793–1880) as the first female standard bearer of abolitionism.

34. "Old Blue," as it was known, had been built by the Annapolis Methodists on the State House grounds in 1789. Black worshipers greatly outnumbered white in the 1790s. Andrews, *Methodists and Revolutionary America*, 132; Williamson, *Annapolis*, 328–29.

35. Job Scott entered this in his journal after attending the MMM with Mary Berry in 1790. Quoted in Carroll, *Quakerism on the Eastern Shore*, 156.

36. "To the General Assembly of Maryland, Now Sitting from Mary Berry and Anne Mifflin." The original address written by Mary Berry and Anne Mifflin has not been found, but a copy, in the hand of John Parrish, is housed in box 9, fol. 26, C-P-W. We thank Nicholas Wood for analysis of Parrish's handwriting. A second address from the SQM, presented by Anne's husband, was published in "Relics of the Past" and can be viewed in Nash and McDowell, *Writings of Warner Mifflin*, 473.

37. Mary Berry and Anne Mifflin, "To the General Assembly of Maryland," below.

38. In his letter to Henry Drinker of December 30, 1795, Anne's husband reported their lobbying efforts in Annapolis. Warner Mifflin to Henry Drinker, Henry Drinker Correspondence, 1760–1806, FHLSC; see also Nash and McDowell, *Writings of Warner Mifflin*, 474–76; and Locke, *Anti-Slavery in America*, 121. The sharp increase of free black people between 1790 and 1800, greater than in Virginia and even Delaware, suggests the effect of the new manumission law. See table 2 in Berlin, *Slaves Without Masters*, 46.

39. Anne Mifflin to Dorothy Ripley, May 31, 1804, below.

40. Warner Mifflin to John Parrish, October 10, 1791, in Nash and McDowell, *Writings of Warner Mifflin*, 382–85. South Carolina representative William Loughton Smith described Mifflin in a letter to Edward Rutledge, February 28, 1790, in De Pauw et al., *Documentary History of the First Federal Congress*, 18:674.

41. Nash, *Warner Mifflin*, 191.

42. Ibid.

43. Warner Mifflin to Henry Drinker, November 12, December 14, 1794, in Nash and McDowell, *Writings of Warner Mifflin*, 467–68.

44. Anne Mifflin to Hannah Townsend, October 4, 1783, quoted in Cadbury, "Negro Membership in the Society of Friends," 172.

45. James Pemberton to James Phillips, November 18, 1794, Gilder Lehrman Collection, New-York Historical Society. Cadbury in "Negro Membership" (172–76) provides details on the case as it made its way from the preparative meeting through the monthly and quarterly meetings and finally to the PYM, where the final decision was made in September 1796.

46. Drake, "Joseph Drinker's Plea," 110–12.

47. John Hunt, a New Jersey minister, farmer, and pump maker, recorded in "John Hunt's Diary" (208–9) that "a considerable number of . . . weighty, wise, solid women" urged the Society to put its racial bias behind it.

48. When the English traveling minister Martha Routh joined a Tuesday worship in April 1796 at Murderkill meeting, she found "a very large mixed gathering in which were many black people." Routh, *Memoir of the Life*, 1.

49. In its first printed "Discipline," the PYM affirmed and emphasized the historic decision. Cadbury, "Negro Membership," 176.

50. Founder of the Nicholites Joseph Nichols, a charismatic landowner, was born near Dover, Delaware, around 1730.

51. Carroll, *Joseph Nichols and the Nicholites*, 3–26.

52. SQM Minutes (1759–1822), November 25, 1797, 294.

53. For the petition of the black North Carolinians, see Wood, "'Class of Citizens'"; for *The Defence of Warner Mifflin Against Aspersions cast on him on Account of his Endeavors To promote Righteousness, Mercy, and Peace*, see Nash, *Warner Mifflin*, 205–7.

54. MMMMM (1788–1830), January 9, 1798; the meeting produced the certificate on February 13.

55. MMMMM (1778–1830), March 13, 1798.

56. Warner Mifflin to Henry Drinker, June 16, June 26, 1798, in Nash and McDowell, *Writings of Warner Mifflin*, 535–36.

57. Warner Mifflin to Henry Drinker, April 1, 1798, in ibid., 532–33. Warner's symptoms may have been due to dental abscesses from bacterial infection, and his complaint of chest pains suggests angina; both afflictions would have aggravated his already chronic, impaired condition.

58. Carroll, *Joseph Nichols and the Nicholites*, 3–26.

59. Warner Mifflin to "dear Children," July 7, 1798, Cowgill-Mifflin Letters, Delaware Public Archives, Dover (hereafter cited as DPA); see also Nash and McDowell, *Writings of Warner Mifflin*, 391n3. When Anne and Warner reached Chestnut Grove, they found eight [black] applicants seeking asylum in Delaware at their doorstep, and others appeared almost every day thereafter.

60. Benjamin Rush described the contagion in *Account of the Yellow Fever Epidemic of 1798*; see also Condie and Folwell, *History of the Pestilence*.

61. Will of Warner Mifflin in Justice, *Life and Ancestry of Warner Mifflin*, 223–28.

62. Condie and Folwell, *History of the Pestilence*, 9.

63. Warner Mifflin to John Adams, September 24, 1798, Adams Papers, Massachusetts Historical Society, Boston; see also Nash and McDowell, *Writings of Warner Mifflin*, 549–52. Warner carried the letter intended for President Adams back home with him, where it laid undelivered for several years.

64. The fever took James Emlen's life in his thirty-eighth year. Emlen, "Memoir of James Emlen," 161–62.

65. In more recent years, a stone in memory of Warner Mifflin was placed in the yard, but the location of his grave is unknown. The stone inscription reads, "Motherkill Burying Ground, within this enclosure are interred the remains of WARNER MIFFLIN Friend, Philanthropist, Patriot. Born. August 21st 1745 Died. October. 16th 1798."

66. Luff, *Journal*, 91–92.

67. Anne Mifflin to "My dear Children," October 25, 1799, below.

Chapter 4

A WIDOW'S MINISTRY IN THE NEW NATION, 1798–1804

At age forty-three, when she returned to Chestnut Grove from her husband's internment at the Murderkill burial ground, Anne faced difficult decisions. Three were immediate and crucial: where to live, how to raise her two young sons, and how to proceed with her remaining years as an acknowledged Public Friend. Returning to the place of her birth to live with the Emlens proved a weighty choice. Despite the horrendous episodes of yellow fever decimating Philadelphians in 1793, 1797, and 1798, Anne chose to spend her final years in the city, where she could shepherd Samuel and Lemuel to adulthood, reestablish herself within the Quaker community of family and friends, and use her Chestnut Street home as the springboard for her religious activity. With pious dedication she put aside mourning and thoughts of middle-age retirement. Because her temperament permitted no less, she entered a new phase, taking on ministry and visitation to Quaker farming communities newly founded on the nation's expanding boundaries and traveling to Native American settlements distanced hundreds of miles from the Quaker city.

This chapter follows Anne's shaky adjustment to widowhood and the launching of her traveling ministry and activism within Philadelphia reform circles, duties she assumed with her characteristic calm intensity. Fully consonant with the PYM's effort after the revolution to regain the respect of the community at large, Anne's labors contributed exceptional service to the Friends' racial and social justice programs designed to create what the nascent Constitution promised in "a more perfect union." But as we shall see, Anne's deepening spirituality would be tinctured with her own share of tragedy.

Mourning the loss of her beloved husband and her younger brother James, Anne's grief was accentuated by a knot of problems. Settling her husband's tangled estate came first, though complicated by the imperfect last will Warner had composed less than a month before he died. The legal haggling that resulted placed a great strain on Anne and caused friction with her stepchildren. Notwithstanding Warner's plea in his final days for her to help him in fashioning a will, Anne had insisted on staying clear of any involvement, knowing too well that dealing with her husband's offspring borne by two mothers might be a recipe for intrafamily disaster. Indeed, the legal disputes that followed Warner's death dragged on and did place more stress on Anne and produce friction with her stepchildren.

The problem was not that Warner's assets were insufficient to provide adequately for Anne, for Warner's five children by his first wife (two of whom were married), and for young Samuel and Lemuel.[1] Warner had intended that the Philadelphia properties Anne brought to the marriage—he reckoned their value at £2,000—should revert to her; that she would also get possession of her dowry furniture as well as the "best riding carriage, her choice of carriage horses, several work horses, a plow and harrow, six cows from the herd, a yoke of oxen and oxcart, three of the best beds with appurtenances, [and] part of the mansion plantation, and an adjacent tract called 'Gainsborough' with its houses and outbuildings." As for the Chestnut Grove home plantation, it would go to her eldest son, Samuel, after Anne died, and Lemuel would have the three-hundred-acre plantation at Cow Marsh when he reached twenty-one, but until then the property would be leased out in order to support his education. The remainder of Warner's estate would go in equal parts to the five living children from his first marriage.[2]

Warner had drafted the will badly, and its terms displeased his grown son and apparently one or more of his sons-in-law, who thought the patriarch bequeathed too much to his second wife and not enough to them. Pointing to the will's incompleteness and inexactitude, Warner Mifflin Jr., assisted by an eminent Kent County lawyer, petitioned the Kent County Orphans Court to declare the will invalid—that is, flawed—insofar as it pertained to the division of real estate. Unfortunately, the resulting family squabble lasted for nearly seven years. Meanwhile, as the court-ordered surveys of the many parcels of land accumulated by Warner and officials sorted through a collection of debts both in favor of and against the deceased Mifflin, his children were unwilling to provide their stepmother with any financial support until the court ruled on the division of property.[3] Anne was deeply wounded by what seemed the hard-heartedness of her stepchildren, whom she had coparented for a decade and who now regarded her as a Philadelphia relative with wealth of her own. Frustrated by almost inexplicable delays in settling the estate, Anne bitterly appealed to the sister of Judge Nicholas Ridgely, an associate of the Orphans Court, for help. "My being excluded totally from receiving one farthing of my deceased Partner's property for my own support or my children's education," she wrote, "was a pitiable example of how a widow and her children were the prey of neglect or design in human transactions unless the hand of benevolence or human sympathy is reached forth for their deliverance."[4] In 1805, after seven years of shuffling ninety pages of documents, the Orphans Court ruled that Anne was entitled to the customary widow's third and that the other two-thirds of the estate should be split equally among the seven living children.[5]

In the meantime, seeking breathing space from her contentious stepchildren, Anne returned to the calming sanctuary of her Philadelphia home and the comfort of Mother Emlen, still hearty at eighty.[6] By May 1799, Ann Ridgely, her Kent County friend, reported that Anne had "left this county entirely."[7] Though she had left the Mifflin clan behind, she had not given up on all of her stepchildren. Accompanying her back to Philadelphia was fifteen-year-old stepdaughter Sarah, who would prove so helpful by forging an almost maternal bond with her half brothers Samuel and Lemuel.

While struggling with her husband's defective will, Anne also felt duty bound to protect Warner's reputation from detractors. Hovering over his corpse like vultures, his critics had wasted no time maligning him almost from the day of his burial. Chief among those dishonoring Warner was William Cobbett who, under the pseudonym Peter Porcupine, used his newspaper to tell his readers that Mifflin "will ever be looked on as the greatest fool or the greatest hypocrite that God ever suffered to let live." Cobbett also paired Mifflin and Anthony Benezet as "crack-brained" opponents of slavery.[8]

To clear Warner's name of any shady dealings with a Quaker entrepreneur whose potash experiments had gone sour, Anne wrote a response to Cobbett defending her husband's reputation and grafted it onto observations about what she regarded as Brissot's mistaken account of his conversations with Warner a decade before.[9] It was one thing that the failed investment had left Anne and Warner hundreds of dollars poorer; it was quite another that the public did not know that a clever promoter had gulled him. Warner was not guilty of unethical dealings himself, which would have been grounds for dismissal from the Society of Friends.[10] She appealed to all who had known Warner that he had been a man of great integrity, and she invited subscribers to repay Peter Porcupine's attempt "to assassinate a character that... did honor to all humanity" by canceling their subscriptions to Cobbett's newspaper. Though it was never published, it satisfied Anne's determination to perpetuate an honorable memory of her husband.

Always on the alert and sensitive to any slurs against her beloved Society of Friends, Anne also cobbled a short response to what she regarded as Brissot's misrepresentation of the Quakers. This, she hoped, would be published in the newspapers—an unusual move in itself for a woman of this era. In his *New Travels to the United States of America*, widely read by this time in English editions, Brissot had lavished praise on the Friends as model citizens, as recounted in chapter 2; however, Anne wanted the public to know that Brissot made Friends look ridiculous by claiming they "put on woolen stockings," regardless of the weather, every September 15, as part of an age-old custom that Quakers supposedly wove into their "system of religion." Anne saw this caricature as disgracing the Society of Friends, who were all too often ridiculed.[11]

Anne also brought closure to the last letter Warner wrote—his plaintive missive to President John Adams, composed in Philadelphia in September 1798 while yellow fever victims were dying around him. Warner had taken a draft of the letter back to Kent County; but falling ill, he left it in his wife's hands to send. In her grief at his death, she had put the letter aside. Two years later, back in Philadelphia, Anne asked Warner's bosom friends George Churchman and Jacob Lindley to forward the letter to John Adams. They did this in January 1801, just as Adams, having lost the 1800 election to Thomas Jefferson, was concluding his presidential term. Churchman and Lindley expressed how they felt impelled to deliver this posthumous letter because of the increase in the "disgraceful traffic in human flesh" and because of the failure of published plans for the gradual abolition of slavery. Sounding much like Warner, Churchman and Lindley asked President Adams, "Why should six hundred thousand fellow-creatures continue from year to year, and from age to age, to groan, many of them under more than Egyptian oppression, without the pity and compassion due from professed Christian rulers?" Echoing Mifflin, they asked whether the president would not lend his voice to stop "the engines of death and destruction that insulted the Christian God and the land of professed liberty."[12]

Anne may have regarded the former president's curt reply as a mockery of her husband's lifelong work. With astounding dissimulation, Adams wrote that "the practice of slavery is fast diminishing" and that "the condition of the common sort of white people in some of the southern states particularly in Virginia is more oppressed, degraded and miserable than that of the Negroes." Yes, he allowed that slavery was an evil and in time should be gradually abolished. But Churchman and Lindley, Adams advised, would better serve the country by focusing on "more serious and threatening evils" that promise "to bring punishment in our land, more immediately than the oppression of the blacks" such as "a general debauchery as well as dissipation produced by pestilential philosophical principles of epicures"—that is to say, deism, atheism, and hedonism. Yet, offering no comfort, Adams warned that "inflammatory publications against the slavery of the blacks"—a thinly disguised reference to the writings of Warner Mifflin—would backfire, bringing more misery down on the enslaved.[13] Anne never mentioned President Adams's dismissal of her husband's dying plea, but it must have disheartened her.

RAISING HER SONS

With the onset of widowhood and relocation back to Philadelphia, Anne regarded the care and education of Samuel and Lemuel as her gravest concern. A few months after returning, she wrote a moving account about Warner that would serve as an advisory text to instruct and inspire her sons as they approached adolescence. It would also provide the youngsters with a thoughtful remembrance of their father. Think of his "virtues and labors," she counseled, and try to imitate "his deep surrender to the work of religion." Lacing her account with some of their father's favorite apostolic exhortations, she urged them to model their father's dedication "to fight only in the heavenly warfare, to obtain the glorious liberty of the Children of God under the banner of the Conquering Lamb or Prince of Peace." She counseled that they should remember "the top-stone of his religious concern was . . . advancing the liberation of the poor oppressed Black People. A trumpet was given him on this subject with other brethren, to spread the alarm within the borders of our society, that we might more and more arise and shake ourselves from the dust of the earth in a departure from this iniquity."[14] While preserving for Samuel and Lemuel a written keepsake of their father's life work, Anne could also take comfort in knowing that raising her boys was not her sole responsibility.

Quaker founder George Fox had redefined the function of family, challenging the long-standing patriarchal tradition. He advocated that wherever Friends gathered, they were one sacred family, one "household of faith." From this belief, Friends justified the submission of all members to the authority of the meeting. Regardless of age or gender, whether acquaintances or strangers, all were regarded as "near relations." This warranted the meeting's responsibility for the sustenance of all its members, for the relief of the poor, the sick, the imprisoned, and for the care of widows and orphans.[15] Friends' adaptation to this radical change had been swift, successful, and remarkable.[16] Their outlook on family met the needs of widowed mothers such as Anne, granting them help and support. To a non-Quaker this might suggest undue dependence or lack of self-reliance, but within the extended family of Friends that support was fundamental.

Upon return to her Chestnut Street home with Samuel and Lemuel in tow, Anne relied on Mother Emlen, stepdaughter Sarah Mifflin, and the Emlen household servants to watch over her sons; moreover, while her finances were bound in the legal entanglements of Warner's will, Anne was beholden to her mother for shelter and provender.

Finding boarding schools for her two sons took precedence. Neither Samuel nor Lemuel had escaped the autumnal fevers that plagued Kent Countians, and that was enough reason to place them in a school elsewhere. As a stopgap measure, she put them in the care of William Jackson in Chester County, enrolled them in a local school in 1799, and would within a few years move them back to a school in Kent County.[17] After learning that Samuel's lameness hampered him in walking to school from the Jackson home, Anne registered him at the newly opened Westtown Friends School. Located twenty-five miles west of Philadelphia, the school embodied the "guarded education" that cut against the grain of the proposed education agenda recommended by Dr. Benjamin Rush and others who sought to create a unified community, faithful whether in times of peace or war. By contrast, educators at Westtown and other Quaker schools encouraged students to think for themselves as semi-separate people and taught "alternative definitions of citizenship and allegiance as well as the resistance to worldly law and authority espoused by the Quakers' Zion tradition."[18]

Following the custom of the well-to-do, Anne had no qualms about sending her boys off from home to be educated.[19] In August 1800, she left ten-year-old Samuel there while Lemuel, age eight, remained with the Jacksons.[20] As a member of the governing board, Anne soon became involved in fundraising for an infirmary and for years thereafter devoted herself to Westtown affairs.[21]

However, with much to recommend Westtown, Samuel's attendance there proved unsatisfactory. Suffering severe lameness, he left Westtown that February, and it appears he was never well enough to return even though Anne claimed that a "pow wow doctor," a practitioner of folk healing, cured Samuel's foot.[22] The fact that Samuel did not thrive like many boys his age would remain Anne's constant worry as her ministry frequently took her away from him on extended trips.

The Society of Friends wholeheartedly supported the itinerating ministry of female Public Friends—in most instances they were mothers with young children—but the separation from family was difficult for Anne.[23] Her letters to her mother while on religious journeys reflect her struggle to balance the duties of the ministry and motherhood. A common request in many of her letters was urging Mother Emlen to have Samuel to write to her.

By 1804, Anne had placed Lemuel in a school in Kent County, where he could get emotional support from his half brother Warner Mifflin Jr. and his half-sister Elizabeth and her husband Clayton Cowgill.[24] But despite his proximity to relatives, Anne chose a boarding school for Lemuel, believing that children's visits with family over the holidays should not be more than two or three weeks; in her mind, "it was hurtful to keep" students long from their studies as it would "lead to dissipation."[25] After withdrawing Samuel from Westtown School, Anne enrolled him in the Stephen Munson Day School in Haddonfield, New Jersey (about nine miles from Philadelphia), and arranged for him to reside there in the home of a worthy widow.

TO THE OUTER BOUNDARIES OF QUAKERDOM

While attending to her sons, Anne launched a renewed service to her Divine caretaker. Only a few months into widowhood, she initiated pastoral visits to quarterly and half-year meetings and proposed a plan to join Mary Berry on a voyage to visit the remnant of several Quaker communities in Barbados "if it should be my lot to take the awful voyage (which I do not shrink from)."[26] Though this proposed voyage was shelved, she found work to occupy her closer to home. Primarily, Anne needed to establish her bona fides with both the women's and men's PMM as well as the Meeting of Ministers and Elders, whose approval was essential for the new life course she intended. That approval came in October 1800, when the ministers and elders tapped her, along with two others, to serve as delegates to their ensuing quarterly meeting.[27]

With her reputation secured in the leadership cadre of the PMM, Anne was ready to embark on her first extended journey in service of the church militant. The timing seemed right to extend her mission to the outposts of Quaker settlement in central Pennsylvania. Eleven days after being asked to serve as a representative to the Meeting of Ministers and Elders, she appeared before her meeting to express how "she has had her mind drawn to visit divers[e] meetings in remote parts of our Quarterly Meeting." Agreeing to travel with her were Ruth Richardson (1756–1829), wife of a wealthy Philadelphia silversmith, and Arthur Howell (1748–1816), the well-traveled minister who often left his business as a tanner and currier to lend his voice at Quaker meetings in Rhode Island and various southern states.[28] Feeling encouraged "to lay the matter before our brethren," Anne did just that, receiving prompt approval. Here beckoned the opportunity to assume the role that Warner had performed for so many years—to strengthen the faith and discipline of Quaker meetings and to offer advice on temporal affairs. This time she would go to freshly settled Friends' gatherings at Muncy, Catawissa, and Fishing Creek that the PYM was eager to bring more closely under its disciplinary purview.

Setting off as early winter ushered in frost and dirty weather, the three Quaker ministers pushed northwest through Germantown to Pottstown, possibly by carriage. Then they continued by horseback across the Blue Mountains, where the road from Reading to Catawissa and Muncy was tortuous. Anne's brother, James Emlen, had made the same trip six years before on his way to a proposed peace settlement at Canandaigua, where the native people had requested a Quaker delegation. His description of the trip likely gave Anne and her party pause because it warned of "the slow and tedious" stone-covered road across the Appalachian Mountains, where Quaker farmers had been taking up new land and building rude meetinghouses in the upper Susquehanna River region.[29]

The new preparative meetings, formed mostly by Chester County Quakers moving west, had been gathered into the monthly meetings of Muncy and Catawissa only a few years before. Now these new preparative meetings would receive the three Philadelphia-based traveling ministers who were on their mission to strengthen their sectarian discipline. To undertake this in December, on crude roads, hazarded risks for the city dwellers; but Anne and her traveling partners returned safely after about eight weeks, reporting "close unity" with the frontier-hardened Friends.[30] For the resolute Anne Mifflin, it was a toughening introduction to further journeys she already envisioned.

Returning to Philadelphia, once again Anne's ministry preempted parental concerns. Back home only a matter of weeks, she appeared again before the women's meeting seeking a certificate to travel with another minister, Mary Gilbert, and other Friends to visit the forthcoming yearly meetings in Rhode Island and New York.[31] Making this long journey, Anne must have been mindful of retracing the steps Warner made two decades before in the midst of war. On her visit to Providence, Rhode Island, she broke bread with Moses Brown[32] and then visited William Rotch of Nantucket,[33] rekindling old friendships with these stalwarts of their monthly meetings. In a series of in-transit letters to her mother Anne recounted many details of this second, six-week extended ministerial journey.[34]

SERVING PHILADELPHIA'S DOWNTRODDEN

Returning to Philadelphia in August 1801, Anne in her forty-seventh year resumed work in the women's monthly meeting and served as an assistant teacher at Westtown for the autumn school term. But the commitment to teach at Westtown School and the work for the women's meeting could not satisfy Anne's boundless energy. She needed new outlets to fulfill her spiritual thirst and expand her reach outside the Society of Friends. For several years she had been part of a circle of Philadelphia Quaker women, most unmarried and half her age, who had struck out to serve poor non-Quakers, black as well as white. In so doing, these Quaker women entered a public sphere heretofore almost entirely dominated by men. Beyond sheer philanthropic urges, good works became a way for Friends in the postrevolutionary era to regain the respect of fellow citizens by serving the community at large.[35]

Anne Parrish Jr. (1760–1800), Anne Mifflin's second cousin, had led the way. Unmarried, in 1795 she founded the Female Society for the Relief and Employment of the Poor. A year later she spearheaded the Aimwell School for the Free Instruction of Females, which provided education for the daughters of poor non-Quaker Philadelphians. Anne soon followed Cousin Anne's lead, joining the Parrish's poverty organization in 1796 and then the Society for the Free Instruction of African Females, the Society for the Free Instruction of Females of Color, and later the Aimwell School.[36] Without directly confronting customary gender relations, Anne Parrish, Anne's cousin (also named Anne Mifflin), and a host of other women pushed beyond these traditional limitations, extending their efforts to non-Quakers in a city crowded with the poor—free African Americans, immigrants, and those drifting in from the hinterland seeking new opportunities.

The inspiration and courage to move beyond the confines of the Society of Friends' charitable activities had come by way of the redoubtable English traveling minister Deborah Darby (1754–1810), who had attended the PYM in September 1794. Darby counseled Philadelphia young women to "seriously consider which of them are called upon to dedicate their time and talents . . . to the useful occupation of instructing children in the profitable parts of school learning," not only to "our youth" but also to "the poor and African race under our notice."[37] It is unlikely that Anne attended the yearly meeting or heard Friend Darby speak; but afterward, when Deborah Darby and her traveling partner Rebecca Young left Philadelphia, they traveled south through Delaware and lodged with Anne and Warner at Chestnut Grove. Then, for the next several weeks, Anne, four months pregnant, along with Warner joined the two English ministers for a journey down the Delmarva Peninsula to bear the Quakers' testimony. Darby noted in her diary that Anne "bore short testimonies" to those they visited as they moved southward and then, after reaching Accomack County, they held a "public meeting" at Pharsalia, Warner's birthplace, where the "Gospel flow'd freely to many of the free Blacks."[38] Surely it was during this extended travel with Darby and Young that Anne was inspired to extend her charitable instincts beyond the confines of the Friends' women's meetings. Entering the dawn of the nineteenth century and the epoch of a new republic, Anne Mifflin would now venture even farther afield.

The move back to Philadelphia had been advantageous, placing Anne in the vital center of Friends' activity and exposing her to some of the most gifted female Quaker ministers of her time. With a new direction for her ministry percolating in her mind, Anne returned to what had been her late husband's consuming interest—the crusade to free slaves and to aid free black people. When the Quaker mystic Dorothy Ripley (1767–1831) arrived in Philadelphia in April 1802, armed with a letter of introduction to Anne, Friend Ripley found herself in good hands.[39] A teacher and the daughter of an English lay Methodist minister, Ripley had undergone a spiritual awakening that called her to travel to America in order to teach the children of slaves, who were then living in Washington, DC.[40] Having broken off a long-standing engagement, Ripley arrived almost penniless; in this straitened condition[41] Anne proved

Ripley's savior, introducing her to the Pembertons and other Friends who might help her reach the capital to seek President Jefferson's support. When the young Philadelphia merchant of means Thomas Cope spurned Anne's plea for funds, others opened their purses.[42] Mindful of how inappropriate and dangerous it was for women to travel alone, Anne and Phoebe Pemberton accompanied Ripley as far as Darby. When Dorothy returned to Philadelphia a month later, she was welcomed by Anne, who invited her to stay at the Emlen Chestnut Street home for a week. For several years, Ripley continued her journeys, facing stern rebukes from many Quakers who opposed single women traveling without male company.[43]

"OUR BRETHREN THE NATIVES"

Toughened by seasons of travel, devoted wholeheartedly to the Divine calling, and fully committed to self-sacrifice, Anne shifted her attention in 1802–3 to what she would later call "the laudable work of improving our brethren the natives."[44] For the next few years, she coupled this concern with visits to the outer edges of Quaker settlements that reached all the way to the northern shore of Lake Ontario.

Anne's interest in the Friends' assistance to native peoples, particularly the Oneidas and Senecas and those domiciled among them, reached back to the early 1790s when Warner and her brother James, along with close friends Jacob Lindley, William Savery,[45] and John Parrish, had sparked the yearly meeting's renewed interest in the Native Americans' well-being. The Iroquois chiefs themselves, struggling to adapt to postrevolutionary reservation life, had rekindled Friends' interest in their welfare when they traveled to Philadelphia to confer with President Washington in 1791 and also to parley with receptive Quaker leaders. Anne, like other Philadelphians, marveled at the native emissaries' camping out in the yard behind Independence Hall—across the street from the Emlen residence. No sources remain to tell us what she heard from Friends who soon became unofficial observers and advisers at a series of treaty negotiations between tribal chiefs and the federal government in the early 1790s. However, knowing that the ever-curious, intellectual Anne was closely bound with the key Quakers involved, we can surmise that she was fully informed.[46]

Building on these early Quaker-Iroquois initiatives, in September 1795 the PYM established a standing Indian Committee for Promoting the

Improvement and Gradual Civilization of the Indian Natives.[47] The mission of the committee was to assist the federal government in promoting what was termed the "civilization" of native people by giving material aid, vocational teachers, and counsel that would nudge them toward adopting white ways, particularly in plow agriculture, female domesticity, and literacy schooling. This, Friends believed, would allow native people to survive the encirclement by ravenous, land-hungry, postrevolutionary white Americans. Because improving their lives rather than converting native people to Quaker faith was the main objective, native people were more welcoming to Friends in the villages of Iroquoia than to proselytizing zealous Protestant missionaries who swarmed onto Indian lands in the 1790s. Though not yet involved, Anne was certainly privy to the plans for the Quaker mission and the roles played by her husband, brother, and close friends on the Indian Committee.[48]

Beginning in the summer of 1802, Anne logged several thousand miles traveling twice from Philadelphia deep into Iroquoia. In the first journey, Anne's traveling companion was the redoubtable Hannah Kirkbride (1747–1826), a minister from Bucks County's Buckingham Monthly Meeting. Eight years older than Anne, Hannah had been approved by her meeting as a minister five months before the signing of the Declaration of Independence and spent much of the war years as a single woman on religious visits to Friends in New Jersey, Delaware, and Maryland.[49]

Anne and Hannah prioritized providing spiritual sustenance and discipline to the remote, newly formed Friends meetings far to the north, and regarded visits to Iroquois people as a secondary matter but far from an afterthought. "She has felt her mind engaged at times for more than two years," noted the minutes of Anne's women's meeting, "to pay a visit to Friends settled at Upper Canada, being now under an appointment of the Yearly Meeting committee." Accordingly, they requested traveling certificates not from the Indian Committee but from their monthly meeting.[50]

What pressed on the minds of Anne and Hannah as they left Philadelphia to visit the Oneida people? "Given that Quakers sought and expected no converts from their missions," asks one historian, "what then, would they do so far from home, traveling intentionally in harm's way and so near peril? What would lead a group of young men and women from Philadelphia . . . to trek hundreds of miles from home into a region that might be hostile, so recently torn by war?"[51] For Anne and Hannah, venturing into this distant territory to Indian country validated their conviction that God required

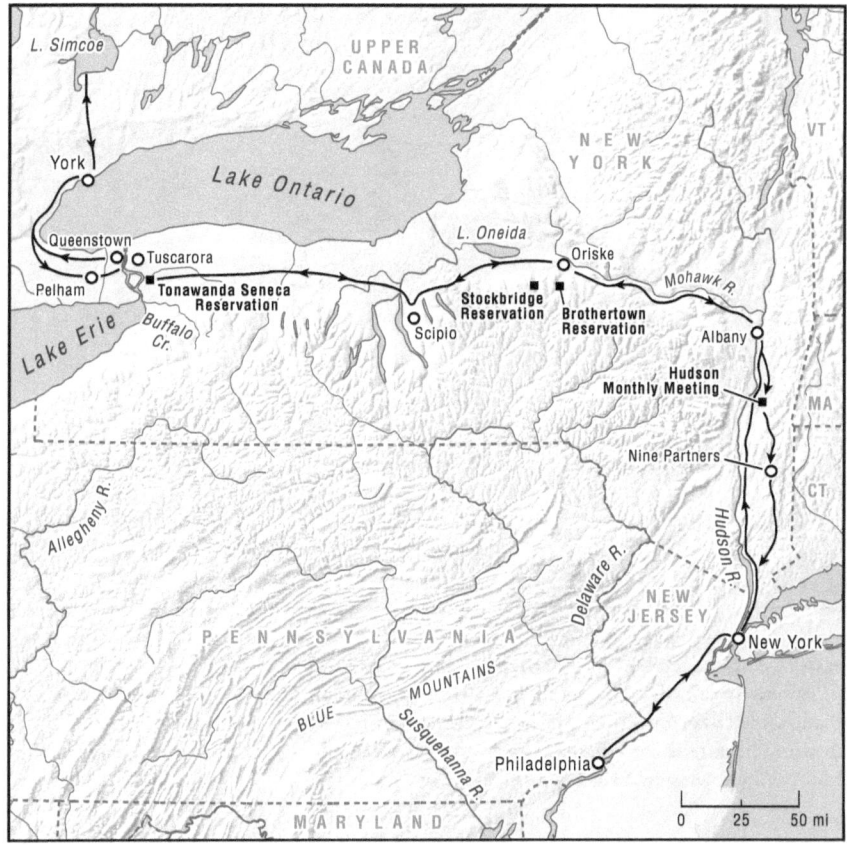

MAP 1 | Anne's August–September 1802 journey from Philadelphia to Lake Simcoe, Canada, stopping at Friends' Meetings at Nine Partners, Hudson Monthly Meeting, and Scipio and visiting the Brothertown, Stockbridge, Tonawanda, and Tuscarora people as well as those at the village of Oriske. Most of the thousand-mile journey entailed travel over rough, overgrown roads. Map by Erin Greb.

Christians to reach out to people across cultural, tribal, and racial boundaries to serve "all God's children"—the core of the testimony of equality.[52] Though they may not have internalized it, they were also contributing to the yearly meeting leaders' call to recapture "a vestige of social and political power and to establish a formal role for themselves and their Society in the new American public sphere." At the same time, this would be a way to reinvigorate the Society of Friends.[53]

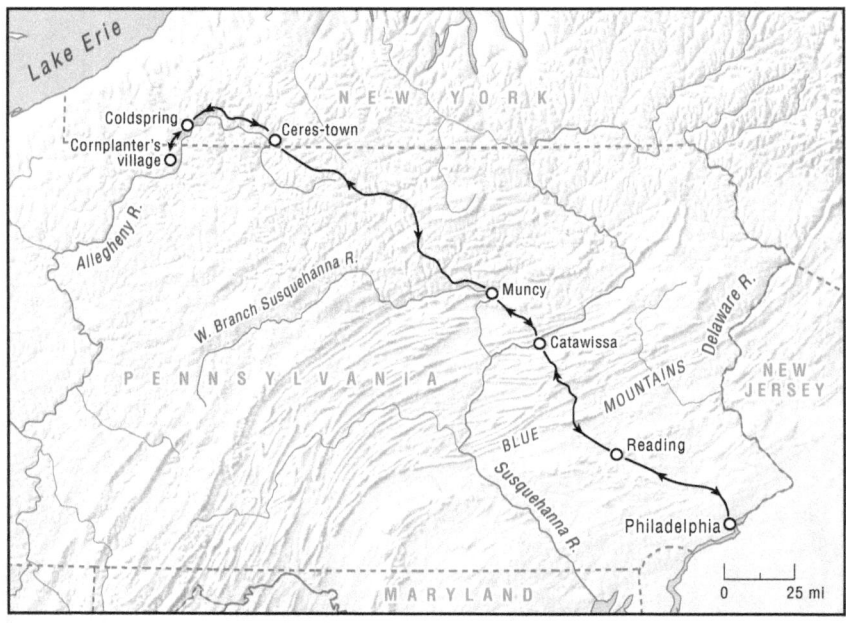

MAP 2 | Anne's October–November 1803 journey to the Seneca villages along the Allegheny River, where she met Chief Cornplanter and his half brother, the prophet Handsome Lake. Covering over seven hundred miles, Anne's group enjoyed the fellowship and hospitality of Friends' meetings at Catawissa, Muncy, Ceres-town, and Half-Moon Valley. Map by Erin Greb.

By planning to fold visits to the Oneida reservation into the strenuous trip to counsel faraway Friends, Anne was certainly informed and inspired by earlier accounts from two Quaker women, Hannah Jackson and Susanna Gregory. In the summer of 1798, Hannah and Susanna, members of the PMM, had enlisted to serve at the Quakers' model farm and at the sawmill sanctioned just two years before by the Indian Committee. They were the first white women to live among the Oneidas.[54]

Though the story of their mission was never recorded, one assumes that Hannah and Susanna shared their experience firsthand with Anne Mifflin and Hannah Kirkbride. Jackson and Gregory had arrived after three young men had been sent by the Indian Committee in the spring of 1796 with orders to establish a model farm that would show Oneida people the advantages of adopting plow agriculture, animal husbandry, individual property ownership, and redefined gender roles. But the Friends' demonstration farm, lasting only three and a half years, was beset from the beginning by social disorder and political factionalism among their native clients.[55] In particular, the decades-old division between the Oneida "pagans" and Oneida "Christians" made it nearly impossible for Friends to reach many of the Oneidas, as the native Christian party had already aligned with the stiff-necked Samuel Kirkland, the longtime Presbyterian minister to the Oneidas. This left the Friends only the "pagan faction," who held to "a creative mix of Christian and traditional" spirituality but also appreciated "the Quakers' relatively non-dogmatic approach to Christianization."[56]

When Hannah Jackson and Susanna Gregory returned from the Oneida reservation after nineteen months,[57] Anne would have heard of their partial success in teaching Oneida women to spin, weave, and study English. But she may also have learned how attempts to encourage Oneida women to leave the fields brought scorn from their husbands, who insisted that seeding, tilling, and harvesting corn was women's work—a position to which the native women generally acceded.[58] Nonetheless, as the nineteen-month experiment came to an end, the Indian Committee in Philadelphia had grounds for some satisfaction from the agreeable exchange of speeches between the visiting Friends and the native leaders.[59] Standing before the small Quaker contingent at Oriske, where most of the "pagan" faction lived, Chief Shenandoah "thankfully acknowledged your kindness, having never heard of any people that has done so much for Indians without a view of advantage to themselves, which is a convincing proof to us you are our real friends."[60]

Knowing that PYM's Indian Committee had aborted the demonstration farm at Oneida while leaving behind all the farm implements and the operating saw and grain mills, Anne and Hannah might have questioned what more they could have accomplished. But perhaps something could be salvaged in reaching out to native peoples.[61] In some measure they might supply encouragement for the exploited native peoples who had been victimized by unscrupulous white people, who, as Anne phrased it, were "invited thither by the country of the Oneidas in their reduced circumstances arising in great measure from their being induced for trifling considerations to part with their possessions to the Whites."[62]

Whatever their hopes and expectations, Anne and Hannah set out from Philadelphia in early August 1802 to progress as far as possible during seasonable weather. Their journey took them ninety miles to New York City, then northward up the Hudson River to Albany, and finally, by one conveyance or another, west along the Mohawk River to the Oneida reservation. First, they visited the Brothertown and Stockbridge people domiciled on the Oneida reservation, then met with the "pagan" Oneida faction living in Oriske village. After traveling farther west along the Genesee Road, they reached the Tonawanda and Tuscarora reservations south of Lake Ontario and northeast of Lake Erie.

In her account, Anne speculated about Native American descent from the so-called Lost Tribes of Israel, included speeches from native chiefs who welcomed them, and described observations on the archaeological remains of ancient mound builders. She also provided poignant accounts of how whites adept in peddling liquor had used alcohol to ravage natives and separate them from their land. Anne made no attempt to hide her contempt for the treatment of the Stockbridge, Brothertown, and Oneida peoples, allies who had fought alongside Americans against the British only to be stripped of most of their lands after the war. Among the first white females to speak to the Brothertown and Stockbridge people and to parley with their chiefs, Anne was gladdened by one of the native speaker's promises that "we shall always remember what she said" about the native peoples origins and by the native women expressing their eagerness to receive other female Quaker teachers willing to live with them.[63]

Though not mentioned in their report, the two women moved north across the Canada border in September 1802 in the Lord's service, ministering to the Quaker farmers and artisans who had migrated to the sparsely settled land between Lake Ontario and Lake Simcoe. In letters to her mother, Anne expressed some anxiety on "the perilous roads which occasions some dread in returning."[64] After visiting the villages of York (now Toronto) and Pelham, Anne and Hannah retraced their steps southward and then eastward through the Oneida reservation to Albany. In the final leg of their long trip, they met with Quakers at the Hudson Monthly Meeting, thirty miles south of Albany, where Friends expressed "their unity with her [Anne] in the weighty work of visiting families and friendly people in their parts." Farther south on the Hudson River in Dutchess County, they communed with Friends at the Stamford Quarterly Meeting at the Nine Partners Quaker settlement, one of the staging areas for Quaker migration to Upper Canada after the American Revolution.[65] Road weary and leaving the Canadian winter behind, they reached Philadelphia in November. They had covered more than twelve hundred miles by carriage, riverboat, horse, canoe, and on foot.

Upon her return to Philadelphia at the end of the 1802 sojourn, Anne submitted her travel certificate from their epic trip to Canada and requested approval to make visitations closer to home. This time Anne and her traveling partner Mary Gilbert cut a wide swath through Bucks and Chester counties in March 1803, visiting four quarterly meetings and many monthly meetings on a trip of several months. "Whilst engaged in their late visit," they reported, "they were favored to feel from time to time in evidence that they were in the right places and were also favored to return home with the answering peace."[66]

By this time, Anne ranked as the foremost Public Friend to come before the women and men's Philadelphia monthly meetings asking for authorization to travel throughout Quakerdom—stretching from Lower Canada to the lower Chesapeake Bay. Her fervent desire to spread Divine truth meant long separations from home and family, and concern for her adolescent sons was expressed in the letters sent to Mother Emlen in Philadelphia with instructions on what the boys were to do, or not to do, while assuring them of her concerns, love, and prayers.

Back in Philadelphia for the spring and early summer of 1803, life could have easily slipped into a routine, but the Jericho Road ever beckoned Anne, who could hardly keep herself from planning the next journey "in Truth's service." She once again sought the meeting's approval to combine a visit to remote Quaker settlements on Pennsylvania's northwestern edge with a stop-off to render service among Native American women. By September, with approval certificates in hand, she was on the road, again with Mary Gilbert, leaving in an amenable season for travel. Much of the primitive road was familiar, for it retraced their 1800 visit to the Quaker settlements at Catawissa, Munsey, Ceres-town, and Half-Moon Valley on the western branch of the Susquehanna and on the Allegheny River.[67]

Having succored the Quaker settlements there, Anne, in company with four others, pushed north to the Seneca reservation villages on the New York–Pennsylvania border. As with the 1802 foray into Oneida country, Anne and Mary were commissioned not by the Indian Committee but by the Philadelphia monthly and yearly meetings. They were surely prepared, nonetheless, by the Indian Committee, which had been involved in the Allegheny River Seneca villages for more than five years.[68] Thus, Anne was entering a region where Friends, backed by encouragement and aid from the federal government, had been urging the Senecas to adopt plow farming practices, alter gender work roles, and wean themselves from the use of alcohol. The partial success of the Friends' exceptional program had been facilitated by Quakers' "impeccable personal conduct," their policy of shunning all profit in their enterprise, and their "discreeteness in their criticism of native religious beliefs."[69]

Over stony, rutted roads, through rugged, mountainous country, and across swift-running river fords, Anne's horse negotiated many hundreds of miles to carry her deep into the reservation lands of the Senecas, where wolves, mountain lions, bears, and elk were more Anne's daily acquaintance than the hardscrabble frontier settlers she encountered along the way. Anne and her small entourage had boldly ventured where few white men, let alone white women, had set foot.

Anne, Mary Bell, and the two Quaker men reached the Senecas at a crucial time for native people in their efforts to adjust to reservation life. The rapid rise of the prophet Handsome Lake as the elected "supreme leader of the Six [Iroquois] Nations," ratifying his code for moral and religious revitalization, had occurred only months before. However, just as Anne arrived, Handsome Lake and his half brother Chief Cornplanter fell out over issues of land sales and money. Intraparty tension would simmer for the next few years; nonetheless the Seneca factions had made some progress, agreeing in general with Handsome Lake's plan to overcome the curse of drinking; adopting technical assistance from Friends; gradually introducing plow agriculture, animal husbandry, grist and saw milling as well as blacksmithing; and, to a limited degree, encouraging native women's participation in the Senecas' domestic economy.[70]

After first reaching Jenuchshadago, or Burnt House, where a group of Quaker men had established an off-reservation demonstration farm and sawmill in 1798, Anne traveled another nine miles upriver to Genesinguhta (Old Town), the residence of Cornplanter, as well as another, unnamed Seneca chief of the Allegany reservation. Perched on his private tract of land, Cornplanter's village, in the words of Anthony Wallace, was "a slum in the wilderness," yet "a unique slum" because this "shabby Shangri-La [was] hidden from alien eyes in the forest of the Allegheny Mountains, where by tradition no white man could enter" and the "Allegany band of Seneca could maintain a greater measure of autonomy than the Iroquois living near Buffalo and Niagara and along the Genesee."[71]

In their welcome, Cornplanter and his sister noted in their speeches to the visiting delegation that Anne Mifflin was the first white woman ever to enter Genesinguhta, a town of about four hundred souls, and the first to meet Handsome Lake, the revered Seneca prophet. Anne's group also briefly visited Tunesassa, the site of a new Friends' 692-acre model farm just taking form in the autumn of 1803.[72]

Upon returning home from this remarkable journey, Anne documented her findings in a report only recently noticed by historians.[73] This account reaffirmed that Friends took care to avoid preaching Protestant belief, especially doctrines that stressed man's innate depravity and the redemption achieved only through the atonement of Christ. Instead, the Quakers opted for a simpler message, an idea far more compatible with native beliefs in the Great Spirit. Friends counseled that the Senecas, like everyone else, could best draw on the Inward Light to better themselves and could best ensure their people's survival through piety, industry, abstinence, and a morality no more complicated than the Golden Rule.

Anne and her friends also recorded the advice they had given to the Senecas. Hemmed in by land-hungry, corrupt whites, the Senecas agreed that they could only save themselves by adopting plow farming. Still, they resisted the Friends' stricture that the native males do the plowing rather than the women. The Quaker missionaries among them had promoted the idea that women's work should be centered in the home, and their communal ownership of property should yield to privately owned, small agricultural tracts. Although this secular conversion, often referred to as a "civilization" plan, caused dissension and some resistance among the Senecas, most could see that Friends were not coming to the Allegany forest to benefit themselves. They earnestly desired to assist the Senecas in finding a formula for survival. As Handsome Lake admitted, his people "saw that the white people would settle all round them; that they could not live unless they learned to farm and follow the white people's ways."[74]

For Anne, the receptiveness of the Senecas had been a heartwarming validation of her trip. She reported how native female leaders had commended her efforts to help natives "promote our advancement in the several improvements of civilized life . . . I know they have a thirst for our knowledge," evident "both from their expressions to us and their flocking around me to see the manner of knitting."[75]

Anne's account of the time spent with the Senecas that autumn, in a landscape incomparable with Philadelphia's, differs from travel narratives recorded by other Quaker ministers. Though she makes mention of the difficulties, she does not dwell on the hardships as other Friends do in their reports.[76] For Anne, this journey, like many she would take, had been not only a spiritual mission and retreat but also an adventure, a step back in time connecting with nature nonpareil. She described lying "encamped on the grass [with] our midnight serenade being the howling of wolves and the screeching of owls," which made her feel "preserved in sweet serenity and peace." Anne was impressed with the Senecas' "sagacity," the beauty of their language, their vow to continue on the path to abstinence, and, most of all, the desire of the women to take up spinning and weaving. She promised that upon returning to Philadelphia she would try to recruit Quaker teachers to live among them as the Senecas had requested.

Passing south through Catawissa to attend Friends' meetings, Anne and Mary Gilbert were back in Philadelphia as winter closed in.[77] Like many travelers to distant places, they returned home with many stories to share and likely were themselves enriched and transformed by the unique experiences of an epic journey. What fascinating adventures Anne must have related to Samuel and Lemuel of her historic meetings with Native Americans! What could beguile these young boys more than tales of Indians in the wilderness or perhaps the receipt of gifts, native mementoes brought back from the trip?

True to form, no sooner was Anne reunited with her family than she set about trying to recruit female Friends willing to leave cosmopolitan Philadelphia to live among Seneca women, to teach them spinning, weaving, and other domestic skills. In a February 1804 letter to Friends who were managing the model farm on the Allegany reservation, she reported not yet finding any women to follow in her footsteps, but in the meantime she was sending fifty needles and 176 yards of thread for the Seneca women.[78] Shortly thereafter, the Indian Committee recommended the recruitment of an unmarried female Friend and a married couple to be sent to work among Seneca women to teach them "the management of dairies, spinning, and other domestic economy." The PYM convening in Philadelphia in April 1804 put their weight behind this effort, hoping "that this benevolent work may be advanced as Truth opens and leads the way."[79]

In the fiftieth year of her life, Anne took to the road again, traveling for several weeks from one monthly meeting to another in southern New Jersey, where Friends were thickly settled. This time, she was joined by Sarah Cresson and her cousin Sarah Mifflin as traveling partners. Visiting the Salem Monthly Meeting, just across the Delaware River from the southern perimeter of Philadelphia, they were pleased to see black worshipers who had gathered quickly upon hearing that traveling female ministers were arriving.[80]

These efforts were by no means Anne's last exercise in her sacred office as a Quaker minister and Public Friend. Still ahead was a decade marked by continued sojourning, always placing the inward calling above outward affairs in her ongoing labor in the Lord's vineyard.

NOTES

1. In the 1798 Kent County tax assessment lists, Warner was assessed for more than 3,500 acres of land. At his Chestnut Grove plantation of more than one thousand acres the tax assessor listed nine horses, a herd of cattle nearly one hundred strong, forty-eight sheep, several sows and shoats, and sixty-eight ounces of plate. Tax Assessment Lists (1798–1801), RG3535.000, microfilm rolls 5–6, DPA.

2. Will of Warner Mifflin in Justice, *Life and Ancestry of Warner Mifflin*, 223–28. Mifflin named his brother Daniel and his brothers-in-law Jonathan Hunn and Samuel Howell to administer the will.

3. Petition of Warner Mifflin [Jr.] to the Kent County Orphans Court, December 4, 1799, RG 3840.006, DPA.

4. Anne Mifflin to Ann Ridgeley, December 11, 1804, Ridgeley Collection, DPA. To the letter Anne appended an account of how she had raised money from her estate to pay the debts that Warner carried into their marriage and how she financed the purchase of Marsh Plantation.

5. According to legal provisions, any debts owed on an estate were paid from the widow's third (her inheritance). Anne had paid sizeable debts for her husband while he was alive, so it stands to reason that Warner left her with residual debt as well.

6. Two months after Warner's burial, Anne visited Philadelphia and called on the Drinkers, apparently while arranging the return to her mother's house. Crane, *Diary of Elizabeth Drinker*, 2:1121 (December 16, 1798).

7. Ann Ridgely to Ann Ridgely Jr., May 5, 1799, Ridgely Collection, DPA. Anne, identified by Elizabeth Drinker as Nancy Mifflin, dined with the Drinkers on April 30, 1799, perhaps upon her arrival in the city. Crane, *Diary of Elizabeth Drinker*, 2:1163 (April 30, 1799). MMM recommended a meeting transfer to Philadelphia's Women's Meeting for Anne, "a minister in good esteem." PWMMM (1783–1802), July 15, 1800.

8. The flamboyant career of William Cobbett (1763–1835) included stints as a soldier, entrepreneur, politician, teacher, translator, and character assassin. He lived in the United States from 1794 to 1800, working as a pamphleteer, controversial journalist, and pseudonymous newspaper owner. Richard Ingrams in *The Life and Adventures of William Cobbett* (2) calls him "the most effective, the most savage, and the most satirical political journalist of his or any age." See Nash, *Mifflin*, 219, for more on Cobbett's attacks.

9. [Anne Mifflin], "An Observer from Kent County," box 9, fol. 7, C-P-W. Anne also sent her screed to Moses Brown for his comments and to John Parrish on the possibility of getting it published in Philadelphia. Anne Mifflin to Moses Brown, October 3, 1801, Moses Brown Papers, Rhode Island Historical Society, Providence; Anne Mifflin to John Parrish, December 12, 1799, box 1, fol. 25, C-P-W.

10. Anne Mifflin to John Parrish, December 6, 1799, box 2, EFP. Anne failed to get her defense of Warner published.

11. Anne Mifflin to John Parrish, December 12, 1799, box 1, fol. 26, C-P-W.

12. George Churchman and Jacob Lindley to John Adams, January 17, 1801, Adams Papers, Massachusetts Historical Society, Boston, also available on Founders Online, https://founders.archives.gov.

13. John Adams to George Churchman, January 24, 1801, Adams Papers, Massachusetts Historical Society, Boston, also available on Founders Online, https://founders.archives.gov. President Adams never favored Anne with a reply.

14. [Anne Mifflin], "A Brief Account of the Late Warner Mifflin: In a Letter to His Sons Samuel Emlen and Lemuel Mifflin," October 25, 1799, box 2, EFP. For the full text of this letter, see chapter 10, below.

15. Frost, *Quaker Family*, 64.

16. In *Daughters of Light* (19–23), Rebecca Larson terms the uniqueness of Quakerism's restructuring roles for men and women as a "unity of gender."

17. Anne Mifflin to John Parrish, November 16, 1799, box 2, EFP.

18. In the Zion tradition the Israelites' experience was characterized by long suffering and a struggle to accept monotheism. Sarah Crabtree notes that nineteenth-century Quakers' adaptation of the Zion tradition emphasized charity and social reform. Crabtree discusses the Friends' turn-of-century school movement on both sides of the Atlantic in *Holy Nation* (chap. 3). Westtown Friends School, the oldest continuously functioning coeducational boarding school in the nation, opened in May 1799 after six years of planning and fundraising by the PYM. Coeducational from its inception, the school appointed Anne to the governing committee in March 1800. Westtown's early history is treated in Dewees and Dewees, *Centennial History of Westtown Boarding School*; and Hole, *Westtown Through the Years*.

19. "I part with both my children for their good to board elsewhere," she wrote Dorothy Ripley on May 31, 1804 (Chicago Historical Museum).

20. Anne Mifflin to Thomas Fisher, March 17, 1800, box 2, EFP. Warner had served on the governing board of Westtown School since 1794 when it was in its planning stages.

21. Crane, *Diary of Elizabeth Drinker*, 2:1322 (July 24, 1800), 2:1338 (September 8, 1800), 2:1360 (December 6, 1800).

22. Ibid., 2:1396–97 (March 31, 1801). See also Kriebel, *Powwowing Among the Pennsylvania Dutch*.

23. Sarah Crabtree, analyzing one hundred Friends' travel accounts between 1750 and 1820, "In the Light and on the Road" (134), concluded that "female ministers consistently portrayed the difficulty of leaving home as the most significant emotional obstacle for them to overcome." In *Daughters of Light* (164–70), Rebecca Larson emphasizes Quaker mothers in the ministry received their meeting's support but suffered stress from being separated from loved ones on ministerial travels. However, for Friends, if a woman displayed spiritual gifts, then public ministry (which might be lifelong service) took precedence over her role as wife or mother.

24. Anne Mifflin to Anne Emlen Sr., October 10, 1805, box 2, EFP. On her way to Baltimore, Anne complained of Lemuel spending money on trifles.

25. In her May 31, 1804, letter to Dorothy Ripley (Chicago Historical Museum), Anne recommended Westtown School for her son and described the arrangements she herself had made for Samuel and Lemuel's schooling.

26. Anne Mifflin to John Parrish, circa March 15, 1799, box 1, fol. 26, C-P-W.

27. PYM, Minister and Elders Minutes (1796–1809), October 20, 1800. The other women appointed were Sarah Harrison (ca. 1744–1812) and Sarah Cresson (1747–1803), both pillars of the women's meeting and senior to Anne.

28. PWMMM (1793–1833), October 31, 1800. On May 31, 1799, Richardson had been recommended to the Meeting of Ministers and Elders "as a Friend who has received a Gift of Gospel Ministry" (PWMMM [1793–1833]). Married to Joseph Richardson (1752–1831) in 1780 and mother of eight children, Ruth was a year younger than Anne.

29. Fenton, "Journal of James Emlen," 265–66. From Philadelphia to Munsey, the four Quakers covered 155 miles in five days. Anne's group probably spent more than a week traveling in insalubrious weather.

30. Anne visited the Drinkers on December 6, so the journey must have begun shortly after that. Crane, *Diary of Elizabeth Drinker*, 2:1360 (December 6, 1800). Returning from western Pennsylvania, Mifflin, Richardson, and Howell, nearly home, stopped at the Haverford and Merion meetings. They submitted their traveling certificates to the PMM at the end of January 1801, indicating they had been on their mission for some four to six weeks. PMMMM (1795–1801), January 30, 1801.

31. Anne received a traveling certificate from the men's meeting. PMMMM (1795–1801), March 27, 1801. Mary Gilbert (1773–?), the widow of John Gilbert, visited Philadelphia in 1794 and again in 1796. After John's death from yellow fever in 1798, Mary moved to Philadelphia with her three sons, all of whom were admitted to the PMM in mid-1800. PWMMM (1793–1805), June 27, 1800.

32. Anne Mifflin to Moses Brown, October 3, 1801, box 2, EFP. Moses Brown (1738–1835), a wealthy Baptist merchant of Providence, Rhode Island, after becoming a Quaker in 1774 participated actively in the Society of Friends. He broke ties with his brothers over their ownership of slaves; and through his efforts, in 1787 the Rhode Island Assembly passed a law banning the slave trade. For Brown's early life, see Thompson, *Moses Brown*; and Rappleye, *Sons of Providence*.

33. Anne Mifflin to Anne Emlen Sr., June 30, 1801, box 2, EFP. William Rotch (1734–1828) (also spelled Roacks or Resch), a Quaker antislavery activist, was the best known of the Nantucket, Massachusetts, Friends. He married Elizabeth Barney, also of Nantucket, and the Rotch family were influential leaders in the Quaker community there for decades. For more on Rotch, see Leach and Gow, *Quaker Nantucket*.

34. See chapter 11, below.

35. Haviland, "Beyond Women's Sphere." Building on Haviland's work, Bruce Dorsey in *Reforming Men and Women* (chap. 1) argues that the efforts of reformist men and women in early nineteenth-century seaboard cities to negotiate "a shared space for benevolent activity in the urban landscape" often brought male disapproval of the women.

36. Margaret Haviland, a teacher at Westtown School, provided information on Anne's work in these organizations. Of the 249 women she studied, only three shared Anne's profile—older women ministers well established in their meetings in contrast to the younger, single women who "channeled their sense of service and caring for others into charitable organizations they formed for the purpose." Email message to the authors, October 31, 2018.

37. PWMMM (1793–1805), November 28, 1794, quoted in Haviland, "Beyond Women's Sphere," 423.

38. Labouchere, *Deborah Darby of Coalbrookdale*, 171–72. Three years later, she and Warner accompanied Richard Jordan, a North Carolina Quaker minister, through the Eastern Shore, stopping at Pharsalia, where free black Virginians gathered on First Day afternoon to audit the testimonies. See Jordan, *Journal of the Life*, 27.

39. "Dorothy Ripley," 36.

40. [Ripley], *Extraordinary Conversion and Religious Experience of Dorothy Ripley*, 61–62, 66. Anne and Dorothy visited the Drinkers on May 12, 1802. Crane, *Diary of Elizabeth Drinker*, 2:1515–16 (May 12, 1802).

41. She arrived in America in penury with her mother, husband, and son, all to be supported by Anne and the Society of Friends for the sake of Dorothy's ministry. See Anne Mifflin to Dorothy Ripley, May 31, 1804, ALS, Chicago History Museum, reprinted in chapter 11, below.

42. Harrison, *Philadelphia Merchant*, 105–6. Cope was astounded at Ripley's account that her parents had confined her "as a lunatic" after she divulged her scheme to come to America "to teach a shanty school for the blacks in the city of Washington." Cope revealed his own prejudice in describing Ripley's "apparently romantic undertaking at a period when the slaves exhibit continual symptoms of insurrections" (107). Reaching Washington, DC, Ripley was received by Jefferson, who gave his "approbation" for her proposed schools, though warning her it was an onerous task to undertake. Ripley also followed Anne's footsteps in 1806 to live with the Oneidas for six weeks. For more on Ripley, see Everson, "'Little Labor of Love.'"

43. "Dorothy Ripley," 36–43.

44. Anne Mifflin to Jonathan Thomas and Joel Swain, February 25, 1804, box 3, fol. 3, PYM, Indian Committee, box 3, fol. 6, QCHC; see also the microfilm edition, reel 1, American Philosophical Society, Philadelphia.

45. A Philadelphia Quaker tanner by trade, William Savery (1750–1804) was acknowledged as a minister at age thirty. Crane, *Diary of Elizabeth Drinker*, 3:2208 (biographical directory). He made ministerial journeys within the United States, to Canada and Europe, a mission to the Northwest Indians, and another to the Six Nations in Canandaigua, New York, where he witnessed the Treaty of Canandaigua in 1794. It is likely Anne read Savery's account of his Iroquoia errand before her travels there. See his *Life, Travels, and Religious Labours of William Savery*.

46. For a brief account of these early efforts conducted under the auspices of the PYM in the early 1790s, see James, *People Among Peoples*, 298–302; and Wallace, *Death and Rebirth*, 217–20. Warner Mifflin's involvement with Indian affairs likely kept Anne apprised of the escalating violence on the western frontier and the Friends' hope for peace. For more on this, see John Pemberton to James Pemberton, February 16, 1790, in De Pauw et al., *Documentary History of the First Federal Congress*, 18:549–51; and Warner's letters to President Washington and Congress, printed in Nash and McDowell, *Writings of Warner Mifflin*, 353–54, 374–78, 412–18, 420–22. James Emlen was part of the Quaker delegation in 1794 to the Canandaigua treaty negotiations between the Iroquois Six Nations and the United States and likely discussed the trip and shared his account with his sister Anne. See Fenton, "Journal of James Emlen."

47. Though the SQM appointed Anne a delegate to the PYM, which had established the Indian Committee (hereafter IC), it is unlikely she attended, having buried her infant daughter the preceding month. The IC was designed to revive the work of the Quakers' Friendly Association for Regaining and Preserving Peace with the Indians by Pacific Measures, established during the Seven Years' War but dormant for several decades. For a contemporary account of the committee, see *A Brief Account of the Proceedings*.

48. Warner Mifflin, James Emlen, John Parrish, and Robert Holliday were among those appointed to the first governing committee in 1795. On March 27, 1798, seven months before his death, Warner had been tasked with three other Friends to "prepare a letter to the Indians" of the Seneca Nation in Cornplanter's neighborhood. Minutes of the IC (1795–1815),

QCHC, 3; we have used the microfilm copy of the IC Minutes at the American Philosophical Society in Philadelphia.

49. The eleventh of fifteen children of the prosperous Samuel and Rebecca (Canby) Wilson, Hannah had married the widower Robert Kirkbride (1740–1798), an elder in her meeting, in 1786, thereby acquiring nine stepchildren. See Buckingham Monthly Meeting Minutes (1763–1782), February 5, 1776, for her acknowledgment as a minister. Her wartime religious visitations, often carried out through combat zones, are documented in in those same meeting minutes; see May 6, 1776, October 5, 1778, July 3, 1780, March 5, 1781, October 7, 1782, July 3, 1783.

50. PWMMM (1793–1805), June 25, 1802. The women's meeting endorsement was approved by the men's meeting and, signifying the importance of the journey, was ratified by the PQM and PYM. PMMMM (1791–1807), July 30, 1802.

51. Quoted from Cox, "Supper and Celibacy," 244.

52. Kelsey, *Friends and Indians*, 14–15, 89–92.

53. Cox, "Supper and Celibacy," 250. For similar formulations, see Dennis, *Seneca Possessed*, 117–47; Wallace, *Death and Rebirth*, 217–28; and Richter, "'Believing That Many of the Red People.'" In his *For the Reputation of Truth*, Bauman emphasizes that whereas in the Seven Years' War Friends had a deep economic and political position to protect, in the 1790s "they had no stake in any partisan position relative to the Indians and held no place in government to vindicate and protect. Nor were they troubled by deviance and opposition within their Society. Thus, their professed goals in advancing the peace testimony and serving the welfare of their country were in no danger of being compromised" (250).

54. Jackson had moved to Philadelphia from the New Garden Monthly Meeting. NGMMWM (1785–1804), March 7, 1795; PMM, Southern District Women's Minutes (1782–1795), June 6, 1795. To accompany her blacksmith husband and young son Azor, Susanna Gregory received a traveling certificate in April 1798. PWMMM (1793–1805), April 24, 1798. Their appointments by the IC are noted in IC Minutes, April 28, May 10, 1798, QCHC.

55. Densmore, "New York Quakers"; Tiro, "'We Wish to Do You Good.'" Tiro argues that the Quaker effort was undermined by the unrealistic expectations that native people would adopt white values, white work routines, white belief in market capitalism, and white gender roles, though internal schisms among the Oneidas seems to have been the major factor.

56. Tiro, "'We Wish to Do You Good,'" 360.

57. After abandoning the Oneida experiment in January 1800, the IC commended Jackson and the Gregorys for their "seasonably useful" service and "steady and exemplary" conduct. IC Minutes, January 22, 1800, QCHC.

58. Jackson reported in January 1799 that "the women in this reservation have need of considerable improvement, and as knowledge must precede improvement, so must instruction knowledge." Quoted in Tiro, "'We Wish to Do You Good,'" 367.

59. The speeches were recorded and presented to the IC when Jackson and the Gregorys returned to Philadelphia. IC Minutes, QCHC, 117–20. The November 6, 1799, report of the IC visiting committee to the Oneida mission, with the recommendation to "draw the concern to a close," is housed in in IC Minutes, QCHC (105–6).

60. Ibid., 107–8. It is not clear why Shenandoah, a leader of the Christian faction, was chosen to make the speech to departing Friends.

61. In "'We Wish to Do You Good'" (373), Karim Tiro treats the five Oneidas who came to Philadelphia in 1801 to meet with the IC seeking help in dealing with federal Indian

agents. "The Oneidas (and the 'pagans' in particular)," he writes, "continued to hold the Quakers in high regard" in the early years of the 1800s.

62. [Hannah Kirkbride and Anne Mifflin], "Relation of a Visit Made to the Indians in 1802 by H[annah] Kirkbride and A[nne] Mifflin with Their Friends in the Course of Their Journey to Upper Canada with Some Observations on Their Origins," box 11, Logan-Fisher-Fox Papers, HSP. For the full text of this report, see chapter 9, below.

63. Ibid. It is puzzling that the IC made no mention of the Mifflin-Kirkbride sojourn among the Oneidas and did not include the report in its files. It appears that until now historians had never consulted this report.

64. Anne Mifflin to Anne Mifflin Sr., October 6, 1802, box 2, EFP.

65. On the Quaker migration to Upper Canada, see Dorland, *History of the Society of Friends*; and Healey, *From Quaker to Upper Canadian*. Anne duly returned her travel certificates and minutes from the Hudson Monthly Meeting and Stamford Quarterly Meeting. PWMMM (1793–1805), November 26, 1802.

66. PWMMM (1793–1805), January 28, 1803; PMMMM (1791–1807), January 28, 180.

67. PMMMM (1791–1807), August 26, September 1, 1803.

68. Mary Gilbert, unwell, remained at Ceres town and was replaced by Mary Bell, a member of the Ceres-town Monthly Meeting. Also accompanying Anne were John Letchworth, a Philadelphia Quaker chairmaker, and Friend Penrose Wiley, of Maiden Creek Monthly Meeting near Reading, Berks County.

69. Wallace, *Death and Rebirth*, 272; for more on the Friends' model farm near the tract of Cornplanter, the Senecas' main chief, see ibid., 272–77; Dennis, *Seneca Possessed*, 60–67; and Swatzler, *Friend Among the Senecas*, 239–46.

70. The tangled politics accompanying the rise of Handsome Lake can be followed in Wallace, *Death and Rebirth*, part 3, "The Renaissance of the Iroquois."

71. Ibid., 184–85.

72. Only two miles north of Genesinguhta, Tunesassa included homes, a sawmill, gristmill, blacksmith shop, and workrooms for spinning and weaving, all on land purchased from the Holland Land Company. Eventually an Indian school arose there. The agreement with the Holland Land Company had been struck on October 6, 1803, a week or so before Anne's arrival. For more on Tunesassa, see Wallace, *Death and Rebirth*, 273, 286; and Swatzler, *Friend Among the Senecas*, 239–46. Correspondence between the Quaker residents at Tunesassa and the IC in Philadelphia can be found throughout the IC Minutes, QCHC. Well into the twentieth century, Friends operated the Indian School at Tunesassa.

73. "Account of a visit to some of the Seneca Nation on the Allegany River in the 10th month 1803 by John Letchworth, Anne Mifflin, Mary Bell, and Co.," ser. 4, box 8A, Logan-Fisher-Fox Papers, HSP. Dennis in *Seneca Possessed* and Karim Tiro in *People of the Standing Stone* are the only historians to have noted and drawn on the Mifflin report.

74. Quoted in Dennis, *Seneca Possessed*, 130.

75. For an anthropological analysis of Seneca resistance, which contrasts with that of Wallace, see Rothenberg, "Mothers of the Nation."

76. See, for example, Herbert, "Companions in Preaching and Suffering"; though she is describing mostly female Friends' who took sea voyages, an overland journey into the Canadian wilderness is comparable in severity.

77. Anne and Mary returned their traveling certificates to their women's monthly meeting with endorsements from the Munsey and Catawissa meetings. PWMMM (1793–1805), November 25, 1803.

78. Anne Mifflin to John Thomas and Joel Swayne, February 25, 1804, box 2, EFP. Anne's hopes were realized in June 1805 when Hannah Jackson, who had lived among the Oneidas from 1798 to 1800, accompanied Benjamin and Rachel Cope of Chester County's London Grove meeting to join the newly established, off-reservation model farm at Tunesessa. They served there for several years.

79. PYM (1796–1822), May 7, 1804.

80. Anne requested a traveling certificate in April 1804 and returned it in July. PWMMM (1793–1806), April 27, July 27, 1804. In three letters to her mother, she reported the details of this whirlwind trip through Quaker New Jersey. Anne Mifflin to Anne Sr., June 18, 19, 22, 1804, box 2, EFP. Not one to be easily satisfied, she requested approval of a return visit to Shrewsbury Monthly Meeting in September, affirming that she was "not feeling disengaged from the concern which had impressed her mind." PWMMM (1793–1805), September 9, 1804.

Chapter 5

SERVING THE CHURCH MILITANT, 1805–1816

In the last decade of Anne Mifflin's life, Philadelphia had grown from a town with a population of about sixty-nine thousand at the turn of the century to a city of more than one hundred thousand by the time of her death in 1815.[1] The rapid expansion of the city westward toward the Schuylkill River was recognized when the PMM responded to its growing membership by erecting a new meetinghouse on Twelfth Street between Chestnut and Market. Though the federal capital had moved to the shores of the Potomac River, and the state capital to Harrisburg, Pennsylvania, the Quaker city remained a center of commercial, cultural, and political significance. By 1805, the scars of a brutal war, and the particular suffering and persecution of Friends, were healing and the enforced payment of war taxes and the use of Continental currency had been tucked away in survivors' memories. Even global events such as the Napoleonic Wars, which triggered the anti-British embargo of 1807–9 that created misery for thousands of mariners, dockworkers, and other Philadelphians, had hardly ruffled the surface of Anne's privileged and religiously centered life. Finally, Anne and her Quaker kin could distance themselves from troubling political affairs. The sixth decade of Anne's life promised to be a peaceful time to spend with her family, attend the women's meeting, and expand her ministerial activities, which distinguished her life as a respected Public Friend.[2] Driven by pious zeal, Anne's willingness to serve the church militant would not falter; she could do no less than her commitment would allow. But age and waning physical stamina limited her journeys—southward, westward, and eastward. Mother Emlen, in her eighties, remained the stately matriarch of the family, but her age suggested that the burden of caring for the physical, emotional, and political problems of Samuel and Lemuel would have to fall more on Anne. This chapter tracks the last decade of Anne's life and addresses the struggles of her two sons as they reached adulthood.

GOSPEL LABORS

In October 1805, Anne embarked on yet another taxing journey accompanied by her "agreeable brave companion," Friend Mary Harper, this time to attend the Baltimore Yearly Meeting (BYM).[3] The plan was to vector westward to visit meetings of newly formed Quaker settlements west of the Allegheny Mountains on both sides of Pennsylvania's borders with Maryland and Virginia.[4] As summer turned to autumn, Anne and Mary reached the BYM, where they found a "very satisfactory" gathering of Quakers from Maryland, Pennsylvania, the District of Columbia, and Virginia as well as an "amiable friend" from Redstone, Ohio, James Cattle, who had traveled to the yearly meeting with some of his own family and graciously guided Anne and Mary as they proceeded westward. Mindful that maintaining Quaker discipline was at risk, especially among the younger Quakers on the raw edge of white settlement, Anne was buoyed by the outcome of the BYM, holding out hope that "through Divine aid we may experience preservation." By preservation she intended that this series of weighty visitations would strengthen the collected body of Friends from any further dwindling of membership.[5]

Thus, accompanied by several Quaker men,[6] the group proceeded for much of the way in a horse-drawn wagon, passing through the same mountain gap where fifty years earlier General James Braddock's expedition of Coldstream Guards and Virginia militia had tragically met their fate trying to cut their way to Fort Duquesne. However, the wagon horse carrying Anne, in no way as fit as mounts of the Coldstream Guards, had a "propensity to run back," which was "considered very dangerous in traveling mountain roads."[7] To ensure her safety, Friend John McKim exchanged one of his more reliable carriage horses as they set out for the Monongahela Valley, a region where Quakers only a few years before had set down primitive outposts.[8] Indeed, "Ohio fever" had infected Quakers from North Carolina, Virginia, and Maryland, drawing sojourners from Pennsylvania and New Jersey as well. The prospect of new territory opening up after Native Americans had been driven from their ancient homelands by federal armies, state militias, and voracious settlers propelled much of the current migration. But for southern Quakers, a major incentive for the move was to exit forever the slaveholding states where the owners of human property held sway in politics at all levels. By 1800, some eight hundred Quaker families had moved into the Northwest Territory.[9] As Thomas Jefferson ascended to the presidency, the migratory flow toward Ohio increased, draining the population of many Quaker meetings on both sides of the Pennsylvania-Maryland-Virginia line that Anne visited.

For nearly two months after leaving Baltimore, Anne and her party endured frigid nights and winter storms reminiscent of her travels to Canada. In the only letter she had time to write, sent from Allegany, Anne cataloged a crammed itinerary. From Baltimore, they rode to New Market, Berkeley, Hopewell, Buck Creek, Bear Garden, Frankfort, Union Town, Redstone, and Brownsville, all before circling back through Frederick, Maryland, for the return home to Philadelphia. At one stop in Frankfort, they arrived with short notice and little time to spend there, but within twenty minutes local Friends managed to gather fifty people together to hold a meeting for worship. Their progress over bad roads in the Allegheny Mountains, covered with ice and snow, was made more remarkable by their averaging trips of thirty miles per day, considered the maximum distance a saddle horse could ride in fair weather over good roads. Anne related how in the Allegheny region, because summer lasted barely two months and winters were so harsh, farmers could not even raise corn.

All along the way, local Friends offered help and hospitality. Anne acknowledged that though they encountered many difficulties and exposure to hazardous conditions, they could never have succeeded without the expert help of Nathaniel White of Hopewell Meeting in Frederick County, Virginia. It was here, near Winchester, some twenty-eight years earlier, that seventeen Philadelphia Quaker men had been exiled.[10] Now in a new century, the gospel labors of visiting ministers such as Anne were welcomed and appreciated for the spiritual comfort and advice they brought to these primitive meetings.[11]

On December 5, 1805, safely back home and nearly one thousand miles the worse for wear, Anne returned the travel certificate to PMM and informed Friends that she "had performed the services she had in prospect and was favored with the consoling reward of peace." The copies of minutes she also submitted from the BYM and the Redstone Quarterly Meeting validated "her religious services among them."[12] This was far from the last arduous journey Anne would make, but for the next year she would curtail her usual lengthier trips.[13]

THE BACK TO AFRICA INITIATIVE

With the trans-Appalachian trip behind her, one might assume Anne would welcome some respite, but true to form she had other prospects in view.[14] For some time, she had been distressed over the condition of the enslaved Americans she observed on many journeys down the Eastern Shore and across the Chesapeake into Virginia. While Philadelphians confronted the economic chokehold that President Jefferson's embargo of 1807–8 had put on American shipping, Anne of her own accord added a new voice to the republic's continuing debate on whether a democracy could survive the continuation—and expansion—of chattel slavery. Contemplating a feasible plan for the "colonization of the black people on the coast of Africa,"[15] Anne seems to have kept her idea quiet until 1805, when she floated a proposal to William Dillwyn, the Philadelphia-born, London-based Friend and key figure in cross-Atlantic Quaker abolitionist communications. Dillwyn conferred with Granville Sharp, the tireless English abolitionist, about the plan. Quite possibly it was Anne's idea that seeded the African Institution, founded in 1807 in London, which aimed to rescue the failing Sierra Leone experiment that had foundered in reformers' efforts to construct a new society of stolen black people who might be resettled on the shores of West Africa.[16]

The repatriation of former enslaved Africans was far from a new idea. Since the late revolutionary period abolitionists, both white and black, had proposed formulas for finding a New Jerusalem for black men and women who had slipped slavery's chains but found little promise for genuine freedom in the new, still deeply divided American republic. Possible sites of relocation ranged from Louisiana to the trans-Mississippi West to coastal West Africa, and the motives of its proponents varied from group to group, including those who were eager to empty the United States of all its black citizens. The Sierra Leone colony, established in 1789 by English abolitionists, had already attracted several thousand African Americans, most of whom gained freedom from the British during the American Revolution and had been transported to Nova Scotia and from there to the floundering Sierra Leone colony. Some Virginians had discussed such a plan a few years before with no results. Now a Quaker woman, determined to assume a role of national importance, was attempting to jump-start the back-to-Africa movement.

Anne had discussed her idea with Paul Cuffe, the Bedford Quaker sea captain and merchant.[17] Incorporating her husband's ideas about reparations, she proposed state-based "returning societies" that would underwrite the cost of shipboard passage to Africa and six months of provisions for former slaves who wanted to relocate. This was not based on the desire to convert black Africa to Christianity, and it was not what would later become a main goal of the American Colonization Society (ACS), founded in 1816, the year after Anne's death. That organization hoped to rid the nation of troublesome free black people, but Anne aimed "for the releasement of this country [America] from the cloud of slavery that hangs over it" and the chance for "such of them [liberated slaves] as were disposed to go to the ancient bounds of their habitation."[18]

Spending several weeks in Philadelphia in December 1807, Cuffe met with black leaders and members of the Pennsylvania Abolition Society to show support for the repatriation of free black Americans. However, later that year President Jefferson's embargo in response to French and British attacks on neutral American shipping squelched any chance of mounting an emigration of American free black people. Anne revived the idea in 1809 when she urged Democratic Pennsylvania senator George Logan, grandson of Philadelphia's famous James Logan, to present the idea to former president Thomas Jefferson and to request that he give Anne an opportunity to make her case in person.[19] Jefferson never granted such a meeting. Not to be denied, Anne sought the help of Virginian John Lynch, asking him to endorse her idea and send it to Jefferson. Choosing not to respond directly to Anne, Jefferson explained to Lynch that it had long been his wish "for gradually drawing off this part of our population most advantageously for themselves as well as for us; going from a country possessing all the useful arts, they might be the means of transplanting them among the inhabitants of Africa, and would thus carry back to the country of their origin the seeds of civilization, which in the end might render their sojourning and sufferings in America as a blessing to that country."[20] However, Jefferson opined that few black Americans would "voluntarily consent to such an exchange of situation" and warned that in his view those of African descent who had been part of the Sierra Leone experiment "had kept the settlement in constant danger of dissolution" through their "idleness and turbulence."[21]

Anne's hopes for a meeting with Jefferson were added to the itinerary of her thousand-mile journey in the fall of 1810 through Pennsylvania, Maryland, the District of Columbia, and Virginia on her way to visit the North Carolina Yearly Meeting to share fellowship with Friends there.[22] Leaving in early September, Anne along with Sarah Zane (1754–1819), a Philadelphia Quaker with deep Virginia connections, made their way first through Baltimore, then

Washington, and on toward Richmond,[23] often covering thirty miles or more in a day with their horse-drawn equipage.

From bayside Maryland to tidewater Alexandria to interior Richmond and Lynchburg, Virginia, they met with every slave owner of any religious persuasion willing to give them a hearing. Anne and Sarah argued that masters should liberate their slaves and assist those wishing to return to Africa—but not send them there "empty handed." Former Virginia governor James Wood, who had freed his slaves, promised to promote the idea, as did John Tyler,[24] the presiding governor. Although during this two-month mission the two women found to their surprise many receptive Virginians, the plan would remain dormant for a half dozen years until revived under the auspices of the ACS.

SAMUEL AND LEMUEL

Looking back over more than two centuries, it is painful to recount how Anne Mifflin's life crumbled as physical, emotional, and psychological maladies marred the growth of both of her sons from adolescence to adulthood. Was there something in the mother-son relationship that lay at the root of these problems? To be sure, she had copied her husband's parenting style of delegating others to keep the home fires burning while taking on the Public Friends' ministry; Anne like Warner prioritized service and obedience to God. Moreover, Anne's maternity, and that of other Quaker female ministers, was not predicated on the prevalent nineteenth-century notion of motherhood and domesticity, an ideal that promoted a mother's complete dedication to her family. In laying out their religious community, Friends had not only allowed women a ministry but also distinguished a different maternal role for female ministers; as discussed above, they also redefined the family as well. These women, Anne among them, were considered first and foremost parents to Friends-at-large, functioning as nursing mothers to what Rebecca Larson calls a "spiritually hungry population." This broader responsibility elevated these women to serve a greater good—the sustenance of the extended family of Quakerdom, but at the cost of relinquishing precious time with their own children. Often this involved being away from home for a year or more.

Yet as Anne saw it, away from home often for months at a time, she answered a higher calling beckoned in the service of everlasting Truth. In the many on-the-road letters to Mother Emlen, she almost always ended with a greeting or instructions to her sons. Her letters are revealing for what they state as well as what they leave out. There is no evidence she ever wrote directly to Samuel or Lemuel in their adolescent years. In all the letters Anne wrote to Mother Emlen, she rarely addressed her sons personally.[25] To judge by her copious writing, she heard the voice of God more frequently than she heard the voices of her sons. Anne's infrequent mention of her boys or specific messages for them suggests some emotional distance. Her correspondence and journal writing reveal a preference for a more engaged life as a Public Friend, which afforded her intermittent escapes from domestic responsibility. In fact, Anne suggested this just two years into widowhood when she wrote, "In our journey I was impressed with the necessity of not saluting any man by the way; or being detained by the affectionate part at any place. I felt this fully as much or more on Mary's account than my own, knowing the demands of her family on her time at home, whenever released from superior engagements."[26] Anne's family made no such demands; she had the means to hire servants and housekeepers. Her boys were looked after by a family that enjoyed all the comforts afforded by wealth; moreover, they had a strong bond with their grandmother Mother Emlen and their half sister Sarah Mifflin. It would be unreasonable to blame the decline of the boys in their adolescent years solely on Anne's absence.[27] She made a determined effort to place the boys in a proper educational situation, and Samuel and Lemuel's moves from one school to another somewhat abated when both were back in Philadelphia by 1807. However, in 1808, half sister Sarah Mifflin, age twenty-four, moved back to Delaware when Samuel and Lemuel were twenty and eighteen respectively. With Sarah's membership at the Philadelphia meeting successfully transferred to the Murderkill meeting, less than two years later she married Daniel Neall (1784–1846), the polymathic son of ardent Bucks County, Pennsylvania, Quaker abolitionists. Samuel and Lemuel, in company with their mother, joined the fifty-three Friends who gathered to solemnize Sarah's wedding on a chilly March day.[28] No doubt this was a happy occasion for the bride and groom but surely a sad parting for the boys from their loving half sister. By the time Sarah and Daniel Neall relocated to Philadelphia, Samuel and Lemuel had already begun to slip into the abyss.[29]

From an early age, Samuel suffered poor health and displayed symptoms of emotional disorder. Though he seems to have acquired no gainful occupation, he made an attempt to work for an urban charity in 1812, joining the Philadelphia Society for Free Instruction of Indigent Boys.[30] He apparently also aspired to become a teacher.[31] But by the age of twenty-two, Samuel had become unhinged, according to brother Lemuel, because of his "excessive studiousness and intense application."[32] A year later, drawing on the vast Mifflin network of cousins, Anne tried—to no avail—to get Joseph Mifflin Jr., who had opened a school in western Pennsylvania, to hire her troubled son by taking him under his wing as a fledging teacher.[33] Lloyd Mifflin wrote to his brother that Samuel "is acknowledged to be in a state of derangement—the symptoms occasionally varying, sometimes violent and sometimes more moderate . . . since his first attack." Lloyd added that Samuel's mother was under a "great misapprehension necessary to render him suitable for the situation proposed for him."[34]

While Samuel remained in Philadelphia, Anne made a last-ditch effort to subsidize a small business he proposed to establish.[35] But Samuel soon lapsed into strange ruminations about his family's history that suggest paranoia. In 1814, perhaps inspired by an inexplicable turn against the Society of Friends, he wrote two rambling, barely coherent letters to Thomas Jefferson. The letters exalted General Thomas Mifflin, second cousin of his father, who had been disowned by the Society of Friends for abandoning pacifist teachings. Samuel also tried to salvage the reputation of Joseph Galloway, his despised Loyalist great-uncle.[36]

Samuel's insanity would impair the rest of his life. And while he suffered recurring attacks of derangement, his brother Lemuel struggled to find his life's purpose, seeking the help of the family of William Jackson, the Chester County farmer and Quaker elder with whom he had lived for several years when he attended school with Jackson's nephew. Lemuel treasured the summers at Harmony Grove, the Jackson home where he was befriended by his near cousin. In a series of letters, he tried to rekindle their friendship and coax new ideas from Jackson while admitting that "I have been very negligent as to the improvement of my mind."[37] When Lemuel turned eighteen, Anne surely felt encouraged when he became secretary of the Philadelphia Hose Company. She could at last hope his life was turning around. To be a member of this firefighting squad was the pride of young Quaker men from some of the city's oldest families. To be chosen secretary while still a teenager was tantamount to entering the inner circle of ambitious young Quakers.[38]

But optimism over this appointment proved to be premature. He had already developed a yen for seeing the wider world—"I am a great friend to traveling," he wrote his cousin when he was sixteen after a trip down the Eastern Shore—and by eighteen Lemuel began distancing himself from his family.[39] Tiring of the city, he made his way across the Allegheny Mountains to Harper's

Ferry, where the Potomac and Shenandoah Rivers joined in a turbulent confluence at the site of a US Army Federal arsenal. Writing from a bookstore, where he may have been employed, Lemuel reported to his cousin the wonders he saw on his travel—vistas such as the towering sheer cliff from which Native Americans threw their victims—or so he was told. Indifferent to his parents' Quaker vision of a better America, he swerved from one scheme to another. First, he hoped to live with the Jacksons as an apprentice farmer and then purchase a farm of his own. With no encouragement from the Jacksons, he scuttled that plan and decided to leave Philadelphia forever. "I have done with this city," he wrote his Jackson boyhood friend. "I have from this moment resigned my citizenship and am determined never to return except as a transient visitor." With that, he made his way to Pittsburgh and from there down the Ohio River to find a new place and a new purpose in life.[40] Curiously, it may have been his mother's own stories of travel and adventure that inspired his urge to get away from it all.

In the summer of 1812, as war with Great Britain erupted, Lemuel made a journey into Ohio that nearly proved his undoing. A month after Lemuel left Philadelphia, his mother received an alarming letter in which he recounted traveling through "the back countries" and seeing settler families in full flight. "Children that was big enough to travel," he wrote, "has a bundle to carry, and that some they met would flee into the woods and hide and could hardly be persuaded that their fears were groundless and the alarms false, although it appeared it really was so." What Lemuel described was the backwash of the Battle of Detroit, where the British and their native allies under Tecumseh overwhelmed the Americans at Fort Detroit. He had witnessed some 1,600 Ohio militia, paroled after capture by the British, headed southward in retreat and disarray.[41]

FINAL JOURNEYS

What became of Lemuel over the next eighteen months is lost to history. It is likely that Anne embarked on a long trip to Ohio in the autumn of 1813, hoping to find him and bring him home. Her two letters to Mother Emlen, recounting the many Quaker meetings she attended along the way, imply that this journey was taken as the latest of her many pastoral visits to the western boundaries of the Quaker migration from Virginia, Maryland, North Carolina, and Pennsylvania. However, this explanation does not entirely suffice because

Anne and her traveling partner, Sarah Zane, had not obtained the requisite traveling certificates requested from the PMM to authorize the bona fides of elders or ministers in good esteem.[42] The more plausible reason is that Anne understood that her monthly meeting would not approve such a long journey considering that her older son Samuel was living on the edge of sanity. She hinted at this in admitting to her mother, shortly after leaving Philadelphia, that "poor dear Samuel under his injured state—my mind was almost constantly with him in sympathy the day after setting out, thinking whether I did right to set out unless he could have come with me till at length I became more relieved."[43]

Anne's itinerary in mapping out her journey to northern Ohio suggests that the trip was intended to search for Lemuel along the places he was last known to be. Rather than traveling directly to Salem, Ohio, her ultimate destination, she added hundreds of miles to the trip by following a sweeping circuitous path west, southwest, and then along a route that she believed Lemuel had traversed to reach the 1812 war zone. Leaving Philadelphia in September, Anne and Sarah Zane set out by horse and carriage to follow the much-improved turnpike west through Lancaster and York across the Susquehanna River. But then, rather than proceed directly west toward Pittsburgh, the gateway to Ohio, she shadowed Lemuel's journey of two years before, heading southwest through Frederick, Maryland, and across the Potomac River to Harper's Ferry and Winchester, Virginia, places where Lemuel had tarried. From there the two women swept north through Wheeling, Virginia (now West Virginia), and across the Ohio River to Pittsburgh and finally to Salem, the newly established Quaker settlement in northern Ohio. On their way they visited many Friends meetings—in Columbia, Pennsylvania, in Virginia near Harper's Ferry, and at Redstone Monthly Meeting, Middleton Monthly Meeting, and others in the Pittsburgh area. Although Anne must have realized that Lemuel, already disaffected from the Society of Friends, probably would not have sought out any Quaker meetings on his journey,[44] Anne nonetheless was anxious for any information she might glean about her son at meetings along the way. Not finding Lemuel, Anne returned to Philadelphia, probably arriving in late November 1813.[45] The following spring, she received the last appointment of her life from her beloved PQM. The meeting had agreed that Anne and three other women should proceed west to attend the inaugural session of the Roaring Creek Monthly Meeting in Pennsylvania's Columbia County. For fifteen years, the Friends who had been obliged to walk many miles to the Munsy-Catawissa Monthly Meeting had pleaded for a meeting of their own.

Now the PYM had at last approved the request. It was appropriate and of special poignancy that Anne was chosen to be there for the first gathering. After all, she was the first Public Friend two decades before to cross the hundreds of miles over primitive roads to minister to the Roaring Creek settlers at their remote setting.[46]

By the time Anne returned from central Pennsylvania, Lemuel was still missing. Eight months later, when she made a short trip across the Delaware River to Burlington, New Jersey, she referred to Samuel in a letter to her mother but said not a word about Lemuel.[47] Finally, her wandering son returned, arriving back in Philadelphia by late July or early August in 1814. Although Anne must have been relieved to have him safely at home again, the joy of reunion was short-lived. To Anne's horror, on August 27 Lemuel enlisted to fight against the British in the War of 1812, then in its third year. Just the day before, Philadelphians received the dreadful news that the British had stormed up the Chesapeake Bay, captured the national capital, and set the city ablaze. Philadelphia's mayor immediately called a mass meeting in the statehouse yard, urging all citizens to come to the defense of the city, which was expected to be the next target of a British attack. Lemuel had only to step across the street from the Emlen house to join the throng and sign up with the First Regiment of Pennsylvania Volunteers, officered by John R. Mifflin, one of his many Mifflin relatives.[48] What had prompted Lemuel to join the fight? Was it the dreadful scene he witnessed in the summer of 1812, in the Ohio back country, seeing families and children fleeing for their lives? Or was it the immediate threat to Philadelphia that stirred the twenty-two-year-old's patriotism and compassion? Certainly, both episodes were enough to arouse his call to duty.

While black Philadelphians and other civilian volunteers rushed to build earthworks on the lower Schuylkill River to defend the city against a waterborne British attack, Lemuel's regiment marched southward to Wilmington.[49] There they drilled at Camp DuPont in preparation for the expected British attack on the nearby gunpowder mills, but that attack never came. Unscathed after a brief four months of military service, Lemuel mustered out on New Year's Day in 1815. Four days later, the PMM, after several months of admonishing Lemuel for violating "our peaceable testimony," declared him "separated" from the Society of Friends.[50]

Extraordinary as it seems, Anne's response to her son's enlistment had been to stand before the women's meeting to request a traveling certificate for travel to North Carolina, passing through Pennsylvania and Virginia to succor meetings along the way. Perhaps she thought this trip would serve as an outlet for her distress, a retreat from family troubles. Or was it the attempt of a forlorn mother to do what she believed her Heavenly Father intended—to bear the cross assigned to her in Christian service? Although the meeting obliged and granted the travel endorsement, no evidence has been found that she actually made the trip. Perhaps Anne was already suffering a weakened condition and realized she could not undertake another exhausting journey.[51]

Six months later, on the first day of spring 1815, Anne closed her eyes and passed away at the Emlen ancestral home on Chestnut Street. A day later she was buried in the Arch Street Quaker cemetery. Had that last anxiety-ridden journey, winding frantically through Maryland, Virginia, Pennsylvania, and Ohio in 1814 searching for Lemuel, proved the tipping point, the final strain? We do not know the cause of her death;[52] but hearing of it John Hunt, one of Warner's close friends, inscribed in his journal a chilling benediction to her life: "Heard of the death of our worthy Friend Anna Mifflin and some think she died of a broken heart. One son went crazy and the other, worse, into the wars. . . . These were the sons of that worthy elder Warner Mifflin." Six weeks later, unable to dislodge sorrowful thoughts from his mind, Friend Hunt again scrawled in his journal: "Some thought the conduct of her sons shortened her days." Then Hunt quoted from Genesis 34:30: "'Ye have made me to stink amongst the inhabitants of the land, among the Canaanites and Perizzites' said good old Jacob."[53]

One wonders who was at the grave for the burial. Unless she was too stricken with grief and physically unable, Anne's remarkable ninety-five-year-old mother would have been there, just a year before her own demise in 1816. Though living at some distance in Bucks County, Anne's stepdaughter Sarah, vital in the upbringing of Samuel and Lemuel, may have been there, too, accompanied by husband Daniel Neall, by then active in the Pennsylvania Abolition Society. Of Warner Mifflin's nine children by his first wife, *only* Sarah and Delaware resident Warner Jr. were still living. Whether Warner Jr. journeyed to Philadelphia to attend his stepmother's burial we do not know. The dashing Thomas Burke, Chloe's Collin, had suffered an untimely death years before after serving briefly as governor of North Carolina. Elizabeth and Henry Drinker, who had hosted the Emlens for many years, had died in 1807 and 1808 respectively. With Anne's passing, only two of her siblings remained, her sisters Margaret Emlen Howell and the widowed Mary Emlen Beveridge, the latter living in Egg Harbor, New Jersey. Of Anne's girlhood friends Sarah Logan Fisher was still alive, and it is safe to assume she paid her last respects to dear friend Anne, but no known evidence confirms her presence. Among the nine female ministers who had shared the road with Anne on her many ministerial journeys, only two, Sarah Cresson Jr. and Sarah Zane, were still alive and living in Philadelphia, but whether either of them attended the burial is not known.

After their mother and grandmother died, Samuel and Lemuel were amply supported by the estates of both Grandmother Emlen and their mother. Anne's estate went almost entirely to them. Aside from the Ohio lands, Anne bequeathed each son a house and lot in the city as well as many other properties and ground rents in Philadelphia and Darby, along with bonds and cash. A modest ten pounds went to the PWM "for the use of the poor." It is inexplicable that to Sarah Mifflin Neall, her stepdaughter, who had so nurtured Anne's boys and been a helping hand to Grandmother Emlen, Anne left nothing.[54]

Few traces of Samuel and Lemuel's lives after 1815 can be found in the records, and the Mifflin family accounts seem to have deliberately left their stories untold. Bearing in mind Samuel's mental state and notwithstanding the poor treatment for the mentally ill at the time, a question lingers—had Anne really understood the gravity of her son's condition and his inability to function on his own? Drafting her own will as her life force drained away, she named Samuel the executor of *her* estate and guardian of *his* younger brother; however, shortly after her death this arrangement was revised in 1815 by court order, naming Lemuel to assume the executor role. Confirming Samuel's debilitated condition, the court appointed a Committee of Lunacy to manage his affairs while Samuel Emlen, Anne's nephew, a Philadelphia physician, did his best to ease his cousin through the six remaining years of his life.[55] The absence of Anne's sons from the city directories of the period as well as the 1820 federal census for Philadelphia suggests the two brothers lodged with others in town or took refuge elsewhere. When Samuel died in 1821, unmarried and intestate at age thirty-one, his estate, virtually all of it inherited from his mother, was adjudicated by the Pennsylvania Supreme Court, which awarded it to his surviving brother Lemuel. Warner Mifflin Jr. and Sarah Mifflin Neall, Warner's surviving children, were allowed only an accumulated appreciation of the assets.[56]

For several years, Lemuel operated a dry goods business in Philadelphia. Dying in 1824, at age thirty-two, he had outlived his brother by only three years. The Quaker internment records report the cause of death as *mania a potu* (madness from drinking; delirium tremens; insanity).[57] To have died in this advanced state of alcoholism at age thirty-two implies that Lemuel was already drinking heavily when Anne was still alive. If this was the case, it must have weighed heavily on her, provoking a sense of shame and social embarrassment. Ultimately, there was some consolation for the Emlen family knowing that Anne's monthly meeting allowed Lemuel to be buried near the grave of his mother and those of his maternal grandparents.

NOTES

1. Gibson, *Population of the 100 Largest Cities*.
2. The only hint of political interest in her letters referred to a Quaker member of the Nottingham meeting who "had become rather skeptical since reading [Thomas] Paine's writing," which Anne dismissed as "but a feeble mind to be overturned by such a flimsy opposer of Christianity." Anne Mifflin to Anne Emlen Sr., October 13, 1810, box 2, EFP.
3. The Maryland Yearly Meeting, sometimes called Baltimore Yearly Meeting, first called in 1672, has continued for more than three hundred years. It was the only yearly meeting in North America visited by Quaker founder George Fox. It includes most of Virginia, Maryland, central Pennsylvania, the District of Columbia, and parts of West Virginia; at the dating of this letter, the Maryland Yearly Meeting had been gathering on the Eastern Shore of Maryland since the creation of the Southern Quarterly in 1790 in PYM.
4. Anne went before the PWMM in August 1805 seeking a certificate to visit Redstone Quarterly Meeting and the preparative and monthly meetings under its care. PWMMM (1805–1814), August 30, September 27, 1805. Redstone Quarterly Meeting, the first west of the Alleghenies, had been established in March 1798 by the BYM. (In 1790, northern Virginia, southern Maryland, and some trans-Allegheny meetings had been transferred from the PYM to the BYM.) For more on the growth of Quakers in northern Virginia and their migration westward across the Alleghenies, see Worrall, *Friendly Virginians*, chap. 11; and Crothers, *Quakers Living in the Lion's Mouth*, 93–94, 99–100.
5. Anne Mifflin to Anne Emlen Sr., October 16, 1805, box 2, EFP.
6. Both Nathaniel White, a member of Hopewell meeting in Virginia, and William White, perhaps also of Hopewell meeting, rendered invaluable aid as skillful drivers; a member of the party whom Anne identified as "a young man from Ohio" also assisted on this strenuous journey. Ibid.
7. Ibid.
8. Concord Monthly Meeting, comprising the Concord and Short Creek preparative meetings, was established in December 1801, the first monthly meeting in the Northwest Territory.
9. The Northwest Territory was especially appealing to the Friends migrating westward since Congress, in the Northwest Ordinance of 1787, forbid bringing slaves into the region.
10. Anne Mifflin to Anne Emlen Sr., October 28, 1805, box 2, EFP.
11. Wayland, *Hopewell Friends History*, 98–112. More than a half century before Anne's visit, John Woolman had made his way to Winchester, Virginia, to visit the newly established Hopewell Monthly Meeting. For a brief view of how visiting Friends provided sustenance for the "inner life of pioneer meetings," see Painter, "Rise and Decline of Quakerism."
12. PMMMM (1801–1807), December 5, 1805.

13. Anne made two shorter trips in 1806 and 1808. Traveling with Rachael Rowland, she attended the SQM and visited Friends' meetings en route for several weeks in May and June 1806. PWMMM (1805–1814), April 2, May 2, and June 27, 1806. Two years later, with Sarah Cresson Jr., Anne received authority to attend the New York Yearly Meeting and to visit Friends' meetings in New Jersey and Long Island. PWMMM (1805–1814), April 28, June 23, 1808.

14. This section closely follows and expands on the discussion in Nash, *Warner Mifflin*, 228–30.

15. John Lynch (1740–1820), Quaker entrepreneur, former slaveholder, and founder of Lynchburg, Virginia, related Anne's early interest to colonization in a letter to Jefferson. John Lynch to Thomas Jefferson, December 25, 1810, Thomas Jefferson Papers, LC, also available on Founders Online, https://founders.archives.gov.

16. For the African return diaspora to Sierra Leone, see Schama, *Rough Crossing*; and Pybus, *Epic Journeys of Freedom*.

17. Paul Cuffe or Cufee (1759–1817) was the freeborn son of a Native American mother and an Ashanti father. See Thomas, *Rise to Be a People*, 35–36, 59, 77, 90, 117, 130n18, 133n15, and 139–40n9, for Mifflin's frequent contacts with Cuffe. Thomas asserts that Mifflin was "an important figure in Paul Cuffe's future as an African civilizer" (128n35). Cuffe undertook such a mission in 1811. John Parrish also suggested it in his *Remarks on the Slavery of Black People* (41–44), just before his death in 1807, and it is plausible that Anne had shared these ideas with him. Younger opens her dissertation, "Africa Stretches Forth Her Hands," with Anne Mifflin's lobbying effort in Maryland and Virginia in 1810. Anne Mifflin to Paul Cuffe, February 2, 1811, Miscellaneous Manuscript Collection, FHLSC; also reprinted below.

18. Anne Mifflin to Anne Emlen Sr., September 19, September 30, 1810, box 2, EFP.

19. Lynch to Jefferson, December 25, 1810.

20. Ibid.; Thomas Jefferson to John Lynch, January 21, 1811, Thomas Jefferson Papers, LC, also available on Founders Online, https://founders.archives.gov.

21. Jefferson to Lynch, January 21, 1811.

22. Anne's intention was to visit as many meetings as possible on her way through southeastern Pennsylvania en route to the Western Quarterly Meeting assembling in Isle of Wight County, Virginia, thence to the North Carolina Yearly Meeting. PWMMM (1805–1814), July 26, 1810. Endorsements for her traveling ministry followed quickly. Sarah Zane's approval to accompany Anne can be found in ibid., August 10, 1810.

23. Anne's three letters on this trip from Georgetown, Richmond, and Baltimore are filled with details about their travel and the Public Friends they met. Anne Mifflin to Anne Emlen Sr., September 19, September 30, October 13, 1810, box 2, EFP. As was usual, the women found lodging and sustenance at the homes of Friends, including that of George Ellicott, the Quaker mill owner at Elkridge, Maryland. Traveling to North Carolina for the yearly meeting there, Anne would return home by way of Baltimore, straddling the Maryland-Pennsylvania border and spreading the gospel message among five monthly meetings. Mifflin to Emlen, October 13, 1810.

24. James Wood (1741–1813), commander of the Twelfth Virginia Regiment during the Revolutionary War, served as Virginia's eleventh governor from 1796 to 1799. John Tyler Sr. (1747–1813), the fifteenth governor of Virginia from 1808 to 1811, was appointed by President James Madison a judge of the US District Court for the District of Virginia, where he served from 1811 to 1813. He was the father of John Tyler Jr. (1790–1862), who served as the tenth president of the United States from 1841 to 1845.

25. Anne Mifflin to Anne Emlen Sr., September 30, 1810, box 2, EFP. Anne directed her sons via this letter to her mother "that they may seek after the best directions, . . . and read sacred writings."

26. Anne Mifflin to Moses Brown, October 3, 1801, box 2, EFP. The Mary mentioned is Mary Gilbert. See Anne Mifflin to Anne Emlen Sr., June 3, 1801, note 10, box 2, EFP.

27. Larson in *Daughters of Light* (161–63) points out that Quaker female ministers when going on a religious mission had their own mothers look after the family or in some cases delegated an older child to care for their younger siblings. Premo in *Winter Friends* (64) found in women's writings from 1785 to 1835 that both parents and children deemed filial care of an aging parent a just "repayment for past services."

28. The marriage certificate is in Justice, *Life and Ancestry of Warner Mifflin*, 136–37. Neall considered himself a disciple of Warner Mifflin and became a devoted abolitionist. After his death, Neall was eulogized by the Quaker poet John Greenleaf Whittier.

29. Daniel and Sarah Neall transferred their membership at Murderkill meeting to Middletown meeting in Langhorne, Bucks County, Pennsylvania, in 1815 and then to Philadelphia in 1824. MMMMM (1804–1818), January 9, 1815; Green Street Monthly Meeting Minutes (1816–1834), November 18, 1824.

30. Rush, *An Account of the Origins*, 57. Mifflin was appointed to the electing committee, perhaps recommended by Caleb Emlen, his mother's brother who was one of the founders.

31. Anne referred in her letter to Dorothy Ripley that Samuel at age fourteen had mastered French under the tutelage of Stephen M. Day, his teacher.

32. Lemuel Mifflin to William Jackson, February 19, 1812, Jackson-Conrad Family Papers (1748–1910), FHLSC. The idea that mental disability would result from too much study follows the biblical injunction in Ecclesiastes 12:12: "And further, my son, be admonished by these. Of making many books *there is* no end, and much study *is* wearisome to the flesh." It is likely Lemuel was reiterating this notion from what he had been taught.

33. Lloyd Mifflin to Joseph Mifflin Jr., November 6, 1813, MS 32, box 3, fol. 3, Mifflin Family Papers, Special Collections, Franklin and Marshall College Library, Lancaster, Pennsylvania.

34. Lloyd's observation that Anne was uncertain how to deal with Samuel's illness should consider the lack of medical knowledge on the treatment of mental illness. Jimenez, *Changing Faces of Madness*.

35. Anne to Jacob Holgate, May 18, 1813, box 2, EFP. Anne asked Holgate (1767–1832), a wealthy mill owner, Philadelphia representative to the state legislature, and director of the Philadelphia National Bank, to pay off the principal and three years' interest on a bond from Anne's estate. The nature of the proposed business is unknown.

36. Samuel Mifflin to Thomas Jefferson, ca. September 26, 1814, Thomas Jefferson Papers, LC, also available on Founders Online, https://founders.archives.gov. Samuel spelled out that his father had married the daughter of Joseph Galloway's only sister. A second letter, ca. September 27, 1814, continued in this vein: "The Mifflin family and the Mifflin name is the greatest in the world as by the authority of the word of God it is testified. The Mifflin family are inspired by the Holy Ghost to protect man from the vanity of the Quakers, to protest America from the contempt of Devils."

37. Lemuel Mifflin to William Jackson, January 10, April 29, 1808, undated letter (probably 1809), August 20, 1811, Jackson-Conrad Family Papers, FHLSC. William Jackson (1789–1864) became active in antislavery activities and later served one term in the Pennsylvania State Senate.

38. The Philadelphia Hose Company was the first fire company to use the new-fangled "hose carriage" engineered by the redoubtable Patrick Lyon. All eight founders, including Roberts Vaux, Reuben Haines, and Samuel Lewis, were not yet twenty-one. Mifflin was listed as the company's secretary in 1810–11. *Historical Sketches*, 62.

39. Lemuel Mifflin to William Jackson, April 29, 1808, Jackson-Conrad Family Papers, FHLSC.

40. Lemuel Mifflin to William Jackson, February 19, February 20, August 6, 1812, Jackson-Conrad Family Papers, FHLSC. The origins of Samuel and Lemuel Mifflin's alienation from the Society of Friends is unclear. Lemuel may have convinced his mother to invest substantial sums in Ohio land, or Friends suggested it was a wise investment. In her will of 1811, she bequeathed 477 acres of unimproved land and two lots in Frankford, Ross County, Ohio, to Samuel and 480 acres of land and a lot in Muskingum County to Lemuel. We have not been able to determine when she acquired these lands.

41. The diary of John Hunt, a longtime friend of Warner and Anne Mifflin, includes the contents of Lemuel's letter to his mother. It seems that Anne shared with Hunt the letter from her son. Hunt Diary, September 22, 1812, Hunt Family Papers, FHLSC.

42. Neither the women nor men's minutes for 1813 contain Anne and Sarah's request for traveling certificates. Sarah was the traveling partner in the lengthy journey to the South in 1810, when Anne wrote she was "a kind and agreeable companion and we get along successfully beyond expectation." Anne Mifflin to Anne Emlen Sr., September 19, 1810, box 2, EFP.

43. Anne Mifflin to Anne Emlen Sr., September 23, 1813, box 2, EFP.

44. In the two letters sent to Mother Emlen on this trip, Anne did not include greetings to Lemuel, almost certain proof that he had not yet returned to Philadelphia but was still planning to quit the city forever.

45. Anne's letter to her mother from Salem, Ohio, dated November 12, 1813 (box 2, EFP), makes no mention of Lemuel, but she expressed her wish that Samuel "endeavors to be a steady and good boy and deserving of my regard."

46. PQM Meeting Minutes (1793–1833), May 2, 1814. The log-style meeting house built in 1795 for the Roaring Creek farmers still stands in Numidia, Pennsylvania.

47. Anne Mifflin to Anne Emlen Sr., July 8, 1814, box 2, EFP.

48. Lemuel's enlistment is recorded in the muster rolls of the First Company of Washington Guards in the First Regiment of Pennsylvania Volunteers. Pennsylvania Archives, Harrisburg, available on GenealogyBank, https://www.genealogybank.com. For an account of the excitement in the city, see Lossing, *Field-Book of the War of 1812,* chap. 40, "The Volunteer Companies of Philadelphia."

49. The African American pick and shovel companies, led by James Forten, are portrayed in Winch, *Gentleman of Color,* 174–76.

50. PMMMM (1804–1818), August 4, August 25, December 1, 1814, January 15, February 2, 1815.

51. PWMMM (1805–1814), August 6, 1814. It was customary to return the traveling certificate granted by the meeting, but this was not the case for the proposed trip to North Carolina.

52. The PMM burial records give "decay" as the cause of death, a general term used at the time for the passing of Friends even in their thirties. PMM Grave Books (1814–1823), March 22, 1815.

53. John Hunt Diary, April 17, May 26, 1815, Hunt Family Papers, FHLSC. Musing on the death of Anne Mifflin, Hunt chose from scripture the betrayal of Jacob by his own sons, comparing that to Anne's experience with Samuel and Lemuel.

54. Philadelphia Wills, nos. 100–149, pp. 170–75, accessed at Ancestry, http://www.ancestry.com. The women's meeting acknowledged her small gift to help the poor two months after her burial. PWMMM (1814–1823), May 25, September 28, 1815.

55. Lemuel Mifflin, Administrator with the Will Annexed to the Estate of Anne Mifflin, April 12, 1815, bk. L, fol. 244, Philadelphia City Archives. For Dr. Samuel Emlen, see Jordan, *Colonial and Revolutionary Families of Pennsylvania*, 1:197.

56. Sergeant and Rawle, *Reports of Cases Adjudged in the Supreme Court of Pennsylvania, Thomas Sergeant and William Rawle*, 460–61. The carefully kept PMM Internment Book (1820–1915) does not list Samuel, nor does the PMM Arch Street Burial Records (1806–1828).

57. PMM Grave Books (1824–1827), 5; PMM Arch Street Burial Records (1820–1872), 24, where Lemuel's death was recorded as August 8, 1824, and where it was noted that he was not a member of the meeting. His papers, donated to HSP by an Emlen descendant more than a century later, include portions of his accounts for his dry goods store. His will, covering an estate of thousands of dollars, left $3,000 to Samuel Emlen and Sarah Mifflin Neall. Lemuel Mifflin Papers, HSP.

EPILOGUE

The death of Anne Emlen Mifflin in March 1815 and that of her mother, Anne Emlen, eleven months later marked nearly the end of the third and fourth generations of Emlens in Philadelphia. The death of Mother Emlen during her ninety-sixth year was reported in Philadelphia newspapers, where it was observed that she could count a total of 147 children, grandchildren, and great-grandchildren. As Zachariah Poulson wrote in his *Daily Advertiser*, she was "an exemplary and charitable citizen fulfilling with much propriety the duties of parent, friend, neighbor, and mistress."[1] She had outlived all but two of her eight children. Except for James, the youngest of the eight, no one in this branch of the Emlens was held fast in Quaker memory. That is understandable insofar as it concerns Anne Mifflin's other siblings. Three of her brothers were disowned by the PMM, as were the husbands of two of her sisters. One brother, Joseph, died unmarried at thirty-seven and her other brother, Samuel, also died unmarried; neither had concerned themselves much with Quaker affairs.

ANNE AND HISTORICAL AMNESIA

What remains a mystery is why Anne Emlen Mifflin vanished from the Quaker annals. Why did history pass her over? This silence in the otherwise detailed records of the Philadelphia meetings on her death is difficult to explain. Why did Anne not merit the customary testimonial from her women's meeting, both in Delaware and Philadelphia, where she served faithfully for so many years as a minister in good esteem?[2] Did her death not merit any mention at all in Quaker magazines, journals, or biographical dictionaries? It was as if the earth swallowed her up.[3] Is this a case of historical amnesia among Friends when a godly life was badly marred at the end, though not through her own misdeeds, unless leaving her sons behind in their adolescent years as she engaged in her religious missions counts as such?

Looking to Quaker beliefs on child-rearing offers some insight. For Anne's generation, perceptions on raising children were changing.[4] J. William Frost suggests anxiety was the source of this evolution. By the mid-eighteenth century, Quakers had not achieved the hoped-for worldwide conversion and still constituted only a small group, further endangered by an increased number of them marrying non-Quakers and consequently being written out of their meeting. Thus, from within the meeting the only way to preserve and propagate the faith was to pass it along to their children. The writing was on the wall: if succeeding generations did not hold the faith with the same spiritual intensity as their ancestors, they knew the "Society of Friends might die."[5]

As a safeguard, the meeting followed certain principles: parents must enforce plain style and plain living; parents must model holy conversation— that is, the devout life in prayer, worship, and behavior; fathers as head of household should rule but with gentleness; a parent should discipline a child but never in anger; children were to be held under continual surveillance, secluded and sheltered as much as possible from the evils of the outside world, "to be in the world but not of it."[6] If a child misbehaved of his or her own volition despite the parent's best efforts, the child was at fault; but if a child through undue "harshness, neglect, or softness" went astray, the parents were held accountable.

Such maxims set a fine line that Anne and many of her sisters in the ministry with children had to walk in serving as Public Friends. They were to prioritize service to God and nurture the faith community as *the* authentic, spiritual family. If this required absenting themselves often from their own family, so be it; but if, in the process, their own children were disruptive or ill-mannered because of parental neglect or lack of discipline, the parents could be harshly judged.

Anne Mifflin was often referred to in Quaker meeting minutes as "Our Beloved Friend," denoting the respect and admiration she had earned in the Society of Friends. But as Samuel and Lemuel's lives unraveled, did Friends hold her in the same regard and feel sympathy for her? John Hunt seemed to think so. His suggestion that she had died of a broken heart and that "some thought the conduct of her sons shortened her days" may have echoed sentiments other Friends expressed at her funeral. Anne, like other women in the ministry, succeeded because she followed the acceptable way for Quaker females to serve as a Public Friend. Moreover, Anne was not continuously away from home, but when she was absent the boys were well provided for, whether at home surrounded by Emlen relatives or under proper supervision at boarding school.

In view of the limited understanding of mental illness in the past, would Samuel have fared any better from his mother's full attention? Anne attempted repeatedly to help him and Lemuel as well. In Lemuel's case, did Anne not recognize the extent of his alcoholism? Or was it too shameful for her to acknowledge the impact of his illness? This cannot be determined. Nonetheless, she had taken extraordinary measures, even risking her own health and reputation as a minister, trying to save him from his own dilemmas.

Perhaps Friends were willing to leave Anne unnoticed, but why had Philadelphia newspapers ignored her death as well? Notices of Warner Mifflin's death in 1798 passed from one newspaper to another up and down the Atlantic seaboard and into the interior. Strangely, Anne's death merited no notice at all.[7] To be sure, newspaper obituaries mostly treated high-placed males. But sometimes the death of a widow of a merchant prince or esteemed politician found a place in the columns of the flourishing periodicals of the era. Such was the case with Elizabeth Drinker, wife of Henry Drinker, the *bon ami* of the counting house and meetinghouse and one of the Philadelphia Monthly Meeting's most resolute leaders. When Elizabeth Drinker died in 1807, *Poulson's Daily Advertiser*'s editor saw fit to inform the public of her demise.[8] Elizabeth, touted as a diary keeper almost from the moment of her marriage, had never traveled thousands of miles to serve the Society of Friends and never entered the public arena giving voice to important issues; at best she was an irregular participant even in the affairs of the Philadelphia Women's Monthly Meeting, but there is little doubt Elizabeth cherished her family and continued to dote on them even as adult children.

If Anne Mifflin was left unrecognized in the records of her meeting or in public print after her death in 1815, then why was the curtain of silence not lifted when some of the causes she championed gained traction in the antebellum era? In 1837, when the brothers John and Isaac Comly launched *Friends Miscellany*,[9] it was filled with remembrance pages of past Quaker leaders, both within and outside the faith community. *Friends Miscellany* gave Warner Mifflin his due, but Anne received no mention at all.

A decade later, Quaker crusader Robert Smith stepped into the shoes vacated by the Comly brothers as the founder of *The Friend: A Religious and Literary Journal*. In eighteen essays—titled "Relics of the Past"—he illuminated the life of Warner Mifflin and published many of his writings and letters in 1844, when the abolitionist movement opened the floodgates of antislavery reform. But anyone reading that extensive material on Warner would not have found any evidence that Anne Emlen Mifflin, renowned in her own time, had ever existed.

The children of those who labor to change the arc of history often give due attention to ensure a parent is not forgotten. This was not the case for Anne, who had no daughters and whose ill-fated sons were incapable of managing their own affairs, let alone carrying on her work or keeping alive the memory of her remarkable life.[10] It was not until four generations later, just as World War II drew to a close, that any possibility of preserving Anne's legacy came when John Thompson Emlen (1878–1955), the great-great grandson of her beloved brother James, gifted the massive collection of Emlen family papers and correspondence to the Historical Society of Pennsylvania.[11]

How John T. Emlen became the custodian of the Emlen family papers is uncertain, since no living Emlen family member can remember how these records were handed down over four generations. It is likely, however, that after the death of Anne's sons in 1821 and 1824, the documents were rescued from the Chestnut Street house by Anne's nephew, James Emlen Jr. (1792–1866), who had lost his mother and father to the yellow fever epidemics of 1793 and 1798 in Philadelphia. James Jr. lived a long life as a farmer and Quaker minister in Middletown, Chester County, spending about twelve years at Westtown, where he had been educated.[12] One of his sons, Samuel Emlen (1829–1920), became an eminent Quaker minister in Germantown and, most likely, carried the family papers back to Philadelphia. It was his son, James Emlen [III] (1854–1922), married to Susan Trotter Thompson (1853–1879), who then acquired these records and passed them on to their first-born child, John Thompson Emlen Sr. (1878–1955).

Although the Emlen family carefully preserved her writing, even so the ultimate price Anne Mifflin paid was ignominy, to become one of history's orphans. No antebellum Quaker abolitionist tried to rescue her from the scrapheap of history. Nor did Elizabeth Cady Stanton and Quakers Lucretia Mott and Susan B. Anthony, all three suffragists, recognize her pioneering efforts, hold her up as a model, or remind readers of Anne's groundbreaking contribution to women's political entitlements when she had stood before the Maryland Assembly in 1795. When the Free Produce Movement gathered momentum in the 1830s, who among that generation's leaders voiced any indebtedness to Anne for the first written appeal to a congregation of Friends to reject fabric dyed in indigo but soaked in the blood of enslaved fellow humans?

BALANCING THE RECORD

How then do we assess the life of Anne Emlen Mifflin, a Quaker born to wealth and privilege, for whom a life of comfort was assured? Like other women of her rank, she might have lived out her days dutifully attending meeting, pouring tea for guests, making light conversation, and managing household servants. That life so typical of her mother and many of her female friends in Philadelphia was not for Anne. Her keen intellect and natural curiosity drew her to other interests. She was well suited for a vocation devoted to scholarship, teaching, or writing, and in this regard as a well-educated eighteenth-century Quaker female she had a distinct advantage over non-Quaker women of her generation.

Anne had received a higher calling from her Heavenly Father and chose a less rewarding path, paved with hardship, sacrifice, and often disappointment. There were early signs of the unparalleled life she would engrave on the history of Philadelphia Friends: indications of a religious vocation began to stir after the death of her father and sharpened when she left her ancestral home over disapproval of her mother's use of Continental currency. One historian proposes that Anne's estrangement from her mother and her defiant spirit recalled the bravery of the early seventeenth-century Quaker converts who had defied their parents, left home, and risked everything to take up the cause of the Lamb's War.[13]

In April 1781, as esteemed Friend Robert Valentine counseled the novitiate Anne on how to proceed in service to the church militant, she took a moment to record her thoughts: "I note down for my more perfect remembrance, some council of my worthy friend Robert Valentine, which was accompanied with the reaching power of truth. His belief was that the Lord would do great things for me and that what had been done was *not for nothing*, for a great work was before me and such things might be required of me, that neither I nor any of my Friends expected of me."[14]

It sounded like a stout-hearted endeavor and a bone-deep commitment but, indeed, our beloved friend Anne Emlen Mifflin in a solid, weighty manner did render service beyond anyone's expectation. Yet it was as if she had never entered the political, religious, and cultural consciousness of her church, her community, or her country. Nonetheless resigned to serve the Shepherd of Israel, she became a minister in good esteem.[15] Providentially for posterity, Anne wrote down for "perfect remembrance" what we now know about her and her life's work. It has been the purpose of this study to retrieve that which was lost, to reinstate Anne Emlen Mifflin, and to reserve to her a merited place in American history as a premier Quaker activist of her generation.

NOTES

1. *Poulson's Daily Advertiser*, February 10, 1816.
2. Testimonials from diverse monthly meetings were recorded in the PYM's "Book for Entering ye severall Testimonies of Friends Concerning our dear friends" and published by the yearly meeting in *Memorials Concerning Deceased Friends: Being a Selection from the Records of the Yearly Meeting for Pennsylvania &c. from 1788 to 1819*. Of 137 testimonials inscribed between 1688 and 1820, thirty-eight memorialized women, including some of Anne's close friends such as Susanna Lightfoot and Sarah Cresson. Also among them was one for Mary Emlen, Anne's Quaker minister grandmother, who had immigrated to Philadelphia in about 1701 and died in 1777.
3. It is not surprising that the wave of biographical dictionaries of the last several decades treating American women have left Anne Mifflin unnoticed since their editors and authors necessarily rely on published historical scholarship. The same is true of *The Dictionary of Quaker Biography*, a thirty-year project launched in the 1950s by leaders of the Friends House Library in London and the Quaker Collection at Haverford College. Based exclusively on published sources, it includes capsule biographies of some twenty thousand Quaker worthies, predominantly male. If Quaker publishers had chosen to print Anne's spiritual autobiography, she might well have been included. Not to be found in published materials of the last several centuries, Anne missed another chance for recognition when, by the 1980s, she began to make cameo appearances in such work as Norton's *Liberty's Daughters*, Marietta's *Reformation of American Quakerism*, Wilson's *Life After Death*, and Lindman's "Beyond the Meetinghouse." Curiously, none of these glances at Anne motivated historians to dip into the two boxes, books, and letters donated to HSP in 1945 by an Emlen descendant.
4. Frost in *Quaker Family* (76) notes change after 1760, evident in advice literature on raising children both in America and in England.
5. Ibid., 75–77.
6. Ibid., 76–80.
7. Searches of the *National Gazette, Poulson's Daily Advertiser, Weekly Aurora*, and other papers yield no notice given of Anne's death.
8. *Poulson's Daily Advertiser*, December 2, 1807.

9. The Comlys intended to energize and lift the wavering lamp of reform. The journal—subtitled *Being a Collection of Essays and Fragments, Biographical, Religious, Epistolary, Narrative, and Historical Designed for the Promotion of Piety and Virtue to Preserve in Remembrance the Character and Views of Exemplary Individuals and Rescue from Oblivion, Those Manuscripts Let by Them Which May Be Useful to Survivors*—was packed into twelve volumes and published from 1831 to 1839. The monthly journal would have been the obvious vehicle to redeem the life and service of Anne Emlen Mifflin.

10. Warner Mifflin's family had little interest in honoring their stepmother Anne, though one might expect that stepdaughter Sarah, or her husband Daniel Neall, a notable abolitionist, might have included Anne in the annals of Quaker history. However, neither Sarah nor Daniel did anything to memorialize her. See Nash, *Warner Mifflin*, 140–44, for Sarah Mifflin Neall and her ardently abolitionist family.

11. Educated at Germantown Friends and Haverford College, John Thompson Emlen devoted his career to addressing the needs of Philadelphia's black community. After working briefly in a Quaker settlement house in New York City, he established the Wissahickon Boys Club in Philadelphia for young black males, the first of its kind in the country. Three years later, he taught African Americans and Native Americans at the Hampton Institute for Industrial Arts in Virginia. By 1910 his commitment to African Americans in Philadelphia assured that thousands of them as part of the Progressive Era's "Great Migration" would leave the South to raise the Quaker city's black population to eighty-four thousand. A century after Anne Emlen Mifflin's death, John Thompson Mifflin served as a trustee of Howard University and founded the Philadelphia Armstrong Association, dedicated to improving the education, housing, and health of black Philadelphians. He received national recognition in "The Movement for the Betterment of the Negro in Philadelphia," published in the *Annals of the American Academy of Political and Social Science* in 1913, with three more decades of service to Philadelphia's black community still to come. For more on John T. Emlen, see Savage, "In Search of a 'Benevolent Despot.'"

12. Emlen had married the widow Sarah Foulke Farquhar in 1816. Her work as a teacher at Westtown School and her ministerial labors in the United States and abroad are documented in the Emlen Family Papers (1796–1866) at FHLSC. An elder in the Middletown Monthly Meeting, her husband James taught at Westtown School for many years.

13. Marietta, *Reformation of American Quakerism*, 61.

14. MRP, April 1781, below.

15. Paraphrased from Little Creek Monthly Meeting Minutes, May 28, 1798, 297.

Part 2
Writings and Testimonies

Chapter 6

MY RELIGIOUS PROGRESS

This account chronicles Anne's spiritual struggles, some of her life experiences, and her call to religious service. She did not intend this journal for publication but only as a memento to pass on to her children.[1]

Having for some time thought it might be right for me to leave some account of my religious progress, and extracts from diaries and journeys for the perusal of my children, if no further, I now take up my pen after some weeks confinement,[2] in which I have [been] led to consider the great uncertainty of our date of life here to make some essay toward it.[3]

About the 20th year of my age [1775], in the midst of my career of company and gaiety, my mind was visited with a sense of the superior Excellency of truth, and feeling my mind drawn by the attractive power of Divine love, I fell into the practice of attending week day meetings.

---

1. This document is derived from two accounts. The first, "Notes on Religion," is the longer version that Anne wrote from 1779 to 1795. The second, started "after some weeks of confinement," was written either before or just after the birth of her third child, Mary Ann. When archived, the second account was erroneously titled "Samuel E. Mifflin's Book" by an HSP librarian.
2. By "confinement" Anne likely meant her third pregnancy in 1795.
3. Henderson in "'Impudent Fellow Came in Swareing'" (147) opines that diary keeping as a "domestic form of publication" was crucial to American women, who were often denied access to literary print publications. This assumption certainly does not match Anne's interest or lack thereof in journaling. Her writing attests she was well-read on a broad range of subjects.

How successful is one act of obedience to lead to another, and one right step to make way for another. One 5th day [Thursday] my state was visited in opening prospects and my good resolutions strengthened by a language from the Galaxy, in which whatever [was] written about Moses was recommended to the adoption of some present: "By faith Moses when he was come to years, refused to be called the Son of the Pharaoh's daughter, choosing rather to suffer affliction with the people of God, than to enjoy the pleasure of sin for a season."[4] This with other pertinent matter dropped had a tendency to strengthen my best resolutions and to prepare me to stand with firmness against a powerful temptation that presented itself in the afternoon.[5] How well is it for young people to give up their time to the attendance of (Friends) meetings where the renewal of best strength is often experienced and how well is it for those to whom is committed the word of reconciliation to be faithful in the little as well as in the much, not knowing what feeble knee or tottering mind they may be instrumental in strengthening in this administration.

My mind was tried from time to time with various exercises and scruples and with different proposals of marriage, which in some instances caused me searchings of heart or deep inquiries to know the mind of truth; for as it is a weighty thing to propose, so is it a weighty thing to decide, where the object appears worthy.[6] These occurrences I kept much in my own bosom when in my power believing it was doing, as I would be done by. One instance in particular I passed through many tossings about from the various voices for and against, and that from religious characters. Some of these things are brought into view in part of a diary,[7] which I kept which it may not be amiss to transcribe.

Being at the house of an acquaintance in the afternoon, a member of Congress,[8] seeing me at the window with the young people, introduced himself, in order to take an opportunity of showing me a letter from one of his fellow members requesting him to inquire of me, whether I would admit of his visits on the fear of a particular attachment. He had been twice at our house, although I happened to be from home, which I thought providential as he had peculiar attractions of person, and other circumstances attending. It would be inviting

---

4. Hebrews 11:23.
5. The temptation was likely an attempt by congressional delegate Thomas Burke's messenger to arrange a meeting between them. See above, chapter 2.
6. On these several proposals of marriage made by unidentified suitors of Anne in her twenties, she did not disclose their names, explaining, "These occurrences I kept much in my own bosom when in my power believing it was doing, as I would be done by."
7. Emlen Diary; see the introduction, above.
8. Likely that same delegate, Thomas Burke.

to a young person whose affections were content in this world, but mine as divine light and love had so far shaken therefrom and engaged in the present of a better inheritance as to be able when the temptations came to stand my ground with unshaken firmness.

I replied after perusing the letter, that as "the person was not a Friend, that was a barrier at once, and I could not receive his visits."[9] "Well," said he, "you will let him come to see you as an acquaintance, young ladies love to have suitors." "No," said I, "that has no weight, the door is shut at once as such is the object." He seemed astonished as I was yet in my gaiety[10] and he acknowledged his surprise, saying he thought before that every woman was a coquette. I felt sweet peace in my candor and glad in one instance that I had vindicated the character of my sex. I felt my spiritual strength increased by this experience.

I made some sacrifices in dress, but the cross in these was trifling to what I had to experience in the open adoption of scripture language in all companies.[11] It had been as a burden of duty laid upon me, till at length being at a neighbor's house in high life, who had paid me much attention and where there were some persons visiting of much respectability in the world, I found then was the time I must make my stand. The surrender afforded me much inward consolation and seemed like building a wall of separation from airy spirits, enclosing me as in the bosom of peace.

One day at meeting we were visited by a friend, Martha Harris, who had a prophetic gift and had walked in a singular path as did some of the prophets of old. As a sign, she had ashes on her head as a token of mourning. [She] walked through the aisles of the Meeting as though she was searching—and with an awful countenance said the Lord was about to scorch Jerusalem as with lighted candles,[12] a statement which a friend had also written but a little before

---

9. Mid-eighteenth-century Quaker reform tightened discipline on members who married non-Quakers. This severe modification coincided with Anne's spiritual development during adolescence. Marietta, *Reformation of American Quakerism*, 56–58.

10. Young Quaker women who had a religious calling typically renounced frivolities such as "plays, balls, fine clothes, jewelry, or playing cards." Larson, *Daughters of Light*, 74.

11. Anne's faith walk began with the adoption of scripture language, such as *thee* and *thou*, and wearing plain dress, a sacrifice for a woman of means. Friends viewed acquisitiveness a distraction from the sacred; as John Woolman explained in his *Journal of the Life* (18), "Every degree of luxury hath some connection with evil."

12. Elizabeth Drinker wrote that Harris "appeared in a very particular manner" at the Pine Street Meeting on May 20, 1778, and at other meetings after the British withdrawal. Crane, *Diary of Elizabeth Drinker*, 1:306, 307, 325, 329. For Harris, see also chapter 2, above.

Martha's entrance. [She] spoke of the wrong things among us, one principle of which as a burden to her soul was Friends circulating the Continental currency, the great sinew of War.[13] She said there was but one step between Friends and death, and in 30 days they would be tried. It struck my mind that in 30 days the English would leave the city,[14] and, if so, I would receive it as a sign that I must as an individual desist from the use of that [Continental] currency, made as the great engine of war, or it would be spiritual death to me. Accordingly in the morning of the 30th day [of June], the English Army took their departure from the city and death ensued to two Friends by the hands of the executioner[15] as an example from government and a warning to others not to take any part with these considered as enemies, as they had done in a civil time.

My soul also became deeply bowed under the weight of an impression [I] received and desirous that, as at the rest of life, I might receive strength to do whatsoever was required at my hands, though under great discouragement that my prospect would be forfeited, according to law, and I should be reduced to labor for my living, which I had not been brought up to [do].[16]

During this exercise, one day at Quarterly Meeting,[17] George Dillwyn[18] visited us as a sign he said to same thine, that if they were faithful this silver would be made gold. I believed myself one whom this little message was for and became strengthened after a time to endeavor to make a stand in humility against that which had become such a burden to me. Soon after, some persons who had part of my money in their hands, came with a witness to enforce it upon me.[19] I spoke of my objections, and offered to give up any claim of interest

---

13. On Quaker radical pacifists' opposition to the use of Continental currency, see chapter 1, above.

14. For fear of an imminent landing of the French Navy, English forces and some three thousand Loyalists left Philadelphia on June 15, 1778. Anne mistakenly dated the British withdrawal to June 30.

15. For the execution of Abraham Carlisle and John Roberts, see chapter 2, above.

16. Anne's father left her considerable properties, mostly in Philadelphia, from which she derived rent. Anne feared that if she were suspected of being a Loyalist, her property might be confiscated, thus depriving her of income from her dowry.

17. The PQM included Abington, Haverford, Richland, Exeter, Gwynedd, Horsham, Philadelphia Northern District, and Philadelphia Southern District worship groups.

18. George Dillwyn (1738–1820), a Quaker minister and head of a prominent Quaker family; his ministerial journeys encompassed Great Britain, Ireland, and Europe from 1793 to 1802.

19. Anne's objection to receiving rents in Continental currency put her at odds with the state's revolutionary government. See chapter 7, below.

for several years. Their hands seemed tied from pushing the matter further, and they fell in with my proposal. This also took place with others, so that our dear friend's sign was verified; having ended favorably to outward interest though before such a scruple, I had lost considerably by money being paid in a depreciated state.[20] Thus is the apostle's declaration verified in our experience through faithfulness, "Godliness is profitable unto all things, having promise of the life that now is, and of that which is to come."[21]

I sought an acquaintance with Martha Harris, before mentioned, and found her a spiritually minded and tried woman. She had predicted for some 20 years before it occurred, the sword entering this land by means of tea, which she thought had become too much of an idol, which afterwards took place at Boston, with the revolutionary war succeeding. And many other things very remarkable occurred which showed she was near in favor with her Maker, whether man could see and own it or not.[22] I administered for some time to her necessities and she afterwards spent some time at our house at the invitation of my mother as her hands were tied from keeping school, acting as a sign which was afterwards fulfilled in many Friends being stopped in that occupation by means of the Test Law.[23]

One day as I entered the Western Quarterly Meeting[24] Thomas Lightfoot saw and felt a considerable bow of Christian Love and tenderness toward me, though he knew not who I was. He inquired into my case, and I received a

---

20. By May 1778 Continental currency had lost 75–80 percent of its purchasing power. The inflated price of flour, meat, coffee, and other table items accelerated after the British evacuated Philadelphia. Bezanson, *Price and Inflation*, 13, 22, 36–39.

21. 1 Timothy 4:8.

22. Anne infers that some questioned Martha's testimony. By 1778, due to Martha's straitened circumstance and the nature of an itinerant ministry, she changed meeting membership frequently. Anne and Mother Emlen provided Martha with shelter and necessities for an undisclosed period of time. For the physical hardship and personal toll female Quaker ministers suffered from their religious travels, see Herbert, "Companions in Preaching and Suffering."

23. In April 1778, the Pennsylvania radical legislature clamped down on Quakers for refusing to swear allegiance to the revolutionary government and forbid all resisters from teaching or practicing other professions. See Mekeel, *Relation of Quakers to the American Revolution*, 189–90; and Brock, *Pacifism in the United States*, 204–5.

24. Probably the February 1779 WQM held at London Grove in Chester County and likely Anne's first encounter with Warner Mifflin. He was reporting on a WQM committee's effort to obtain the manumission of slaves still held by Friends and to visit families of free black people previously held by monthly meeting members. Western Quarterly Meeting Minutes (1758–1799), February 1, 1779. At this meeting Anne also conversed with Thomas Lightfoot, who offered her refuge at his home.

kind invitation from him and wife [Susanna], a valued minister, to spend some time at their house.[25] This opening was very grateful, to retreat from city life under the shelter of a father and mother in the church.[26] If more such characters were to turn their sympathy toward the early awakened travelers from Zionward and consider in what way they might afford them a hand of help, great good might often result therefrom and be fulfilling the true disciple part—"I was naked and ye clothed me, a stranger and ye took me in."[27] When the young inexperienced mind becomes stripped of its former clothing and exposed to the gaze and observations of the light and superficial, when it sets out as a stranger and pilgrim in the earth there to find the hand of Christian sympathy stretched out to lead them as under shelter, till they become more strong in the Lord and in the power of his might; how comforting it is to the tried mind, how rewardable the act. Not that we are to place our dependence on human aid alone but that it is very needful at times, as our state of dependence [is] are upon another. Were it withheld from infant years, how desolate would be the state of children and so in a spiritual sense, if the tottering knee is not strengthened in due season, how may they fall and become crippled. I have understood William Penn's thought, if friends had some place of retreat for young converts it might be useful. This may be difficult to come at though worth attempting but if all Christian characters did their parts in the line I have mentioned and considered the great importance to their own souls of fulfilling the Christian duties mentioned in Matthew 25:35–36, there would be an ample remedy. For wisdom and stability, is not in the affectionate part, "And to him that knoweth to do good, and doeth it not, to him it is a sin."[28]

My sympathizing friend Thomas Lightfoot brought his carriage when he came to the Meeting for Sufferings and took me to their peaceful habitation, which always resulted in the renewal of my strength. In a little diary kept on that occasion, I find this note, "Having experienced the benefit of school education, I have earnestly wished it might be more generally extended to poor as well as rich, both of city and country and under that concern, have felt an engagement to render some service therein. If individuals dare to

---

25. Thomas and Susanna Lightfoot are treated in chapter 2, above.
26. It is not surprising that Chester County Friends supported Anne. They were the vanguard of Quakers professing radical pacifism and forbidding payment of war taxes in any form, including the use of Continental currency, regarded as stained in blood. Marietta, *Reformation of Quakerism*, 258–59.
27. Matthew 25:35–36.
28. James 4:17.

embrace the occupation of school keeping from choice and a sense of duty, who were under no temporal necessity of doing it, I believe it might have a tendency, in showing respect to a profession that ought in policy to be considered one of the first offices in life, of encouraging some to pursue it who are better qualified to engage in the weighty undertaking than many now employed therein."[29]

I apprehended from the operation of those impressions, deeply fixed on my mind, that it might be my duty to set an example of dedication herein and desire to stand wholly open to the pointings forth of divine wisdom, and to comply, though in the cross from its confinement, to whatever might be laid upon me. These exercises introduced me into sympathy with those occupied in this employment and ended in a sense, that if I aided a widow in the neighborhood in the writing department in her school, it would be all that was required of me at present. This exercise I was not alone in from what has occurred since. As [this is evidenced in] the increased attention of the Church to reformation on those points and the valuable dedication of many of our young friends in this city for the voluntary instruction of Whites and Blacks, with their [giving] additional concern and disposal of time, in forming associations for the inspection into the needs and relief of the poor.[30] [It] has been in my view, very memorable and praiseworthy and has happily paved the way or helped I trust to excite similar associations with those not of our Society in this city and elsewhere, who with an active zeal go forward in a work which no doubt affords them an enriching reward. There has likewise [been] several other associations taking place among young friends in different towns in this country.[31] Thus does good example have a prevalent effect as well as the evil, which is an encouragement to those reflecting minds to attend to the leadings of best impressions.[32] During this visit I had the privilege of accompanying our friends on a visit to [Third] Haven, [and] Maryland Yearly Meeting, which was a season of deepening and instruction to me.

---

29. Though the cause of comprehensive public education was promoted in the revolutionary period, Anne's vision would not come to pass in Philadelphia for another half century.

30. Haviland, "Beyond Women's Sphere."

31. On the rise of charitable organizations in the new republic, see Dorsey, *Reforming Men and Women*.

32. A "leading" is an *individual's* sense of God prompting them to a particular course of action, whereas a leading arising *from the corporate spirit of the meeting* might require a Friend to submit to the meeting's general guidance.

My Religious Progress | 147

7th Mo. 3rd day [July 3], 1779

Paul exhorted the people of Antioch to "Beware lest that come upon you, which is spoken of in the prophets. Behold ye despisers and wonder, and perish for I work a work in your days, a work which ye shall in no wise believe, though a man declare it unto you."[33] A language which may be fitly applied to many in this day, wherein I believe the Lord is about to exalt the mountain of his holiness, above all the mountains of worldly mindedness, even those who despising the little instruments, by which he may bring it to pass and wondering at their scruples and lowly walking, may perish in their contempt and unbelief. "For they that dwell in Jerusalem and their rulers because they knew him not, nor yet the voices of the prophets which are read every Sabbath day they have fulfilled them in condemning him" (Acts 16:27). Not only [had] the Master suffered by this Spirit of unbelief but the servants also on their turning to the Gentiles, excited the envy and invective reflections of the Jews. And I wish we of the profession of Friends, may not be disposed on any degree to spurn at or despise the risings of the work of truth in others, though it may appear peradventure in ways different from our sometimes more cold and insensible state.[34] And though we cannot own the lengths to which many of the people called Methodists proceed to in their religious convocations, neither can we countenance the hypocritical appearance of unfelt sensations.[35] Yet must we acknowledge from the approvable fruit of piety in many, that the blessed work of awaking hath taken place and insures their right procedure and establishment therein; let it not gainsay what therein may be of the Lord, lest we be raised among those of whom a late writer says, "The Lord can bring

---

33. This is the first dated entry in Anne's journal, coming after weeks of militiamen brandishing clubs and searching houses of merchants and shopkeepers for hoarded goods to force those suspected of price gouging and monopolizing scarce commodities to lower their prices. For more on this, see Rosswurm, *Arms, Country, and Class*, chap. 6. Anne cites Acts of the Apostles 13:41, St. Paul's address to the church at Antioch, to caution Friends not to despise the work of truth in other Christians, such as the Methodists.

34. Anne's premonition in her diary, July 5, 1779, notes, "I have lately been told I shall suffer, by a Prophetess (likely Martha Harris) and that in the cause of God. I am not dismayed at the news" (Emlen Diary).

35. On the rise of Methodists and their efforts on behalf of black Americans in the revolutionary era, see Andrews, *Methodists and Revolutionary America*. Methodists appealed largely to underclasses and African Americans, both free and enslaved. Methodists' class meetings and revivalist "love feasts" increased even as they were attacked and maligned as Loyalists. Female members, though denied the pulpit, were essential as leaders and network builders.

forth no birth of his Spirit, but the zealous professor hates, reviles and seeks to destroy it."[36]

7th [July 7, 1779]

It was the sense of a wise man (George Mason)[37] that the serpent being consigned to live on dust all the days of his life is descriptive of that craving part in us after indulgence of the palate in food, which whilst one is chewing, the indulgence is never satisfied. He is said to be more subtle than all the beasts of the field. And it may be that many modes of subsistence which have their origin in the subtle property, which are carried on merely by the invention (and cogitation) of man and not by a moderate application to useful industry. I believe therefore inseparable from true virtue, a disposition to labor and without it when the body is of ability is in danger of actually bending its course in the broad road to destruction towards Babylon. This subtle disposition when relied on for the suggestion of means for subsistence and not on the virtuous application to really useful branches of employ has a tendency to draw and center those who are so influenced under its dark dominion, and it may be covered the spring of every custom, profession and branch of trade that have not their foundation in utility. May I then be redeemed from any dependence on the ensnaring reasoning's or contrivance of the head and not on the hands for support, and then if my allotment is to labor for my subsistence, I shall eat my morsel with sweet content in the consciousness of its cleanness from oppression or injury to others.[38] For every wrong thing in life arising from this serpentine property hath a tendency to bring under the bondage of sin those who are partakers thereof and spread its oppressions in creation. <u>And Oh! Saith my soul that may the affectionate part never weaken my hands by an undue regard to compliance with pleasing the creaturely part on false peace that should not be cherished.</u>

---

36. Anne quotes from Isaac Penington's work *The Jew outward, being a glass for the professors of this age*. Penington (1616–1679), an English Quaker and apologist, was frequently incarcerated for defending Quaker beliefs.

37. George Mason (1706–1774), a Quaker minister and member of the New Garden Meeting in Chester County, had died five years previously; Anne remembered him as a wise elder.

38. Anne's belief that honest labor is done by the hands, not by "contrivance of the head," echoes the labor theory of value expressed by Benjamin Franklin in the "Nature and Necessity of a Paper Currency" (1727). Aiken, "Benjamin Franklin."

14th [July 14, 1779]

I believe the Lord God of all truth has a mighty work on the wheel in promoting his everlasting truth and that as the affectionate part hitherto cherishes received relations in all states because of that relationship, so the spirit of found wisdom and discipline may change the ideas of the times some and cause the faithful to uphold up to view those two. That regard which the Savior of men did to his kindred that it was only as they and others walked in obedience to the will of God that he could own them as parent and brethren. It is a great thing to espouse this doctrine in the world as it is a principle so contrary to the general spirit of it; but I have long conceived it had the stamp of right in it and I pray the Father of light and well spring of life that he will preserve me firm to the teachings of his grace.

<u>I know it is declared that cursed is he that curseth Father or Mother and that we are not to turn our backs upon our own flesh,</u>[39] <u>but when an adherence to the council of any connection or even abiding with them for a season is inconsistent with the Testimony required of us to bear, then is an attention to the voice of the Shepherd and Bishop of souls and not to the world's ways, maxims, and customs, laudable and necessary.</u> And as the example and words of him who was set as a perfect pattern for us, will support in such a belief and practice, we may build therein when called to it, nothing doubting, seeing it is on the immutable rack and pillar of truth.

11 Mo. [November] 1779

My mind being sunk under discouragement of how from an apprehension I was like to be a dwarf in Israel[40] when I became clear in the remembrance of a dream pointing out my child like state in religious growth. I thought I was a little plump naked boy about 2 or 3 years of age, led by a Friend out of a city and over a green plain.[41] This friend has been and is a helping father to me in leading out of Babylon, into the green pastures of life.[42] The healthy and growing appearance of the child afforded me comfort which I well remember, raised my admiration in my dream that I should be that boy. Thus the Almighty

---

39. Deuteronomy 27:16.
40. See note 53 in chapter 2.
41. For the spiritual significance of Quaker dreams, see Bacon, *"Wilt Thou Go on My Errand?"*; and Gerona, *Night Journeys*. Gerona suggests that "extreme pacifists were the most prolific dreamers," helping such Friends as Anne "come to terms with Quaker divisions and justify her behavior" (192).
42. As Thomas Lightfoot apparently entered Anne's dream work, she considered that enough justification to leave home to reside with the Lightfoots.

is pleased to raise the drooping mind by an impression of encouragement and warn the unwary by midnight visitations. And Oh! That he who can sustain the feeble mind, as well as tottering frame of infant years, may be pleased to preserve this birth in a true growth in wisdom, holiness and purity.

As the Almighty appears as in thick darkness, so hath he been pleased to approach my soul in his blessed manifestations. For after a season of wading exercise, yea anguish of Spirit, I was relieved in a manifestation of duty to forbear partaking of what was purchased with Continental currency which being accompanied with the evidence of sweet peace. As the Lord's people are a willing people in the day of his power, my whole will became melted down into resignation, provided I might be favored with further confirmations of this being a required duty which appears needful as the putting into execution this scruple will be attended with a cross and difficulty.[43]

A religious person had a vision of children wading through a Sea of blood, crying for bread, when a table was spread of it unbaked and mixed with blood of which they could not partake and went away weeping. Some of small growth, children in religion have been led off the use of this money and we know not how deep our wadings may further be, in rejecting this mark of the bestial spirit of war as in the right hand or otherwise by the mark on the forehead.[44] Yet is there great encouragement in remembering the promises annexed to a perfection of true faith, though but as a grain of mustard seed.[45]

1 Mo. [January] 1780

The hand of the most High is upon me in a diseased state, sent I believe in love that it may tend to spiritual refinement and greater subjection of will. Before its approach something offered advancing to outward interest, but it could not be proceeded in without dealing with authorities derived from present powers of government. I remembered what Paul said about civil government being for the punishment of evil doers and [the] praise of them that do well.[46] But this being set up in, or founded on a basis of blood, very different therein from that established by William Penn, in peace, it does not bear

---

43. For Anne's struggle over the use of Continental currency, see chapter 2, above.

44. Rejecting the "mark of the bestial spirit of war," Anne quotes Revelation 13:12.

45. The parable of the mustard seed is related in Matthew 13:31–32, Mark 4:30–32, and Luke 13:18–19.

46. In Romans 13:1–7, St. Paul states that as a matter of conscience, governing bodies divinely established should be obeyed. However, Anne's refusal to tender Continental currency was based on the belief that a revolutionary government founded in violence was illegitimate.

enough the stamp of a punishment to evil doers, etc. The cause I must leave, but I felt the guardian wing of divine peace extended for help in the faith that I should be sustained and enabled to endure hardness in a life of labor rather than for greater ease to suppress my apprehension of our being called as a people into a separation from these mixtures. Believing that the 5th Monarchy spoken of by Daniel;[47] or that which superseded all others in the government of Christ and the establishment of his church discipline under the regulating influence of truth will be found a sufficient government for a Christian. And this spirit which is gone forth, is I fear, a restless search after a licentious liberty, not of the Spirit but of the flesh.

Since my indisposition, I have been impressed with an apprehension of duty in leaving my dear Mother's house until she can see her way to forsake the use of Congress currency and by the support thereof in the payment of taxes.[48] Oh! That I may be able to endure the change should not a resignation of the will be accepted for the deed.

2 Mo. [February 1780]

The above mentioned exercise is accepted at present as a waive offering, but it tends further to establish me in a non-compliance with the payment of the War-Taxes.[49]

3 Mo. [March] 1780

Bodily indisposition is shook over me as a load and these are my breathings of soul. Oh! Lord, thou powerful God of mercy, be pleased to stop the current of my affliction and I covenant to guard with increasing care through thine holy aid against indulging in what may come through the channel of a polluted currency.[50] I have felt scrupulous in the regulations of temperance for partaking

---

47. Daniel 2:36–44; the prophet Daniel interpreted King Nebuchadnezzar's dream that four successive empires would fall, and usher in a fifth—the Kingdom of God. During the English Civil War (1642–51) some Christian groups believed the execution of Charles I indicated the imminent end times with the end of the fourth monarchy.

48. In paying the 1779 Provincial Supply Tax on her property and that of her deceased husband's estate, Mother Emlen was among many wealthy Friends who complied with the imposition of war taxes.

49. Anne apparently agreed to postpone rents due on her Philadelphia properties in order to avoid accepting payment in Continental currency.

50. Two months previous, Anne described being ill and that she had not yet recovered in March. Usually in good health, she may have suffered anxiety disorder from the terrors of war, the constant peril for Quakers, her financial concerns, the distress of separation from Mother Emlen, the scandal in the Emlen family, and the social opprobrium she

with customary freedom in the use of butter believing too great of portion of it is corrupting to these Tabernacles and the same substance will afford better nourishment without the unnecessary labor in the creation, to procure so great a portion thereof.

Favor me dearest Father with a further confirmation of the rectitude of my declining yesterday's proposals leading to a change in life on the ground of not being supported by an Estate in part collected through the aid of Congress currency. And though I believe these tender sensations flow from thee, yet being a testimony highly refined for me, I fear not near enough the kingdom through obedience and purity of soul. I entreat thee. Oh! Blessed that thou would make of me, what thou would have me be.

5 Mo. [May 1780]

Making covenant and offering petitions is like solemn mockery without a daily cane to walk answerable thereunto. Yet I feel centered in humble resignation to endeavor for the maintenance of a faithful testimony against the currency before mentioned though to the loss of much outward substance which I have apprehensions may be the case. Yet [I] would rather encounter the danger of this trial than forfeit that sweet serenity which covers my mind whilst writing this.

Half Year Meeting, [March] 1781

An exercising period to me wherein my heavens have been made to dissolve my earthly mind to quake and elements to melt with fervent heat. Some powerful gospel ministry hath had this tendency. Proposals for a change in life that also had a shaking effect on my mind in earnestness of desire to know what is the good and acceptable will of the most High concerning me.[51]

---

experienced for her hard line on Continental currency. With Quakerly sensibility, Anne accepted the illness as a Divine test and promised that if God would end her affliction, she would continue to avoid use of the "polluted currency."

51. Ten months had lapsed since Anne's last journal entry. During this time she journaled about the religious journey with the Lightfoots in May 1781 to Little Creek, Uwchlan, and Goshen meetings, meetings in Delaware at Duck Creek, and the Maryland Yearly Meeting at Choptank and West River. Anne spoke at several meetings and elders invited her at Third Haven to attend their meeting for ministers and elders. There, Cousin Samuel Emlen gave her the salutation that Friends used to acknowledge one with a religious calling. "This was repeated to my comfort among the Ministers and Elders where I was invited and introduced," she wrote. "May they never see occasion in me to repent of this indulgence, for such it is, as any small growth in righteousness entitles me not to a seat there." Emlen Diary, May 8–11, 1781.

3 Mo. [March 1781]

After being favored to arrive at what I believe [is] a clean view of how to decide on the above-mentioned subject, [I] wrote accordingly and trust the proposition might be right, though not its acceptance as it furnished an opportunity of discharging some hints of council weighing on my mind towards this friend.[52]

4th Mo. 13th [1781]

At Pikeland,[53] where I find a peaceful release from some conflicts [I] had in the city, yet [I] pray for preservation from setting down in a polluted nest. I feel much humbled in spirit and ending contentment with a lowly path in life; so that it be removed from the want of poverty; that having food and raiment, I may therewith be content. I have at the present taken shelter under the roof of endeared Friends <u>who feel to me as parents</u> and the object of whose tender care have heretofore with gratitude, I <u>know myself to have been</u>. With open arms and Christian loving <u>parental tenderness</u> did they receive a little one thus led forth by the hand of a heavenly Parent, from an earthly parents' house for the advancement of His own testimonies. May my way not only be made in the minds of my friends, for the singularity of my steps but also may they be led instructively to ponder the same.

The prospect of losing a tender nursing mother in dear Susanna Lightfoot is affecting. May I retain with due care every instructive hint from her.[54] My conflicts are peculiar; may I never reject the openings of true light, through the suggestions of the reasoner that they arise not from a right opening, when their weight and long continuance testify their soundness.

The singularity of conceiving it, might be right, passed to resign to certain overtures of marriage some time past, and then again to resign to it on the suggestion of some Friend to that end, hath been [the] cause of difficulty to reconcile the contrary sounds. Yet if these turnings and overturnings, siftings and provings are designed to center deep, may there be a building on that foundation which is not of man. I desire to profit by every lesson intended for my good. Perhaps there might have been a danger of human will becoming

---

52. For Anne's clean break with Jacob Lindley, see chapter 2, above.

53. The township in Chester County where the Lightfoots resided.

54. Susanna Lightfoot had been ill on the trip to Maryland Yearly Meeting in June 1779. In a further declining state of health, she had not attended Uwchlan meeting for worship since January 1781. "The Testimony of Uwchlan Monthly Meeting concerning our Beloved friend Susanna Lightfoot," PYMM.

incorporated with prospects that might have issued from a right spring, and so it was frustrated that the divine will might singly predominate. Perhaps as the Friend[55] had in view who interfered, there might be a danger of my being too much absorbed by the encumbrances of the world. In either case, there is cause of thankfulness for whatever tends to redemption and preservation.

20th [April 1781]

My esteemed friend [Susanna Lightfoot] continues ill. Yesterday I was bowed in spirit, even to a measure of distress, when not being able to account for it and patiently abiding under the exercise till evening. It unfolded to my view to return to Philadelphia when [an] opportunity offered and my spirit became relieved. And though it be to the city of my birth and near connections, where resides a worthy and beloved mother, yet is it attended with a cross on account of my scrupulous feelings about partaking where war requisitions are complied with. But as David Sands said "Those who are to be as signs must endure it."[56] And though my thus walking under the cross should not be availing to engage any to a due consideration of the cause, yet if I may be favored with the continued evidence of divine support so as to be able to adopt the language of the prophet, "Though Israel be not gathered yet shall I be glorious in the eyes of the Lord, and my God shall be my strength."[57] This is the enriching penny of the kingdom, which I shall have great cause to be content with, seeing its excellent and permanent nature, is far above the delusive and fleeting enjoyments of sense.

Holy Father if thou see meet (and a trying reverse is not necessary to prove my faithfulness unto thee) reconcile the minds of my friends to thy pure mind in the path of my walking. When my love unto thee and thy blessed cause of truth, binds me with the strong bond of a divine love, to comply with what I believe [to be] the requisitions of thy Holy Spirit. At the risk not only of this world's friendship, but also of many conveniences and pleasant accommodations of life. And should I ever come to want its necessaries, be pleased, oh! Father of mercies, to fill me with the peace of thy kingdom, which will make the most sparing diet and mean attire wholly reconcilable. For what more

---

55. Here Anne may refer to Martha Harris.

56. David Sands (1745–1818), charismatic minister from Nine Partners Monthly Meeting in New York, traveled widely along the northeastern seaboard and across the Atlantic. In 1780–81 in Philadelphia he joined Henry Drinker in planning a Quaker community on Pennsylvania's frontier. For more on Sands, see Godbeer, *World of Trouble*, 218–19.

57. Isaiah 49:5.

pinching nakedness can there be to one who has tasted of the good word of life and the powers of the world to come than to be stripped of thy blessed presence. And what can be more joyous or supply the want of any external comfort than basking as in the sunshine of thy favor or being embosomed in thy heavenly love and life.

27th [April 1781]

A few days having been passed usefully to myself in the great valley, I note down for my more perfect remembrance, some council of my worthy friend Robert Valentine,[58] which was accompanied with the reaching power of truth. His belief was that the Lord would do great things for me and that what had been done was not for nothing, for a great work was before me and such things might be required of me, that neither I nor any of my Friends expected of me. Exhorting to keep in the humility where safety is, and not to take too much in hand at once that he had oft thought my preservation depended on. He asked me whether the Ward's report of [my] having [a] marriage in prospect was well grounded.[59] I told him my desire was to fulfill my Heavenly Father's will, whether that should be to marry or not. He said he did not mean to discourage any thing of the sort but believed it would be best not to hurry, until my feet were firmly established on the Rock, and so founded in the truth that the very Gates of Hell should not prevail against me for many and deep trials of preparing baptisms were probably before me. He thought my path narrow and trying in the city and that a good companion might be a strength in seasons of deep wading, and as a brook by the wayside and he would encourage me to settle in the right time, but he believed my growth depended on not taking too much in hand at once. That I had got out and he wished me to hold on and if humble and faithful, I should be made an instrument of help to many souls. That the concerns of a family alone were weighty and he wished me to move in clearness, without any doubt or jealousy remaining when I entered that state.

---

58. Robert Valentine (1717–1786), an Irish Quaker minister, immigrated to Chester County in 1747 and married Rachel Edge of Uwchlan meeting. Rachel bore ten children and solely parented their family during his religious visitations to Virginia, England, and Ireland.

59. The editors have not identified Ward.

This led me to those high notions of justice I have imbibed of not accepting temporal accommodation from any without endeavoring to make ample returns by application to labor. That being rigidly bound to this principle might so crowd my mind and time with temporal business, that the earth would perhaps get too much between me and the Son of righteousness and so engage my attention from things of a spiritual nature, as not to afford opportunity for duly seeking after and doing my little part in contributing to the propagation of divine wisdom and knowledge. And this was as Robert Valentine observed, the children of disobedience might triumph, and he remarked one who made such high professions did not get forward in her religious growth. I stand therefore convicted; it is best not to be over strenuous in making abundant returns for kindness but where the Lord opens hearts to accommodate in any shape they may receive such favors with grateful acknowledgments to the first great Author of all our blessings and toward the instruments who are thus subject to his influence in making Christian contributions to our comfort. Nevertheless, in all my movements [I] should desire to be as little expense as possible to any one and to shake my hands from holding of bribes, not suffer favors from any to blind judgment, or assume bound to any authority over me not of the Lord's sanctifying and bring under bondage from that spiritual liberty in which I trust Christ my Savior hath in good measure set me free to follow him clear of the contrary influence of human fear or favor.

5 Mo. 2nd in the morn[ing] [May 2, 1781]

[I] arose at cock crow and sat in a holy silence with some of the family. [We] may style it holy, as it was graciously favored with the Master's presence. As a seal to a former impression of it being right to repair to visit before the customary time in city life and with the rest of creation arise before the glittering sun appears in the horizon to shame our indolence. That we may join in the general chorus of rejoicing nature in giving thanks to the Author of all good for the renewed refreshment, returning light to our earthly tabernacles and in waiting to be renewed in spirit we may also receive qualification to discharge our several duties in the course of the day, and present a secret mental petition to be directed and preserved aright therein. We shall receive direction from the enlightening beams of the Son of Righteousness, if we do but open our hearts to receive the same. It is the great want of attention thereto, or maintaining the holy watch, by which so many errors on the right hand and on the left are produced.

At noon

My nursing friend [Susanna], after a season of close conflict, broke forth into a baptizing prayer that the most high would be pleased to do for her offspring as he had done for her, and could bring them that were furthest off, near unto himself. She tenderly and weightily also prayed for the youth; that the Lord would be with them and direct their steps before the uncircumcised in heart, who did not seek unto him. That he would relieve the oppressed amongst them who saw the secrets of all hearts and knew the conflicts of some and prayed the Almighty would be pleased to show them the snares of Satan, and his transformations, though it should [appear] to be as unto an angel of light. My spirit was so bowed from the power attending and my feelings so corresponded with a sense of the necessity of such a petition (much of which I cannot repeat) being offered by the faithful, whose fervent supplications avail much on account of such as myself who are often "tossed with tempests and not comforted," that I felt the constraining power of truth to bow me on my knees before the throne of might and majesty and power. This reminded me of a scene to which I was summoned at the request of a dying neighbor where the Minister and family knelt together and though it was then an unfelt form, yet I now believe it originated in the spirit and like many forms, the substance remains supported when the leading principle or life dictating the form, is much departed from.

One evening, when my dear friend lay very ill and all around seemed to stand in expectation of a great change, I felt the bowing power of truth, to engage me to kneel by her bedside, in silent reverential breathing unto God in which surrender with the present, I felt the answer of peace. Which brought to my remembrance an account of the frequent practice of Mary Peisley and Catherine Payton;[60] when one broke forth into public supplication, the other would kneel in company. And it may be, that through the turnings and overturnings of humbling judgments on the hearts of the people that more of these

---

60. Mary Peisley (1717–1757), a domestic servant, became a minister in 1744; after marrying Irish Quaker minister Samuel Neale (1729–1792), she died three days later. See Lawson, *Daughters of Light*, 314; and Neale, Neale, and Barclay, *Some Account of the Life*. Catharine Payton (1726–1794), an English Quaker minister, forestalled marriage until age forty-five, when she married English Friend William Phillips, a noted London printer. She authored several treatises on Quakerism. Lawson, *Daughters of Light*, 315. See Herbert, "Companions in Preaching and Suffering," regarding the hardships Peisley and Peyton endured on their faith journeys.

fruits of obedience may appear. For as is the shadow of thy substance so is the binding posture of the body, natural to a bowed down state of supplication. Yet for any to comply with it in a form without truly joining in the spirit of prayer is but solemn mockery.

Evening of the day

My dear friend has just given me directions concerning her burying clothes in which she is no less exemplary in death than in life having separated such as were thinner and less fitted to be useful to survivors, yet decent. It was deeply affecting and teaching to me and I desire never to forget the lesson. She wished the holy hand would be with me perpetually until everything was conquered that would conquer me. Her reasons being this particular in directions was that there might be no hurry. Being her friends might perform the last offices of respect with quietness. Observing there was a comely order in the truth, it directed us what to do in life and in death, and that the Everlasting Truth should stand when all deceit was done away. Uttering many living expressions to individuals present and recommending them to gather up the fragments for there was much in it.

20th [May 1781]

My nursing friend is no longer here. Her burial was respectfully large at which we had an edifying meeting. She had set a pattern of humility in desiring a coffin made of the wood most commonly to those parts, saying she did not see the necessity of importing costly wood for such purposes, this [one] being of oak and made neat looked very well. I was humble under a sense of my own unworthiness and afresh incited to duty. Oh! That the loins of my mind may be kept girt about, and in readiness to do my heavenly father's will. Sincerity of heart, firmness and soundness of judgment under divine guidance is the girdle which will strengthen and qualify to promote the work of truth in the earth. Great is my friend's gain, may I follow her as she followed Christ, that in the conclusion, I may be centered with justified and glorified spirits.

My time passeth sweetly on, much in the love of God which may be maintained I trust through vigilance. My kind and worthy Friend Thomas Lightfoot is truly father to me in whom I hope a blessing may descend for his parental tenderness. The housekeeper here joins me in reducing to practice my prospect of it being right to wait in reverent acknowledgment on the great dispenser of all our benefits at morning dawn.

[May] 26th [1781]

I have not so uniformly observed the waiting in silence at the showing of the day as expected.

The young bees ushering forth this day to form a new habitation reminds me of my present situation. Departed from a tender mother's house, to seek a habitation not made with hands, since it was in obedience to my heavenly leader and for the sweets of peace that I came forth. Oh! That like the industrious bee I may be diligent in a faithful application to wholesome labor (both spiritual and temporal) by which I may obtain my daily supplies of celestial nectar. And that in moving and staying only with my King and Leader, may I finally be hived with him in the fold of peace and joy. E. Lauden[61] called me to behold them and learn the lesson they taught. The king bee having lodged in a wrong place, the rest were discomposed not knowing which way to turn. So it is with the leaders in the camp of Israel, how awful is the station if such [be] mislead, [then] how many are bewildered.

The other day being under a close exercise of spirit I felt as if a meeting was near at hand, but could not tell where, as the week day meeting here was still some days' distance. When intelligence came there was to be one amongst the Methodists at the next neighbors and I was queried with whether I would go? When feeling myself authorized by those previous impressions, I was most easy to do so and Friend [Thomas] Lightfoot bore me company. The people soon gathered and when the young minister came, the first act in religious exercise was to sing a hymn.[62]

Upon conclusion of this hymn he knelt down to prayers, others accompanying him and I felt a degree of the spirit of prayer arising as he expressed himself that those collected might be helped in speaking and in hearing that day having, I judged, some regard toward us who were strangers and desiring so to acquit himself, as not to disgrace but advance his cause in our view. And he was, I thought favored with a portion of help in his discourse beyond his own human understanding which was well adapted to our principles and recommending to the word of God within and that if we were not led by the Spirit of God we were none of his. Instantly upon his conclusion he says, "let us pray," and they again knelt in a short supplication. But I felt nothing of the Spirit of prayer as before.

---

61. The Lightfoots' housekeeper.
62. Methodist hymn singing began with founder John Wesley (1703–1791) and brother Charles Wesley (1707–1788), who together composed some 6,500 Christian hymns.

When they broke up he came and sat pretty near us and most of the people remained as if waiting in expectation that something would be said. There was a solemn stillness and I addressed him in substance as follows: "I have good unity with those who in sincerity of heart endeavor to gather souls to God, and I wish thy labors this day may be blest. But [I] must own I could not unite with that sudden transition from singing to praying and from exhortation to prayers."[63] [For] though I felt something of the spirit of prayer in the first petition, yet in the second I did not. And as every acceptable act of worship must proceed from the Author of all good or help, and from leadings of his Holy Spirit, we should witness that to go before us ere we attempt anything of the sort especially in so solemn and awful an act as that of prayer we should feel inward and something of necessity. [I said] "The Apostle said it was from necessity he spoke and in prayer I think great care should be used not to run in our own time and will."[64] He modestly replied, "We were told to pray without ceasing and to be constant in season and out of season."[65] I mentioned that "As there are diversities of operations but the same Spirit, we should wait for and discern its distinct operations ere we put forth a hand to act." I had heard their professors met with a loss on speaking too commonly on religion, which being a weighty subject should be weightily treated on. And I had heard likewise from a friend who had traveled to the southward that he had met with a young woman who had been so wrought upon through the influence of the Spirit to whose guidance the people had this day been recommended, that her teeth should even chatter together from a concern to impart the exercise of her mind. But their rules admitted not of it and that if any appeared so concerned, it would be well to make way for them, seeing male and female are declared to be one in Christ. He said they were not all of one mind respecting women's speaking, but it was allowed in private meetings. I observed if any draw conclusive arguments from any one part of scripture against it, another part could be produced in contradiction. That it was a practice among the Jews to oppose or reason with the speaker if they did not like his doctrine but from the communicative turn if some of our sex, the weaker part might

63. Anne's criticism of Methodist liturgy stems from Friends' custom of silent meetings. Friends regard singing or music during worship a distraction; however, one so moved by the Spirit may break silence to sing, pray, or speak spontaneously during worship. "How Can I Keep from Singing?" a hymn expressing such joy that one cannot keep silent in God's presence, erroneously credited a Quaker original but was in fact composed by the American Baptist minister/hymnist Robert Wadsworth Lowry (1826–1899).
64. Acts of the Apostles 13:46.
65. 1 Thessalonians 5:17.

be troublesome, where unlimited liberty was granted. And the Church which the Apostle wrote to when he said he suffered not a woman to speak in the Church, but to ask their husbands at home, was remarkable for its confusion and want of order amongst the women.[66] That Philip's daughters were Prophetesses and scripture testifies that prophesying is speaking to edifying, exhortation and comfort.[67] The meetings he alluded to I supposed were what is called class meetings and a young man who had led a profligate life, but was now mercifully turned to seek more permanent good, informed me that in his days of wandering, he was at one of those meetings and it reminded [him] quite prophetically of the confessions made to this Priest among the members, the leader of the class going about to inquire of each one the state of their souls.

I believed they had in meeting together (as it was right for Christians to have communication one with another for the strength and comfort one of another) been owned with the divine presence as the "promise is to the sincere that though but 2 or 3 are gathered in the name of Christ, there he will be in the midst.[68] That finding this, there was a danger of increasing those meetings in a formal line." The man of the house thanked me for coming there and I believe there is danger, [and] should be great care in such establishments of drawing some who love to make a show in religion of taking expressions of things beyond their genuine experience and so infringing on the truth. Some were refreshed with the waters of a supernatural life. After leaving the house some paces, I felt constrained to go back and take the young speaker [aside] by himself, exhorting him to let his life and conversation preach as well as his words that no lightness nor lewdness might appear inconsistent with so solemn an office as he filled for it was weighty. That I knew nothing of him but [I] begged he would be careful and dwell inward and wished him to be made an instrument of good. He seemed touched with my hints and said he thought they should not be lost.

Those class meetings[69] remind me of my concern to wait at morning dawn. And [I] find care must be used when that is practiced, to dwell under that daily exercise, which prepares the mind to render acceptable offerings in worship.

66. 1 Corinthians 14:34.
67. Acts of the Apostles 21:8, 9. Anne cites the disciple Philip's daughters as an example of women who prophesied and ministered in the early church.
68. Matthew 18:20.
69. Early Methodism permitted small groups of about twelve to fifteen to meet weekly. See Manskar, *Accountable Discipleship*.

Those seasons of solemn waiting[70] may renew strength and promote in word, recollection, and care that may operate through the day in preserving [us] from deeds of vice and error.

Oh! Thou merciful God whom at this time I adore in the inmost of my soul: keep me I pray thee; and never suffer me long to stray unreproved from that holy watch and travail of spirit, to know and feel thee near, which will be as walls of defense around me, from objects without, of wrong influence or ensnaring temptation. So shall I live to praise thy great name who is forever worthy.

8 Mo. [August 1781]

Oppressed in the night season with a great weight on my spirit, it was not lessened by the sudden appearance of what is esteemed a token of death, when this thought presents: If providence works by various ways for the instruction and warning of the children of men and intimations are given in this way of what is approaching, [then if] it is my tender <u>indulgent</u> Mother I am to be deprived of, oh, thou Rock of Ages, support me and [I] pray thee in patience and calming resignation [for] whatever trials beset me.[71] In this state, I am brought into deep sympathy with the case of orphans who are left destitute of near protecting friends, and without a temporal dependence. The income of my patrimony being much cut off not only from the impediment of Congress currency[72] but also tender scruples on the score of interest money, or at least as high an interest as is customary, being desirous to guard against everything that may tend to the oppression of mankind.[73]

9 Mo. [September 1781]

Instructed this morning by intimations arising, I believe from the teachings of the heavenly Shepherd, in which I had to view the necessity of guarding

---

70. "Seasons" in Quaker speech denote a period of waiting, about a month, to discern whether a decision or action conforms to God's will.

71. A dream portending the death of Mother Emlen likely frightened Anne of the possibility it might negate any chance of her making amends.

72. Anne at cross-purposes feared that refusal to accept rent payment in Continental currency would result in a loss of income. By April 1780, Congress began withdrawing the depreciated currency when it had reached near-worthlessness. By May 1781, it was no longer circulated. Bezanson, *Prices and Inflation*, 12, 14, 20–21, 46, 48, 215.

73. Anne reiterates concern over the possible loss of income. For her view on the practice of money lending (usury for Christians), see her letter to Thomas Burke, March 3, 1779, in chapter 10, below.

against superfluity in every shape: in conversation, preaching, reading, writing, working, dressing, etc.[74] Oh! May I treasure up every illuminating ray, issuing from the source of all truth, as those who are faithful in a little shall be made rulers over more wisdom and consolation.

10 Mo. [October 1781]

The past Yearly Meeting has been a season of deep exercise to me in the revival of what had weighed on my mind to deliver to the brethren at their Yearly Meeting in 1779.[75] But waiving it then, on its present renewal I essayed to comply, when the time for moving seemed enforced on my understanding as [it] came. And though I had intended to consult some valuable friends, yet the ministry of David Sands at that juncture, who remarked that our ancestors when bid to go anywhere, waited not to consult a brother and Ann Moore,[76] who stood up with fiery words and desired a state there, not to smother the babe they could not give life to. I became urged in spirit to go immediately from the close of the 5th day Meeting (Thursday). After my arrival, having to wait awhile in the adjoining apartment until the business of nominating a committee on the subject of taxpaying was finished, it opened on my mind, that if Friends were not easy to hear what I had to say, I should be clear and my burden should rest on them, or those who should prevent me. And as I found it to my soul's humble rejoicing, the few Friends who were called out by the doorkeeper to consult on the occasion declined it from my not having conferred with my sister. But this proceeded entirely from conviction of duty not to delay and no contempt of the care of those I prefer to myself. Robert Valentine and some others I found since, who perhaps knew me better, and

74. Anne reflects on the testimony of simplicity: to avoid excess in all things. The word "conversation," or holy conversation, denotes proper Quakerly behavior, deportment, interaction with others, or good deeds.

75. In 1778, the PYM on the problem of paying war taxes determined that each member should decide. In August 1780, the Western Quarterly Meeting implored the forthcoming PYM to "do more to advance the testimony against taxes for warfare." Marietta, *Reformation of American Quakerism*, 266. After appointing a committee to deal with this sensitive matter, the PYM reaffirmed the 1778 decision to leave it to every Friend's individual's conscience. PYMM (1780–1798), March–December 1778, 25–30, and September 1780, 80.

76. Ann Herbert Moore (1710–1783), a strict pacifist, preached in war zones during the Seven Years' War and the American Revolution. Moving from Pennsylvania to Maryland in 1753, she was a prominent member and "gospel minister" in the Gunpowder Monthly Meeting near Baltimore. A testimonial for her is in BYM (1783–1842), 3–8. Her life and vivid nocturnal visitations are explored in Gerona, *Night Journeys*, 152–57; and Gerona, "Ann Moore's Secrets." See also Bacon, *"Wilt Thou Go on My Errand?"*

confided in my integrity of purpose, said friends were exceeding wrong in preventing my being heard. The message I believed myself commissioned with was remarkably apropos to the subject of the committee [and] was then separated on, which was doubtless the cause I felt them so impelled to go though unacquainted with the movements of men friends.

11 Mo. 30th [November 1781]

For two years past my mind hath travailed under a concern on account of the use of gold and silver from the oppressive channel through which it comes, and its being a capital spoke in the destructive wheel of war. And [I] have solid reason to believe the period is now arrived in which I must be willing to encounter whatever difficulties may rise from the disuse thereof; rather than break my peace with my heavenly Guide this disobedience who administrates to my soul consolation on this surrender.[77]

I believe a standard of purity if called for to be held up to the nations from our Society [of Friends], and to advance this, humbling dispensations may be meted out for "Zion shall be redeemed through judgement."[78] And to accomplish this great purpose, we must stand more in the resignation of whatever tends to unless in a gratification of the lusts of the flesh, the lusts of the eye and the pride of life.

12 Mo. [December 1781]

My mind being fully given up to bear the foregoing testimony not many days elapsed before, like Abraham's offering, it was restored in the use of the necessary part in those articles, provided I coveted not more than was needful for the common purposes of life; whether in the use of silver vessels or money.

12 Mo. [December 1781]

Yesterday [I] received a letter from a solid youth who has mistaken imagination for revelation, in conceiving I should be his partner and as he is fearful of his own ground in the proposition desires secrecy, which I shall duly observe, believing it most consistent with Christian kindness in doing unto others as

---

77. Having forsworn tendering Continental currency, Anne's refusal also to use hard money leaves the editors to wonder how she imagined society could function, or did she consider return to a simple bartering economy? In the next entry, Anne abandoned this impractical idea.

78. Isaiah 1:27.

we would they should do unto us [and] to observe a conduct of this sort on such delicate subjects.

3 Mo. [March 1782]

The youth before spoken of has explained that cause of his mistake; that once in meeting it weighed on his mind, that if he was faithful, he should be a comp[anion]n with me, which he now believes with myself signified a companion spiritually Zionwards. But that as Thomas Elwood[79] speaks of a natural fire, he was not sufficiently void of that for the will of the creature to be raised into a belief that favored his inclination from one large in the ministry. A proposal on the subject hath been renewed with weight from one who in years past laid the prospect before me but endeavors to act as I thought to the best of my understanding was induced to pass it by. This renewal was very unexpected but as it is from one of considerable weight and experience, the subject remaining so with him demands my serious attention.[80]

One day after a state of conflicting uncertainty [on] how to decide it, Martha Harris, a friend who believed herself authorized to encourage me therein, addressed me in the language of Abraham's servant when sent to procure a companion for his son: "Tell me now yea or nay, that I may know whether to turn to the right hand or to the left."[81] After which in viewing it, I concluded, if I had gone counter to best wisdom in putting a negative on it before, in desiring to cast off what felt so weighty, I would now assent thereto, and she became relieved. Sometime after she compared herself to one of the three valiants who passed through the host of the Philistines at the peril of their lives to fetch water for David and he afterwards poured it out unto the Lord: as she had past thro[ugh] perilous opposition in pleading for this matter.[82] In former ages a plurality of wives appeared lawful [but] since the prevalence of Christianity, one wife or husband in succession, and if a dispensation should

---

79. Thomas Ellwood (1639–1714)—an English Quaker scholar and associate of George Fox and William Penn who was frequently imprisoned himself for his faith—and in turn he visited many Friends in prison. Ellwood's numerous works include his autobiography, *History of Thomas Ellwood*.

80. A previous suitor proposed again, even though Anne had tried to end the matter.

81. Martha Harris, speaking for one of Anne's suitors, relates the story of Isaac and Rebekah in Genesis 24.

82. 2 Samuel 23:15–17. Martha Harris cites a biblical incident to illustrate how she, too, faced danger acting as messenger for Anne's would-be suitor.

be approaching, in which those who are left in a state of widowhood will have to make it an occasion of seeking a marriage more closely with an heavenly husband dedicating their time to his service. Dispensations vary in succeeding ages [and] we should not be stumbled at the past, nor limit the holy one of Israel in the future as Isaac Penington says in speaking of the day about to break forth, "Take heed of retaining or setting up anything which the Lord is coming forth against and take heed of slighting or appearing against that which the Lord is preparing to set up."[83] And if it be his will and I should ever set an example therein during this life of vicissitude, I desire to walk in the wisdom of his council and safe directions.

18th [March? 1782]

My mind hath been clothed with sorrow under a sense of the great deficiency in a spirit of sound discipline in many families. And the erroneous conduct and benighted mind of a brother has affected me with fearful apprehensions lest he should be forever lost.[84] Oh! Thou who canst turn the heart of man as a man turns his water course in the field, I pray thee to turn his captivity. Comfort my tender Mother amidst all her exercises and enable her to steer along consistent with thy righteous will in deed and word. And Oh! Lord, arm me with unshaken resolution and perseverance in clearness of sight respecting thy divine will to tread the path most pleasing unto thee. Give me strength to stand amidst the floods of obloquy that may be poured forth. Change the hearts of the obdurate towards me and cause the sorrowing bosom of thy little one to be filled with divine consolation. As thou in mercy hast visited our family, forsake them not I pray thee until judgement has brought forth victory over everything that separated from thee. Turn and overturn until thou comes to rule and reign in our hearts, and bring us into the daily participation of thine eternal peace. That if, in the disposal of thy Wisdom, I should be separated as was Joseph from his Father's house,[85] we may be yet again restored to each other's company in the cementing love of Christ.

Affecting difficulties present to my view as at the door. Oh! That the great preserver of men may keep me from bringing reproach to his name under

---

83. Quoted from Penington, *Church or the State of the Church*.

84. Anne refers to one of her brothers who had been disowned. Regarding Emlen family troubles, see chapter 2, above.

85. Genesis 37–49. Reflecting on the separation from her mother, Anne cites the story of another estranged family, implying hope for reunion with her family.

proving conflicts. This overturning hand of power is leading me, for even as a preacher of righteousness to others in conduct, to leave my birthplace and near connections on account of the Congress money and payment of taxes rather than subsist on a plenty, in part arising from such compliances. May the arm of divine power be underneath to sustain amidst the inundations of reproach, overflowing every bank of tenderness, from an uncharitable world, that sees not into the cause and tendency of these exercises.

The subject of weight, to which I thought best to submit, and leave the event to Providence, engaged the attention of David Sands and others who advised both parties to drop the matter as though it had not been, leaving it to the wise disposer of events, whether ever to revive it or not.[86] We were mutually prepared to accord with the proposition having felt an intimation to exchange letters, which took place and the friend passed on homewards.

19th [March 1782]

Martha Harris being a guest at our house some time past had a view of the visitation extended to our family, seeing a table spread of dainties and a green vine running over it. This morning she had the affecting account to give me that she saw the vine dried up and a serpent's head got in the top.[87] A lamentable case, that the serpent's power should take [the] place of the living power and vine of life. She believes herself sent to pluck me as a brand from the burning or as Lot out of Sodom. Oh! That the inhabitants of this city were more redeemed from the Sodomitish[88] state of pride, fullness of bread and abundance of idleness. The view of this state, being too prevalent with many, has been embittering to my life for some years past and for some days and nights, I have been heavily oppressed with fears that the day of light is closing with some individuals. Oh! That the God of Jacob may yet arise and bruise the serpent's head in these. And should I have to flee as for my best life from this city if a little Zoar[89] is provided, [I] shall be content with a small though quiet habitation, if free from the pollutions of Sodom.

---

86. The editors have not discovered the nature of the contention.
87. The language here and in the next paragraph suggest that Anne had returned to Philadelphia. See the entry for March 2, 1783, below.
88. Sodomitish—that is, like Sodom, the notoriously sinful city described in Genesis 18 and 19.
89. A city in the lower Jordan Valley, Israel, that was spared the destruction that fell on Sodom and Gomorrah. Anne, too, prays for a retreat from her troubles in Philadelphia.

9 Mo. [September 1782]

My heart is filled with thankfulness [to] the Father of every mercy, for his added one to me this day; in being favored with the sympathetic company of diverse clean-handed friends on the subject of my removal into the country and our conference settled with peace to my mind, in resigning as they proposed my application for a certificate not to be renewed unless it should revive again with weight.[90]

12 Mo. [December 1782]

We who profess to be led and guided by the spirit of truth should in all things be subject thereunto and not to the reasoning spirit in man, in ourselves, or others: I find the contest between these two powers considerable in my bosom. The world and human inclination might dictate an adherence to the council of near connections, but divine grace influences to believe that in so doing, I should lose sight of that path of faith which I have seen cast up for me to walk in.[91] Keep me Oh! Father near unto thee, in humble obedience to thy requirings! And either reconcile my mind more triumphantly above the changeable opinions of men. Sure there is great room for a loud testimony to be proclaimed through the borders of our camp against the workings of the man of sin and blind acknowledgement of his power. At a time when the beastly spirit of war is placing its mark on all who will receive it, and bow to its dominion, instead of the power of the living God, therein departing from the true Spirit of worship and [a] fulfilling scripture declaration "And all that dwell upon the earth shall worship him whose names are not written in "the book of Life" <u>of the lamb slain from</u> Rev: 13.8.[92]

Agreeable to the testimony of a friend lately brought under deep baptism, thro[ugh] which she was cured of fits to which she had been subject for years:

---

90. This conference likely took place at the PYM in late September 1782. The year before, Anne had requested the PWMM issue a certificate of good standing so she could join the Concord Monthly Meeting in Concordville, Chester County. A committee of five women denied Anne's transfer, apparently concerned for her radical positions on Continental currency and the payment of war taxes. When Anne renewed her request, she was told it "was not the proper time for her removal." PMMWM (1781–1792), August 31, October 4, 1781, February 22, March 29, 1782.

91. After the PWM's rebuff to transfer her membership to the Concord Monthly Meeting, Anne reaffirmed her radical opposition to the War for Independence. While complying with the steps for transferring membership from one meeting to another, she stood firm on her pacifist position.

92. Underlined in the original manuscript.

believing in that restoring word of life through the operations of which she had many remarkable sights in a kind of trance or vision. After which to her neighbors and the people who visited her on report thereof from far and near, she spoke to their states in a striking manner. She said she has been in heaven and saw the book of life opened and well was it for the Quakers and Menonists[93] and all who renounced having anything to do with war, in even paying war taxes or being [in] any other way concerned, for their names were written therein and she saw them in the road to heaven but many others she saw in the path to hell where she had also been.

1 Mo. 14th [January 14, 1783]

Greatly am I exercised in mind on beholding the dangerous path of my walking. Grant me patience, dearest Lord in every conflict and probation refine me as thou sees meet but Oh! Father I beseech thee suffer me not to fall and become a reproach to thy holy truth. Keep me in thy pure council. Oh! Forgive I pray thee and blot out my past transgressions, that I may be restored to the joys of thy salvation. Having a right fight not to hardness towards [illegible].

3 Mo. 2 [March 1783]

I am in straits and encompassed with difficulties; Lord Jesus make me wholly thine and remove not the hedge of thine Holy Spirit from me. Keep me in the enclosure of thy peace.

> Deliver me from fear of man
> Who would my inward life trespass
> Oh! Set me now a captive free
> Then shall I strive to follow thee
> Then shall it be my great delight
> To call upon thee day and night
> Grant then Oh! Lord a list'ning ear
> And ransom from enslaving fear

---

93. Mennonites, or sixteenth-century Anabaptists, historically a peace church, professed adult baptism and like Quakers refused to swear an oath. See Estep, *Anabaptist Story*. Tolles in *Meeting House and Counting House* (239) notes that by the time of the Revolutionary War, Quakers had withdrawn from mainstream society and took on a "pattern of behavior, characteristic of sects like the Mennonites, who in many particulars they came more and more to resemble."

Strengthen to follow thy command
That I may reach to Canaan's Land

I have revived the proposal of leaving the city, I see no other way for true peace.[94] Oh! Thou ransomer of thine own, show me the way in which I should go, lead steadfastly eyeing the same, [that] the whisperings of the stranger may have no power over me to decoy from the right path. Turn many Oh! Lord from the paths of deviation and self-seeking turn the captivity of Zion and be pleased to remove every obstructing thing from before me, to the full performance of thy holy mind and will and cause the sincere hearted so to be brought into a sympathetic view of my exercises that they may be led to administer a word of consolation and encouragement that I faint not.

16th [March 1783]

My sister[95] coming to reside with us during her husband's absence on trade, I feel secret breathings that our dwelling together may be in that heavenly fellowship which is of the father and brings forth fruit to his praise, as my friends discourage my yet moving into the country which judgment I feel resigned to and though with a secret inquiry why is it thus with me? Yet am I encouraged by the experience of others and pious David who when his faith and love was sufficiently tried, the all-wise disposer of men was pleased to say it is enough. And so I believe now as of old, he will bring his dependent children in his own time as on the banks of deliverance with thanksgiving and the voice of melody.

I was lately communicant as at the Lord's Table, with a sincere hearted young woman and baptized seeker when with floods of tears, we felt that between us which is better than greatness, wealth, or human favor. She related a dream of her taking up a new born babe that almost smothered [and] it felt to me [as if] I was that babe, having witnessed extraordinary refreshments to the best life in me. Which was almost choked indeed by her company and she said on awakening she immediately thought of me. Whatever was the cause, I felt more enlargement afterwards in partaking of the necessaries of life without asking questions. Blessed forever be my gracious benefactor for the various turnings of his Love my heart is touched with humble gratitude and [I] desire

---

94. Anne apparently had returned home the previous December 1782, then proposed to leave the city again.

95. Anne's older sister, Margaret Emlen Howell, the wife of Samuel Howell.

to exercise moderation and temperance in the restoration of this great privilege.

We had a solid meeting attended with divine quietude and instruction and humbling to that part which would work of itself and without the cross of Spirit and power of Christ its only redeemer. I was tenderly bound in the fear that I had at times perhaps, done more than was required of me. This led me from one degree to another almost a condition of despair and I saw clearly that what had led some even to the attempting of the natural life, in feeling the accuser of work in others who were cast down. This was poor Martha [Harris]'s condition in some of the later days of her pilgrimage here, but there is no doubt but she has entered into that rest which is prepared for the righteous. Amen.[96] We lodged at Isaac Massey's[97] in company with William Savery[98] and wife, Thomas Lightfoot, Thomas Savery,[99] and our caretaker out of town the esteemed Benjamin Smith[100] he is a hopeful young friend and Thomas Savery professes such integrity and singleness of heart God-ward as will I trust in [the] future make him as well as his brother very useful in the family of the faithful. May we all be faithful to our particular concerns or allotments in life, then shall we be made as pillars in the house of our great Architect that shall go no more out. So be it. We got to breakfast at Doctor Morris's[101] and so came to Derby [Darby][102] and home that day. Since which I have been frequently

---

96. Goshen Monthly Meeting approved eight pounds for the funeral expenses of Martha Harris in February 1785. Goshen Monthly Meeting Minutes (1773–1798), February 1785, 345.

97. Isaac Masseya, respected member of the Goshen Monthly Meeting, was descended from a Chester County pioneering Quaker family.

98. William Savery Jr. (1750–1804), a Quaker minister and tanner by trade, made ministerial travels in the United States, Canada, and Europe; a mission to the Northwest Indians in Sandusky, Ohio, in 1793; and a visit to the Six Nations in Canandaigua, New York, in 1794, where he witnessed the Treaty of Canandaigua. In 1778, he married Sarah Evans, daughter of Pennell Evans of Berks County, Pennsylvania. Crane, *Diary of Elizabeth Drinker*, 3:2208.

99. Thomas Savery, younger brother of William Savery Jr., was a member of the PMM and a skilled furniture maker like his father, William Sr.

100. Benjamin Smith (1762–1793) married Deborah Morris in 1790. Crane, *Diary of Elizabeth Drinker*, 3:2213.

101. John Morris (1759–1793), a Philadelphia Quaker physician, married Abigail Dorsey in 1783. In 1787, he founded the Philadelphia College of Physicians and died six years later in the yellow fever epidemic. For his biography, see Bell, *College of Physicians of Philadelphia*.

102. A town on Darby Creek in Chester County, founded by Quakers in 1684; it was an easy carriage ride of five miles southwest from central Philadelphia.

attacked with that Spirit which would sink into the pit, but a gracious arm of support hath been in mercy extended to help me therefrom in pinching moments of danger. Blessed be the great name of him.

21st [March 1783]

Gracious fountain of preserving mercies! Thou knowest my many conflicts, and thou alone knowest what baptisms are meet forces. Preserve me I pray then in pinching moments unhurt that through every temptation I may pass along to the glory. My soul hath been bowed in deep probation this day as we [are] heretofore of late, under a sense of close trials before me. Oh! That I may pass over those difficulties that await leaning upon thy holy staff of support, as well as seriously reading the language of thy word. What there is before me I know not, but must rely solely on thy divine sufficiency, gracious Creator, who hath hitherto sustained me and know how to deliver safely out of, as well as lead into Jordan.

23rd [March 1783]

Having met with some close proving circumstances of late, from others, I find it of consequence to my peace, to bear all things calmly and with resignation, not suffering any hardness or censorious dispositions to arise concerning any who have injured me but looking to the Great Fountain of inexhaustible Love and Light, endeavoring to seek after goodness and view all things in a right light. That I may be qualified to return good for evil, blessing for cursing. Those wherever I may not be disposed to lean repose fresh the apprehension they so not always confide in the counsel of omnipotence singly and alone but [rely] too much one on another.

6 Mo. [June 1783]

I am persuaded in the regulations of temperance, that two moderate meals a day and a draft of milk at night is sufficient for the general sustenance of nature and [I] desire to walk in that line. I also believe it is right to offer a morning and evening sacrifice in a little portion of time in waiting on God. This was part of the family discipline of William Penn. Some might think it would too much interfere [with the] time demands of temporal duty, but I believe mankind are more apt to miss their way, in a too earnest pursuit of the outward than the inward life and if there was more generally an abatement of one and increase of the other [this] would greatly advance our happiness. The appetites of persons being brought into subjection, our wants would be fewer and there would not be the prevalent hurry in business in the attainment of abounding wealth to supply artificial wants.

7 Mo. 3. [July 3, 1783]

Enjoyed great sweetness this day after partaking of a frugal meal in a sense of thankfulness and bounding my appetite by a stop when I felt a secret intimation that I had taken enough. If we thus endeavor to abide under the regulating hand of wisdom, it proves a leaven leading to heaven, or joy and comfort in the Holy Ghost. Oh! That I may never quench by acts of disobedience that light of Christ which is precious to profess nor yield to him the pearl of inestimable value by yielding to any gratification of [the] senses.

5[th day] [July? 1783]

Passed through much bitterness of spirit this day to prepare me[103] I believe for openly declaring my feelings to some, whom I have feared would sustain great loss by resting too much unredeemed from a party spirit, with whom it appeared my duty to forbear, partaking until they are more leavened into a disposition consistent with our high profession which, as it is maintained in purity, leads out of all parties or anxious promotions of any government but his own who is the Prince of Peace. Which although a stone of stumbling to the formal profession, yet shall be found to be that stone of mighty power that shall subdue all things unto itself.

6[th day] [July? 1783]

[I] dreamed last night [that] an elderly friend queried of a person whether I partook at a certain house observing as I was a dweller in the deeps. She thought in the deeps I might see they were not clear. I felt rejoiced I could answer in the negative, having so lately to bear my testimony as above mentioned.[104]

9 Mo. [September 1783]

The Friend concerning whom there was such various advices on the subject of marriage, sought an opportunity with me that we might look over some past

---

103. This and the two previous entries in March show that Anne was still personally criticized for her position on war taxes; however, by 1783 with the fever of war winding down, Continental currency was no longer in use. Levying war taxes continued through the 1780s as Pennsylvania tried to pay off its revolutionary debt.

104. This dream and Anne's reaction suggests someone accused her of associating with unsuitable company, for which "having so lately to bear my testimony" she was happy to deny any connection.

circumstances. We both concluded if we had kept near the guide ourselves, and not leaned so much to the council of others, <u>perhaps it might have been.</u> But the right time was over, and we parted good friends; he was exercised to trembling on speaking it.[105] Whatever was the cause, in the various timing of Omnipotence toward us, I felt more enlargement in partaking of [the] necessaries of life without asking questions and felt thankful for the privilege.

1 Mo. 18th [January 18, 1785]

Of most unequaled magnitude art thou, Oh! Holy wedlock, in contributing to the comfort, or producing the affliction of thy votaries according to their wisdom in entering upon or conducting under thy engagement. In a renewed weighty sense, that of myself I cannot take one right step therein [or] be preserved from missing my way or acting in any degree to thy glory. Oh! Blessed Father of Lights! I implore thee on the bended knee of my spirit to keep me in an especial manner herein, in the way thou wouldst have me to walk in, that whether in high or low degree thou tries me, with riches or poverty, marriage or celibacy, widowhood and desolation, stripped and comfortless, be however thou tries me in coming allotments. Enable me I entreat thee to keep the word of thy patience, that in the humbling hour of temptation,[106] I may be kept, and all my goings may acknowledge that thou alone art all sufficiently able to direct aright and to uphold in thy holy warfare. Thus Oh! Merciful Parent of Light, cause thy enshining Spirit to manifest itself in <u>darkness</u>.[107] In which state, I now fit, and as in the dust implore thy holy aid. That seeing clearly thy right way before my goings, I may pursue the same with obedience and alacrity of heart. Being with the offers of thanksgiving praise and holy prayer, [I am] thy humbled and I hope in measure, dutiful grateful servant. Amen. Amen.

3 Mo. 9th [March 9, 1785]

Since the above ejaculatory expressions of my concern on an important subject, I have been favored clearly to see my place in respect to some presentations

---

105. Anne likely refers to a marriage proposal that had discomfited her previously.

106. Anne could not entertain a marriage proposal lacking God's approval. Frost notes how Friends contemplating marriage sought Divine approval. Depending on the inward light, the Spirit might direct not only "whom to marry, but when," though trying to achieve spiritual clarity on an upcoming marriage was often difficult. Responsibility fell to the Women's Meeting to discern God's will and to iron out any difficulties, Frost, *Quaker Family*, 150–55.

107. Underlined in the original manuscript.

and apprehended presentations of that kind. Oh! The mercy of that power of light and love who unveils himself in darkness and bestows upon us in his own time, as we become humbled before him, a clear sense of our duty and proper allotments, both in spiritual and external matters. May the feet of my mind be preserved as on the Rock of His salvation, that no unforeseen waves of trial on these or other concerns may carry me as into an ocean of confusion, perplexity, and difficulty, but that by his gentle hand of love I may be led along to His praise who keeps us.

4 Mo. 30 [April 30, 1785]

This day having arrived at 30 years of age, I suppose commences that period of time wherein I may be styled what is called an Old Maid. May I through divine grace be so favored to conduct in my future path as to furnish one evidence to different ranks, that it is not marriage or celibacy [that] gives merit or demerit to a person but a life ordered in the fear of the Lord and seeking his glory. I cannot fully account for the respectful mode of speaking sometimes used respecting persons advancing in a single state. It is not founded in reason, neither in our holy religion. Seeing a great Apostle recommend or approve of it in many of the believers in Christ, as being thereby more disentangled to serve him. It often proceeds from light and superficial minds and sometimes may from the dark spirit of human policy which to promote its fancied strength by increased population may encourage marriages, which are so far from being typical of that uniting harmony subsisting between the bridegroom of souls, and his spiritual church, which every Christian marriage should resemble that they sometimes prove as thorns one to another. But those who are actuated by such policy should remember, that all governments are under his power, who when he sees meet can dash them to pieces as the vessel of a potter.

5 Mo. 1 [May 1, 1785]

At meeting James Thornton[108] stood for some time under divine influence. Before he arose, [and] the descendings of heavenly power, covered as a canopy

---

108. An English Quaker minister, James Thornton (1727–1794) immigrated to Philadelphia in 1759 and became an active member of the Byberry Monthly Meeting and inspired minister by age twenty. He served with Warner Mifflin in the peace delegation in October 1777 to meet the warring British and American generals after the bloody Battle of Germantown. Thereafter, Thornton's religious visitations included Maryland, Delaware, New Jersey, and New York. He was deeply involved in the PYM and the Meeting for Sufferings. See the testimony for James Thornton in *Memorials Concerning Deceased*, 44–47.

the Assembly which compared a little to ancient time, when the glory of the Father appeared in dignity and bade Moses put off his shoes from off his feet, for where he stood was holy. Thus must all selfishness and all human dependency be parted with, even [the] instruments one prepared to receive [as] sacred intelligence for the peoples' sake. He opened the clear prospect, clearer than ever; he then had, of the truth of that declaration, that "Male and Female are one in Christ," there being no sexes in souls [and] giving great encouragement to some forward in our several duties, keeping rank, for some were behind in their duties. This seemed a loud call to me, having wrote to this very friend, on something of weight relative to the Churches but though with him.

6 Mo. 28th [June 28, 1785]

This day in our Women's Monthly Meeting southward we had seasonable doctrine delivered from a visiting friend. He spoke of the superior privilege we [women] enjoyed to others of the nations, an effectual bar being placed between other women and any service they might be in the Church Militant. He wished therefore we might suitably improve it; which might be a means, through our wise conduct and improving our gifts, of opening the way for others. He spoke of the various gifts there are in the Church and that of the ministry, enjoying it was a common saying, they have marred their gifts through want of giving up in faithfulness, but it was often owing to a want of professing their vessels in sanctification more than a want of willingness that the Lord would not dwell in or speak through an unclean vessel. Therefore he wished them to come more to that live coal which cleanses and fits for service believing the Lord would fit and prepare some and advising to a faithful discharge of duty though he desired not to encourage a forward disposition in any and remarking there were various dispensations to pass through. How Moses being called as a leader to Israel went forth at first much in his own Spirit when he smote the Egyptian and offending the people had a season of retirement of forty years [when] he was made a fit leader for the people, to wear out that unfitting part. Here was a place of retirement he chose; had he gone and told anyone, the work [would have] been marred. He feared some who like Moses had seen something to do and was too hasty in this execution thereof—for like children, the spiritual birth as the natural, it feeds things before it is able to go—had suffered less by going to some who might be weak brethren to make their complaint. On not finding any evidence of peace in which they had done who told them, they had done very well and thus were they hurt!

He spoke in the preceding meeting of worship of the great work of the Lord how he sets as a refiner with fire and [a] fuller with soap. That as in the outward, if we send a garment to the fullers, we do not like it to be returned with a grease spot or dirt on it, so we should abide under the operating power till all things offensive were done away. That the women had a part of the work to do and speaking to the children encouraging them to be willing to wait with their parents in reverence in setting down to their meals; and that parents would not give room for others to remark of us that we sat down to eat like hogs that look not up to the tree from whence the fruit falls. That mothers keeping their places in the families with their children were like doing a part of the work, as the needle work formerly, etc. He spoke in our meeting of the subjection due to parents in the church and advising to a regard of what they should say. As also of the subjection of wives to husbands as how by a gentle, much loving and faithful conduct they gained upon their husbands whom they could so govern almost through affection, but did they attempt to bear the sway they were not as the virtuous woman who is a crown to her husband's but they were put under foot.

12 Mo. [December 1786]

Oh thou inconceivable source of excellence, who refines thy children as silver is refined and purifies them as gold. I pray thee in and through the inexhaustible riches of thy goodness to make known unto me and lead me safely in the way thou wouldst have me to walk. Preserve me on the right hand and in the fire, keep me from consuming. Oh! That thy quickening power may do its office upon me. Redeem me from evil and through thy fiery baptisms let me clearly see the rays of true light concerning me. Preserve me dearest Lord, that if length of days be portioned unto me, they may be spent to the exaltation of thy saving truth, for thou art sufficient for thine own work. Blessed Lord, keep me from falling and show unto me thy safe direction in the case of a youth of integrity who makes professions of regard, let the light of thy countenance illuminate our understandings and discover to us safely and in thine own time, thy sacred will concerning us. Let every exercise of soul [be] redeemed to thy glory and give unto us the peace of thy kingdom in a dedication of heart unto thee. Whatever or with whomsoever our future allotment may be, Amen Lord Jesus—bless him I pray thee as one of thy children. Amen.

Blessed fountain of light and love who knows every [one] of my secret conflicts, and that I am at this time peculiarly tried from the profession of one,[109] who says 4 years ago in walking the street, I stopped and shook hands with a friend [as] he was with walking on some public business. That my meek and plain appearance had a considerable effect on his mind and feeling unity with me he thought I was of the true spirit. On returning home he acquainted his wife of the appearance he saw, and she informed him who I was, that I was a young Quaker who had taken a very religious turn. So he had been then for some time dissatisfied with some things in their mode of worship, that of the Baptists and had been reading Friends' books. It was a means of leading him in a closer examination in the merits of the principles I professed from whence he hath at length become a Quaker.

Though he hath passed through the same deep provings since, the death of his wife pretty soon after and a singular trial to his virtue even as Joseph was tried about five months after that. When a woman of credit to the view of the world with whom he was little or not acquainted sent him a note requesting his company. When he went, she took him upstairs, dressed in all the allurements of the fashion with her bosom bare; and said she wanted to consult with him about some painting. After he had given her his judgment on them, he came away but felt the force of the temptation very much. It dipped him into a humbled state of mind, under a prospect of the danger single men were exposed to, and he saw that it might be right for him some time to think of marrying though he had rejected the thought as not being acquainted with a woman whom he could unite with when the young friend he saw in Fourth Street was brought to his remembrance. But he thought, how could he call at his friend's house by whose means he conceived we should become acquainted? He there accordingly met me in the shop. The few minutes we stood there, I knew his attention much. He said [that] on returning home [and] pondering the matter, a passage of scripture came into his mind that he knew not was contained there, till on examining he found "Houses and riches are the inheritance of father and a prudent wife is from the Lord."[110]

This he believed pointed to me and from that time became professed with a belief that I was to be his companion. How far this may be founded on the Rock I know not, but if it be a seed of faith, sown by the everlasting Shepherd and holy seedsman, I wish it to flourish and increase with the increase of God. If not, that it may be rooted up, the plant springing therefrom of Love

---

109. We have not identified this Baptist turned Quaker.
110. Proverbs 19:14.

and tender attachment to me having believed it was under divine function, he cherished it. If it is indeed so, I wish an abiding blessing to rest upon it, to the praise of that God who brought Abraham thro[ugh] difficulty to his promised inheritance, hoping against hope this must be his case, if ever he obtains me for a companion, this the conflicting scenes of human life and Christian warfare. For there would likely be much outward opposition and inward doubtings also at times in my mind, to combat with, for if he had courage and faith to proceed, it must be well founded.

I may perhaps write in reply to him from which as he lives in a distant city, to be steadfast in the faith given him of God—meaning his religious faith—as to this concerning marriage.[111] It remains to be proved whether it be of the right part, as it is a singular kind. If it be so interwoven with his religious or doctrinal faith as to be inseparable, he has conceived it to be almost so, for if that passage of John was brought to his remembrance, John 1:33 is applicable to his case testifying that one and the same spirit directed him in both matters. For the same that convinced him of friends' principles also told him that I was to be his wife. "He that sent me to baptize with water, the same said unto me, upon whom thou shalt see the spirit descending and remaining in him, the same is He which baptizes with the Holy Ghost. He may be under a mistake, I cannot yet determine, time must prove it. It is good to prove all things and hold fast to that which is good. I wish to do so, in this case as well as on all occasions not to hold fast that which is wrong but to teach me how to walk herein and lead me safely along that I may not stumble as the dark mountains. Amen. I have for this time desired the matter wholly to drop, I before warned him of it. And he also in a meeting had it represented to him as a deed of writing with the dates in order and all prepared which he had to give up.[112]

---

111. Anne noted in her diary, "Have wrote this day to a friend [Warner Mifflin] on his addresses for marriage. I know not what is before me, may I be humbly submissive and patiently endure trials that I feel are approaching. And Oh! May I not flee from the furnace but wait the holy hand of gracious deliverance to bring me forth in the night season. Many, very many have been the evidences I have had of the divine will concerning me; Gracious Father preserve me in the way and bring me into the way wherein I may duly perform the same to thy praise, the help of thy cause and benefit of mine own soul's salvation. I have seen myself as on the brink of a precipice, deliver me blessed father and keep me from falling" (Emlen Diary, May 6, 1788). This entry indicates she felt pushed to her limit and feared it might be difficult to reject his proposal.

112. This apparently refers to Mifflin's appearing before his monthly meeting to give first notice of intention to marry Anne Emlen. For more on this, see Nash, *Warner Mifflin*, 156–57.

He did so and felt after resignation and it was withheld him for a season which was a state of painful suspense but it was said to him "My Grace is sufficient for thee"[113] when after a while it was returned to him with the dates as before. I told him <u>it must be so, it was necessary for him to resign it and if [it be] of the Lord, he could restore it in his own time, which was the best time but that</u> it might be restored perhaps signed with another name some listed in spirit <u>not mine. Which name as from male friend I mentioned</u> and that may be, I was only a waymark to that as a means of pointing him thither as a people when passing through deep places look to beacons or a waymark set for their direction. He is a man of wealth being thus did not move me without the right offering. <u>Whatever the Lord doeth is right and I wish it to be as he sees meet herein one way or the other.</u>[114] Amen.

10th Mo. [October 1788]

This day is the expected time of my second espousal, not unto God as formerly, but unto one of his devoted servants.[115] May the connection be a happy one but if the gloom that has overspread my mind at this season, with plenteous tears flowing from mine eyes <u>like the gloom of the day perhaps denotes but a solidity</u> and if [there be] any peculiar trials before me <u>and disconsolate time for me throughout this marriage</u>. If it be fired in time of some heavy (illegible)

---

113. 2 Corinthians 12:9 most closely follows this scriptural passage: "And he said unto me, my grace is sufficient for thee: for my strength is made perfect in weakness. Therefore most gladly I will rather boast in my infirmities, that the power of Christ may rest upon me."

114. Underlined in the original manuscript.

115. Some twenty-two months had lapsed since Anne's last entry. Here, Anne is referring to Warner Mifflin, whom she had first met in 1779 while traveling along the Eastern Shore with the Lightfoots. Anne Emlen Diary, May 7, May 14, May 16, May 18, 1779. Warner seems to have considered Anne as a possible mate after the Philadelphia midyear Meeting for Sufferings in 1787. Ibid., March 28, 1787. In May, the following year, Anne wrote to him "on his addresses for marriage." Ibid., May 6, 1788. Warner first requested approval to marry before the Duck Creek Monthly Meeting on July 26, 1788. DCMMM (1705–1830). His request was premature as Anne was apparently still undecided. That Warner had been pressing his case for months is noted in his father's letter that was presented when Anne finally appeared with Warner before the PWMM on August 29, 1788, accompanied by her mother and friends, Anne Howell and Elisabeth Rogers. Daniel Mifflin, Warner's father, in a letter dated April 20, 1788, attested to his son's "clearness" in proceeding with this second marriage. The second request before the women's meeting came on September 26, 1788. Anne entered the wrong date by a few days in this October 1788 entry. PMMWM (1781–1792), August 29, September 26, 1788; PMMMM (1782–1788), August 29, 1788. The marriage was solemnized on October 6, 1788.

My Religious Progress

to me therein, may I be able to endure to the end in the fire and in the furnace. Jesus Lord be with me, Amen. Now A. Emlen but no longer is after this day. May the change be at best for my soul's good, though outward trials of rather a sore nature should be my portion, now as hereafter. Amen.

7th Mo. [July 1791]

Three years are nearly elapsed since my marriage, which hath at times been attended with a sweet comfortable union of spirit with my dear partner to solace by the way and sometimes been attended with some very close outward provings. I have been nearly united with him who is my partner and my friend. Those [women] who [have] become wives of such who have offspring may expect conflicts at times from the forward officiousness of seeming Friends and children, although they may with a conscientious steadfastness endeavor to discharge their duty towards them. [In] this I have been deeply proved but the Lord hath mitigated my trial by showing the daughter the malicious spirit of my prosecutor[116] by which they cast off her influence and we have dwelt in comfortable unity. Granted deliverance to my oppressed soul when the bands of mine heart with secret (sometimes hidden) grief were ready almost to bring asunder. He [God] then graciously made way for his little one[117] and caused me to rejoice on the banks of deliverance giving me a heart through his own saving grace even to love mine enemies. The one affected by her spirit[118] was reparably addressed in a family setting [at] Darby[119] when she said "Warner, thy Mother seeks thy goodwill," thinks I, this is no less than [in] the past

---

116. The incident suggests the prosecutor was a family member causing a rift between Anne and a stepdaughter and that the conflict was resolved when the stepdaughter "cast off" the malicious charges. Wilson in *History of Stepfamilies in Early America* points out that stepfamilies were common in colonial America because the prevalence of disease and death necessitated remarriage, causing frequent domestic disruption. Though blended families were common, some regarded stepparents as unfit and a bad influence. If this perception typifies Anne's role in the Mifflin family, that social stigma would have minimized any efforts she made toward family harmony or bonding with her stepchildren.

117. Anne likely means herself; in several instances, she refers to herself as God's little one or as his loving child.

118. This may refer to one of Warner's daughters whom Anne has mentioned above.

119. This may refer to a family gathering in Darby, where both Warner and Anne had friends. "Thy Mother" may denote Anne herself, implying that Warner was insensitive to her reconciliation efforts; this family squabble likely caused some disagreement between them.

year—language of inspiration, to love mine enemies—I do intimately seek it but he is not sensible thereof.[120]

He hath also given me a son whom I have dedicated to him[121] if he will be pleased to accept him as his servant. Oh! That he may indeed be as one of the faithful Tribe of Levy ministering about the holy things of the Temple whose inheritance is the Lord of Hosts. There are many means of oppression in the earth. The Lord is rising to me to plead the cause of the oppressed; may all who love Him and desire to serve, fear His holy name and any attentive ear to the pleadings of His immaculate Spirit on the account of such, for oppression appears in many shapes in the world both amongst the white, black and tawny race. Amen.

4 Mo. 13th [April 13, 1792]

Deliver me, oh! Lord from the hands of the extortioner, from merciless men who make a prey of the poor and the needy! I have been exercised under a sense of the many wrongs and means of oppression, that there are in the world many waking moments and hours have I had in the night season from this subject; particularly before the birth of this my son Lemuel born the 23rd ultimo [April 23, 1792]. Should he have to experience oppression and wrong through friends, relations, or foes, Oh! That his soul may be preserved in patience and mind also for hard is it to see wrong at times and yet keep the seal of silence upon our life.

Samuel Emlen Mifflin born 4 Mo. 5th [1790]

A Thanksgiving Prayer
"Be careful for nothing: but in everything by prayers and supplication with thanksgiving let your request be made known unto God." Phil[emo]n: 4.6.

Thanks be to my Sov'reign Lord
For mercies thou hast sent

---

120. In the last two pages of the manuscript, Anne's writing becomes more illegible and more words are crossed out. This may indicate distress as Anne intimates that although "her grief was sometimes hidden; it nearly brought her asunder." The deletions suggest she was taking precaution about what she wrote, concerned someone might be peering into her journals.

121. Emulating the Jewish tradition, Anne dedicated her first son, born April 5, 1790, to the Lord, and then named him Samuel after the priest and prophet. 1 Samuel 1–2.

Who with the blessings there affords
Adds that of sweet content.
The boy thou'st given to my arms
My offring is to thee
Oh! Keep him spotless from all harms
In sweet simplicity.
Preserve him midst each dang'rous ill
That oft encounter youth
And thro[ugh] thy Grace his bosom fill
With righteousness and truth
That he a pattern forth may shine
Of wisdom and of love
Where in assemblage may combine
The serpent and the dove
That Solomon's superior choice
And Samuel's purity
May raise with usefulness his voice
And with his life agree
Thus to thy Throne of heav'nly grace
I bring my infant son
As Abram and Elkinah's Wife
In faithfulness hath done
And in like faith which they professed
As ancient records tell
A name is giv'n in which I rest
And call him Samuel

**Written 12 days after the birth of my son Lemuel Mifflin—
born 3 Mo. 23rd [March 23, 1792]**

"Thus saith the Lord, stand ye in the ways and see and ask for the old paths, where is the good way, and walk therein, and ye shall find rest for your souls." Jer[emia]h 6.16.

The unequal'd mirror of thy Word
Oh! Lord My heart reveres
Which doth true wisdom ere afford
Surpassing length of years
The perils of a lying-in

Are many, great, and sore
Thou has preserv'd from wreck therein
And I'll thy name adore.
Thy word was giv'n, a son was sent
Preserve him if thy will
With thy pure mind to be content
Thy precepts to fulfill
Instruct him in thy royal law
Make him in love therewith
That he may move in holy awe
And dread offence to give
Thus if his life continued is
Retain him in thy fear
That his first fruits he may thee give
And to thy Throne draw near
Yet, if for time, but a short space
His life be lent to me
Oh! May I through thy calming Grace
To thee resigned be.
Thou knowest how to portion out,
The bitter and the sweet,
And in each turn we need not doubt,
But mercy we shall greet.
As names significant were giv'n
By ancient Israel
Not without cause I'll do so ev'n
And name him Lemuel.

Chapter 7

RADICAL PACIFISM

Some Notes on the Payment of Taxes Appropriated for Military Purposes

This unpublished essay was probably composed late in 1779, just as Anne took refuge with Thomas and Susanna Lightfoot in Chester County; it was seemingly inspired by Anne's reading of John Churchman's pacifistic and widely circulated "An Account of the Gospel Labors and Christian Experiences of a Faithfull Minister of Christ," published in September of that year. By 1778–79, tax collection for military purposes was in full operation. For a young woman to undertake such a politically and historically minded brief against the policy of the revolutionary government is unparalleled so far as the editors know.

With respect to the tribute paid by our Savior at Capernaum,[1] Stackhouse in his *History of the Bible*,[2] page 1357 says every Jew that was 20 years old was obliged to pay a [illegible] Drachma or half a shekel, about 15£ Sterling for the use in the Sanctuary to pay for sacrifices etc., and this was the tribute which the collectors demanded of our Lord, and not a tax payable to the Roman Emperor, as some imagine, which appears not only from our Savior's argument, viz. that he was the son of the Heavenly King to whom it was paid

---

1. The tribute passage, "render unto Caesar," appears in Matthew 22:15–22, Mark 12:13–17, and Luke 20:20–26; however, Anne takes the opposing view that Jesus did not endorse paying taxes. Gross in *American Quaker War Tax Resistance* (xxi–xxii) explains Friends' position on tax payment, stating that they refused "to pay any tax levied expressly for the purpose of conducting a war."
2. Stackhouse, *New History of the Holy Bible*.

and consequently had a right to please his attention, but also from the Greek word which according to Josephus (the most noted of the Jewish writers)[3] was the proper word for the capitation or head money tax for the temple, etc. Bishop Taylor in his *Life of Christ*,[4] page 307 fully confirms the above operation, also William Burkett, I. A. Smith, and Daniel Whitby in their several commentaries on the scripture[5] and likewise Alexander Crudence in his Concordance.[6]

As to our Savior's answers to the tempting questions put to him by the Pharisees and Herodians,[7] it was adapted to defeat their design of ensnaring him, but by no means conclusive upon the rectitude of paying those taxes. He did not say the money was Caesar's; nor did he bid them give it to him, for it did not argue that because it bore his image it was His; no more than the money in the Kingdoms of Europe, which has the image of reigning Princes can be said to be theirs. Our Savior by this declaration strongly enjoins us to be faithful to what the secret monitions of truth require of us, whether in paying or refusing the payment of taxes or anything else, as to pay Caesar that which was his just due. Thus we rightly fulfill the injunction, "Render unto Caesar the things which are Caesar's and to God the things which are God's."

And with relation to the advice given by the apostles to the believers to "submit themselves to every ordinance of man for the Son's sake; as unto them that are set by him for the punishment of evildoers and praise of them that do well"[8] for this cause pay you tribute. For what cause did they pay tribute? This is more clearly explained in [1] Timothy 2:2, where he enjoins submission to kings, etc. "that they may lead a quiet and peaceable life in all Godliness and honesty." Now it is plain from the text as well as from the reasons of things that this injunction to the believers [is] only related to the civil authority, which was established for the peace of the community and by no means referred to taxes for the support of the wars so destructive of all order and good government. This is clear from the words of the apostle in the same chapter, where

---

3. Titus Flavius Josephus (37–100 CE). See *The Famous and Memorable works of Josephus, a man of much honour and learning among the Levis*.

4. Taylor, *Great Exemplar*.

5. Burkett, *New Testament*. I. A. Smith has not been identified by the authors. Whitby, *Paraphrase and Commentary on the New Testament*.

6. Cruden, *Complete Concordance to the Holy Scripture*. Anne's familiarity with these books is notable.

7. The Pharisees, a Judaic sect in 167 to 73 BCE, espoused the oral tradition of the law that became the foundational belief of Rabbinic Judaism.

8. Paraphrased from 1 Peter 2:13.

after enjoining the believers "to render to all their dues, tribute to whom tribute is due, etc." he adds, "owe no man anything but love to one another; thou shalt not kill; thou shalt not steal; thou shalt not covet."

Now these evils, which the believers are enjoined to avoid, are all efforts and attendants on wars, and the apostle further adds, "If there be any other commandment, it is briefly comprehended in this, namely, Thou shalt love thy neighbor as thyself." And even if it could be supposed that in early times under the government of Heathen Emperors, the believers thought themselves excused in their compliance to such requisitions. Yet now that the powers under which we live profess to be followers of Christ in doctrine and practice, it seems very strange that we should freely pay taxes for the prosecution of bloody wars which have been prosecuted in our nation, either in Europe or America not only in defense of their own territories but also for the purpose of crushing those they esteemed enemies and of enriching themselves through devastation and destruction in other lands. Read the history of modern time and see what horrible destruction of human beings many poor men by means of wicked laws [were] dragged against their wills to the field of battle and forced to slay or be slain. What corruption of manners; what waste of substance has not been made through the many years. Wars carried on in Germany, sometimes jointly with the Queen of Hungary with whom the English united to wage war, was maintained against that Queen and France in conjunction. What expense has accrued to the nation in order to get possession of the territories and wealth of the East Indies by every murdering art of war? Whereby thousands and hundreds of thousands have by sword and famine been brought to an untimely end. In Africa, also by acts of Parliament, a military power, forts, etc. have been maintained the better to enable the heathen in conjunction with the professed Christians to make war with and make merchandize of their Brethren. And in America how often have the Indians been instigated to acts of violence and murder, [or] Christians against Christians mired with scalping Indians have stained the earth with human blood for a miserable share in the spoil of a plundered world. A world, which a late pious author well remarks, should have felt nothing from the followers of Christ but Divine love, indeed a love which had impelled them to visit strangers with the glad tidings of peace and salvation.

Now if we deal truly with ourselves, if we desire to act on the purity, sincerity and [the] plainness of our profession, can we with truth assert that taxes for these purposes are such as the Apostle had in view when he required of the believers that they should submit to every ordinance of man for the Lord's sake? Will they tend to act for every good work to enable us to live a quiet and peaceable life in all godliness and honesty? Can the use of these taxes be said with truth to be for the punishment of evil doers and for the praise of them that do well? Are they agreeable to the general advice given not to covet, not to kill, not to steal? Nay are they not expressly for these purposes and in direct opposition to the direction to the injunction: owe no man anything but to love one another and thou shalt love thy neighbor as thy self. Will our pretense that we are ignorant of the use excuse us when indeed we know, and it is known we know, these taxes are put to uses the most inconsistent with our principles? Shall not we, as has hitherto been the case, be justly reproached as acting in opposition to the simplicity of the gospels to the sincerity and plainness of our profession? That our Friends did not formerly see these matters in this light is no argument in opposition to what is now made manifest; our Savior himself declared [in] John 16:2 "I have yet many things to say unto you but ye cannot bear them now."

By the 6th query,[9] we are required to bear a faithful testimony against war. Will not a query arise in every honest mind whether the voluntary payment of taxes which we know are appropriated to warlike purposes is indeed bearing such a faithful testimony as we ought? Whether we do not therein, in effect, support that which we profess in words give strength to the Spirit, strive to refuse and in a great measure deny him before and who commands us to love our enemies and has declared he came not to destroy men's lives but to save them? Luke 11:47

Great are the promises made to the Church that the kingdoms of this world are to become the kingdoms of our Lord and of his Christ, and that he shall reign forever and ever. The Prophets Isaiah and Micah describe the prevalence of the peaceable kingdom in a more so-called degree than the church has hitherto experienced, under which military achievement or requisitions can have no place in any character, for as saith the prophet (Malachi 1:9): "From the rising of the Son even unto the going down of the same my name shall be great among the Gentiles and in every place incense shall be offered unto my name."

---

9. The sixth query, a spiritual exercise on the peace testimony, is a Quaker meditative practice and teaching. See *Discipline of the Religious Society of Friends*.

When ye all hear of wars and rumors of wars, saith our blessed Savior, "See that ye be not troubled for all these things must come to pass but the end is not yet."[10] Hence Christians are admonished not to be concerned with wars and indirectly informed that they shall come to an end. Let us seriously consider how far the name of a tax because often applied to civil war can sanctify a military requisition or how far the opinion some Friends have adopted that our Savior's declarations and example as well as the Apostles' doctrine will justify their paying such taxes.[11] Let the unprejudiced judge. Why is a fine more obnoxious to our testimony than a tax for the same purpose? A tax that is not even applied to the sinking of a currency.[12] It is objected we which gave rise to it; but to prevent as far as possible we cannot pay a fine because in lieu of a personal service making more by which we contribute for the immediate to this, it may be answered if we were required to anything in support of war equally with the payment of kings and is constant with our duty as followers of Christ, we aiding human policy in its subterfuges to maintain should not refuse. So that our refusal is not because desolation lay waste indeed the building up of that peaceable kingdom which ought to be the business and duty of every true and baptized Christian. Christians cannot own even to destroy those for whom Christ died whose lives he came to save and whom he contrary to the dictates of the pure Spirit of God but commands us to love even as we love ourselves. It is like splitting a hair must discover to the warts.

How can we justify actively paying men for [left blank] that not him but the mammon of unrighteousness doing what we say we cannot ourselves do, the tax we serve; and by thus exposing our nakedness to behold differs from the fine only in name but not in [crossed out]. For these times are to strip us and discover ever the purpose. It is the same power [that] demands it and for the [his] wounds that they may be healed. We crucify the son of God afresh and put him unto open flame. Or if I see a man going headlong to destruction, we premeditate thy proposal being deceived in meditating the ruin of others and bring into suffering his body, the church, or money to bear

---

10. Matthew 24:6 and similar passage in Luke 21:9.

11. Anne's dismay was leveled at several Philadelphia Friends, including her mother and brothers, who paid the war taxes to avoid having their property distrained. In Chester County, where Anne was living, Friends who led the resistance to war taxes suffered the loss of property valued at thousands of pounds. Brock, *Pacifism in the United States*, 251.

12. Anne refers here to the galloping depreciation of the paper currency printed by order of the Continental Congress in order to finance the ongoing War for Independence.

the expense in the design on any pretense who are truly devoted with a single eye of guilt to him whatsoever; certainly [we] cooperate in his [crossed out] service and are united to him in Spirit on that which shall be, in a great measure accessory to the consequences [which] is the seed of life and it not at enmity with, but is obvious how able even well-disposed people are to suffer themselves to be blinded and deceived in matters that flatter their passions and humor but more especially their interest. We have a glaring instance of this in the so long continued slavery of the Negroes and in the displeasure which for a great number of years prevailed in the minds of the people otherwise well-disposed against those who ventured to oppose that most iniquitous practice.[13]

The prophet in the name of the Lord declares that where in our enquiries to know the Divine will there is a predisposition from worldly attachments in the mind, he will suffer the individuals to be deceived by giving them an answer of peace where there is no peace. See Ezekiel 14:4: "Every man of the house of Israel that setteth up his idols in his heart and putteth the stumbling block of his iniquity before his face and cometh to the prophet I the Lord will answer him that cometh according to the multitude of his idols."[14] The case of Balaam who from worldly considerations for temporal gain sought for argan only to establish that which he from the first answer had received, he had reason to be persuaded was not agreeable to the divine will is also fruitful of instructions, see Numbers 22. [margin words illegible][15]

As the society has generally paid such taxes as were demanded by government without inquiring into the application (and many still favor the same prospect), it ought to be treated on with discretion and great kindness, entreating such not to suffer custom nor interest to influence their judgement, to weigh the reason of things and open to the secret monitions of truth in this weighty consideration. Lest it should fare with them as with those who had been invited to the supper but from worldly consideration or ease or interest refused and

---

13. Most non-Quaker Philadelphia slave owners had ignored Quakers' efforts to cleanse themselves of slaveholding and their pleas for others to follow their lead. In some denominations, the number of slaveholders increased between 1767 and 1780. For more on this, see Nash and Soderlund, *Freedom by Degrees*, page 81, table 3.1 and chapters 3 and 5. Several of Anne's brothers were among those impervious to the pleading of Friends on the antislavery issue.

14. The prophet Ezekiel warned against ignoring genuine prophetic spirit and choosing instead to consult false prophets. Likewise, Anne cautioned that idols of self-will were not pleasing to God.

15. In Numbers 22, Balaam had sold his soul in order to buy argan oil.

were not found worthy whilst others who were comparatively, as stones, were raised up to lift up an ensign to those who sit in darkness.

There has long been a growing uneasiness in the Society with regard to the payment of taxes for the purpose of war. It is now between 60 and 70 years since it first appeared amongst Friends in this city.[16] On occasion of a tax then laid on the people for raising a sum of money for the purpose of the war, which was then carrying to take Canada which some Friends refused to pay;[17] and in the year 1756, the like concern was renewed in the payment of taxes for carrying on a war against the Indians when a number of Friends remonstrated to the Assembly on that head as it [is] particularly related in our Friend John Woolman and John Churchman's journals.[18] We also find by what is mentioned in our Ancient Friend John Richardson, Journal,[19] page 119, that there was a concern of the same kind amongst Friends in England, when it was inquired of him by Friends at their Yearly Meeting at Rhode Island what Friends in England did in the case of paying taxes for the carrying on [of a] War with France, and he replied: that "He had heard the matter debated both in inferior and superior meetings in England that many Friends there were not easy in the payment of those taxes but did it on account of the difficulty which attended the separation from other taxes for a civil use."

As it is an awful season wherein the judgements of God are sent forth to humble and bring us into righteousness, it concerns every individual to know whether their proceedings are in that line which has a tendency to appease divine vengeance and not from a rebellious disposition against his holy will in the gratification of our own corrupt wills be instrumental in drawing down

---

16. Anne's memory was somewhat blurry. The first challenge to Quaker pacifism occurred after the outbreak of King William's War (1689–97), when Quaker legislators appropriated £760 for the colony's defense on the assurance that it "shall not be dipt in blood," but used to pay officers' salaries rather than to purchase arms and ammunition.

17. In Queen Anne's War (1701–13), Quaker politicians stretched pacifistic principles again when their colony's governor responded to the king's insistence that the assembly contribute to equipping military expeditions to Canada to be conducted by the New England colonies. Most Friends paid the war tax and a few noncompliers had property distrained. Brock, *Pacifism in the United States*, 97–111, 103 for quoted phrase; Davidson, *War Comes to Quaker Pennsylvania*.

18. With the onset of the Seven Years' War (1756–63), the payment of war taxes and the accumulation of wealth came sharply into focus again. Many Friends heeded the warnings of John Hunt and Anthony Benezet, who advocated a return to simplicity and pacifism. Marietta, *Reformation of American Quakerism*, 103–5; Brock, *Pacifism in the United States*, 133–58; Woolman, *Journal of the Life*.

19. Richardson, *Account of the Life of* [. . .] *John Richardson* [. . .].

yet heavier punishment. The deeply thoughtful generally unite in the belief that there is a great work on the wheel, and if we too ought to be in the foremost rank in carrying it forward according to our high profession should through willfulness or luke-warmness omit our indispensable duty therein, no doubt but a double portion of tribulation will be justly allotted to us. Yea in vain may we petition heaven or sue to man for address of grievances in that state, for our answer must not be deafness and renewed scourges for disobedience.

It is very evident that we are not only called to rebuild the worst places of the walls of our Zion to repair the desolate state of religion amongst us through a long weakening state of ease and indifference but also to build up a person's house which shall be more glorious than the former in that the testimony of pure righteousness will be advanced to a degree superior to what it has hitherto to have been. May more therefore be so far fighters against God and his sacred purposes and their own great enemies in incurring his displeasure as to check or retard this work by shrinking from the cross and hugging former indulgences when they are called for at our hands by him who was to be humored with the first fruits of all our increase; for so, "is it time, O ye, to dwell in your circled houses and this house lie waste."[20]

EFP, box 1.

---

20. Haggai 1:4. Anne cites the prophet's reprimand of the Jews for adorning their own homes and neglecting God's Temple at Jerusalem.

Chapter 8

ANTISLAVERY

This epistle, with its admonition on the use of indigo, was the first of its kind in the United States and a forerunner of the movement to boycott products brought to market through the toil and suffering of enslaved Africans. Quaker reformers such as Benjamin Lay, John Woolman, Anthony Benezet, and Warner Mifflin avoided dyed cloth, wearing only white or drab clothing; their objection, insofar as they expressed it publicly, was not to indigo per se but to wearing flashy, ostentatious displays of color.

TO FRIENDS OF THE MONTHLY MEETING OF NEW GARDEN

Philadelphia 1st day of the mo. 1791[1]

Dear Friends,[2]

Having past [passed] thro[ugh] the families of your Monthly Meetings to a good degree of satisfaction, or relief to our minds,[3] nevertheless when we

---

1. Dated the first day of an unspecified month in 1791, this letter of advice was written after Anne Mifflin and Philena Lay spent several weeks visiting families of the Nottingham and New Garden monthly meetings in August and September 1791. Philena and likely Anne as well attended the PYM on September 27 as a representative from SQM. This suggests the epistle was written on October 1, 1791, but endorsement by the ministers and elders is uncertain. Miscellaneous Manuscript Collection, FHLSC.

2. On June 11, 1791, Anne and Philena asked the Murderkill Women's Meeting for permission to visit members of the monthly meetings in Nottingham and New Garden in Chester County, Pennsylvania. The men's meeting endorsed this on July 9, 1791. MMMWM (1788–1845). On August 6, 1791, the New Garden Monthly Meeting also endorsed these visitations. NGMMM (1790–1802).

3. Anne and Philena reported to the New Garden Monthly Meeting on October 5, 1791, upon completion of their visitations, to "nearly all the families of Friends . . . to a

take retrospective view of what appears to us may be the too general state of things among you, we do not feel quite clear without endeavoring to hint a little thereat. And the like prospect we doubt not many of you have at times and that it hath caused some to go mourning in their way, crying "Alas for us." Weeping as between the porch and the altar saying "spare thy people O Lord and give not thine heritage to reproach."[4] New Garden has appeared like to what is mentioned in Isaiah, Ch. 5, a vineyard in a very fruitful hill, for whom the most High hath done great things. "He fenced it and gathered out the stones thereof and built a tower in the middle of it, and also made a winepress therein."[5] And looked for fruits according to favors bestowed. But oh! Friends is there not cause for the complaint that was then uttered "When I looked that it should bring forth grapes, it brought forth wild grapes. And now, oh inhabitants of Jerusalem, and ye men of Judah judge between me and my vineyard: What could I have done to my vineyards that I have not done in it?"[6] Read the passage, beloved Friends, and compare it with your own experience of the Lord's dealings with you and his favors to those of your parts to those above many others. Look whether the seed of life is not oppressed even as a cart under sheaves.

Oh Friends, come down into sympathy with the seed; get as into the low valleys where the stocks will be watered. It was on the high mountains that the beauty of Israel was slain, where Saul fell and was slain as though he had not been anointed. "Ye mountains of Gilboa, let there be no dew neither let there be rain upon you"[7] was expressed by one lamenting the loss at that time sustained.

And dear Friends may the lessons of divine instruction and the prospects of religious duty, which have been unfolded to many in the hours of deep humiliation and adversity, as in the valley of vision never to be bartered away for trifles nor lightly esteemed and forgot in a time when greater prosperity might lead into improper indulgence and vanity unless the holy watch is kept to. For these prospects and duties being the Lord's previous testimonies given

---

good degree to the peace and satisfaction of their own minds and by the sentiments of many friends expressed, it appears to have had a uniting tendency." NGMMM (1790–1802).

4. Joel 2:17.

5. This passage compares the Israelites to a vineyard yielding sour grapes unfit for consumption.

6. Isaiah 5:4. Anne and Philena use Isaiah's metaphor to warn New Garden Friends that though their recovery after the war brought prosperity, they must avoid the "lavish and unnecessary use of indigo as a dye" produced by the labor and suffering of slaves.

7. Samuel 1:21.

to his called and chosen ones to bear, as proof of their fidelity and obedience to him when they are trifled with and trampled on, he may "laugh at our calamity and mock when our fear cometh"[8] for those who obey and "honor him he will honor but those who despise him and his requirings concerning them shall be lightly esteemed."[9]

It is well known that many in your parts as well as some others have been thus favored in clear prospects and tender scruples concerning matters relative to the law and the testimony, and sorrowful would it be if there should appear even a more conspicuous declension there than in some other parts.

One matter, which though it may seem small to some, yet as the lives of a number of our fellow creatures are concerned in it, the mention thereof may prove relieving to our minds, which is the lavish and unnecessary use of indigo as a dye[10] when there are so many things produced here that may be had in a more innocent channel than that. It may be a cross to some who have practiced it to give it up;[11] yet seeing truth leads out of contributing towards the taking of men's lives; this also we believe has a share therein as well as that of keeping them in bondage and misery whilst life is afforded; for the poisonous exhalations issuing from it whilst manufacturing by accounts bring hundreds and thousands of poor slaves to an untimely end.[12]

---

8. Proverbs 1:26.

9. Samuel 2:30.

10. We know of no earlier denouncement of indigo dyed apparel, bed linens, and the like because of the lethal effect this production had on enslaved workers. In what would later be the Free Produce Movement, sugar was the focus of boycotts of products made by slaves. The cultivation of indigo, second to rice as a moneymaking crop in South Carolina, spurred increased importation of enslaved Africans and enriched many planters. The boom in indigo production in South Carolina and Georgia was brief, peaking in the early 1790s. Nash, "South Carolina Indigo"; Edelson, *Plantation Enterprise in Colonial South Carolina*, 110–13, 122–23, 159–61, 213–14; Feeser, *Red, White, and Black Make Blue*, 159–66.

11. At what point New Garden Friends, or Friends generally, began wearing indigo-dyed garments is an unexplored topic. The first mention we found of it is noted before the revolution when wealthy Philadelphia Friends such as Sarah Logan Norris and Rachel Budd Collins wore deep blue gowns. Gummere, *Quaker*, 158, 160. Such a fashion, apparently rare, was in disfavor by mid-eighteenth century during the "Quaker reformation." This effort to cleanse Quaker society of its growing materialism and conspicuous display of wealth was built into the PYM *Rules of Discipline*, which warned against "all superfluity in furniture of house and apparel whatsoever." Quoted in Caton, "Aesthetics of Absence," 248–49.

12. In stifling heat and humidity and amid swarming flies, slaves working with indigo inhaled toxic, deadly fumes and were in constant danger of being burned. A soldier in Washington's Continental Army, witnessing the toil of plantation indigo workers, reported

And dear young people, of whom there are a large number in your parts, some of you have felt very near to us we desire your encouragement in the way of well-doings. Look not back at the conduct of others nor start aside because of the seeming difficulty of the way; but be concerned to look unto the Lord with all your hearts and lean not unto your own understandings. And some of you may if faithful become instruments of use in the Lord's hands. We wish for the preservation of those who are engaged in something of a scholastic institution lest they should be led aside, blinded and betrayed by that wisdom which puffeth up and is earthly and sensual, and we believe the care and attention of solid friends will be helpful to preserve them out of the snare and point out clearly to their understandings the beauty and excellency of that wisdom which cometh from above.

With the salutation of much love and affection which we now as heretofore have felt towards you, we remain your friends,[13]

Philena Lay
Anne Mifflin

Miscellaneous Manuscript Collection, FHLSC.

This address presented by Mary Berry and Anne Mifflin was prompted by the rapid rise of the postrevolutionary internal slave trade as cotton cultivation intensified in the Lower South. Alarmed at how the trade wrenched husband from wife and parents from children, Friends began petitioning state legislatures to halt this domestic slave traffic. Maryland Friends, operating through the SQM and the BYM, had been petitioning Maryland's legislature since 1787, even advancing a bill for the gradual abolition of slavery in the state. These efforts were renewed in 1790, then languished, and were not revived for several decades.

---

that "such is the effect of the indigo on the lungs of the laborers that they never live over seven years." Roberts, *Narrative of James Roberts*, 28. For more on the life-sapping indigo production regimen, see Sharrer, "Indigo Bonanza in South Carolina"; Morgan, *Counterpoint*, 159–64; Feeser, *Red, White, and Black Make Blue*; and Holmes, "Indigo in Colonial Louisiana."

13. Whether Anne and Philena's epistle had any effect is an open question; but of note, the New Garden Monthly Meeting ordered copies of "the Epistle" printed on December 3, 1791, for distribution among preparative meetings. NGMMWM (1785–1804).

TO THE GENERAL ASSEMBLY OF MARYLAND, NOW SITTING FROM MARY BERRY AND ANNE MIFFLIN

Early December 1795

From present impressions of religious duty, and being part of a Committee[14] to whom was referred by our sisters on the Eastern Shore of Maryland &c. the consideration of the late affecting subject, which hath claimed the attention of our brethren in their Memorial,[15] we beg leave, earnestly to solicit your attention to the subject matter therein contained so that as men endowed with the upright principles of Christianity and the tender sensations of benevolence, you may become honorably instrumental in promoting that work of righteousness and equity in the Earth, which we believe it is the divine purpose to accomplish.

Often have our feelings of sympathy and deep commiseration been awakened, in hearing of and beholding the sufferings of our own sex of the African race[16]—the enfeebled mother, through oppressive toil, and helpless child, torn from each other's embraces, with other separations of the nearest connections in life, have, we apprehend with their uplifted cries, pierced the very Court of

---

14. For a capsule treatment of Mary Berry, see chapter 3. Anne and Mary, authorized to travel to Annapolis, were appointed to the SQM in November 1795. MMMMM (1788–1830), November 12, 1795; MMMMM (1770–1805), December 11, 1794; SQM Men's Minutes (1759–1822), November 12, November 23, 1795.

15. The memorial referred to here was from the SQM, titled "To the General Assembly of the State of Maryland, November 1795," See Nash and McDowell, *Writings of Warner Mifflin*, 472–73. The manuscript copy has not been found but has been transcribed from "Relics of the Past." Two earlier drafts are in PYM, Meeting for Sufferings, Miscellaneous Manuscripts, 1794, QCHC. After a yearlong effort, the SQM secured approval of the memorial from the Philadelphia Meeting for Sufferings, which directed the drafting committee to present the petition to the Maryland legislature. Warner Mifflin, probably the author of the male memorial, accompanied his wife and Mary Berry to Annapolis, where both memorials were read by the clerk of the legislature on December 5. For this lengthy process of procuring the approval of the Meeting for Sufferings, see Warner Mifflin, Daniel Mifflin, and Jonathan Hunn to Henry Drinker and Thomas Morris, November 24, 1794, in Nash and McDowell, *Writings of Warner Mifflin*, 463–64, which describes their effort to move the memorial through the chain of Quaker committees.

16. Anne and Mary had many opportunities to hear directly from black Marylanders. Reaching Annapolis in late November, before the legislative session, their group "had two public meetings in the State House and one in the Methodist meeting house appointed principally for the blacks." Warner Mifflin to Henry Drinker, December 30, 1795, in Nash and McDowell, *Writings of Warner Mifflin*, 474–76. Holding a public meeting in the Maryland statehouse to discuss the abolition of slavery and the internal slave trade was highly unusual but certainly encouraging to the Friends' delegations.

Heaven; from whence a decree may issue from him who ever remains to be the refuge for the oppressed, that retribution for these things shall be made.[17] Therefore we implore your denouncing a close to that traffic, which will one day or other, with an unshaken confidence be considered as a shame to humanity, or an indelible blot in the annals of human history, when that degree of Christian fortitude is attained as to reject with religious, as well as national firmness, the unsatisfactory gains issuing from so corrupt a spring.

We hope the affecting occasion, may sufficiently apologize for the female character, thus approaching your presence[18]—for it is under a solemn sense of the necessity of our generally fearing and obeying the God of Heaven and the whole Earth, so that we may bow in mercy, and not awaken the extension of his chastising judgements that we are impressed with the necessity of discharging our religious duties in their relative capacities—and with all due respect to the dignity and importance of your station and breathing to the God and Father of all our Spirits, that He may incline your hearts to the performance of his blessed Will, do we subscribe ourselves,

Your friends,
Mary Berry
Ann Mifflin

Copy of an address by Mary Berry and Ann Mifflin, to the legislature of Maryland, persuading them to a speedy abolition of the inhuman commerce in slaves, C-P-W, box 9, fol. 26.[19] The folder at HSP is marked 1800 but the document is from 1795.

17. The separation of slave families is a major theme in the literature on the internal slave trade. See, for example, Pargas, *Slavery and Forced Migration*; Deyle, *Carry Me Back*; and Gudmestad, *Troublesome Commerce*.

18. As implied, Anne and Mary knew by entering the public arena they violated rules prohibiting such bold female intervention. Almost certainly they witnessed from the gallery the reading of their memorial by the clerk of the House of Delegates. We are indebted to Jennifer Abbott at the Maryland State Archives for information regarding women's admittance to witness legislative sessions from the gallery. It is historically significant and important to point out that Anne and Mary were the first women on either side of the Atlantic to have petitioned a legislative body on the subject of slavery. Historians have accorded that honor to Angelina Grimke, who forty-three years later delivered before the Massachusetts legislature an impassioned antislavery address. Even in Angelina's era, women on the public stage at antislavery meetings had to endure the "sneers of the heartless multitude" and were charged with "infractions of the laws of female delicacy and propriety." Quoted in Sinha, *Slave's Cause*, 279.

19. We are indebted to Nicholas P. Wood, who determined that the copy is in the hand of John Parrish, Warner Mifflin's kinsman and close friend. Wood is the first to write about the petition; see Wood, "Considerations of Humanity and Expediency," 283.

Chapter 9

OUR NATIVE BRETHREN

Approaching fifty years of age, Anne made two onerous trips northward to reservations where a remnant of indigenous peoples had survived the long revolutionary war. This undertaking marks Anne as one of the most reform-minded women of her generation. In this report, she expressed great respect for tribal peoples and gave detailed description of their origins, customs, behavior, and struggle for survival.

[August–September 1802]

Relation of a Visit Made to the Indians in 1802 by H[annah] Kirkbride and A[nne] Mifflin with Their Friends in the Course of Their Journey to Upper Canada with Some Observations on Their Origins

Our first visit was at Brothertown within the Oneida reservation, a settlement formed of the scattered fragments of seven different Nations invited thither by the country of the Oneidas in their reduced circumstances arising in a great measure from their being induced for trifling considerations to part with their possessions to the Whites.

A great example [of] this, to our color which if not issuing from a measure of the like brotherly love which prevailed in the Apostle days when all things were held in common we may at least consider it as a trait of their descent from the Israelites, in whose law they were directed to cherish their brethren who had waxen poor amongst and fallen into decay.[1]

---

1. Anne refers here to the first-century CE church when members lived communally as described in Acts of the Apostles 2:44–45 and 4:32. Anne shared the widely held belief

They have embraced the Christian faith and are chiefly of the Baptist profession.² No interpreter was necessary in our meeting here as they understood English. They have a decent meeting house in which a school was kept by a valued Friend deeply interested in their welfare who has since relinquished his post from occurring difficulties.³

They are chiefly governed by five of their brethren called Peace Makers chosen to settle all cases of difficulty: some of whom we saw whose countenances were marked with a degree of wisdom and solidity. A lesson to the Whites who judge for reward and from exorbitant salaries rolling in splendor often prove oppressors instead of benefactors to the people. Although some are careless and indolent yet from the appearances of their little farms, others are industrious and advancing toward the condition of sober white inhabitants.⁴

Our next visit was at Stockbridge, a people from a place of that name in New England, in like manner invited here by the Oneidas and a valuable portion of land assigned them.⁵ In the evening their chiefs waited on us with an interpreter and one of them delivered the following speech:

---

that Native Americans were direct descendants of the Israelites, a so-called Lost Tribe of Israel.

2. Anne was mistaken that the Brothertowns had accepted the Baptist faith. Eleazar Wheelock (Congregational), Samson Occum (Presbyterian), and Samuel Kirkland (Presbyterian) were the main missionaries to them before the war. By 1802, John Sergeant Jr. (1747–1824), commissioned by the Society for the Propagation of Christian Knowledge (Anglican), was their primary minister. At age nineteen, John Jr., a Princeton-trained teacher fluent in Mohican, had continued his father's work as missionary and teacher to the Stockbridge community, but he was not an ordained minister. For a biographical essay, see Harrison, *Princetonians*.

3. The PYM IC in 1796 sent Henry Simmons to serve as a schoolteacher on the Oneida Reservation. Swatzler, *Friend Among the Senecas*, 22.

4. Five years before, New York Quakers Edmund Prior and Thomas Eddy reported to John Jay that the Brothertowns "made some improvement in agriculture, industry and sobriety" as evidenced by their "good cattle, cows, and working oxen" and their "good disposition . . . to improve their moral conduct and agricultural knowledge." Quoted in Silverman, *Red Brethren*, 124.

5. The Stockbridge numbered some four hundred and, like the Brothertown, were served by missionaries and teachers. In 1796, visiting Massachusetts ministers reported that "two-thirds of the men and nine-tenths of the women are industrious. Agriculture and the breeding of cattle and swine are their chief employment by which they procure a sufficiency of food; and by selling a part of their produce they are able to purchase their clothing." Quoted in ibid., 123–24. The next year, two visiting New York Quakers reported to the IC in Philadelphia that the Stockbridge and Brothertown people had no need of aid or instruction from the Friends. Ibid., 124.

Brothers, we rejoice to see you come among us. We have cleared the path for you and opened doors to receive you. Thank the Good Spirit who hath put it in your hearts to come and see us, and preserved you so long a wilderness way. We bid you welcome and so make a plain path for you to pass. We clear your throats and loose your tongues that you may deliver clearly and distinctly those things ye have to say to us. What ye feel from your hearts for the good of our souls and our well-being here. The path is open between us: we wish it may continue so: and hope the Good Spirit may often put it into the hearts of Friends to come and visit us and speak good things to us.[6]

Their meeting house is a commodious building where enlargement was given beyond expectation; and way opening at the close to impart some counsel on cleanliness and the renunciation of spirituous liquors.[7] Their minister, a missionary who resides near (whose salary is derived from a part of their income due from the government for the sale of land)[8] expressed to us his satisfaction therewith desiring Friends would embrace every opportunity of enforcing such advice and observing that we had influence with them but they [he?] had not.

An aged chief whom we had not before seen sought us out and inquired after several Friends who had formerly visited them;[9] [he] expressed a feeling and desire once more to see them, adding, "I have heard this day, which makes me feel good here" laying his hand significantly on his breast. We were afterward informed they complained of being weary of their stationed minister

---

6. In *Seneca Possessed*, Dennis describes how Natives used ceremonial cleansing rites to express grief for those who suffered loss. Merrell in *Into the American Woods* (20–22) explains Native visualization of the power of the woods and how weary travelers were affected. Host natives prescribed rituals to cleanse visitors' eyes, ears, and throats in order to communicate clearly.

7. Anne addressed the importance of sobriety for Native Americans and supported their efforts to abstain from alcohol, which by 1802 was a serious problem for many tribes. For a historical, ethnographic, and cross-cultural analysis of drinking among Native Americans, see Edgerton and MacAndrew, *Drunken Comportment*.

8. Almost certainly John Sergeant Jr., who in June 1803 wrote to President Jefferson requesting receipt of the annual overdue payment of $354 for "the general public benefit of the tribe." Sergeant to Jefferson, June 25, 1803, Thomas Jefferson Papers, LC, also available on Founders Online, https://founders.archives.gov.

9. We have not identified the "aged chief." Friends who had "formerly visited" were probably Edmund Prior and Thomas Eddy, New York Quakers who visited the Brothertown people in 1796 and 1797. Silverman, *Red Brethren*, 124, 247nn79–80.

and that his discourse was the same thing over again feeling to them I suppose too much in the oldness of the letter.[10]

Our visit to the Oneidas[11] was frustrated by a traveling missionary having possession of their meeting house before our arrival who proposed a junction; but from its being in the afternoon it would probably have been too late for us to clear our minds and reach the nearest inn, after he had [illegible] -sed through his accustomed rites in worship and we deferred it until our return. That nation speaks the most beautiful language I ever heard uttered.[12] At Tonwata village we found Blue Skie, their respectable chief,[13] and several others were from home; and while the rest were summoning to collect in the Council House, we visited the wife of Owenessee, their speaker, who lay ill; several female Indians coming in divine love and power overspreading and commanding stillness we had a precious little opportunity with them and words were given I believe suited to their conditions. [A] French Canadian being our interpreter who resides there and keeps a small inn.[14] It was scarcely over before

10. The traveling minister likely refers again to John Sergeant Jr.

11. Anne and Hannah traveled from the Brothertown and Stockbridge settlements westward to Oriske and Kanonalohale, the main Oneida villages. Numbering about six hundred, the Oneidas divided into two factions, designated by historians as "Pagan" and "Christian." The Pagans who dwelled at Oriske, just east of Kanonalohale, were most receptive to Friends, while a greater number at Kanonalohale followed Kirkland, who preached strict observance of Christian doctrine. For the bitter relations between the two groups, see Silverman, *Red Brethren*, 155–56; Campisi, "Oneida Treaty Period," 60; and Tiro, *People of the Standing Stone*, 72–76. Tiro emphasizes the fluidity of religious beliefs and allegiances, arguing that for both factions "eclecticism and syncretism prevailed" (72). Three years after Anne and Hannah completed their visit, the Christian and Pagan factions split, with Pagans receiving the land east of Oneida Creek. Anne's account does not specify if she visited both, but it seems reasonable she would have spent time at Oriske, the center of the Quaker Oneida experiment.

12. Characteristic of the Seneca language is soft pronunciation, polysyllabic words, and linguistic rhythm, all rendering a harmonious sound. Various videos on YouTube demonstrate a vocal pronunciation of the Seneca language.

13. Before reaching the native village, on the Tonawanda Seneca reservation, Anne and Hannah traveled 148 miles farther from the Oneida settlements to the westernmost limits of New York in Niagara County. The reservation was a refuge for Seneca prophet Handsome Lake (half brother of Chief Cornplanter), who retired to Tonawanda in autumn of 1808 and died there in 1815. Two months before Anne and Hannah's visit, Blue Sky, a Seneca chief at Tonawata village, traveled to Washington, DC, with Cornplanter and Handsome Lake to treat with President Jefferson. For an account of the trip, see Wallace, *Death and Rebirth*, 266–70. In the War of 1812, Blue Sky emerged as the heroic chief protecting what remained of Seneca land. Hauptman, *Tonawanda Senecas' Heroic Battle Against Removal*.

14. The French innkeeper/interpreter was possibly Pierre Penet, identified by Tiro as a French trader with his eye on Oneida land. Tiro, *People of the Standing Stone*, 78, 80–82.

word came that the Indians were assembled in their Council House whom we found smoking their long pipes, a token of welcome and friendship.

After a little season of silence and waiting, H. K. [Hannah Kirkbride] arose and spoke on the nature and effects of internal religion, the teachings of Christ who is light and life to the soul, etc. and I had to enlarge on some historical points: how in the beginning God created the heaven and the earth and said let there be light and there was light, etc. That in the process of time he chose a people to shew forth his praise to whom he appointed Moses as a leader; who was inspired with a knowledge of things past, so as to write on the formation of the beautiful creation we inhabit; as well as to look into future events as the Lord's prophet which has been since evinced in the fulfillment of many things by him pointed out.[15] But that people proving disobedient to the laws laid down under the Divine direction by Moses, he forewarned them that should such rebellious disposition prevail they should be cast off from peculiar favor and become a scattered nation; which has actually taken place, and I believed they were some of the offspring of that people that Divine Mercy was now again calling to them to enlist under a new and pure dispensation which Moses had testified should come to pass saying, "a prophet shall the Lord your God raise up unto you"; that this was no other than Christ, the son and sent of God who since appeared with Divine power and instruction as the Redeemer of mankind. For it was as easy for that power which in the beginning said, "Let there be light and there was light," to say, "Let a son be miraculously born unto me," as pointed out in the Scriptures and it should be done. He came a light into the world, and was an example for mankind to follow; who were now required to walk in his footsteps and obey his precepts which would lead out of all strife, bloodshed and ill will; into love, harmony and true peace, universally, etc. and that the gospel message was now sent unto them and they were called to embrace these divine doctrines and imitate the holy example of Christ, our blessed leader as a means of their present happiness and soul's eternal peace, advising them to seek an acquaintance with the Scriptures.

Abraham Lapham,[16] who is much interested in the natives' good who accompanied us thus far from Farmington, spoke a few sentences with trembling; and before we separated a young counsellor of rising worth delivered

---

15. Tradition assigns Moses authorship of the first five books of the Old Testament.

16. Abraham Lapham (1754–1836), a farmer in Ontario County, New York, and leader in the New York Monthly Meeting, where he served on the Indian Affairs Committee. Farmington is located in the northern portion of Ontario County, New York.

the following speech: "We give you many thanks for this day's opportunity; we are sorry our chiefs and so many of our nation are absent. We are glad to see you come among us; yet they are not the people to instruct us—they teach us with kindness. We have been very wicked and ignorant and had nobody to instruct us. We never heard the ways of the Good Spirit and the Scriptures so opened to us before. We are desirous to learn the ways of the Good Spirit, and to be instructed in the Scriptures.[17] We have renounced the use of strong drink and are determined to maintain our resolution of not taking anymore. It was hard at first yet our children will not know the difficulty as we are resolved not to return to it again, and to try to learn to do better. We have heard that Friends are a sensible people and understand the Scriptures and we need a minister among us and a young man to teach our children and give you a thousand thanks for your visit to us and other nations of Indians." In reply to which they were told, "Consistent with our principle, we could not appoint a minister to come among them; but if it appeared to be the duty of any they would probably be encouraged, and if they endeavored to mind the dictates of the Good Spirit in their hearts it might be a means of some being influenced to visit them. As to a schoolmaster, if any believed it to be their place to come they would likely also be encouraged."[18] I could not but wish that the Friends provided for the benefit of the Natives would enable and induce friends to do something for this settlement and encourage that spirit of reformation and improvement so laudably begun.[19]

On our arrival at the outlet of Lake Erie and near Buffalo, a large Indian village,[20] we beheld what further confirmed my former opinion that they are of the stock of Abraham, near forty of them were returning from hunting, Indian file fashion following one another in a line (single file) carrying seven deer and other game to celebrate their annual festival of thanksgiving for a

---

17. Given the three-and-a-half-year Quaker presence on the Oneida reservation, the young Oneida councilor's disingenuousness is hard to explain; however, it seems apparent he belonged to the "Pagan" faction in Oriske.

18. Quaker teacher Henry Simmons (1768–1807) had taught at the Oneida reservation between 1796 and 1799. PYM IC (1791–1802), March 17, 1797, quoted in Swatzler, *Friend Among the Senecas*, 22.

19. "By so laudably begun" Anne refers to the 1796–99 demonstration farm established at Oriske terminated almost two years before her arrival.

20. Buffalo, New York, is located at the juncture of Lake Erie and the Niagara River. They had traveled twelve miles from New Stockbridge to the Oneida reservation, then 148 miles to Tonawata village, on to Farmington for sixty miles, and then another eighty or so miles to Buffalo on Lake Erie—a journey comprising approximately three hundred miles on horseback trekking along overgrown and muddy roads.

beautiful harvest. Doubtless a relic of the Jewish Feast of Tabernacles instituted for like purpose. And as that began with a solemn convocation, so in their passing along, they called to us to allow where we stopped to attend the next day and have a meeting with them at the opening of it.[21]

We being indisposed, it would have afforded a suitable opportunity for us to have seen many collected together and might have been very relieving to my mind from secret sensations of duty to see all the natives in that way which situation and circumstance would admit of. But some of our men Friends not being resigned to go three or four miles out of the way for that purpose, particularly our guide, we did not urge the matter: yet may acknowledge being disappointed of an interview with them, both going and returning produced in the right season inexpressible sensations of distress. I do believe that if faithfulness is yielded to the heavenly guide the number will be enlarged of those who have to visit the inhabitants of the wilderness.

An Indian in this neighborhood having in liquor slain a white man, for being he believed one of the seducers of some of their women, an offence which above all others raises the indignation of the natives;[22] the minds of the people were in a great ferment and for a time it bore the gloomy appearance of an impending Indian war; a fit season to urge the necessity of their abstinence from spirituous liquors.[23] But on that point I relieved my mind by a letter to one of their brethren engaged as a school instructor whom we met with on a visit to Tuscarora village, the next Indian settlement we were at. Which being accomplished under some discouragements the master was pleased to reward for the exertion by more abundant aid in testimony and supplication.

At the close, a well looking young man, the Chief of Warriors with eyes uplifted, addressed us as follows: "Brothers, the Quakers and sisters also, we bid you welcome to this place and we are glad you have had us in remembrance and thank the Good Spirit who hath put it in your hearts to visit us. Brothers, we are sorry our chief sachems are absent but although none but the war chief are present, we bid you welcome and are glad to hear the word spoken. We receive the council of our brethren and also of our sister; we shall always

---

21. The Jewish Feast of the Tabernacles, a thanksgiving commemoration of the sojourn forty years in the wilderness described in several places in scripture (e.g., 1 Kings 8:2).

22. This incident is noted in Tiro, *People of the Standing Stone*, 103.

23. On crime and drunkenness, see Mancall, *Deadly Medicine*. In *Seneca Possessed* (47–48), Dennis examines tragic episodes connected with alcohol and the degeneracy in the Seneca camps in the postrevolutionary period, as well as Handsome Lake's own struggle with drinking and his conversion to abstinence.

remember what she said brothers. We shall be glad to be kept in remembrance by Friends and always pleased to receive their visit.[24] We may inform you we drink no more rum in this place and are determined not to admit of it again. We have received the Gospel (pointing to his forehead which we thought implied water baptism) and are desirous of having our children taught to read having it in view to procure a schoolmaster that they may be instructed in the good book (the Bible) [that] you have recommended." We expressed our satisfaction with their disuse of spirituous liquors and [with a] view to acquire knowledge of reading and desiring [of] their religious perseverance therein. A travelling missionary who understood the intention of our visit had followed us from Queenstown and during the meeting surveyed us with rather a jealous suspicious countenance.[25] Before their speech he took out some of the Indians, and we believe endeavored to infuse something into their minds, to say to us, they did not relish as they looked ruffled on their return.[26] Perhaps it was we need not visit them, they had already rec'd [received] the Gospel message in his [this?] way; but their speech and behavior bore a very different aspect.

The day following, as we rode from Niagara Town, we met a respectable looking Indian and his wife from Tuscarora who shook hands very affectionately with us and with a pleasant countenance nodding his head at me said, "It is good to hear you."[27] I thought there was encouragement in the simplicity of the expression in hopes the feeling part was touched and that they were open to receive the Gospel message notwithstanding any contacting influence even from [a] female, the man friend who had joined us [previously it] appeared was not present.

24. Though antagonistic toward Friends, Samuel Kirkland, Presbyterian minister to the Oneidas, described the Friends contingent's departure at the end of 1799 as "like the attendance of a funeral." Pilkington, *Journals of Samuel Kirkland*, 332.

25. Queenstown, located three miles north of Niagara Falls, in Ontario, Canada. This region was settled in the 1780s by Loyalist refugees of the Revolutionary War. See Moore, *Loyalists*.

26. Anne and Hannah witnessed what Dennis in *Seneca Possessed* (56–57) calls "an interdenominational strife of a bitterness scarcely to be paralleled" when ministers of various sects competed for converts in the early nineteenth century.

27. Situated adjacent to the famous Niagara Falls, Niagara was officially founded in 1812 in the southwest corner of Niagara County, New York. The Tuscaroras, a tribe of the Iroquois Confederacy, had migrated to North Carolina. After the Tuscarora War (1711–1713), a lethal conflict with English colonists, native survivors resettled in Pennsylvania and New York. Because their common ancestry and language aligned with the Iroquois, the Tuscarora became the Sixth Nation of the Iroquois in 1722.

On our return from Canada [we] were informed a person had inquired why so many Quakers had gone thither? Another replied, "They are the Quaker missionaries who ride the circuit once a year," which renewed my reflection on the extensions of Friends care in the civilization of the natives and thought as other societies expend large sums in sending forth missionaries in lieu of these expenditures,[28] the faithfulness and liberality of our Society [of Friends] towards the outward improvement of the Indians may prove an acceptable substitute, it may render them more comfortable and help to prepare the way for the reception of the Gospel truths: and both temporal and spiritual improvement may progress together as Divine influence engageth obedient minds in their respective lines of service.

At Scipio near Lake Cayuga [we] collected the newly settled members of our Society and held a meeting,[29] where we have the satisfaction to hear they continue to hold them ever since being near forty in number, minors included. The evident loss to remote settlers, not being organized into regular religious society and the wilderness too often contracted by the youth when thus circumstanced as well as the more savage barbarity of manners too frequently apparent in the frontier inhabitants when dependent on a hunting life will readily account for degeneracy of the natives, after such a length of years and loss of those arts they once possessed from traces yet remaining in the wilds of America and the destructive effect on all improvement of repeated wars among themselves being also considered.

In this neighborhood was the evident remains of an old pothouse from a quantity of broken fragments of potters' ware since chiefly carried off by travelers piece by piece as curiosities. And not many miles distant are the ruins of an ancient fortification near four miles square with a strong wall on part of it: within it was found the rusty remains of a smith's anvil, hammer and pipe

---

28. Anne was apparently unaware that the Indian Committee expended more than £2,000 in building and supporting the demonstration farm at Oriske. See Tiro, "We Wish to Do You Good," 371.

29. A town near in Cayuga County, New York, Scipio was part of a two-million-acre tract reserved for revolutionary soldiers. White settlement began around 1790 when the federal government awarded land to the veterans, but out of dire necessity some indigent veterans sold their government-issued land warrants to land speculators. See Cayuga County NYGenWeb Project, http://www.cayugagenealogy.org. Scipio Meeting House was built in 1810, and other Friends meetings sprang up in the area.

of a bellows; and trees grown therein four feet in diameter which shows its ancient date.[30]

From the miserable effects of wars which are often excited by a spirit of avarice, and from the frequent disputes between offspring in the division of property, is probably the cause why the Indians have adopted their present custom of burying with the dead the most valuable articles they possess (an opinion sanctioned by their own declarations).[31] This practice seems to have been adopted before they had wholly lost the use of letters from what appeared in a cave or sepulcher in this neighborhood, discovered by a hunter in 1801 who observing an arch, on the top of which grew a tree above, two feet in diameter showing its antiquity: he [the hunter] having procured and opened it at the side, from whence an intolerable stench for a time issued. They discovered the skeletons of eight persons, placed in a sitting posture with their feet meeting each other.[32] Their hands had fallen between their knees and the arm bones remaining in the shoulder sockets and elbows resting on the ground, kept the back bones erect leaning against the sides of the cave: from the size of the bones, there were four men on one side, and four women on the other, with bracelets on their arms and other trinkets. There were scissors of a curious workmanship discovered in those most preserved from the damp and rust by a very nice kind of fire: axes on the French construction and inscriptions on stones they could not understand. The bones crumbled to dust on the entrance of the air and from the weight of the tree on the top and the side walls being taken away it soon caved in. I expressed a wish these inscriptions could be procured for the Philadelphia Museum, as subjects of investigation, and the Friend who informed me of these matters said he had thought of taking hands [helpers], felling the tree and digging to see what further could be procured.[33]

---

30. The ruins of a fortification near Scipio, New York, purported to be the site of a people known as the Allegans, or mound builders, who had occupied the area long before white settlement. See "From the French's Gazetteer of the State of New York, 1860," transcribed by Steve McKay and Pat McKay in July 1997, Cayuga County, https://www.cayugagenealogy.org/books/french/index.html.

31. The burial custom described in Richter, *Ordeal of the Longhouse*, 81–83.

32. An example of the body's seated position and preparation of the burial site is featured in ibid., 84, plate 12.

33. The Philadelphia or Peale Museum, one of the first successful national public museums, was founded by the artist, naturalist, and patriot Charles Willson Peale. Nash, *First City*, 136–40.

By the great road leading through the Oneida reservation[34] is the meeting house where we had an opportunity with that deluded people the Oneidas, almost ruined with the effects of strong drink.[35] We had some close labor with them on that point at which the men held down their heads and the women looked solid; also the necessity of cleanliness, and that Christians should pursue a life of industry, etc. referring them to the Divine witness in their hearts, which would lead into every regulation necessary in followers of the Lamb, etc. etc. They appear as the fallow ground which hath need to be ploughed for receiving the seed of the kingdom. Their sale of lands on the state road for the accommodation of taverns gives them ready access to spirituous liquors which keeps them poor and miserable, and brings them into this besotted state. This sale was opposed by some of more regular lives, who resided near Friends, once stationed there, for the instruction of the natives who foresaw the consequences.[36]

But the more corrupted majority represented them to the New York government as heathens because they did not embrace the forms of worship they were in and that prevailed. We saw how they elude the law made against the sale of distilled spirits to them. A White man came into the inn with an Indian, called for spirits, paid for it with the Indian's money, drank of it and handed it to him. Thus are "a people robbed and spoiled" by the evil example and mercenary ways of the Whites and too often I fear dispossessed of their native soil for the consideration through the prevalence of human policy both under the old government and since the revolution; and where shall we find an atonement for the frequent injuries done to that people by our Nation? Shall the sacrifice of bullocks from the wealthy with turtle doves and young pigeons from those of lesser ability either in personal pecuniary aid in the advancement of their civilization help to do away the guilt and prove an

---

34. Anne uses the metaphor for Christ as the Lamb of God.

35. In 1796, the State Road, or Great Genesee Road, began at Fort Schuyler and cut through Whitestown to Geneva, New York, via Auburn; in 1800, completion of the Cayuga Bridge opened the route to a flood of white settlers ready to seize what land belonging to the Oneidas and other native people remained.

36. Dennis in *Seneca Possessed* (248n48) explains, "Alcohol also functioned as a trade good that promoted Native American dependency and debt, cultivated consciously by white traders and officials to necessitate Indian payment in the form of land." Anne's reference to "some of more regular lives" is the Pagan faction.

acceptable atonement offering in the sight of divine justice?[37] I trust it may be available.

Their sense of the advantages too frequently taken of them was conspicuous some years past when Colonel Hawkins[38] was stationed southward by [the] government on their borders for their civilization. Dubious of the white peoples' integrity of intention, they [native peoples] at first slipped the proposals among the expressions observing, "When we see the countenance of a white man his color bespeaks deception and his tongue a lie."[39] And in consequence of a treaty made since the revolution by which the Seneca Tribe[40] considered themselves aggrieved, Cornplanter,[41] with a magnanimity becoming a chief, remonstrated it with the head of our nation and called for justice, part of which was in the following terms: "Your speeches are like the morning, when the sun riseth to a sick man whose pulse beats high in his head. He sees it but he is not eased. We have heard you are wise and you are strong and we come to see if you are just."[42] And to the credit of the respectable man in his line addressed [as] General George Washington: men in their power it may be mentioned were not deaf to the voice of entreaty; in that spirited application,

---

37. Anne notes for the ancient Jewish temple sacrifice, the wealthy could purchase a bull but the poor could barely afford a turtle dove as a burned offering.

38. Benjamin Hawkins (1754–1816), North Carolina planter, slaveholder, and Continental Congress delegate, was appointed by President Washington as general superintendent for Indian affairs (1796–1818) for the region south of the Ohio River. In 1786 and 1790, Hawkins, a skillful negotiator with fluency in French and multiple Indian languages, concluded treaties with the Creek and Choctaw nations. He promoted the "civilization plan," advocating the teaching of Euro-American agriculture and husbandry to ease Native Americans' adjustment. For more on Hawkins, see Florette, *Southern Indians and Benjamin Hawkins*.

39. Native Americans charged that white men's deception and lying was second nature, but we have not been able to trace this quotation.

40. The Second Treaty of Fort Stanwix signed in October 1784.

41. The exploits of Cornplanter, the Seneca War Chief (aka Johannes Abeel II), span a critical era of American history. His birth date is uncertain, but his death is recorded as 1836. Born of a Seneca mother and Dutch father, Cornplanter became a key participant in pre- and postwar events. See Abler, *Cornplanter*.

42. This is a modification of "The Speech of the Corn-planter, Half-town, and the Great Tree chiefs of the Seneca Nation to George Washington," December 1, 1790, available on Founders Online, https://founders.archives.gov. Washington's December 29, 1790, reply is also on Founders Online.

a large tract of country was retained or ceded to them, a part of which is their settlement on the Allegheny River.[43]

Logan-Fisher-Fox Papers, box 11, HSP.[44]

Account of a Visit to Some of the Seneca Nation on the Allegany River in the 10th Month 1803 by John Letchworth, Anne Mifflin, Mary Bell and Co. Mary Gilbert Being Weary With Her at Liberty to Visit the Indians, Who for Some Time Had Felt Inclined So to Do

On our arrival at Usqueshanadarqua, the first Indian town we stopped awhile at the general family resort of Joesa, our canoe man and his relatives as they thus dwell in families, like their forefathers the Israelites, the distinctions of tribe and families being more observed than among most nations.[45] His wife was a Chiefess[46] in whose countenance was a majestic gravity and solidity beyond most of her sex: and the softness of her voice and manner when she gave her husband a relation of the past illness of a beloved grandchild which she held on her lap, far exceeded the harmony of our language. Divine love overspread and commanding a degree of stillness, it would have been grateful to me to have embraced the opening as it was first day morning, but we had no interpreter; it was therefore judged best to defer an opportunity till our return.

---

43. Anne's mention of Cornplanter's meeting with Washington affirms that the Chief was well-known and admired among Philadelphians. For the full text of the Cornplanter land grant, see Wallace, *Indians in Pennsylvania*, 174.

44. This account appears to be written in several handwritings; pages 1–3 show finer penmanship: on page 6 the top three lines are crossed out; pages 4–7 more closely resemble Anne's handwriting; and page 8 again shows finer penmanship. The editors are unable to explain the differences.

45. The title of this piece refers to the domain of Senecas and some Cayugas in what is today Cattaraugus County, New York. The Allegany reservation encompassed forty-two square miles, bisected by the Allegheny River. John Letchworth (1759–1843), a craftsman, merchant, minister, and weighty member of the PMM, may have been on the mission to teach the Senecas carpentry. For Mary Gilbert, see chapter 4, note 31. Ceres is a township in McKean County, Pennsylvania. Mary and husband John Bell were members of the newly formed Catawissa meeting.

46. The Senecas' matrilineal system gave the eldest women of the living generation the status of matrons and the power to rule "to some degree politically" within the longhouse. They could nominate or remove chiefs and decide the fate of prisoners. Richter, *Ordeal of the Longhouse*, 20.

We then proceeded to the house of our brethren stationed in that reservation for the instruction of the Natives,[47] whose morning opportunity of religious retirement being over we sat with them in evening oblation.

On our proceeding the day following to Geneshato, the town of Cornplanter's residence[48] we passed a place where an image had once been erected to which they paid adoration; thus sliding at times into idolatry as [did] their predecessors. Cornplanter's son,[49] a sensible young man who has been educated by government disdaining the absurdity of it threatened its destruction, they dared his procedure supposing he would not presume to meddle with anything so sacred until at length filled with indignation at the folly of his people in pagan reverence to a senseless block of wood he cast it into the river. It was this young man, who in a shrewd manner queried with a person respecting their diverse modes of worship, "Whether there was any difference in offering worship to the Deity with the sound of bells and organs or the rattle of deer's hoofs and turtle shells as they did."

Being collected after sitting a little while in silence, Cornplanter arose and addressed us as follows

> We were informed last night of your intention to pay us a visit we are very glad the Good Spirit hath preserved you in health from any damage in the journey I believe it was the Good Spirit hath helped you on the way in coming so far to see us. We take your visit very kind; I speak on

---

47. The three Quakers living among the Senecas since 1798 were Halliday Jackson (1771–1834) and Joel Swayne (1775–1850), both farmers, and teacher Henry Simmons. Since the three had no missionary experience, the PYM IC designated committee member John Pierce and elder Joshua Sharpless to accompany them. Swatzler, *Friend Among the Senecas*, 22–23.

48. Geneshato, or Genesinguhta, the Seneca village on the Allegany reservation north of Jenuchshadago, which Anne mistakenly identified as Cornplanter's residence, though it probably was his temporary home in 1803. When Jackson, Swayne, and Simmons arrived May 17, 1798, they surveyed the area and chose Genesinguhta, a nearly abandoned site nine miles up from Cornplanter's village on which to build. Swatzler in *Friend Among the Senecas* (22–25) provides a full account of the model farm.

49. Cornplanter's oldest son Henry Abeel (1776–1848) served as interpreter for the Quaker missionaries in 1798. Swatzler, *Friend Among the Senecas*, 31. According to Wallace in *Death and Rebirth* (188, 285), by 1803 Henry, the only English-speaking Seneca, became an official interpreter. Henry was the individual Anne claimed had tossed the wooden idol into the river. Wallace explains that after Henry's schooling in Philadelphia, he openly opposed Seneca beliefs as superstition. Ibid., 293.

behalf of us all both men and women. We are much pleased to see you and you are at liberty to express whatever may be on your minds. [After clearing ourselves of such doctrine and counsel as presented, which terminated in a season of supplication, on our withdrawing they conferred together and we were invited to return when Cornplanter spoke as follows]:[50]

We are glad you are come among us. I believe it was the Good Spirit that moved you so to do and hath put it in your hearts what to say to us. It was under the direction of the Good Spirit you were appointed to come so far and see us and this was the day appointed for us to meet. Your visit is very acceptable and satisfactory, and we desire your friends in Philadelphia may be informed of it. This [is] the first time any women have come to see us and give us any instruction;[51] we take your visit very kind and hope your coming may be an encouragement for others. We thank you for the information concerning former and present time, what has been said agrees with what our prophet has told us; therefore it must be true. He has told us that we should live in peace and good will and that if we drank whiskey we should never go to heaven. I believe the Good Spirit never intended the grain which is given us to live on should be made into whiskey. The white people have been wrong as well as us in the making so much whiskey and in buying up lands of the Indians for a trifle to speculate on. Land was not made to speculate on for the gain of individuals but for the general good of all. The white people have taken so much of the waters to make whiskey is the reason the waters are now so much dried up.

This prophet is [half] brother to Cornplanter of much influence. Another mark of the Israelites who placed great dependence on the word of their prophets; although he may possess some mixture of error and superstition in his ideas. Yet is, I believe, a spiritually minded man and has been a principal instrument in recovering them from the misuse of that dreadful man bane distilled spirits.

50. The bracketed text here indicates an aside by Anne in the midst of this Cornplanter quotation.
51. Before Anne's sojourn to Indian country, the IC had sent Friends Hannah Jackson and Susanna Gregory to work at the Oneida demonstration farm in 1798; however, Anne and Mary Bell were the first women to visit the Senecas. Tiro, "We Wish to Do You Good," 367.

To which they were told, "we rejoice in the firmness of the testimony against spirituous liquors and wished thee to go on and prosper therein, that we disapproved of it as all of our members dealing in lands after that sort in taking advice of the Indians; and if any of our society did so they would be turned out of our community."

Cornplanter's sister, a Chiefess with a grave countenance, on behalf of her sisters, spoke as follows,

> We are very glad to see you and take kind the visit. We believe it was the Great Spirit that helped you on the journey and preserved you from any injury on the way. You are the first women who have come to see us, and we are thankful to the Great Spirit for helping you on the way. We have left drinking whiskey for this four years and are resolved to drink it no more.

To which I remarked, they should say, "with the help of divine Grace or the Holy Spirit; they would do so no more, for ourselves we can do nothing."[52]

At the close of an opportunity at Genesinguhta the house of our brethren, a family of white neighbors and neighboring Indians present, Blue Eyes,[53] a principal sachem spoke as follows.

> We are thankful for the opportunity of seeing you here this day at our friend's house: we are very thankful for the pains you have taken in coming so far to instruct and enlighten us, and wish that others may do the same, for we are very deficient. Many of us are of the same opinions that have been delivered. I believe it was the Good Spirit that influenced you to come and see us and we thank you for your information and for the good advice given and hope we shall improve thereby.

They were reminded of their being less incitements to hunting than in past times and of the necessity there is of continuing increasingly to turn their attention to agriculture and other useful employments and by so doing, their women would have time to learn spinning and the management of dairies and men and women could learn weaving by which they might have suitable changes

---

52. John 15:5.
53. The Seneca chief Blue Eyes, still alive in 1809, was then identified as a Christian. Wallace, *Death and Rebirth*, 330.

of raiment and keep themselves clean. Thus men and women could fill up their several departments in business and help one another, in which consists the harmony and the true peace of society. To this they replied, "We are sensible the game is decreasing in our country and we will endeavor to instruct our children, as far as we know how to get a living by useful labor."

The Indians settled at Cold Springs[54] sent a request by Cornplanter's son that we would call on our return towards Usqueshanadarqua and have an opportunity with them as it would save them several miles travel to that place, and they had to go there the day following to attend council. Although it would occasion some more unexpected detention, yet the proposal met a feeling of approbation especially in the minds of our brethren stationed in that reservation for the instruction of the natives who observed they spent much time in ranging about to attend councils, and they thought the example might be useful in bringing council to their own homes. At the close of our opportunity in which Divine aid was near and weightily attended although through the medium and difficulty of two interpreters, what was communicated was conveyed. Thompson[55] at whose house we were at, better made and more cleanly than many of his brethren spoke as follows,

> I am glad we have met together today. [I] believe it pleasing to the Great Spirit. I am pleased with what has been said and it is by the help of the Great Spirit we have met and believe it is also satisfactory to the people and approved by the Great Spirit you know more than we do and I hope you will continue your instruction to us. I think the Great Spirit has been pleased with what has been said and has been present in instructing us in this council.

An elderly woman followed us out with a grave countenance said she was most easy to express a few words, viz.

> I am thankful to the Great Spirit we have met together today. I believe our meeting is pleasing to the Great Spirit and that he directed what was

---

54. This clearing on the Allegany Reservation where Cold Spring Creek and the Allegheny River merge was the site for generations of a Seneca longhouse, a central meeting and council lodge. In 1811, at the Senecas' request, Quakers built a schoolhouse there. Instruction was interrupted during the War of 1812. In 1816, the school reopened and operated until 1822. Swatzler, *Friend Among the Senecas*, 230–31, 238–39.

55. Not identified.

said in council. I am thankful I have lived to see this day. I never heard the like before, nor never felt the like before. I believe the presence of the Great Spirit has been with us in council and I never heard the right way so clearly pointed out before, we will endeavor to walk in the way that has been pointed out. And I think it has been by the direction of the Great Spirit we have been together today.

At Usqueshanadarqua we found the men were from home, gone to prepare a sacrifice to be offered next day as an earnest of success in their winter hunting; which were about to commence.[56] The proposed opportunity was therefore necessarily deferred until the next day; feeling not easy to pass them wholly by, and it was also believed it would be considered by them as a slight.

But the minds of the men appeared to be so afloat on the object of their approaching sacrifice and dance, they seemed in no state to be brought into seriousness; and indeed I believe they rather secretly warred against it, as a spirit that should innately testify against the pursuit of such follies.

I thought if they offered any serious reply at the close it must be hypocritical; but to our satisfaction they did not, which rather enhanced the value of those speeches which had been made to us, as further establishing a belief they spoke from feeling. The remembrance of the state the men were in sat some on the feeling mind for some time. Yet it was reconciled in the reflection that such views of their yet wild unregulated state, must tend to enforce the evident necessity there is for their cultivation; and bringing them into the light and knowledge of the Gospel of peace and Salvation. The opportunity was also hurt for want of a suitable interpreter; but the women were solid and a few of their principal women seeing the state [that] the men were in, [the women] did not wait for them to offer anything; but consulting a few minutes together, spoke through a Chiefess as follows:

Brothers and sisters I am very glad to see us together today. I think it is a council of the Great Spirit's appointing. We have nothing but love one towards another. Your sisters the Indians are about to reply, and we wish

56. Swatzler in *Friend Among the Senecas* (207–8, 226–28) describes the White Dog ceremony. This thanksgiving sacrifice to the Creator was a petition for Divine protection. Dennis in *Seneca Possessed* (120) notes that congregational minister Jacob Cram criticized Quakers' tolerance for such Seneca practices; their sacrifice of an unblemished victim resembled Passover and would have reinforced Anne's notion that Native Americans were descendants of a lost tribe of Israel.

you to attend. We are generally come together of this settlement; and are thankful we have heard what has been delivered. It must be the Good Spirit that has called you from your habitations on the business you have come about. We wish all may join in pursuing the path pointed out, you at home and we here. We wish you would think of us when at home, and endeavor to promote our advancement in the several improvements of civilized life.

Another one with a countenance impressed with deep concern said,

I hope our eyes may be opened to pursue the way laid down for us. As friends have been kind and friendly to us, I wish some Women Friends would come and instruct us in spinning, etc. And should be glad to know whether such help could be had soon; as we wish much for it and desired Anne Mifflin would endeavor to promote it.

To which she [Anne Mifflin] replied, she "would inform the brethren of your wish (who have the direction of these things) and enquire among the Sisters if any feel it their duty to come. And if any do, I doubt not they will be encouraged."

It appears to me that after the removal of the ten (lost) tribes of Israel from their former possessions by captivity, they passed through the extensive country of Asia and from thence a larger part of them into America, by then narrow passages pointed out in late discoveries made by Capt. Cook[57] and others and agreeable to McKenzie's[58] account they profess the Ancient tradition that they came from Siberia. And according to 2nd Esdras Ch. 13 from the 29th to the 45th verses,[59] which describes their immigration here and the motives thereof, they were divinely aided in their progress by the streams being stayed for with God nothing is impossible and though every part of creation may be said to abound with miracles when compared with the sufficiency of human

---

57. Explorer James Cook (1728–1779) thought Pacific Islanders migrated to the Pacific islands by canoes but never determined a plausible navigational route. See Beaglehole, *Life of Captain Cook*.

58. Anne refers to the Scot Canadian Sir Alexander Mackenzie's (1764–1820) account of his epic journeys across North America. See Mackenzie, *Voyages from Montreal*; and Hayes, *First Crossing*.

59. The First and Second Books of Esdras, considered apocryphal literature, not to be confused with the Book of Ezra, part of the biblical canon. See Bruce, *Canon of Scripture*.

reason to prove or even account for them, yet if in the pride of that reason any treat lightly this account they may at least from Cook's report and others allow their passage to America practical in canoes, small boats all by them made of one stock of a tree and some I have seen very neatly made of bark and ornamented. I saw an Indian crossing Lake Ontario thirty miles over in one of them and several of us travelled to Genshato (Genesingutha) in a canoe of 50 feet in length that would carry considerable loading.[60]

The idea of their being thus removed without divine revelation was entertained by observing characters many years before the late discoveries sanctioned the opinion. Previous to which account of them was confirmed in the sentiment on seeing the portrait of an inhabitant of the extreme parts of Asia, called Samoides,[61] exactly corresponding in color too with our Indians. The account also some years past received strengthened with the prospect of an Indian trader meeting in Asia to his astonishment an Indian woman whom he had been acquainted with who informed he [him] she was taken captive from one nation to another and travelled over a great extent of country until at length she had arrived there. The 46th or 47th verses of the before mentioned chapter [Esdras] seem to point out their retreat to their former possessions, and as the other passages in sacred writ savor much such an event and the present state of things seem gradually verging towards it by the Indians parting with their country and removing farther back. I do not know why we should dispute the possibility of such an occurrence. They were chosen a peculiar people not because divine mercy did not regard the rest of his workmanship but that they might show forth his praises in being living monuments to the world of divine revelation in the fulfillment of prophecies respecting them both ancient and new as well as in these memorable events which shewed forth the divine power in their departure from Egypt [and] their passage through the Red Sea, Jordan River.[62]

Esdras [Ezra] describes them as being gathered to the Prince of Peace but that gathering not as affected until their return by which they might still remain monuments of the divine power and continue a separate or

---

60. Explorers and navigators attest to the reliability of the canoe on waters with swift currents. Archibald McDonald of Hudson Bay Company noted, "I have never heard of a canoe being wrecked, upset, or swamped. They float upon the water like ducks." Kellogg, "Portage Trails in Minnesota," 4.

61. Anne's description of these people living in Asia; however, no portraiture of this ethnic stock has been identified.

62. The epic escape of the Hebrews from Egypt, in Exodus 12–24.

distinguished people. But those who may be truly gathered to Christianity, redeemed from a dependence on hunting and established in regular habits of civilized life may not flesh with the majority but be content to remain improving their portion of the Reservations. They seem described in the 48th and last verse on that subject. They who are left behind of thy people are they that are found within my borders. How laudable then the endeavor to gather them within the inclusion of true faith and to facilitate this work by leading them along in useful employments and rendering their outward situation settled and comfortable. In coming from Canada, I met a deputation of Chiefs from Stockbridge, the places we visited where they complained of being weary of their minister,[63] though we conceived he was a well intending man in his line going towards the Wabash to hold a council with the Indians there who had invited them to remain and dwell with them where there was more hunting ground.[64] Habits of idleness with many and inclinations to a roving life may engage the larger number to accept the proposal and being gathered for the most part perhaps more to the form than the substance of Christianity will be no sufficient stay to visit the temptation.

Thus all these circumstances both those that move from place to place and those who stay may feel it the words of this prophecy should this view of the subject prove right. Their annual sacrifice of a dog (an animal they most value having no sheep in the wilderness state) seems a strong relict of the feast of the Passover; their festivities after harvest both as to the season of the year, manner of holding it a week, and the declared purpose for which it is held bears a strong resemblance to the feast of the tabernacles, the sign of covenant instituted under Abraham agreeable to McKenzie's late travels in the remote parts of America and the practice of some in this province on its first settlement. Their aversion to touching the dead, the rites of burial[65] being left wholly to the women, their erecting altars of 12 unhewn stones, some of them observing certain ceremonies at the new Moon, they're not eating a part of

63. The minister is likely John Sergeant Jr.
64. Probably the Treaty of Vincennes, June 3, 1803, which settled American claims to the Vincennes Tract that stretched across the Wabash River in the Indiana Territory. Horsman, *Expansion and American Indian Policy*, 143–48.
65. Under Seneca matrilineal kinship, women performed burial duties. Halliday Jackson observed in 1800 Seneca burial customs where a wooden coffin or boards are laid beneath the wrapped body and articles meaningful to the deceased are buried with the corpse. The Senecas, believing in spiritual resurrection, left an opening in the coffin to give the spirit access to come and go. Jackson, *Civilization of the Indian*, 27.

hollow of the thighs, like unto the Jews, in memory of Jacob's wrestling; and other striking features of the Jewish dispensation are presumptive proofs of their origins, they are of chaster lives than the whites in a state unmixed with them and as to correction of language they have no terms for swearing [as] the worst expression they can use of another being. There is no redemption for them, this bearing an illusion to the soul's immortality and I saw an evidence of their holding that faith as we approached Cornplanter's residence in the tomb of the beloved child of a Chiefess, his sister neatly made of wood and painted with Indian coloring in the front was a little hole for the spirit to come out and [laid] beneath it a small table for it [the spirit] to rest upon—[a] strange idea! But this the fond mother pleased herself with the thought of being visited at times by her darling. And Wm. Savery in the year 1793, when spending some time with the Indians, queried with a sober tone [one] of the Potawatomy tribe[66] what he thought of the soul's immortality and of a future state and to which after a solid pause, he replied,

> I believe all good Indians who do not steal other Indian's blankets, get drunk or do any bad thing will set near and round the Good Spirit, smoking their pipes, and them that steal a little and get drunk a little will set in a circle further off. But those who steal a great deal and get drunk every day shall be so distant they can neither see him nor hear him, nor have any comfort from him.

How consonant this with scripture testimony concerning the disobedient. "Cast ye the unprofitable servant into outer darkness: where there shall be weeping and gnashing of teeth." Matthew 25:30.

The apparent improvement of the men in what related to their branches of business, the pleasing appearance of their improved buildings, enlarged fields, and increase of cattle since the superintending care of our brethren in that reservation, has excited a spirit of imitation in other settlements, who are reaching forth their hands for aid, from friends in the same line of instruction beyond what their present funds may admit of. And if any who have not yet

---

66. Native Americans of the Upper Mississippi, Great Plains, and western Great Lakes region, the Potawatomy were members of the Illinois Confederacy, one of the "Three Fires" along with the Chippewa and Ottawa. According to Wallace in *Death and Rebirth* (42), the Three Fires "at least minimized warfare among themselves." For much of the seventeenth and eighteenth centuries, they allied with the French.

put their hands to the work who have been favored in a large degree with divine bounty should feel their hearts enlarged to extend their corn, wine, and oil towards nations waxing poor and falling into decay, for the bettering of their conditions, it will be an oblation to the cause of humanity and I doubt not acceptable in the eyes of Divine Mercy. For when among the Oneidas, I beheld the emaciated [state] of some, often feeling the keen bite of hunger from a miserable subsistence picked out of the woods, now almost void of game from the coming of the whites, my feelings of human sympathy were deeply touched, and I thought what need there is for a friendly hand to be reached forth to lead them into fields of agriculture and houses of useful employ where pale want may be chased away and peace and plenty preside in the room thereof.[67] For towards such a condition must all the nations of Indians verge who from one sale after another part with their territory unless they are thus instructed in the school of useful industry.[68]

The reformation has begun at the right end with the men who hold the reins of power who by being awakened to see the utility of forsaking their wilderness roving and settle down in the pursuits of husbandry are brought to a feeling for their women, heretofore drudging alone in the labors of the field and by lightening their burthens leave a space of time for them to improve in branches suited to our sex, which if not engaged in the work must become marred, as it is not likely the men will bend their attention in contented pursuit of the object unless the women are brought forward to bear up their end of the yoke.[69]

Friends having found some disadvantages attending their residence on Indians' lands have purchased a tract adjoining for their continued instruction;[70] and should it be put on the hearts of females of property or any other

---

67. The Oneidas sought the government's help to act as trustees overseeing their leased land, but the commissioners sent pressured the Oneidas to sell the land to the government. Tiro, "We Wish to Do You Good," 368–69.

68. Anne mirrors the view of the IC and others that native survival depended on their adopting plow agriculture and animal husbandry.

69. As Swatzler and almost all historians who have recorded the Friends' work among the Senecas maintain, "although Friends were not religious proselytizers, they were definitely cultural proselytizers," and "neither the Quakers, nor the government expected an immediate transformation" of the Senecas. Swatzler, *Friend Among the Senecas*, 238, 244.

70. Anne refers to Tunesassa and a small acreage the IC had purchased from the Holland Land Company to build another self-sustaining model farm like the first at Genesinguhta. At Tunesassa, Seneca males could learn skills such as building fences,

persons to lend their aid in the establishment of another house near the brethren's or rather a manufacturing school to instruct in spinning, weaving, knitting, and sewing and in addition to effect this work should a couple of men, whether from far or near, feel it their duty to commence instruction they would be moving on a foundation likely to sustain in patient endurance under every occurring difficulty or discouragement, and such an establishment might prove a blessing to that people and the promoters of the work. The work would not be grievous for they are a ready people at taking learning, and I know they have a thirst for our knowledge both from their expressions to us and their flocking around me to see the manner of knitting; indeed were I a person suitably qualified in those respective branches and felt it required of me, I could freely devote a portion of my time in such an institution for I believe all meet their reward who are engaged in different departments of the work. [To] those who devote a share of their property to its promotion, the committee in their attention to the great outlines the brethren in their active station there and myself may thankfully acknowledge. I have felt my share of satisfaction in the little sacrifices made on their behalf. And when passing through the wilderness and lay encamped on the grass our midnight serenade being the howling of wolves and the screeching of owls reminding me of man in the wilderness of rude unregenerate nature, when passions like unto the dispositions prevalent in wolves, bears, and panthers infest the soul. Even here was I preserved in sweet serenity and peace: neither did I fear assail on hearing one of them pad around our camp, taking a gradual survey of us knowing this fear of approaching fire which we had kindled for our comfort and to guard against the beasts of the forest: in like manner, thought I am not of those wild dispositions [illegible] at the appearance of true gospel fire?

And now may I not render the tribute of thanksgiving and praise to the hand of adorable help, which not only putteth forth but goes before his dependent children and supports them amidst every extremity whatsoever to fulfill their little portions of duty in bearing the glad tidings of his peace and salvation and to proclaim liberty to every soul darkened and captivated by erroneous customs and opinions, who will avail themselves of the grace and mercy offered.

---

caring for livestock, planting, and harvesting; native women could train in the domestic arts of dairying, cooking, sewing, housecleaning, and making soap. Wallace, *Death and Rebirth*, 271–73.

The sagacity of the Indians and disposition to judge of men's faith by their works [is] discoverable in the following anecdote:[71]

Two Presbyterian ministers under the patronage of Princeton College of New Jersey who were chosen by the Missionary Society to go and propagate the Gospel among the Creek Indians,[72] accompanied by several members of the Congress to give weight to the embassy who took with them a number of Bibles; on their arrival a conference was held with some of their Chiefs. It was agreed they should call a council. Upon meeting they informed the Creek chiefs that the delegation had brought two ministers of the Gospel to preach the Gospel of Salvation unto them and a number of books which would learn them the way to heaven. The Indians after a pause said they would consider of it, which took fourteen days. The Ministers proposed preaching, but the Indians said they must first consider of it. They inquired of the members of Congress if they had any dark people among them? Whether they preached the Gospel of Salvation unto them? Whether they gave them those good books which would learn them the way to Heaven? Whether they treated them as Brothers or as slaves? Being answered in the negative, the Indians said, "Go home and preach the Gospel of Salvation unto them give them those good books, which will learn them the way to heaven, treat them as brethren and not as Slaves, and then come preach unto us."

In consequence of this unlooked for retort, they returned, and one of the embassy E.B. a well-known character in [New] Jersey who had fourteen slaves, set them all at liberty.[73]

71. We traced this account to the journal of Joseph Clark, a Philadelphia Quaker schoolmaster and Pennsylvania Abolition Society stalwart. Clark recounted hearing the Indian account in 1797. See Clark, "Account of a Journey to Indian Country," 374–75. Anne possibly heard the account from Clark, her neighbor on Chestnut Street. A copy of this anecdote and moving letters between Clark, the Stockbridge, and the Tuscaroras are in the Miscellaneous Manuscript Collection, 004/Oct. 1800, FHLSC. We are indebted to Pat O'Connell, archivist at FHLSC, for providing access to these manuscript copies. The copy varies somewhat, stating that seven members of Congress accompanied the two Princeton-trained Presbyterian ministers to preach among the Creeks. It is also possible Anne read the Indian account in *Anecdotes of Christian Missions*, 160. It was thereafter published in London as *The Christian Observer Conducted by Members of the Established Church for the Year 1806*, 254, where it appeared with an added sentence, "This occurrence took place among the Creek Indians."

72. The Presbyterian ministers and members of Congress who carried the Christian mission to the Creek Indians have not been identified, nor have we been able to document this mission before 1797. For the Creek Nation at that time, see Ethridge, *Creek Country*.

73. This passage calling out "E.B." is not in Joseph Clark's journal. Though E.B. calls to mind Elias Boudinot, he did not serve in the House of Representatives at this time. No

Logan-Fisher-Fox Papers, ser. 4, box 8A, HSP. Another manuscript of this 1803 visit is at Cornell University Library. This compressed version includes Penrose Wiley, a Quaker from the McDonald Monthly Meeting near Reading, Pennsylvania, as one of the members of the Quaker group. See "Account of a visit made by Penrose Wiley," no. 9001, Division of Rare and Manuscript Collections, Cornell University Library, Ithaca, New York.

New Jersey member of the House of Representatives in the 1790s had the initials of E.B. It remains a mystery how Anne received information about "E.B." since her account precedes the *Christian Observer* article cited above by three years.

Part 3
Correspondence

Chapter 10

LETTERS AMONG FRIENDS, 1776–1799

The letters in this chapter begin when Anne was twenty-one. They cover the years of the American Revolution, when she was searching for her life's work, and they continue through the years of her marriage, the birth of her three children, her efforts on behalf of the antislavery movement, the death of her husband, and the first year of her widowhood, when she worked to rescue Warner's reputation and guarantee his legacy.

TO HANNAH PEMBERTON

March 6, 1776

This letter to Hannah Pemberton,[1] written just two months after the death of Anne's father, responds to Hannah's note expressing her condolences on Anne's loss. Anne and Hannah had been friends and schoolmates since childhood and were part of a female literary circle.

The tender sympathy expressed in my dear Hannah's note, excites the warmest emotions of gratitude in the bosom of her friend, partaking of another's affliction without reluctance is the sweet mark of a heart replete with all the softest feelings of humanity, let me then admire the commiserating turn of my

---

1. Hannah Pemberton (1755–1788) was the third child of merchant Quaker James Pemberton (1723–1809) and Hannah Lloyd Pemberton (1734–1764).

Hannah: There is no substantial blessing in life but a clear conscience or that peace of mind expressed by self-approbation

> To no peculiar lot of life
> To happiness confined
> But in the self-approving hour
> And firm contented mind

This truth has made a deep impression on a mind not long since depress'd with grief at parting with an earthly blessing which I was little apprehensive of being so shortly deprived of many happy hours of instructive entertainment did I pass with my dear deceased father in his favorite study, supremely blest were those moments in the society of an affectionate and intelligent parent and many more such did I promise myself. May the locks of my friend's be silvering with age ere' she meets with such a trial and when that awful day arrives which shall forever exclude from thy sight the presence of so beloved a protector summons all thy fortitude and reflect there are many partakers in the loss.[2] The idea of company in distress sometimes helps to alleviate favor and as thy father acts more in a public capacity the loss will be more publicly felt. On the contrary my father's natural bent was for reading and retirement, he indulged it and lived a stranger to the affairs either of a general or particular body.

I have just read of the death of Tommy Fishbourn.[3] I lament with his near connections this fatal stroke which separated from their bosoms a very promising youth who never lost an opportunity of improvement and rarely ever said a foolish thing. His unquenchable thirst after knowledge has unhappily hastened his end, as too deep study is a great enemy of the human frame.[4]

I thank thee for the perusal of those verses I now return. Fidelia's merit great praise;[5] indeed, all her performances display a bright and capacious genius

---

2. Hannah could empathize with Anne on the death of her father. At age nine Hannah had lost her mother. She married Robert Morton at age twenty-nine and was widowed by age thirty-one.

3. Thomas Fishbourne (ca. 1758–1776) was the son of Philadelphia Quakers William and Mary Fishbourne. Thomas's grandfather, William Sr., had served as mayor of Philadelphia from 1719 to 1722.

4. Anne's notion that Thomas's untimely death was exacerbated by his "too deep study" reflects a belief in Ecclesiastes 12:12: "Of making many books *there is* no end, and much study *is* wearisome to the flesh."

5. Fidelia's verses from the memorial poem written by Hannah Grifitts (1727–1817) honor Sarah Morris (1702–1775), an esteemed, widely traveled Philadelphia Quaker minister.

whose lines methinks show her great skill in delineating characters; they are the just strokes the high coloring of an excellent painter:

> The heart benevolent, with judgement join'd
> And easy converse showed her generous mind
> Where Christian virtues did with social blend
> And form'd the instructor in the cheerful friend

The familiar epistle of Essex is not without its beauties;[6] some lines may be deem'd exceptionable by an American, as she seems to hold in contempt many things here to be met with; she cannot certainly be vain of coming from a great metropolis that conveys no honor to her; the advantage there is not superior nor equal to ours when the difference of time is considered that has part in improving each place. Her notion of our looking with admiration on the State House is highly envious as no person who is the least acquainted with books or the world can think it extraordinary. Children may look on it in that light, but she has too great a share of understanding to draw an illiberal character of the Americans from such ignorance but she is a pitiable object of disappointed expectations, her mind sore with misfortune dwells only on the dark side of prospects, add to that the reception she first met with was rather inhospitable. Often have I pitied and wished to promote this woman of adversity, but power often falls short of inclination. If it did not, I should command my dear Hannah Pemberton to make me a long and immediate answer to this.

I recommend to thy notice these Vols. of advice[7] the bearer will deliver; they are well worth the attention of every girl please to send them back soon as thee has done with them as I want to return them to the owner and believe me to be,

Thy sincere Friend
Nancy Emlen

Autograph letter signed (hereafter ALS), vol. 128, fol. 77, Pemberton Papers, HSP.

In *Friends Miscellany* (1838), 11:392–94. The full poem is in Blecki and Wulf, *Milcah Martha Moore's Book*, 253–55.

6. Not identified.

7. In trying to identify the advice volumes, University of Leeds professor David Fairer suggested the source may be Croft's *A Brother's Advice to His Sisters* or John Gregory's better-known *A Father's Legacy to His Daughters*.

TO THOMAS BURKE

Philadelphia
3 mo: 3rd 1779
[March 3, 1779]

Living across the street from the State House, where the Continental Congress met, Anne encountered many of the delegates, Thomas Burke foremost among them. In this letter she sharply criticizes Burke. The political consciousness she expresses here is exceptional for a young woman of this period.

In no small degree [am I] shocked at thy operation that "Luxuries are necessary to employ for their support [of] the laboring poor." I cannot rest easy without endeavoring to vindicate the cause of truth, "which the gates of hell shall never prevail against." In offering a few objections to so mistaken a sentiment, which if they are not capable of convincing it is erroneous; may awaken reflections that shall seriously and weightily point out its evil tendency, if thou art not too much blinded by a false reasoning or biased by the politicians' plans to receive the enlightening rays of unstudied verity. But it suits not with the politics of America, if interest is the prevailing principle in that study.

Are men the riches of the nation?[8] Then stop the channels of luxury by limiting trade to the necessaries of life, and by so doing prevent the misuse of that happy means Providence bestowed on mankind for their mutual help and intercourse; draw down a blessing on our sea adventure and invite numbers hither to seek assistance from the culture of our yet unexplored wilds, who might otherwise be employed at a distance in preparing the means of our undoing.

Were I a man, [I] should think it my indispensable duty to prefer an honest simple life of husbandry rather than by joining in unlimited trade, become polluted in handling those things to others which I approved not in

---

8. They had previously dallied in poetic exchanges; see chapter 1, above. Burke's remark that "luxuries are necessary to employ for their support [of] the laboring poor," which prompted Anne's reply, would have instigated a similar response from Quaker elders such as John Woolman, who believed the "evil effects of avarice [to be] among the most pressing problems of his day, including wars, slavery, racial prejudice, usury, exorbitant rents, drunkenness, debility and cruelty to animals." Quoted from Marietta, *Reformation of American Quakerism*, 101. Anne's opening statement and words that follow suggest familiarity with Smith's *The Wealth of Nations*.

myself, and thus be painfully accessory to their hurt in feeding a vanity and excess, destructive to true peace and that must finally ruin hundreds who now dance the giddy whirl of thoughtless dissipation, if the prevailing extravagance continues.[9]

Is money deemed the riches of a nation? Then forbid the importation of a thousand gee-gaws, that greatly drain the country of its gold, the recompense of its produce and there will be no longer a necessity for so many money changers as it will lessen the demand for that article and politically enhance the value of your own currency. Yet money is but a nominal good, in reality a great evil; and heartily should I rejoice if it were banished [from] society as its most subtle and insinuating foe. Trade would be thereby so shackled that acquisition of superfluous wealth and with it a thousand artificial wants that destroy the true felicity of our existence must vanish with it, the useful part alone remaining; for people would be almost obliged to confine their bartering to the conveniences of life, which being very practicable cannot be objected against the utility of such a treasure. The groans of the distressed would no longer be heard were gold and silver in disgrace who are now confined to unwholesome mines effectively laboring for them. Those who call themselves "Enthusiasts in liberty" should not countenance anything that remotely tends to deprive others of their natural freedom.[10]

The profession of being a friend to simplicity in everything is inconsistent with a position immediately subversive of it. Simplicity will ever prove the most pleasing where the taste is not vitiated by habit: Is it not merely from being under the denomination of a Friend that I divest myself of inconvenient ornaments? Though the beauty of consistency might alone induce me thereto, it is from an inward conviction that is requisite in all the followers of a meek Savior, and being in a manner, the shadow of the cross may serve as a constant monitor to live under the control of its holy influence, remembering the sacred injunction, "If ye will be my disciples ye must take up your daily cross and follow me"[11] and without some degree of it in the subjection of our evil propensities,

---

9. Some in the Continental Congress, especially New England delegates, had been making this charge since 1775. For the Massachusetts standard-bearer who decried "luxury and extravagance" as "totally destructive of those virtues which are necessary for the preservation of the liberty and happiness of the people," see Maier, "New Englander as Revolutionary."

10. This was Anne's first-known statement protesting the enslavement of Africans and how this contradicted the natural rights philosophy undergirding the Declaration of Independence.

11. Luke 9:23.

it has been the acknowledged opinion of the wisest that virtue is but a name. There is a perfect harmony in the doctrines of Christianity; care for the poor is an essential one, but distribution of charity from the source thou mentions clashes with its requisitions of humility, moderation and self-denial, deceitfully rendering folly and excess a merit.

Where are the moments of leisure for mankind to discharge the duties of worship by acknowledgement of a protecting Providence in contemplating the wonders of creation and aspiring to become acceptable in the eyes of perfect purity, whilst one half are bond slaves to the others, who are daily resting in the means which the unremitted labor of those furnishes of flattering unbridled passions whom chance or avarice has placed beneath them?[12] Thus is that time which ought to be disposed of to better purposes unprofitably engrossed by the works of their own hands, the superiority of a part proving their corruption, whilst the other bends beneath the weight of oppressive toil.

It is high time in this state of strain for some valiants[13] to arise, animated with the genuine spirit of liberty, who shall plead the cause of truth and equity, point the defects in government, and generously seek to restore the original rights of mankind. There are certain righteous and wholesome limitations in the use even of lawful things, which the upright must witness in themselves to be right, whose minds not clouded by the subtle arts of the lawyer, are open to the voice of unerring wisdom. The bondage of sin is above all others the most dangerous as the stupefied captives hug their chains and will not know it is from them they are oppressed. This is the foundation of all outward slavery; the cause must cease 'ere the effects can totally. Yet to restrain the violent perils of this still unconquered principle, laws have been made and are still instituted. Why not that of a sumptuary one[14] to be in full force at the end of ten or twenty

---

12. That the desire for wealth was tied to slaveholding was a constant refrain among the early Quaker abolitionists, whose work circulated widely in Philadelphia. Anne would have read them and known that the PYM heeded their call by making slaveholding a disqualifying offense by the onset of the American Revolution.

13. Anne's call for "valiants" to rise up recalls the seventeenth century male and female itinerant preachers, the Valiant Sixty who spread the Quaker message of truth. Some of them charged with speaking against the Anglican Church suffered corporal punishment, imprisonment, or loss of property. See Martin Williams, "Ancient Friends: Quakers in Wales and the Marches," Hereford Wales Monthly Meeting at Abergavenny, 2006, http://www.quakers.hyperphp.com/ancient_friends.htm.

14. Sumptuary laws restrained extravagance in dress and other personal luxuries in order to reinforce a class system by limiting what commoners could wear. See Hunt, *Governance of the Consuming Passions*. Anne's proposal was rooted in an insistence that slave ownership reflected a desire for worldly goods but that through training the younger

years? In the intervening space of time to operate on the rising generation at the decease of their sires, in order to be gently entered on, and prevent the confusion and cruelty of wishing that redundancy they have always been accustomed to, from the aged. Limits thus being presented to each one's possession, the curb will be placed on a mad horse and a better opportunity afforded to the generality of procuring a comfortable subsistence.[15] [Thus], there would be the same virtuous motive for industry, which is attaining a sufficiency to set down easy in old age; at the same time a damp would be cast on ambition and oppression, for the thriving part knowing they would not possess more than a stated sum, would have no incentive to joy in the poor, hastily to aggrandize themselves or attain those vanities which if openly discountenanced by rulers would leave no motive for the pursuit of needless wealth.[16] Was there no respect paid to the riches, no deference to pomp or pride, covetousness must then drop and depart for what can induce men to grapple for a little more dirt than their neighbors, but to become bowed down to by them; an unjust distinction when it is only virtue that indeed ennobles man.

The rich, it is to be feared will ever prove interested bars to this eligible establishment, those only in whom selfishness is overcome by a desire for the good of all men. Usury[17] appears to me another aspiration to gain ingenious treasure and is as reverse to the spirit of Christianity as to make promises that we know not that we shall be able to fulfill, for he who commanded to "swear not at all" hath said, "Lend and look for nothing in return."[18] Was this prevented, it might serve to avert a thousand acts of tyranny now experienced towards the poor, with a view to amass sums for this too profitable method of disposing them.

---

generation into new habits, to acquire only necessities, society might alleviate the oppression of the poor who worked for meager wages and slaves whose labor was unpaid.

15. A curb is a device on the bit and bridle that controls the horse.

16. Anne's proposal to cap the amount of wealth anyone could legally accumulate put her on the extreme of Quaker reform. In drafting Pennsylvania's constitution in July 1776, radical members of the drafting convention argued that "an enormous proportion of property vested in a few individuals is dangerous to the rights and destructive of the common happiness of mankind," and proposed to limit ownership of large tracts of farmland or urban property. Benjamin Franklin, not radical in most respects, had reasoned earlier that "what we have above what we can use, is not properly *ours*, though we possess it." See Nash, "Philadelphia's Radical Caucus," 80–81.

17. The church objected to the practice of usury—that is, loaning money with interest in order to profit the lender.

18. Luke 6:34.

When civil power becomes promotive of righteousness, how will it invite the smiles of heaven in its favor? Zion then shall rejoice, for "Kings shall be thy nursing fathers and Queens, thy nursing mothers."[19] Invite then thy companions in power, to clothe themselves as in humility and ask [for] counsel from above, that in turning to the guidance of the "Spirit of truth which will lead into all truth,"[20] they may take the safe and narrow path and be led to restrain the hands of those who torn by the spirit of war and violence themselves, seek to tyrannize over such churches or people who are redeemed therefrom and wish to maintain their principles of harmless quietude. We of the North are, I believe, from various corresponding prophesies appointed to raise a more exalted standard of righteousness than has hitherto been erected[21] to the fulfilling [of] that prediction, "I will lift up an ensign to the nations from far."[22] Oh then that none may hold back from doing part of the work, or impiously dare to oppose its progress in others by vainly striving to counteract the designs of Providence, lest sudden vengeance overtake them, "they perish from the way."[23]

The sensualist may wonder, the willing laugh at such expressions as these, but let them remember, their mirth shall be teemed into bitterness, for the Lamb and his followers are ordained to have the true victory, and however flattering the prospect, I would not that any should think to say, "I sit a King, and shall see no sorrow" left there, "plague come in one day, death and mourning and famine, for stronger is the Lord who judgeth us,"[24] but bear in mind the language of the inspired psalmist, "Be wise now therefore, ye Kings, be instructed ye judges of the Earth. Serve the Lord with fear and rejoice with trembling. Kiss the son lest he be angry, and ye perish from the way."[25] Let the upright intention of this communication excuse its freedom, it was dictated by a heart replete with those feelings which seek the good of all men, desiring for myself, so to conduct as to obtain, "that peace the world cannot give nor take away"[26] a joy that will support and comfort, when the midnight gloom of distress shall make sad our land.

I hope that if ever I have an opportunity of conversing with thee again, it will not be 'ere the unlawful opinion which gave rise to this, be eradicated

19. Isaiah 49:23.
20. John 16:13.
21. For such prophetic thoughts, see Bloch, *Visionary Republic*.
22. Isaiah 5:26.
23. Psalms 2:12.
24. Revelation 18:7.
25. Psalms 2:12.
26. A paraphrase of John 14:27.

from thy bosom, choosing to withdraw from the society of those who are willing to entertain such corrupting notions, as there may be moments of weakness like as when the sentry of a garrison slumber, when not being on that watch enjoined on every Christian to observe, evil may creep into the heart and sway over the feeble building of virtue already erected; for no person can boast of being able to stand in the hour of its assault especially when transformed as into an Angel of Light.

From one who wishes to see the process of darkness and confusion, overcome by true religion, directing the assemblies of rulers and presiding in the breasts of those whom they ought tenderly to care for and watch over as delegated shepherds, so shall tranquility and good-will take place of malice, revenge and all hateful things, and having our outward concerns regulated into a happy order, enable men to set down as "under their own vine and own fig tree"[27] fulfilling the great end of their creation by building each other up in the most holy faith, promoting brotherly love and good works and glorifying God in the beauty of holiness.

Truth and sincerity will ever be preferred by me to compliment; in that disposition of mind, were the foregoing lines penned. And in that I subscribe myself.

Thy Friend
Nancy Emlen

ALS, C-W-P, ser. 4, box 10, fol. 52.

FROM JOHN PEMBERTON

Philadelphia, 6 mo. 6. 1781
[June 6, 1781]

The advice of John Pemberton[28] urging Anne to return home to her mother stemmed from his concern that her disapproval of her mother's use of Continental currency would bring more opprobrium on her than on Mother Emlen.

27. Micah 4:4.
28. John Pemberton (1727–1795), son of Israel Pemberton and Rachel Read Pemberton, married Hannah Zane in 1766. During the Seven Years' War, he and his brother Israel resigned from the Pennsylvania Assembly, and he continued to seek better relations with Native Americans. A key reformer, he promoted restoring Friends to their earlier spirituality

Dear Friend,

As it was [a] matter of true joy to me and [to] many more who love the truth to find some years past thou had submitted to its humbling power, that thou were bound to see the emptiness and vanity of the world and its friendship and thy youthful mind turned to aspire after enduring substance, so strong desires attend for thy preservation and establishment in the truth, and by a watchful attention to the pure Spirit, thou may be enabled to see the enemy in all his appearances and transformations and wisdom and strength be given to show every device and snare.[29] But nothing may be able to separate or turn [you] aside from the Holy Path of the redeemed.

Given that love thee have, and pious thoughts and much sympathy knowing that various exercises have attended thee but comforted in a belief that the Lord hath been gracious and mercifully bore up and sustained and I doubt not will as thou keeps a single eye and in a watchful state. It was when Israel abode in their tents[30] that neither divination nor enchantment could prevail. Here indeed is ever of our safety.

Thy tender care and attention to our worthy deceased friend, Susanna Lightfoot, who having fought the good fight and kept the faith finished the course in love and peace.[31] Comfortable to her and manifested a truly Christian benevolent friend, and the season afforded thee instruction and the reflection of thy endeavor to serve her peace and comfort. She is now released. Thou hast

---

and was one of the first to initiate home visitations of members. He was among Philadelphia Friends exiled to Virginia in 1777. In *The Diary of John Pemberton* he recounted that incarceration of Friends. Like his brothers Israel Pemberton (1715–1779) and James Pemberton (1723–1809), John was an abolitionist. He died in 1795, during his last ministerial sojourn, in Pyrmont, Germany, where he was buried. For more on Pemberton, see Hodgson, *Life and Travels of John Pemberton*.

29. In this letter of June 6, 1781, esteemed Friend John Pemberton takes the initiative to write to Anne about her leaving her home and taking up residence with Thomas and Susanna Lightfoot. Within the close-knit circle of Philadelphia Friends, Anne's decision to separate herself from her family on the account of mother Emlen's trading in Continental currency was regarded as an extreme measure. Pemberton had known Anne from infancy. As a young woman, he had witnessed firsthand her spiritual transformation and adoption of more austere habits in speech, dress, and deportment. His fraternal correction, takes a more tactful approach making reference to her religious piety and devotion as well as her great care and compassion in caring for Susanna Lightfoot during her last illness. After Susanna's passing, he appeals for Anne to return home. Succeeding letters give no indication that there were any hard feelings between them.

30. Pemberton draws on Israel's faithfulness to Yahweh, suggesting that Anne likewise be faithful to God and honor family.

31. See chapter 2, above.

paid the last office of respect and as one who truly loves thee, I would advise thee now to return to thy mother's house to avoid any censure which an uncharitable world may cast out; conscious innocence may cause us to despise censure. Yet the eyes of many are watchfully attentive on thee and as thy happy turn of mind and prospect has had a reach of influence on some. So I am solicitous no step or conduct may cripple their goings or cause any to stumble. [three lines crossed out]

It is in much tenderness to thee I send this, accept dear friend the hints, and if thou calmly resign to the voice of pure wisdom, I believe thou will comply with this request.

With dear love to my disconsolate valued friend Thomas Lightfoot[32] and desiring thee to accept the same, I am thy cordial friend.

J. P. [John Pemberton]

ALS, vol. 35, fol. 143, Pemberton Papers, HSP.

TO JOHN PEMBERTON

Pikeland[33]
6 mo; 12th, 1781
[June 12, 1781]

Considering that in 1781 Pemberton served as an esteemed minister and clerk to the Yearly Meeting of Ministers and Elders, Anne's adamant tone and willingness to withstand criticism is all the more remarkable.

Dear Friend,

I take kind thy well-meant advice, as it is intended to preserve me from the shafts of calumny; but if, as thee says, it yields my friend's satisfaction that I have seen the emptiness of vanity of the world and its friendship would it not forfeit any just claim to their regard as well as the peace which the world gives not. If I were so far to bend to this world as to forsake known duty either this fear or for the favor of that world. This would not be the clothing of the Lamb,[34] which is slain by the world, the true church Spirit which hath the moon or changeable things under foot, for the fickle varying and often groundless

---

32. The husband of Susanna Lightfoot, in whose home Anne had taken refuge.
33. Anne continued to reside in Pikeland with Thomas Lightfoot after the death of his wife Susanna.
34. A reference to the crucified Christ as Lamb of God.

opinions of the deceitful and unstable heart of the unregenerate would then be above my head and bear tyrannical sway. I have of late been much the object of censure yet am, and fear I may be, unless I can look to the world and not to the light of that Eternal Word speaking in the heart which formed the world for the regulation of my conduct. Holy help has, with thank fullness I say it, been with me and if I keep the word of patience during the winter season of reproach, [I] hope it will carry me safely [over] this Jordan and I shall land in peace rejoicing that no specious argument whatever frustrates me from an humble obedience to divine requiring. For depend on it, my dear and very kind friend it is not in mine own will but in the cross thereto that I have submitted to become as a mark to shoot at having anticipated before many difficulties that might accrue and the prospect would have effectually turned aside my obedience had not a very deep necessity been laid upon me.

However, it may appear in the eye of human prudence a [illegible] in the justification of paying taxes by a kinsman whom I wish to make haste admit? Of the mixture in this respect for me to this absent myself from a dear parent and expose myself to many difficulties that may arise, and hard sayings that have been uttered, yet sensible I am that whomsoever makes that the governing principle of their lives is led by the world's spirit not the spirit of truth. I therefore dare not quench nor grieve the Spirit[35] by disobedience and must bear with the darts of the uncircumcised until the power of the highest shall unstring their bow by judgment or weaken the nerves of these hands that would crush the little ones in mercy to both.[36]

My attention to Dear Susanna Lightfoot was inconsiderable,[37] [and I] wish it had been more. Her memory is sweet her counsel was excellent and her sympathy for my situation was precious may a blessing light upon those with whom she was connected in, her counsel would not I judge agree with thine. Do not dear friend have an ear too much open to the slanders and vague opinions and reports of a deluded world. But to the voices of inspeaking wisdom, I take affectionately thy hints, but hope thou wilt further

---

35. In Ephesians 4, St. Paul lays out how a believer can grieve the Holy Spirit by anger, bitterness, disobedience, or vulgarity in speech and behavior and thus obstruct the Spirit's efficacy.

36. Anne refers to the less faithful as the uncircumcised, those outside of the circle of believers, nonmembers of God's covenant.

37. During her stay with the Lightfoots, Anne attended and cared for her beloved friend Susanna Lightfoot as she was dying. See MRP, May 2, 1781, above.

recommend or insist on acquiescence with what they require—peace. I am sensible [that peace] would be broken and surely thee must think if my own inclination was consulted, it would be to have a fixed abode in a beloved and very tender parents' house, rather than to be an alien therefrom, exposed to the sufferings of malevolence and the shallow harsh judging of the too superficial. I have felt the depths of this testimony and those who are careless and feel not its necessity, are not fit judges of any steps that are ordered for its promotion. The weight not falling on them, they are incapable of feeling for others there, but I freely forgive their censure and pray that he who seeth in secret and knoweth the spring of motive for every action and argument may forgive also.

I have felt some openings to return to the city but the circumstances attending will make it a Cross; however, safety depends on submission and I must endeavor to stand my ground, knowing in the depth of some painful experience on what ground and foundation I do stand in matters that to some may appear considerable. With love to thy dear companion, father and sister in law, I conclude with acknowledgements for thy care and tenderness, thy affectionate Friend,

Anne Emlen

P.S. Thy intimation of my example influencing some by their having a watchful eye toward me feels awful.[38] Oh! That I may not in any shape administer cause for stumbling. I have been filled with a solemnness of the necessity to have true wisdom for the guide of my tongue and conduct when in company with young, converted Friends and hope I have in a degree been made able to attend to the weight of such sense, and that with the help of such spirits as I have now the satisfaction of addressing. I shall be made more of a conqueror over everything that would obstruct the growth of the precious seed in me or prevent any fruitfulness therefrom. Thomas Lightfoot's love is to thee and companion.

ALS, vol. 35, fol. 144, Pemberton Papers, HSP.

---

38. The postscript suggests she is resolute with a "solemnness of necessity" in defiance of Mother Emlen's use of Continental currency, but Anne is also conflicted. The notion of a watchful eye gave her concern that she might set a bad example for newly converted youth.

TO JOHN PEMBERTON

>Philadelphia
>1 mo: 15th: 1785
>[January 15, 1785]

It is evident that Anne and John Pemberton maintained a kindly relationship despite their differences during the war. Pemberton had arrived in Great Britain in time for the London Yearly Meeting in 1783, where he played a key role in convincing Quaker leaders there to join in the growing antislavery movement.

My Esteemed Friend,

A suitable opportunity offering, I am willing to embrace it to show forth my sympathy and unity with thee in thy almost untrodden path of walking. The dear Lamb of God who taketh away the sins of the world trod the wine press alone, and shall we profess to be his followers, forbear from yielding up to follow him. Even in the regeneration or helping forward through humble obedience to all his requirings [for] that great and essential work, both in ourselves and others. The grapes are ripe, the fields are whitened indeed unto harvest, and many there are who may yet be fitted to join the already enlisted troops, the Captains, Generals, and Commanders in chief of the heavenly militia whose King and awful ruler and commissioner is the Majesty on high.[39] These I tenderly wish encouraged whether of the aged, middle aged, or tender youth; may they be enabled faith, my soul to wax valiant in [the] fight and under the influences of the gathering arm and extended hand of unequaled holy power [and] become instrumental to gather in the sheaves which shall be reaped and which thou art now as a foreman[40] made to help bind up in the harvest field of the divine power that so many may come. Through the store house of gracious provision and help and the barns of Zion as it were being filled, may come to experience the blessed effects thereof, when their bread shall be given them and their waters shall be sure.[41] And when the new wine of the Kingdom shall replenish, yea be even handed forth from such as

---

39. Anne's call to arms mirrors the spiritually zealous prose in MRP. But clearly her adherence to simplicity in dress, diet, and speech did not extend to her florid writing.

40. Anne is referring to Pemberton's status as a mainstay of the PYM and Meeting of Ministers and Elders.

41. Isaiah 33:16. The reference is to the Church Militant, in this case the Friends' Lamb's War. Anne is assured by Isaiah that God will provide for those who follow the religious life.

made us instruments under God's appointment (who can work instrumentally as well as immediately) to the comfort and refreshment of some now perhaps barren souls who may not yet have learned the alphabet or even [the] first rudiments in religion, or holy, sanctifying, preserving self-denial. For as the "New wine is in the Clusters"[42] the ripened feelings of tender seeking souls requires the faithful children of the mighty God, but to gather them together, that the new wine may flow forth from or in their gatherings and that the great name of the King of heaven and the whole earth may be glorified, acceptably worshipped or renowned in the way that he hath appointed for his ransomed and redeemed ones to walk in.

A way in truth of purity and peace, altogether unadulterated by the human policy, wisdom, or artificer of designing men, which too many alas! Poor things have unwarily or traditionally abode too much for their essential advancement in the work of real religion under the darkening influences of especially, perhaps, amongst the Catholics as well as others or those who look to the dominion of the Pope or his decrees and dispensations, as to a holy authority indubitably derived from God the Father.[43] Though no doubt but these are many of them, poor things, who seek aright and can and do worship in the temple, notwithstanding their ignorantly and unwittingly joining hands with what is of man's devising and not from the Author of all purity and therefore to weak minds, who cannot distinguish things from things or discover some difference between the secret hid workings of the mystery of iniquity as well as that of Godliness, by dwelling steadfastly under the preserving enlightening or animating spirit of God to such who dwell not here as worshippers in the sacred temple and before the holy altar. Wrong influence becomes exceedingly dangerous, like unto the time formerly when in Israel of old, "The leaders of the people caused the people to err and they that were led of them are destroyed."[44]

I tenderly and ardently wish to preserve my integrity (if favored to have any) Godward, that no erroneous influence whatever may ever cause my feet

---

42. Isaiah 65:8.

43. Anne deems that the papacy is leading Catholics into error; she echoes anti-Catholic sentiment evident from the sixteenth century onward. Wolfe, "Comparative Historical Categorization of Anti-Catholicism." The Pennsylvania Constitution of 1776 declared that "all men have a natural, and unalienable right, to worship Almighty God according to the dictates of their own consciences and understanding," but anti-Catholic resentment persisted among Protestants in America. Shea, *Lion and the Lamb*.

44. Anne's choice of Isaiah 9:16 points to religious leaders who, promoting error, lead their followers to destruction.

to slide from the beaten path of Christ's companions. It is, and ever remains to be, a way of self-denial, or abasement of self and whatever tendeth to lead or whomsoever striveth to divert from a steady perseverance in this path when pursued from internal conviction or necessity, becometh a kind of minister of Anti-Christ to us. Let their name to religion or profession be whatsoever it may, or the phylacteries[45] of their garments be ever so conspicuous to the view of men. Oh! May I be preserved, mercy gracious goodness preserving me, for I cannot of myself do one jot towards the same. On Him alone I have relied, I trust, and he is indeed a never-failing preserver unto them that seek diligently unto him.

I recollect in thy former letter thou queried of me concerning poor Martha's expressing some tender sympathy in a Christian concern I believed towards or for that Friend, or exercised deeply tribulated Pilgrim.[46] May [I] acquaint thee she is gone lately to Joshua Hoope's,[47] a person I expressed something to thee about in my reply (whether thou ever got it or no, I cannot tell). He had far above two years or more desired his wife and family to invite her [Martha] up, as well as himself which he thought it his religious duty to do. They did not consent freely for a great while but at last, he importuned them so much, promising to keep at home and not go abroad so much, calling aloud to Friend against blood guiltiness, against mixing with human government, and a good deal so on, which he thought it his duty to proclaim as a trumpet against, until he got (like Benjamin Lay was I suppose about slavery,[48] though perhaps

---

45. A phylactery or *tefillin*, a small box containing Hebrew prayers.

46. This is likely Martha Harris, whom Anne described as a prophesying minister. See chapters 2 and 6, above.

47. Joshua Hoopes (1734–1809), from one of the founding Quaker families in Pennsylvania. The Bradford Monthly Meeting recorded, "The overseers laid before this meeting for consideration the situation of Joshua Hoopes and his frequently taking up most of the time of our meeting to the great disturbance thereof which being attended to it is agreed to lay his case before the monthly meeting for advice." An appointed committee visited Hoopes "to convince him of his error and disgrace him from rambling about disturbing the peace and quiet of Religious meetings, yet he still persists in this disorder endeavoring to lay waste all order and government in society and notwithstanding he appears in some measure disordered in his natural reason." Bradford Monthly Meeting Minutes (1782–1787), March 6, August 15, 1783. After wandering from one meeting to another, shouting his imprecations across Chester County, he was disowned in February 1788 by Uwchlan Monthly Meeting.

48. Benjamin Lay (1682–1759), an English Quaker, immigrated to Philadelphia in 1731 and was a zealous early opponent of slavery and the slave trade. Disciplined by Friends in

more fiery [and] zealous or rather [had] more to say) about them. Perhaps to be quite noisy and talkative in meetings for public worship, and though his matter might perhaps on a close scrutiny be good, yet his manner being too earnest for us to accept in this day as yet. However, he was by no means acceptable to Friends. Though diverse acknowledge what he said in a great many expressions or things is the truth. His family was at last desirous of having Martha under their roof but she would not consent to go, not only their coolness at first for it might have indisposed her mind for going there, but she did think Joshua had got into a far too great zeal or talkative spirit on a subject he otherwise had an honest wish might prosper, though he did not choose the proper way to promote it acceptably.

Martha told him candidly he was wrong and seemed resolved not to go to his house. Thinking, too as she expressed that it might give concern to some friends. Until some of the Goshen Friends, where she is [has] right of membership came and acquainted her that Friends[49] of that meeting had consulted together and appeared quite satisfied with her going (though by his actions in the way I have been speaking of, like Benjamin Lay also he had got himself disowned;[50] otherwise his conduct had been quite unexceptionable as a good neighbor, husband, friend, etc.). They thought it might perhaps be of some use if she could be clear to go, and to their great satisfaction it hath appeared so since for he hath kept at home [and] hath not gone any that I have heard of two meetings to harangue or importune Friends as before and had applied his hands to useful labor, insomuch that he [illegible] his family it would have been 200 pounds in his pocket if [paper torn, missing] had invited her at his first proposing it from an apprehension as he thought of duty. So it appears best to deal gently with such people; they did try force and put him in the hospital, though his companion, who is a distant cousin of mine, a Garrett, was almost broken hearted about consenting to it when solicited. Till at last, a magistrate in his neighborhood or assembly man came down and took him

---

England and Pennsylvania for his boisterous behavior and antislavery protests, Lay, though controversial, inspired late eighteenth- and early nineteenth-century abolitionists. See Rediker, *Fearless Benjamin Lay*.

49. In March 1784, the Goshen Monthly Meeting placed Martha Harris, in poor health, in the care of Isaac Thomas. Goshen Monthly Meeting Minutes (1773–1798), March 1784.

50. In late 1737, the Abington Monthly Meeting ordered Benjamin Lay out of the meeting for business, though he remained a member. Abington Monthly Meeting Minutes (1682–1746), November 30, 1737. Rediker in *The Fearless Benjamin Lay* provides full details.

out and by force also, some others joining him, saying the man was not crazy, it was an unjust imposition of Friends for that it was only his doctrine which they thought truly Christian, if but come up to that, Friends could not relish. So we see how some see more than they practice.

I spent a few hours with thy dear wife, the other evening very pleasantly, and we drank a dish of sage tea alone together. She seems brave and happy in the prospect of seeing thee sometime, though quite gives thee up until the Lord's best time.[51] Farewell, and in his own time may he be again restored to the company of thy Friends here as well as to that of thy affection, though when thee goes to England, I should ever be glad, worthy Friend, to hear of thy going to visit Jos[ep]h Galloway and daughter or any other Friends.[52] I am greatly mistaken if thee has not been a secret hand at work with Elizabeth.[53] [next line illegible] Our family is well in health. Dr. Mott's[54] love is to thee. My love is to Samuel Neale,[55] if thee is nigh hand to him or thinks it worth giving. Farewell W. [William] Strahan[56] whose company hath been quite agreeable to his friends here. I only wish he may give up more fully to what I conceive he sometimes believes he should do. Farewell.

AE [Anne Emlen]

ALS, vol. 42, fol. 162, Pemberton Papers, HSP.

51. Pemberton spent almost thirty months on a transatlantic sojourn, not returning until September 1789. His seven-year journey can be followed in Hodgson, *Life and Travels of John Pemberton.*

52. Leaving with the British in June 1778, Loyalist Galloway and his daughter Elizabeth went to New York and then a year later to England, where he served as adviser to the American Loyalist Claims Commission. Full details are in Norton, *British Americans.* Galloway also withdrew from the Quaker faith, but Anne and her mother retained a close friendship with him, his wife Grace, and their daughter Elisabeth.

53. Anne may refer to Galloway's attempt to protect his widow Grace's dowry property. She died in Philadelphia in 1782 amid a legal battle to bequeath the estate to her daughter Elizabeth. After many years the Pennsylvania Supreme Court granted daughter Elizabeth a small fortune.

54. Not identified.

55. Samuel Neale (1729–1792), an Irish-born Quaker minister, married minister Mary Peisley. His service to truth was published as *Some Account of the Life and Religious Labours of Samuel Neale.*

56. William Strahan (1715–1785), a Quaker publisher, American Philosophical Society member, friend of Benjamin Franklin, and member of Parliament.

TO JOHN DICKINSON

December 21, 1787

In this letter to the statesman John Dickinson (1732–1808), famous for his "Letters from a Farmer in Pennsylvania to the Inhabitants of the British Colonies" (1767–68) and his political role as delegate to the Continental Congresses (1774–76), president both of the Delaware (1781–82) and Pennsylvania (1782–85) legislative assemblies, and delegate to the Constitutional Convention of 1787, Anne expresses great concern regarding education even as the states were debating ratification of the Constitution.

Respected Friend,

I attended to thy requests and send some patterns of flannel. Thy brother Dickinson[57] was set off for Wilmington before I sent the letter as I did not arrive in town till yesterday.

I am pleased with thy charitable intentions of being a capital contributor towards a free school established on suitable principles.[58] The Great all-Wise Being in considering the happiness of mankind, doth not distribute his talents amongst them but according as they are capable of improving them. Shall we not then controvert or at least not consider the wise order of his Providence so far as to bestow an abundance of manure on a barren soil that can never repay the cultivator for this labor and expense. Shall we branch forth in this establishment into high academic learning; depart from a plain English education and indiscriminately apply great labor on minds not capable of much improvement? Or shall we keep to the common and essential parts of learning by which it can be extensively useful by affording help to a greater number than if it were otherwise and where a peculiar liveliness or strength of genius or in other words where many talents appear, then to have a certain part of

---

57. Philemon Dickinson (1739–1809) was John Dickinson's younger brother. A dedicated Federalist, he represented New Jersey at the Continental Congress.

58. Dickinson and his wife Mary Norris Dickinson supported educational efforts as early as 1782 when Quakers launched efforts to establish a school for poor non-Quaker children. Eight years later, the Dickinsons deeded a lot at Seventh Street near Market to create a charity school in Philadelphia for children of poor Friends rather than children of non-Quakers. Dewees and Dewees, *Centennial History of Westtown Boarding School*, 23. The plan, it seems, did not materialize.

the funds appropriate to their more extensive culture of such when the institution becomes strong enough?

At present, considering the infant state of the country compared with others, and the difficulties some ever good livers are encompassed with at times in procuring an ample subsistence, I make no attempts at a very rapid advancement in this matter, but be content to witness a gradual growth such as the state of the country and minds of its inhabitants are capable of bearing under with ease. As it is a voluntary matter, they must feel themselves easy in it, or it is impossible it can advance. There must be a secret persuasion of mind in favor of anything before it openly assents to it: If we attempt to force it into conviction, it will shut the door if its will against us, for as free agents we naturally love everything that is voluntary; whatever appears to the contrary is to our feelings as impositions and burthens, though in their nature and tendency they are not. Hence it is necessary in forming the building to consider the materials by which it is to be raised and supported. The minds of the people must be considered as these materials or the furnishers of them. Time only can prepare, by suitable labor bestowed upon them. Thou mayst be a suitable laborer in the work if disposed to. It is a worthy act, not only to do good ourselves but to induces others thereunto.

If thou was to become a member of society[59] thou might with joint assistance of others also be yoked in mind to the service and become as Doctor Fothergill[60] a vigilant advancer of it into execution. But that must depend on thy own feelings. Perhaps human wisdom is not yet sufficiently reduced in subjection to the "simplicity that is in Christ" to make thee as yet willing to stoop to the foolishness of the Cross sometimes appearing in the Quaker. I do not mean an irrational or unchristian foolishness, but what appeareth foolishness to sophistry. I suggest these things respecting thyself. I do not say they are so. Forgive my great freedom. And burn this if I do not conclude to save thee that trouble. If it goes, let the veil of charity cover its defects.

And thou may persevere through time in that which shall induce us to address the[e] in the character of John Dickinson the worthy not John

---

59. Anne notes that Dickinson was not a Quaker, though his wife was. Dickinson admired Friends' principles but served in the Revolution as a private and a colonel. Nonetheless, his philanthropic support of Quaker causes was notable. For more on Dickinson and his family, see Calvert, *Quaker Constitutionalism*, 189–95; and Flower, *John Dickinson*.

60. John Fothergill (1712–1780) was an influential London Quaker doctor, botanist, philanthropist, and friend of Benjamin Franklin. In 1779, Fothergill was instrumental in creating and financing Ackworth, a Quaker-only School in northern England.

Dickinson Esquire or the Great. Thou wilt say I suppose I am a strange girl to write as I do.

Farewell! However thy Friend
[Ann] Emlen Jr.

[P.S.]
Philadelphia 12 mo. 21st '87

26th of the Mo: from the departure of [Jos.?] West from town a day before I expected missed an early opportunity for this. A pattern Samuel Rhoads had, if flannel may suit thee better than the enclosed perhaps. There is no great variety in town I believe. I feel not very well from a renewed cold attended with some fever. But come life or death sincerely wish thee would attend to the matter spoken of above if my indisposition should increase, I think I shall secure something to the institution myself, according or in proportion to what I may be possessed of.[61]

ALS, Society Collection, HSP.

TO SUSANNA MIFFLIN

Philadelphia
8 mo 4th '88
[August 4, 1788]

Shortly after Anne pledged to marry Warner Mifflin, she wrote this letter to his daughter Susannah, soon to become one of her stepchildren. The letter provides insight into how Anne's thoughts about parenting had formed.

Dear Young Friend:

The kind of respectful expressions contained in thy letter is very pleasing to me.[62] Without knowledge of thy person, or of thy character, I felt sensations of hope in thy account, that if thou art mindful to please thy Maker, remembering

---

61. As early as 1777, Anne considered working in a charity school for poor children, and at age forty-seven she taught briefly at Westtown school. See chapter 4 and MRP, above.

62. Born on August 24, 1779, Susannah had not quite reached her ninth birthday. Perhaps with her father's encouragement Susannah had previously written to her prospective stepmother Anne, but that letter has not been found.

him thy Creator in the days of thy youth, it will indeed be well with thee in the land and state of being which the Lord thy God giveth unto thee and thou may be made an useful friend in thy day, which is my wish. Thee uttereth kind intentions of acting to the best of thy understanding to please me. Dear Susannah seek to please thy heavenly Father and in that thou will please me by being [brackets enclosing blank space] thereby through his presence dwelling with thee into every right thing, which will doubtless afford me much pleasure. I shall rejoice to see you do well as much as though you were my own dear children, for I shall consider you as such and I hope you will allow me to treat you as such.[63] That affectionate concern implanted in the breast of a parent for its child leading to the freedom of true friendship and regarding where advice, admonition, counsel or even reproof might be wanting, it is not afraid to administer it in that. I hope we shall dwell in love dear Susannah and go hand in hand therein. A good man's steps are ordered of the Lord as is a good woman's and child's also. I wish ours may be such that the peace of heaven be with and seal us to the end. You that are younger as you will need more of a mother's care and attention and may more immediately come under the direction of such than those who are arrive or arriving to years capable of reflection for themselves, though not less objects of anxious solicitude for their safe stepping along in the path of wisdom, that they may be happily as examples and way marks unto others and the example of those where parents like thy father are looked at and often followed. May this consideration induce thee dear Susannah to endeavor to keep near to that which is right and in matters where thy inclination leads one way and duty to thy parent and Maker, another, rather to take up the cross in which thee will have sweet peace and a reward that can never be taken from thee.

I send thee a little bag of shells to view in the variety and beauty thereof, the wonderful works of Providence. A little parcel of raisins and a book containing pieces that will please and edify if attended to [by] children and young people. I send also Warner[64] a little parcel as a sample of love and good will, though they are far inferior in sweetness to friendship and true Christian

---

63. Anne was perhaps hoping to ease Susannah of any fears of the trope of the cruel stepmother; at the same time, Anne makes it clear that an affectionate mother did not stint in strict parenting. Wilson in *History of Stepfamilies in Early America* offers insights into the "wicked Stepmother" and "through the eyes of a stepchild." For a treatment of Quaker family relations, see Levy, *Quakers and the American Family*.

64. Warner Mifflin Jr., age eleven at the time, was Warner's only son from his first marriage.

fellowship. I wish this may prevail when we meet together under one roof[65] and in that [I] wish [to] conclude, thy affectionate Friend.

A. Emlen Junr.

ALS, Cowgill-Mifflin Papers, DPA.

TO JOHN PARRISH

3Mo: [illegible] '99
[March 1799]

This first surviving letter written by Anne after her husband's death five months before shows how quickly she reengaged in Quaker affairs. That she contemplated leaving her young sons to accompany Mary Berry on a voyage to the war-torn Caribbean attests to her unflinching desire to take up the cross.

Esteemed Kinsman:

Believe it may be right to inform thee that in my late visit to our Quarterly Meeting[66] I find our Friend Mary Berry continues her concern for Barbados and views to going this spring if way may open.[67] I hope if it is the Lord's will this should take place—that a door may open. Mary said she would as leave go from Baltimore from which place a trade is kept up to that Island; [and]

---

65. They would be under one roof shortly after the marriage of Anne and Warner on October 16, 1788, but Susannah only lived at home until 1794 when she was apprenticed to Josiah Bunting, a Chester County Quaker farmer, to learn housewifery. For more on this, see Warner Mifflin to Susannah Mifflin, November 2, 1794, in Nash and McDowell, *Writings of Warner Mifflin*, 422–23.

66. The Southern Quarterly Meeting was usually held in Easton, Maryland, in early March.

67. Anne's frequent companion on ministerial journeys, Mary received a traveling certificate in June 1798 to visit the scattered Friends on hurricane-ravaged Barbados. Though her husband's health was failing, Anne, determined to accompany Mary, had presented a traveling certificate from her monthly and quarterly meetings to the ministers and elders, who authorized the trip. Nicholas Waln to "Friend in Baltimore," March 28, 1798, in *Friends Miscellany* (1834), 5:141; Parrish to Phoebe Speakman, June 16, 1798, in *Friends Miscellany* (1835), 6:262. However, the 1798 trip was postponed, probably due to the disruption of ship traffic in the West Indies during the Anglo-French War then in progress. For more on this, see Gragg, *Quaker Community on Barbados*.

John McKim[68] was concerned in it. Perhaps it would not be amiss to write to him if thee see the way and enquire if any vessel without guns[69] was like to sail from there sometime after our yearly meeting.[70] Mary and I propose being in town a few days before Yearly Meeting at Samuel Clark's[71] or my mother's; thee may hear of us.

There is a Woman's Collection in our Quarterly Meeting; what is gathered of it we shall give to Mary Berry for pocket expenses in the journey and the men I expect will contribute something in addition. The Yearly Meeting treasury no doubt will discharge her sea expenses and maybe some small addition of clothing. What cash I may not be able to command, for my necessary expenses by land and sea if it should be my lot to take the awful voyage (which I do not shrink from),[72] I propose borrowing of our female treasurers in the city and giving my note for it to the treasury, to be paid soon as I can with convenience without intending [that] which will be proper enough as no part of it is put out to interest. Mary said she never could think of going to be an expense to them she went with; and I feel glad our little treasury may help to relieve. If thee hears of any probable conveyance, thee may leave a letter at my Mother's on the subject. I thought of asking Henry Drinker or some Friend of benevolent attention to the cause of truth whether they thought there might not some be excited, if the matter was spread to fit out a vessel and load it on a trading voyage to that place. Perhaps some from here would be willing to help load it; it may do no harm to suggest the idea to any in thy freedom of

---

68. A Quaker Baltimore merchant.

69. Quaker traveling ministers may have refused to travel on armed vessels; but it's possible that Anne and Mary's concern was to reach Barbados on an unarmed vessel flying under a neutral flag. A few weeks before this letter, President Adams had nominated William Vans Murray as the US minister plenipotentiary to France in an attempt to defuse American hostility to French after the XYZ Affair the previous year.

70. After the devastating yellow fever epidemic in late summer and autumn of 1798 that had claimed Warner Mifflin's life, Friends moved the yearly meeting to mid-December; however, after briefly convening, Friends decided to move yearly meetings to April each year until the outbreaks abated.

71. Samuel Clark (ca. 1735–1802) was a Quaker carpenter and elder of the Philadelphia Monthly Meeting.

72. The women's minutes of the Murderkill Monthly Meeting are silent on endorsing this trip; but Murderkill Meeting was probably satisfied with the former approval from the Philadelphia ministers and elders the previous June. On April 1, 1789, Warner wrote to Henry Drinker, "The Monthly Meeting's certificate for my wife is thought by her to be among the Meeting papers in thy possession. If so, thou will please to send it to [Anne's] Mother." Nash and McDowell, *Writings of Warner Mifflin*, 532.

way opens. Mary thought much of Captain:Gill her cousin[73] for a Captain; some time ago he seemed rather disposed to try a sea voyage again. I received thy letters some time since they were written. I am not tenacious about finding my dear husband's letters; I can acquiesce with [a] Friend [in] mind in its suppression, [though] being wrote from a concern had they seen the way suitably to correct the exceptionable parts, it might not have been without its use in strengthening a right mind in him.[74] My love to thy children, from thy Friend and relative.

AM

ALS, C-P-W, box 1, fol. 26.

TO WILLIAM COBBETT

Kent County
Delaware State
[ca. April 1799][75]

Warner Mifflin was never attacked in the press more viciously than by William Cobbett, the firebrand journalist who had emigrated from England to Philadelphia in 1794. Anne's restrained reply was never published in any newspaper at that time.

To withhold tribute due to merit is to disregard the scripture injunction of rendering to all men their dues; from this view of things I am induced to vindicate the character of one, whom long acquaintance had confirmed to me was worthy, against the public opprobrium cast on it by Wm. Cobbit [Cobbett],

---

73. Possibly Joseph Gill, of Berry's Third Haven Monthly Meeting.

74. Anne's closing strongly suggests a reference of Warner's letter to President Adams, penned just before she and Warner fled the yellow fever outbreak in Philadelphia the previous September. See Warner Mifflin to John Adams, September 24, 1798, in Nash and McDowell, *Writings of Warner Mifflin*, 549–52. Warner had taken the letter back to Chestnut Grove, intending to transcribe and polish it, but left it in Anne's hands. Two years later she asked George Churchman and Jacob Lindley to send it to the president, which they did in January 1801 as Adams was completing his term. For more on this, see Nash, *Warner Mifflin*, 224–25.

75. Since Anne did not leave Kent County until May 1799, to move to Philadelphia, we have assigned this document an approximate date of April 1799.

who I am confident was not acquainted with the genuine traits thereof, a sketch of whose unjust reflections I have lately met with in one of Brown's papers.[76] He appears to have been for some time piqued at a conversation that Brissot represents as having past [passed] between Warner Mifflin and him: when various parts of that writer's letters will prove his inaccuracy in the English language and the rapidity of his ideas and free expression of them, from whence great mistakes arose. Witness his describing it as a part of Friends discipline to put on worsted stockings the 25th of September,[77] which must produce a smile on every one of that community who know better and an emotion of contempt perhaps from observers who might justly esteem it trifling for the adoption of so large and respectable a body of people. From misapprehension on the part of Brissot a misrepresentation hath taken place without design in the writer, being evident he would not wish to depreciate the Society [of Friends] or the individual in the view of any, as he speaks highly of both. I have ever believed since the publication of his Travels[78] that his bad English had produced this mistake and have been lately confirmed therein from the declaration of a particular acquaintance of Warner Mifflin, whose word may be relied on as valid and who was present at the interview[79] and says no such discourse passed, nor could I before believe he ever meant to exalt

---

76. Brown's *Philadelphia Gazette and Universal Daily Advertiser* published Cobbett's feverish attack on Warner Mifflin on November 22, 1798, a month after Warner's burial. Cobbett had attacked Mifflin and Brissot as "precious hypocrites" in his *A Bone to Gnaw for the Democrats*. Cobbett's "Peter Porcupine" continued his attacks on Mifflin (and on others such as Anthony Benezet, Benjamin Rush, and Thomas Paine) in subsequent editions of *A Bone to Gnaw*. Within weeks, Mathew Carey defended Mifflin, publishing *Plumb Pudding for the Humane, Chaste, Valiant, Enlightened Peter Porcupine*. Carey deplored Porcupine's "cowardly and billingsgate attacks" on a man "whose exemplary humanity had acquired him the plaudits of all who knew him."

77. Anne's notice written for publication pointed out errors she believed Brissot made in his depiction of Philadelphia Quakers. The unpublished remarks are in box 1, fol. 25, C-P-W. Hoping to have it published, Anne sought the help of John Parrish. Anne Mifflin to John Parrish, February 12, 1799, box 2, EFP.

78. Brissot de Warville's *Nouveau voyage dans les États-Unis de l'Amérique Septentrionale, fait en 1788* (Paris, 1791). For Brissot's favorable treatment of the American Quakers built on the ideal of the legendary good Quaker, the embodiment of religious toleration, pacifism, and benevolence, and his meetings with Warner and Anne, see Nash, *Warner Mifflin*, 149–51, 224. Brissot's *Nouveau voyage* translated by Barlow *New Travels in the United States, 1788*. Anne's perturbance with some of Brissot's descriptions of Philadelphia Friends speaks to her protectiveness of them. Brissot, *New Travels in the United States of America*, 301.

79. Not identified.

the character of the French Nation at the expense of the English.[80] He was a man of the most enlarged benevolence of as much as any man I ever knew. His love (as his religious professions also dictated) was universal and extended to the whole bulk of mankind without respect to nation or color. I have heard him on the early revolutionary procedures of the French Nation suggest that peradventure Providence might favor their then prospects from their disposition to emancipation.[81] But of latter times when power seemed productive of corruption, as it eventually does in all nations and individuals where it is not restrained by a principle superior to man, there is no doubt left with those who had the pleasure of his acquaintance that he disapproved of their politics. It is to be hoped therefore that this very decisive writer who stamps him [Warner Mifflin] as hypocrite and fool without hesitation will in justice to himself calmly investigate the grounds of his association; and he may discover from the account of these who were personally acquainted with him and from his writing that he was no <u>fool</u>. And the many conflicts, besetments, persecutions and revilings that he passed through in the promotion of rectitude in various shapes, particularly in the liberation of the Blacks, which none but these who were intimately acquainted with the history of his life can have any competent idea of: and which abundantly proves his integrity was on no slender foundation. Therefore, that he was no <u>hypocrite</u>. Should Wm. Cobbit fail to make this investigation and offer some atonement for attempting to assassinate a character that in many respects did honor to humanity, he may expect some of the moderate part of his subscribers who disapprove of such rash methods of expression will withdraw their names from his list as a testimony against them.

An Observer

Manuscript copy, C-P-W, box 9, fol. 7.

80. Warner's remarks in his conversation with Brissot (as reported by the Frenchman) that aroused Cobbett were "I love thy nation. I must admit I used to be greatly prejudiced against the French. But when I actually saw them, a secret voice told me to know them and love them. I have therefore sought out their company. I have learned to know them, and it is with pleasure that I have found in them a kindness and a universal benevolence which I had not met among the English." Brissot, *New Travels in the United States of America*, 165.

81. Anne refers to the 1794 decree by the French Constituent Assembly's emancipating slavery in France and in Saint-Domingue, Guadeloupe, and Guyana, the largest of the French West Indies colonies.

A BRIEF ACCOUNT OF THE LATE WARNER MIFFLIN:
IN A LETTER TO HIS SONS SAMUEL AND LEMUEL MIFFLIN

October 25, 1799

Anne writes the following based on advice letters, a particular genre in seventeenth- and eighteenth-century English literature, but hers is intended solely for her boys. Just one year and nine days after the death of her husband, still grieving and cognizant of her own mortality, she composed this as a treasured keepsake that described their father, his character, his virtues, and his monumental work. She intended to give her sons a tangible recollection of him as well as a memorial that might inspire them to imitate their father.

My dear Children,[82]

As your infant years deprive you of the benefit that might be derived from a particular and personal knowledge of the merits of your dear deceased parent: I proceed to leave with you, this little, monumental epitome of his virtues and labors; that should I not be continued on this stage of being, to recite them with my lips, you may have an opportunity of eyeing this small delineation of the features of his conduct and be engaged to imitate. So that the loss to civil and religious society, in the removal of so valuable a character, may be regained; by an abstract of the like worth reviving in his sons.

His early life was marked with uncommon exposure, being the eldest son of a family respected in a part of Virginia remote from the settlements of Friends. His manners affable and conversation cheerful and pleasing, he became early an object of attention by people in gay and high life; which, though it introduced him into some of the vanities and levities prevalent, yet he was in a singular and providential manner wrested as from the jaws of temptation at different periods, so as to be happily preserved from the commission of things gross and polluting. May such be your blessed experience, that your souls may be maintained in innocence before an all-seeing God who can, if he sees meet, preserve you as vessels for service in his holy house, bearing the inscription of holiness unto him.

His first connection in marriage was to Elizabeth Johns (descendant of a respectable Friend of that name, one of the first settlers in Maryland);[83] and

---

82. The title appears in Anne's hand, at the top of the manuscript.
83. For the family of Elizabeth Johns and the long-standing confusion about this in the historical and genealogical literature, see Nash, *Warner Mifflin*, 28–30.

from circumstances of supposed difficulty in their proceeding by Meeting in a fit of youthful inconsideration they went out of the order of Society in accomplishing their marriage. But no sooner was the ceremony past, than he became deeply smitten with remorse for his precipitation. And though they afterwards returned to the fold, and became baptized and living members of Society, both filling the important station of elders in humility therein, yet he frequently expressed apprehensions that this misstep might be suffered to have a crippling effect on him all his days.

Previous to his more deep surrender to the work of religion, he was possessed of a Commission of the Peace, and though he endeavored to act an upright part, in the full discharge of his duty therein, yet, not finding it productive of true inward consolation, he believed it right to relinquish the office and therein set an example of the convicted necessity he felt, for Friends to resign their active stations in civil government in enforcing the mixed laws of human policy and enlist themselves more unshaken under the divine control,[84] the directing influence of the Law of God, the Spirit of Life in Christ Jesus, which redeems and sets free from the law of sin and death.[85] Under the operation and progress of which work, he was made an eminent instrument in promoting and advancing many of the precious testimonies of truth, which the Lord hath entrusted us as a people with the guardianship of; and in the exercise of a lively and vigorous faith and belief that the most high was indeed come to teach his people himself; that, as in a season of memorable deliverance from the Egyptian host, when the highest commanded Moses, "Speak unto the Children of Israel, that they go forward,"[86] on their moving in the faith, the Red Sea was made to divide for their safe passing along. So, he believed, the Almighty was commanding through the manifestations of the light of Christ, of whom Moses was a type, that his spiritual Israel should go forward from the entanglement of every improper yoke of bondage to the Pharaoh spirit of hardness and darkness too prevalent in the world, to the perfecting of holiness in his fear—believing in the propriety of Apostolic exhortation, Hebrews 12:25: "See that ye refuse not him that speaketh: for if they escaped not who refused him that spoke on earth, much more shall not we escape, if we turn away from him that speaketh from heaven." Nor was his enterprising spirit [or?] established mind daunted or diverted from the pathway

---

84. The appointments of Mifflin to Kent County justice of the peace from 1771 to 1774 are presented in Justice, *Life and Ancestry of Warner Mifflin*, 110.

85. Romans 8:2, paraphrased.

86. Exodus 14:15.

of duty; even when Goliaths in might presented to [bid] defiance to spiritual Israel, or those whose weapons are not carnal but spiritual, and who desire to fight only in the heavenly warfare to obtain the glorious liberty of the Children of God under the banner of the Conquering Lamb or Prince of Peace, of the increase of whose kingdom and government there shall never be an end.

May the prime object of your pursuits, my children, be to advance the harmonizing and blessed influence of the redeemer's kingdom, which breathes "Glory to God in the highest, on earth peace, and good will to men,"[87] rather than to mix with the pursuits of human policy, in the jangling parties amongst men; and so deprive yourselves of that tranquility of soul which is witnessed in Christ, who amply fulfilleth his promise to his followers, "Peace I leave with you, my peace I give unto you: not as the world giveth, give I unto you. Let not your heart be troubled, neither let it be afraid." John 14:27.

He was steadfast in a faithful and zealous testimony against the pernicious use of spirituous liquors, endeavoring to extirpate the abuse thereof from harvest fields, tables, and etc. And he maintained an animated testimony against war, not only in striving to cleanse his hands of whatsoever related thereto and withholding from aiding others in their exertions therein by voluntary contributions, but also in his conciliating disposition, showing abundant instances of the meekness of Christian condescension in matters wherein he was aggrieved and of his peculiar talent at reconciling differences; often no doubt being rewarded with the blessing descending on peacemakers who witness the owning presence of our heavenly Father as his <u>children</u>.

But that which most engaged the uniform exercise of his mind for a number of years, as the top-stone of his religious concern, was a laborious travail of spirit and free disposal of his time and substance in advancing the liberation of the poor oppressed Black People. A trumpet was given him on this subject with other brethren, to spread the alarm within the borders of our society, that we might more and more arise and shake ourselves from the dust of the earth in a departure from this iniquity. And when our camp was in a good degree purged from the filthiness thereof, his commission was enlarged to go forth among the people and powers of the earth to labor and dissuade them from such an unrighteous practice, delivering their own souls from the indignation that will be poured forth on the actors of such abomination.

87. Luke 2:4.

For some particulars of his progress in this benevolent work, which engaged his persevering attention for a number of years, I [refer] to his *Defence* published in 1796, which was necessary to appear for the removal of those various aspersions and misrepresentations, which the enemies of his pointed testimonies against error and iniquity labored to propagate, though he patiently bore their contumely in the experience of that blessing devolving on those who are persecuted for righteousness sake. His laborious exercises on this subject, as well as others, towards the latter part of his time, had evidently a wasting effect on his frame, which hastened the period of a life much devoted to the self-denying path and close religious engagements of a faithful disciple of the Lamb; so that it might be truly said, he <u>wore out</u>; his talents did not <u>rust out</u> for want of use.

He was not only frequently engaged in person to plead with those in power on behalf of the injured Black People but his pen was oft drawn out on this and other subjects, remonstrating against oppressive laws in military fines on the tenderly conscientious, against horse-racing and other vices, being of a good understanding and qualified to point out the distinctions between virtue and vice. And as an experienced elder remarked, he thought few could with more propriety adopt this language than himself: "The blessing of him that was ready to perish came upon me: and I caused the widow's heart to sing for joy. I put on righteousness, and it clothed me: my judgment was as a robe and diadem. I was eyes to the blind, and feet was I to the lame. I was a father to the poor: and the cause which I knew not I searched out. And I break the jaws of the wicked and plucked the spoil out of his teeth."[88]

He discharged his portion of duty in the government of the church, as an elder worthy of double honor, being not only especially qualified to partake with those called to the ministry in their inward travail and provings, strengthening them by secret sustaining sympathy, as Aaron and Hur upheld the hands of Moses. And was qualified suitably to counsel those who stood in need. But was frequently concerned to drop a word of exhortation in Meetings of Discipline, and at the close of Public Meetings, particularly in the one of which he was a member, and in [their] families.

He was distinguishably useful as an able disciplinarian in support of the good order of Society, in which service he visited in the year 1777 the Quarterly Meetings belonging to this Yearly Meeting, in company with a committee for

---

88. Job 29:13–17.

that service.[89] And by the tenor of his notes in that journey,[90] he appears to have travailed under many renewed baptisms of soul, in a Godly exercise for the advancement of mankind out of the fall and the progress of our church toward the standard of more perfect purity. In 1780, he rode about 340 miles in visiting the Quarterly and Monthly Meetings in Bucks County, with a minute of approbation from the Monthly Meeting; in which he appears to have been exercised to labor with a disposition too apparent in many, of settling down at ease, inattentive to the concerns and travail of the body. In 1782, he traveled in company with other Friends down this peninsula advocating the cause of the Black People, which labors appears to have been blessed.[91] In 1780 [1781], he united with a Friend, in like station with himself, in visiting Friends' Meetings in New England, and left behind him a good favor as a useful instrument in the Lord's hand, in repairing the waste places of Zion.[92] In the year 1787 he joined a Friend in the ministry, in paying a religious visit to the Yearly and many other Meetings in Carolina and attended the Assembly there on behalf of the Blacks.[93]

He was a dutiful son to his parents, when living; an affectionate husband and tender father, and was religiously and industriously exercised in the discharge of other relative and social duties.

He possessed in himself a testimony against the too free use of tobacco. But having occasion sometime to use it medicinally, it produced a warfare to guard against the excessive, or merely habitual use thereof; and this led him to lament the imbecility of human nature. When upon your elder brother[94]

---

89. For five weeks, from October 30 to December 8, Warner journeyed on horseback through the counties of Chester, Bucks, and Philadelphia.

90. His notes for this trip have not been found, but the journals of his traveling partner, George Churchman, cataloged at QCHC as "Churchman Diaries," provide copious details, including harrowing attempts to enter British-occupied Philadelphia. For more on this, see Nash, *Warner Mifflin*, 69–72.

91. On this trip, with traveling companion cousin John Parrish, Warner crossed the Eastern Shore to spend nineteen days successfully lobbying the Virginia legislature to pass a bill allowing manumissions by individual slave owners.

92. Anne rates this as the longest, most difficult of Warner's many journeys, beginning on May 4, 1781, and ending on his return home, about August 24. With George Churchman, David Cooper, and James Thornton, Mifflin traveled about 1,400 miles, mostly on horseback. The trip is covered in Nash, *Warner Mifflin*, 82–91, with a map on page 86.

93. Anne refers to a trip in October and November to lobby the North Carolina legislature to revoke the law forbidding the manumission of slaves and to halt the practice of seizing men and women already liberated by Quakers to sell at auction back into slavery.

94. Warner Mifflin Jr.

entering the chamber with a cigar in his mouth, he warned him against the practice, even when he could scarcely articulate the words clearly, desiring he would not be backwards and forwards in it as he had been, that he knew what it was. May you my dear children be warned by the experience of the wise; for habits once strongly contracted are hard to subdue, and nothing but that subjection to the cross, which is not pleasant to the natural faculty, and persevering self-denial through holy help, will redeem or deliver from the thralldom thereof. Therefore, we only increase our difficulty in the path of life, and shackle our souls with improper burthens, when we unguardedly embrace any custom which hath not its foundation in true wisdom. And though a degree of the use of this powerful and intoxicating plant may be serviceable to the complaints of some who may be advanced or advancing in years, yet for the young and strong to adopt its consumption (I will not say the use, for it is the abuse of it) is running either blindfolded or willfully into that which is really injurious to body and mind. So I hope my sons will carefully guard against the encroachments of corrupt custom, in this as well as in other respects, especially when they are now informed of the dying injunction of a worthy parent. For those who reject or slight the counsel of such, [they] will not be likely to be attended with a blessing in their footsteps through life.

His anxiety was great on account of many Black People who unworthily applied the privilege of their freedom, causing thereby gainsayers to vaunt over their follies, who are opposed to the good work of their emancipation, when he expressively broke forth in this language: "Oh! That the Black People could be persuaded to do better."

This and a concern for the accommodation of some Friends in reduced circumstances seemed the only objects of anxious concern on his deathbed except the not having his will completed, which was the daily, almost hourly burthen of his soul, frequently calling for his Friends to come and assist in the finishing of it. But an attention to it was neglected too long, although he had prepared a rough essay of what he had proposed and had expressed the same in substance to his grown children, in a solid opportunity with them before setting off to attend the Yearly Meeting, in which accustomed act of dedication it was thought he received the messenger of his death in a prevalent infection.[95]

95. Warner had not completed his will before leaving for Philadelphia to attend the PYM on September 24, 1798. What instructions he did leave were imperfectly drawn and ultimately declared invalid. This incomplete document is reproduced in Justice, *Life and Ancestry of Warner Mifflin*, 223–28. For family disputes over the disposition of the estate

So that this omission by no means appears to have arisen from a negligent oversight of that salutary part of our discipline which requires Friends to settle their affairs and make their wills whilst in health. He had been anxiously concerned on that score, as he told me. Had I known what he had gone through on that account for some weeks past, I would have pitied him by which it appeared he had a foresight of what was approaching. Difficulty attended a hasty settlement, as his affairs [lay] wide, from circumstances proceeding from his benevolence; as beyond men in general, he fulfilled that apostolic injunction, "Look not every man on his own things, but every man also on the things of others. Let this mind be in you, which was also in Christ Jesus."[96]

He indeed exceeded most I ever was acquainted with in the pure disinterested love of mankind. And he was far from building up himself by the oppression of others but would rather submit to suffer than be the instrument of suffering; and feared rather than coveted to be possessed of great riches, from a like pious motive with Agur, "Lest I be full, and deny thee, and say, who is the Lord."[97]

The situation of his affairs in some respects and his desire of seeing all concerned together that things might be settled with general consent and acquiescence with his mind had been a means of retarding the business of fully completing his will. And now, some of the parties being at a distance, and some fearful of approaching the house from the expected malignancy of the disorder; and the Friend whom he twice sent for to execute his prospects, from same motive or other rather evading the office, it remained unfinished. But this event, not arising from willful or reprehensible neglect, his portion of exercise therein closed; and his soul was favored to mount as on the wings of seraphic love and heavenly enjoyment, above all things changeable, after repeated looks of inexpressible concern on my account, desiring me not to grieve for him, and, I believe, tenderly fearful that the unsettled state of affairs would be a means of adding gall to my woodworm. But I could freely excuse the omission and apply it in part perhaps to mine own doors, as he had several times in past seasons suggested a desire that I might sympathetically aid him in forming a will, which I regularly declined, expressing my belief that if people would center deep to the gift of grace in their own minds—asking for aid—they might be even divinely aided in a matter of such magnitude. And in the present

---

and the final ruling by the Kent County Orphans Court, see Nash, *Warner Mifflin*, 222–23.

96. Philippians 2:4–5.
97. Proverbs 30:9.

circumstance, as there were offspring by two mothers, I had not a freedom to dictate, but left it entirely to the pointing or wisdom in his own mind, which restriction felt in myself I have had cause to be truly thankful for attending to since.

I was his steady nurse, with your brother Warner and sister Susan. Not very long before his departure, wearied with loss of sleep, grief, and attendance, I retired to another room to see if I could be sustained by a few moments of rest. But sleep was far from me, and when about to return I received a message that he wished to see me. I went; and with a look filled with tenderness, he said he loved to have me by him. A most affectionate embrace took place, and soon after a change beginning to appear, he calmly lifted up his hand to show me how the blood was settling.

Not long after, with much composure, though with some evident increase of pain (as he had laid in much quietness and without much apparent suffering for the greater part of his sickness), the solemn change took place. But Oh! The imbittered pangs of separation, even at this time, and many times when the waves lift up their heads; how doth mine eyes run down with tears; how am I depressed with inexpressible [rendings?] of soul, in feeling of and contemplating my great loss and striped state; and your deplorable one, my children. "Poor fellows" said he one day on your entering the room, with a look of unspeakable feeling and pity, no doubt contemplating your approaching exposed state without a father's care, and the floods of temptation you would be assailed with in passing through time [wherein?] ye must seek for your defence by watching against their attacks and praying for deliverance from their prevalence, that your souls may be preserved in a state of purity and acceptance with an all-seeing God. May the God of all mercy and consolation be a father to you, guide you by his blessed spirit, and raise in your breasts a confidential trust in his goodness and sufficiency, similar to what possessed the mind of his servant David, when he said, "When my father and my mother forsake me, then the Lord will take me up."[98] And if he is pleased to implant a concern in the minds of Godly disposed Friends for your preservation, and they may at any time feel engaged to drop a word of caution or counsel, may the ear of your souls be opened to receive instruction.

Oh! the state, above all sense of pain and trouble I had a view of, as that in which the soul of your worthy parent was about everlastingly to enter in. It excluded for a season all sorrow on his account. Yea, I was made even to rejoice

---

98. Psalms 27:10.

in the prospect of his approaching happiness—I wondered at my feelings forgetful of my own state—I reflected, could I crave his continuance under the many exercises that loaded at times his spirit and desire longer to withhold him from the blessed fruition of such peace? I felt the sustaining presence of my redeemer who when about to leave his disciples said, "Peace I give unto you: If you loved me, ye would rejoice, because I said, I go unto the Father:"[99] And it is the truest mark of love to rejoice with our Friends in their occasions of joy, though we ourselves be losers thereby. It is self that speaketh another language.

But Oh! when the voice of this self-began to be heard, when reflection was turned to view my deplorable loss and striped condition without his society, who had been to me as a husband, father and friend; and who had often remarked his regard to me was like unto that borne by Jonathan to David, "passing the love of woman." Well therefore might I adopt the language of David on his loss, "I am distressed for thee my brother—very pleasant hast thou been unto me."[100] Into what a flood of grief was my spirit overwhelmed; and now in reciting these circumstances, my wound bleedeth afresh. And though thirteen moons have revolved their course, yet sorrow's sword seemeth at times as poignant to my mental feelings as the first day it entered. Well for us, succeeding time blunts the keen edge thereof, and these returns of overpowering grief are less frequent and mercifully mitigated by some alleviating circumstance [and?] reflection: as nature could not sustain the conflict, the natural life would fall a prey thereto, and spiritual also. And would it not be rebellion against the wisdom of divine decrees to admit a spirit of murmuring against even piercing events. For though we may deeply deplore our losses, yet as we repair to the healer of breaches with prostrated spirits, he will regard our secret petitions in like manner with Jonah's in his conflicted state: "When my soul fainted within me I remembered the LORD: and my prayer came in unto thee, into thy holy temple."[101]

Oh! My dear children! Dwell as at the footstool of Jesus, ask counsel of him the unerring Guide and Counsellor. Delight to read instructive and good books. Don't pass over time in idleness and dissipation of mind that ought to be better applied. Delight to wait on God in spirit. Delight in good company. Thus, may you peradventure, should some length of days be your portion, and

99. John 14:27–28.
100. 2 Samuel 1:26.
101. Jonah 2:7.

it proves the Lord's gracious purpose to fit you for service in his holy house of prayer. Become as polished shafts in his sacred quiver and prepared to fill up the place of your honorable father, who is doubtless now reaping the blessed and joyous reward of a well spent life. And that his may be your happy progress and conclusion, is above all other objects that which liest nearest my heart and to the fervent petition on your account of your very affectionate mother,

A. Mifflin

Kent, 10 month 25th, 1799
ALS, EFP, box 1.

TO JOHN PARRISH

11 Mo: 16th '99
[November 16, 1799]

Still living in Kent County, Anne preoccupied herself with family affairs, Quaker meetings, and safeguarding the reputation of Warner thirteen months after his death.

Esteemed Relation,

I continued my prospect of visiting my children[102] about the time of the Western Quarter,[103] until [a] way seemed to close for want of company after which Brother Daniel[104] informed me he proposed going to Philadelphia before very long and he would go round there with me, if I would wait till then. I embraced the prospect, remarking I had felt my mind turned lately towards the city and could not tell why but I thought I should be willing to proceed that far with him. I might send thee that essay of my husband's[105] but know of no certain conveyance, the present being uncertain; [I] can bring it when I come (or if I should not reach there, send it) which would be after the

---

102. Her sons Samuel, age nine, and Lemuel, age seven.

103. Anne frequently visited the WQM, which usually convened in London Grove, Chester County, Pennsylvania.

104. The younger brother of Warner Mifflin and owner of various Kent County properties.

105. The essay concerned Warner Mifflin's dispute with Samuel Hopkins, whose potash scheme had attracted investors, including Warner.

marriage of our daughter, who passed meeting the fore part of this week.[106] I am now on my way to our daughter Raisin's to tarry with her till our Quarter, as she expects to be confined[107] and shall be glad thee will inform William Jackson and my children[108] of the circumstances of my detention. With my dear Love; also to thy Company and conclude thy Friend: and relative.

Anne Mifflin

Duck Creek
ALS, EFP, box 1.

TO JOHN PARRISH

12th Mo: 6th day, 1799
[December 6, 1799]

Mindful that shady business practices were grounds for dismissal from the Society of Friends and aware that she might be held liable for any of her late husband's debts, Anne was eager to bring Warner's defense of a failed business transaction before the public.

Esteemed Cousin,

I have not been unmindful of thy desire in attending to the last little legacy of my dear partner, for the public, which bore some weight on his mind. I enclose [for] thee the transcript of his essay[109] but do not know that the few alterations in it may be of any advantage, being transcribed rather in haste previous to my coming here. Had I the original [I] would send that also. I

---

106. Susannah Mifflin (1779–1801), Warner Mifflin's daughter who would shortly marry John Cowgill, the son of one of Mifflin's close Kent County friends. Anne mentions the appearance of the couple before the Murderkill meeting to state their intention to marry.

107. Anne is referring to her stepdaughter Ann Mifflin (1774–1799), who in 1795 had married Warner Raisin (1763–ca. 1805), a Kent County, Maryland, Quaker abolitionist and esteemed member of Cecil Monthly Meeting in Lynch, Kent County, on the Maryland Eastern Shore. Ann Raisin died on December 19 after giving birth to Elizabeth, her second child.

108. Anne had placed her two sons in the home of William Jackson, Warner's close Chester County Friend, so they could attend a nearby school.

109. We have not found Mifflin's essay.

intended to have finished a little addition after coming here; but my mind and time have been so much other ways occupied, that I have not been able to give it that coolness of attention the subject demands, and also feel discouraged that although the thought presented to me, I conceived a little in the opening of that which is pure perhaps of giving forth with my dear companion in his life time by way of postscript to endeavor to clear myself of my part of the debt or charge if any rests with me, as I thought some did on this subject. Yet if it should prove that, this postscript then must be made verbally, I hope to be resigned, whether in writing or verbally, [and] I hope to see it in clearness, yet [I] have not felt qualified to pen my mind to my own satisfaction, and cannot hope therefore it will be to another's, and feel discouraged so far from attempting to forward anything. Yet if thee feels encouragement to think further upon it, and opportunity of a little time suitable should offer, [I] would yet endeavor to attend to the matter, and bring it with me should I proceed as far as Philadelphia with Brother Daniel after visiting my children.

At present I am at Warner Raisin's, where I have been—tomorrow will be three weeks. [I] came on his wife's account[110] but found him ill with the catarrh fever, and ever since has kept his bed, most of the time delirious but is now some mending.[111] His wife much amiss with fevers and chills and in her lying in, having a son called Abraham[112] and we have found business enough. It seems likely from present appearance I cannot be released from here to attend Susan [Susanna] in her second passing[113] but hope I may not be prevented from being at the marriage on the 17th of this month.[114] Sometime after which Daniel is proposing moving towards the city, when I can furnish with the original. I was fearful I should say something that would not go down if I offered an attempt, and it might to some appear like presumption in me to expose my name to the public, as it could not be done without, consistent

---

110. As noted in the letter of November 16, 1799, above, Anne went to Third Haven, Maryland, to attend her stepdaughter in the last weeks of her pregnancy. Ann Mifflin Raisin died shortly after giving birth.

111. Raisin would outlive his wife by only a few years. After his death in about 1805, their two children were placed under the guardianship of their uncle, Warner Mifflin Jr. See Brewer, *Kent County Guardian Accounts*, 163.

112. Abraham Raisin, Warner and Ann Raisin's first child, had just passed his first birthday.

113. The second appearance before the Murderkill meeting seeking clearance for their marriage.

114. Susanna Mifflin (1779–1801) and John Cowgill (1773–?) were married at the Murderkill meetinghouse on December 31, 1799.

with our discipline, to offer my sentiments; but if thee still thinks there would be no better way of introducing it to the public than through my hands, as I had the thought before, [I] am willing to endeavor to put it in practice. I remain with respect to thy Daughters Family and self.

Thy relation, A. Mifflin

I cut off the addition made by me, not being satisfied with it, and being impressed with those fears I have mentioned. Ann's Love to thee.

ALS, EFP, box 2.

Chapter 11

LETTERS TO FAMILY AND FRIENDS, 1800–1813

The letters in this chapter cover the thirteen years following her husband's death when Anne relocated to Philadelphia and, while raising her sons, served as a Public Friend. In Truth's service she logged thousands of miles, traveling to newly formed remote Quaker settlements as far north as Canada and westward across the Appalachian Mountains.

TO ANNE EMLEN SR.

New York 6 Mo. 3rd. 1801
[June 3, 1801]

This letter is the first of a series Anne wrote to her mother on a long road trip northward. Leaving her sons behind, apparently in the care of their grandmother, she traveled with a sizeable group of Friends and was eager to visit fellow Quakers along the way from New York to Nantucket.

Beloved Mother

Before leaving this city I again take up my pen to visit by a few lines and inform of our continued [good] health and that after the close of the Yearly Meeting, the day following we were at the State Prison,[1] which is a spacious

---

1. Anne and her retinue visited Newgate State Prison, which had opened in 1797. Newgate's first director, Quaker Thomas Eddy (1758–1827), endorsed humane rehabilitation.

noble building in a pleasant situation on the North River out of the bounds of the city. It is only for criminals so that they have a better chance for its more perfect government than that in Philadelphia. The next day we were at the Poor House (John Hall, the women Friends from Maryland, and us), which is a good building on a strong situation. But I question if it is conducted with such attention and management as ours.[2] Then attended their First Day Meeting here and visited two days [waiting] for a fair wind, our wagon having gone forward with Richard Lermon,[3] Nicholas Waln,[4] and William Fisher[5] as we preferred going by water to riding above 200 miles over rough country. We propose going today if the wind will any way admit of it.

Friends here are very kind and we lodged at James Parsons[6]—valuable Friends who are very able and bountiful having but one child, an amiable youth the rest having been [missing] by the fever, which has made a deep impression on [missing]. I will enclose a few lines to James Jones,[7] which truly are glad thee would please to have left at his brother Richard's near Samuel Howell's.[8] If my lines for Lemuel are left at Cousin Ann Dawes', they will be likely to go; and I wish Samuel to write also.[9] And that he would write to me at Newport. If Anne Emlen[10] inquires at John Martens[11] she will know when a vessel sails for the port; I hope she will not fail to write. I should take it unkind knowing she is ready with her pen and it is a hardship on thee to

---

Eddy's own incarceration by the British during the Revolutionary War likely affected his treatment of prisoners. His program was based on the system of Philadelphia's Walnut Street Jail built in 1773, which is considered the first penitentiary in the United States. For an analysis of evolving penal institutions in Philadelphia, see Meranze, *Laboratories of Virtue*; and Manion, *Liberty's Prisoners*.

2. For a treatment of the Bettering House, see Nash, *First City*, 70–71.

3. Richard Lermon or Lerman (1762–1822), a Philadelphia Quaker.

4. Nicholas Waln (1742–1813), Philadelphia Quaker minister and leading member of the city's Quaker patriciate.

5. William Fisher (1752–1845), a member of Chester County Monthly Meeting, worked for the rights of Native Americans as well as enslaved and free black Americans.

6. A wealthy Quaker and New York merchant.

7. Richard Jones, a wealthy Quaker lumber merchant in Merion.

8. A Philadelphia Quaker mariner disowned by Friends during the Revolutionary War for his military service but reinstated in 1797. Samuel married Margaret Emlen, Anne's sister.

9. Possibly Ann Miller of Chester Monthly Meeting, who married Jonathan Dawes in 1775.

10. Probably Anne's niece, the daughter of Anne's oldest brother, George Emlen IV (1742–1812).

11. Likely a Philadelphia Quaker and acquaintance of Anne and her mother.

attempt it. Should be glad she would write on receipt of this and leave it at John Marten's. I wish particularly to hear how Samuel's health continues as it seemed precarious [and] thine and Sister Mary's. Mary Gilbert joins in love to you all and requests it to her family; she is stronger than when she came out. I am thy affectionate daughter,

Anne Mifflin

ALS, EFP, box 2.

TO ANNE EMLEN SR.

Newport, 6 Month 8th 1801
[June 8, 1801]

In this diary-like letter covering seventeen days, Anne expresses concern for Samuel, her eleven-year-old son, and provides details on the network of Quakers known to all Friends who conducted such ministerial journeys.

Beloved Mother

We arrived here on the 4th of this month after about 30 hours turn of a pleasant passage by water of 200 miles. We spent 2 days in resting ourselves and going to some families of the lame, the blind and the infirm and yesterday attended their First Day Meeting here in company with John Hall and Stephen Grellet[12] and this day we are going to cross a ferry about 3 miles onto a meeting at Conanicut, an island about 2 miles in length and so on to some meetings at Narragansett on the mainland before the yearly meeting comes on.[13]

I have been thoughtful dear Mother about my son Samuel whether his health will be suitable to remain the summer in town and whether it would not be a relief if most agreeable to thee for him to go in the country.[14] I thought

12. Stephen Grellet (1773–1855), a French Catholic, became a convinced Quaker in 1796 under the ministry of English Quaker minister Deborah Darby. He served as a Quaker minister and missionary in the United States, Canada, the West Indies, and Europe. A widely read Friends' inspirational account is Seebohm's *Memoirs of the Life and Gospel Labours of Stephen Grellet.*

13. Conanicut, Rhode Island, an island in Narragansett Bay, could be reached by ferry by 1725. Narragansett, Rhode Island, gathered an active Friends Meeting in the eighteenth century. For its early history, see Hazard, *Narragansett Friends' Meeting.*

14. Suffering recurrent health problems, Anne's son Samuel probably lived with his grandmother after the school year.

it best to mention it, that thee might consult thy own feelings and if his health seemed likely to require it, or a want of health in the city, that thee might act as felt most easy under circumstances. Whether to send him to William Jackson's,[15] which might be done by sending him in a Wilmington Packet[16] the day before their market day and if Anne Emlen[17] would write to Samuel Canby[18] that I should esteem it a favor if he would please to send him to Friend Jacksons by some of the market wagons. This might do if no better a conveyance offered, and there was a prospect of his returning in the winter; but if thee should think best to send him to Westtown.[19] Thomas Stewardson[20] can be spoke to who made no objection to his being kept out for some months on account of attending to his ankle, which I hope Joseph is so kind as to do in aiding him in rubbing it. Any time in the 8mo: I expect would do to return him whether first or last.

[June] 14th Yesterday we attended the opening of the Select Yearly Meeting at Portsmouth, where were a number of solid valuable Friends and today first day meeting here.

[June] 21st after attending the Yearly Meeting we are now on our way to Nantucket,[21] though would have been glad to have met with a release to return at the close of the Yearly Meeting. Among several other meetings on our way to Bedford,[22] we took one at a settlement of Indians in company with a travelling friend from New York State.

---

15. Jackson is identified in chapter 4, note 54, above. Both of Anne's sons had lodged with him in 1799.
16. In the early 1800s, the *Wilmington Packet* mailboat transported passengers from Philadelphia to Wilmington, Delaware. See Bounds, *Postal History of Delaware*.
17. The daughter of Anne's oldest brother, George Emlen IV.
18. A wealthy Wilmington, Delaware, miller and leading figure at the Wilmington Monthly Meeting.
19. Westtown School is treated in chapter 4, above.
20. A Philadelphia merchant and Quaker elder, he served as treasurer of Westtown School.
21. Nantucket, in the state of Massachusetts, thirty miles south of the mainland. Quakers were the island's majority religious sect for much of the eighteenth century and thrived in the whaling industry. Their devotion to simplicity influenced the city's architecture, fashion, and social behavior. See Leach and Gow, *Quaker Nantucket*.
22. Bedford, Massachusetts, served as the major nineteenth-century whaling port.

[June] 22nd We are now arrived at our worthy Friend Wm. Racks at Bedford, who seems indeed as one of the Princes of the people, though surrounded with every convenience in the most genteel line and clothed with power in a great degree.[23] Yet he is a pattern of true unaffected humility. This amiable family around him are goodly and bright examples in their day.

Dear Mother, I often think of thee thy advanced years and trials yet surrounding. May the Lord in the unspeakable riches of his mercy be pleased to sanctify them and not suffer their continuance unto unsupportable discouragement but that he may be pleased to reveal his Holy arm of power for thy consolation? And such is his bountiful care of his humbled dependent children that he so works for them that "the rod of the wicked shall not rest on the lot of the righteous, but (lest) the righteous put forth their hand unto iniquity."[24]

I received Samuel and Lemuel's letters which were very acceptable and took kind Margaret Howell's addition.[25] I had laid the charge on Anne Emlen[26] knowing she was ready with her pen and thought she had leisure. But it's no matter how the information comes, so [long] as I obtain it, of your welfare, was glad to hear Samuel's health mends.

[June] 25th Bedford. After attending meeting yesterday and the day before chiefly among the feathered of the flock carried off by Timothy Davis[27] and others not distant from this place we attended the week day meeting here and tomorrow set out for Nantucket.

May the gracious helper of Israel be near to crown thy advanced years with the enriching incomes of true peace and reward thy labors as a faithful Wife, Mother and Friend;

In which I now conclude thy loving child,
Anne Mifflin

ALS, EFP, box 2.

23. William Racks (also spelled Rotch or Resch) is treated in chapter 4, note 33, above.
24. Psalms 125:3.
25. Anne's older sister.
26. This Anne Emlen is Anne's niece; see page 272, note 17.
27. A Quaker who during the Revolutionary War urged Friends in a published essay to acknowledge the Continental Congress and pay taxes to support the war. See chapter 7, page 191.

TO ANNE EMLEN SR.

Bedford, 6 Month 26th [1801]
[June 26, 1801]

Anne describes ministerial travels through New England and meetings with notable Friends there; but with miles between her and home, concerns over family and affairs in Philadelphia occupied her dreams as well.

Beloved Mother,

Yesterday I closed a letter for thee written from place to place, giving a concise account of our journeying though there is not much writing time. And now before quiet day being summoned to fall in about an hour, I thought I would embrace a leisure moment in addressing a few more lines to thee.

Last evening I received Anne Emlen's[28] acceptable letters and one from Robert Jones.[29] Am pleased to hear such good accounts from my son and that you are all favored with the continued mercy of health, except Sister Mary with whom I tenderly sympathize; my love is to her and I wish she may be favored to draw near to those springs of consolation in herself, which Christ told the woman of Samaria,[30] whosoever asked of him shall receive; that may she be favored to have access to that peace which the smiles of prosperity cannot not give nor the frowns of adversity take away.

I awoke an hour or more past covered with exceeding anxiety, having seen thee in my dream and thought thee was displeased with [me] and for not doing something which I told thee had I but known it was thy mind I would have done. It just struck me whether thee thought amiss of not receiving more letters but may inform, though I have embraced what private opportunity offered yet was diffident of sending much by post unless thee had told me to from the apprehension my letters would not be worth their price unless I had something of consequence to communicate, I thought also an accusation was advanced or rather a surmise against me which was utterly without ground; and I was entreating with thee against it and thought if thee received it as truth whether thy eternal happiness would be at stake; I did not expect to

---

28. Anne's niece, the daughter of her brother George.
29. Not identified.
30. The woman of Samaria, John 4:10.

mention only the first circumstance as it is presented; strange thoughts arise in sleep at night. May the Lord in mercy preserve us in our places. There are many handsome buildings in this place and it commands a view of a bridge near a mile long which is a credit to their manly exertions.[31]

If thee could put pen to paper and favor me with me with some lines, to the care of Samuel Parsons,[32] New York, it would be very pleasing.

Probably after Nantucket Quarter [Quarterly Meeting] we shall cross over to some more meetings also to see another settlement of Indians and then turn homewards by the way of Nine Partners [Meeting] and New York.[33] With the tenderness of affection, regard to thyself in which dear Mary [Gilbert] joins, to my dear son, to Anne Emlen, Mary Howell, etc. etc.[34]

I conclude they loving daughter Anne Mifflin

ALS, EFP, box 2.

TO ANNE EMLEN SR.

Nantucket
6 Month 30th 1801
[June 30, 1801]

Anne marveled at the wealth of Nantucket Friends displayed in elegant homes, greater than those of the Quaker grandees in Philadelphia.

Beloved Mother,

A conveyance offering tomorrow for Philadelphia and [I] am glad to embrace it in communicating the information that we are all well. We reached

---

31. The Bedford-Fairhaven Bridge built by Quaker William Rotch and associates; when opened in 1800, it linked Bedford and Fairhaven villages. See Demanche, *Bedford–Fairhaven Bridge*.

32. A New York Quaker who conveyed mail and messages to Anne on her travels.

33. Nine Partners Meeting in Millbrook, New York, built in 1780 by wealthy Quakers from Nantucket. In 1796, they added Nine Partners Boarding School in the Hudson Valley.

34. For Anne Emlen and Mary Howell, see Anne to her mother, June 8, 1801, see note 17 above on page 272.

here on the 27th after a pleasant sail from [New] Bedford of about 7 hours, being 60 miles passage. Next day attended their two meetings at the North and South house, most of the inhabitants living in the town;[35] the rest of the island being held in common for pasturage, etc. On second day attended the Select Meeting and this day comes the Quarterly Meeting for business; tomorrow and next day comes their two Weekday Meetings and Monthly Meeting; after which we expect to cross towards the Continent;[36] although we have been solicited to stay longer, this being the only time of the year almost that they got to see their Friends, very different from those who are frequently having them to pass and repass.

Yesterday the heat here was up to 91 [degrees]; although there being a sea breeze made us not so sensible of its intensity the like has not been known here for some years, we were thoughtful how it might be in Philadelphia.

My love to my dear Son and am pleased to receive good accounts of him, I believe I must write to Lemuel consider how I can expect and wish he would add one to it enclosing mine; it will be grateful to his brother so remote from his connections and will be useful to Samuel.

My love is to our relations and inquiring Friends. There is a kind set of Friends here as well as in other places where we have passed. At [New] Bedford they live in such a degree of elegance that we compared William Resch [Rotch] and wife to a King and Queen in a mere palace of a house and his children round him in buildings little in favor to young Princes; and as they seem to honor the truth as a prime object; so this beautifies and enobleth them; a very pleasing sight this, to see those who are high in this life, yet lowly and humble in the pursuit of that life which is hid with Christ in God. Many of the buildings in this country are neater than what is termed elegant in their appearance than in our parts.

I conclude with the tenderness of near and affectionate regard thy one
Anne Mifflin

ALS, EFP, box 2.

35. See chapter 4, note 33, above.
36. The mainland.

TO ANNE EMLEN SR.

Warwick, Rhode Island State[37]
7 Month 21st 1801
[July 21, 1801]

Following visits at the Bedford and Nantucket meetings, Anne and Mary Gilbert completed their round of visits to Friends Meetings in Rhode Island and then headed for Hartford, Connecticut.

Beloved Mother,

As we are now about to leave these parts, proceeding tomorrow towards Connecticut and so on to some meetings in [New] York State and homewards; I will embrace the present opportunity of sending some lines from Newport, informing of our being favored with health; though Mary [Gilbert] has been some indisposed. We came from [New] Bedford where I last wrote thee, to Berkley and Swansea Meetings, the latter near the favored residence of Patience Brayton,[38] then to Providence, a handsome town form containing a number of elegant buildings, though our stay was mostly at Moses Browns who resides in a large commodious mansion near it. There we spent two days, part of the time. Mary poorly, and part going to some Friends' families. Next day being 1st of the week attended Smithfield and Providence Meetings the day following Cranston, today Wickford and tomorrow Greenwich, the day following Foster, and then to the settlement of newly convinced Friends at Hartford in Connecticut,[39] where Thomas Roach and his wife[40] went to reside merely as helpers to them and the cause; from whence we expect if nothing hinders to go by the way of Nine Partners to New York.

---

37. On Narragansett Bay, south of Providence.

38. A Quaker native of Portsmouth, Rhode Island, wife of John Gray Ross and the daughter of Isaac and Mary Brayton. See Crabtree, "In the Light and on the Road."

39. Dutchess County, New York, Quakers established their first meeting for worship in Hartford, Connecticut, in 1788; by 1800 their preparative meeting formed part of the Oblong Monthly Meeting of the New York Yearly Meeting, a group Anne described as newly convinced Quakers.

40. Thomas Rotch (also spelled Roacks or Resch) and his wife Sylvia of New Bedford.

We have cause thankfully to acknowledge we have got along more prosperously than we could have expected aided by the agreeable Society of kind Friends. On 7th day Samuel Redman[41] and Sylvia Roach left us to return to [New] Bedford, and we are now joined by their kind Friends.

Mary proposes writing a few lines to enclose, but as we have some miles to ride today to attend a meeting, time does not admit of saying much. Must therefore conclude with the tenderness of affectionate regards to thyself, to the family and inquiring Friends.

Thy loving daughter Anne Mifflin

The time being short it is too hurrying for Mary to write as she is feeble from the air [and] from the salt water. Though it is bracing to me, [it] is rather prejudicial to Mary, her lungs being weak; but expect she will be better as we are about to turn from it. She desires her love to her family and will write at a more convenient season as she requires rest at present between meetings a good deal.
To: Anne Emlen
Requested to be forwarded by John Morton

ALS, EFP, box 2.

TO MOSES BROWN

Philadelphia, 10th Month 3rd day, 1801
[October 3, 1801]

Back home after an extended trip through New England, Anne shifted her attention to family matters and personal correspondence. Two years after Warner's passing, she continued to protect his memory.

Well Esteemed Friend,

Being often thoughtful of the engagement entered into of sending a certain manuscript account of my dear companion[42] for thy perusal as I have been hitherto deprived of that through the neglect of a Friend returning it who had

---

41. A Friend not identified.
42. Anne is referring to "A Brief Account of the Late Warner Mifflin," presented above.

it in possession, I believe it may be right to embrace the present conveyance of mentioning it by Joseph Howell whose further detention since I closed some lines to Dorcas, furnished me with an opportunity so to do.[43] When I have it at command and have taken time to make some little corrections, purpose forwarding it. I have committed to Joseph Howell's case my little account of our valued daughter Ann Raisin and if there should be a choice in transcribing any part of it, should be glad any corrections that might presently be made and inserted also in the back with a pencil.[44]

I did not know but another engagement would have engrossed my time and prevented an attention to my promise; but on my return[45] found the subject which had claimed the religious attention of another Friend and myself, had so come under view of the church not knowing of [missing] our private concern that it had rather passed hands into the service and we found ourselves agreeably released for the present.

If thou sees our dear Friend John Hall,[46] offer sympathetic love. I hope Stephen tries to eat a little more, or he may be disqualified from doing what his master may require. I have successfully prescribed to Mary Gilbert in the nourishing line. She did better afterward perhaps now may prove as dear in the other case. Richard Mott and Hugh Judge are on their way to Baltimore; but though Sarah Stevenson was looked for on that course, it appears she is yet [illegible] to New York Government.[47]

Nothing in particular further presents to communicate at present but the offer of tender regard to thyself and wife and her daughter, who kindly helped to take care of us when at your house; poor Mary has met with a great change

---

43. Members of the Quaker community in Providence, Rhode Island.

44. Ann Mifflin Raisin (1774–1799), second daughter of Warner Mifflin who by the age of eighteen had served as clerk of the Murderkill Women's Monthly Meeting. After marrying Quaker abolitionist Warner Raisin from Kent County, Maryland, she was appointed an overseer of Cecil Monthly Meeting, a duty that required monitoring marriage intentions, member discipline, and other affairs.

45. Anne refers to her long trip to New York, Rhode Island, and Nantucket.

46. Probably a Providence Quaker whom Anne met in Newport or Providence.

47. Richard Mott (1765–1856), a member of the Purchase Monthly Meeting, entered the Quaker ministry in 1787 and visited friends in New England, New York, Philadelphia, Baltimore, Ohio, and western Pennsylvania. Hugh Judge (1750–1834), Quaker minister of the Wilmington Monthly Meeting, visited parts of New York and New England. Judge, *Memoirs and Journal*. Sarah Stevenson (1754–1837), a Quaker of the Burlington, New Jersey, meeting, married Stephen Comfort of Neshaminy, Pennsylvania.

since our return on the removal of her husband[48] as mentioned to Dorcas but way will be made for her I believe.

In our journey I was impressed with the necessity of not saluting any man by the way; or being detained by the affectionate part only at any place. I felt this fully as much or more on Mary's account than my own, knowing the demands of her family on her time at home, whenever released from superior engagements; and am glad we adhered to this pointing as she had so short a time [with] her companion's company after our return and he had expressed before our arrival to my dear mother that if we did not return that week we did, he should be out of patience almost, he so much needed his wife's company under the weight of their business.[49]

Poor Mary will feel an increased load I fear doubtless indeed it will be so now.

From thy sincere Anne Mifflin

ALS, Moses Brown Papers, Rhode Island Historical Society, Providence.

TO ANNE EMLEN SR.

Young [Yonge] Street between Lake Ontario and Lake Simcoe, Upper Canady[50]
9th month, 1802
[September 1802]

With her characteristic curiosity Anne describes the Lower Canada region with engaging detail.

Beloved Mother,

A Friend about setting off for Muncy, I am glad to embrace the opportunity of forwarding thee a few lines. We have now nearly finished our visit on this

---

48. Shortly after her return to Philadelphia, Mary's husband Robert died on September 20, 1801, and was buried the next day.

49. The "weight of their business" may refer to the three Gilbert sons' difficulties adjusting to life in Philadelphia. PMM, Arch Street, Certificates of Removal (1772–1800), December 26, 1800.

50. Yonge Street, a historic road stretching some sixty miles from Toronto (formerly York) to Lake Simcoe. Quakers had settled from Holland Landing to the town named Upper Yonge Street but later renamed Newmarket.

side [of] the lake and are about [to] return to Pelham[51] where we expect to meet others of the committee.

Our passage in coming around the head of the lake was over perilous roads which occasions [us] some dread in returning. It is through an Indian country where there is a whole day's ride and now no sight of human habitation.[52] But, we think of going to York Town,[53] the seat of government about 30 miles hence on a straight line—a street called Young [Yonge] Street, the center to see if we can get a passage by water. The roads are to be laid out in straight lines in squares like our city each square consisting of 1,000 acres and divided into 5 farms.[54] It is very rich land and looks very inviting to people who are farmers and have no land. The laws have been so unfavorable an aspect we apprehend on inspection as has been represented; the people in power seeming well disposed towards Friends at present.

I am favored with good health and have got along bravely so far. [I] was once thrown off a horse by a wasp stinging him we believe but [I was] not hurt. Hannah was thrown off by an attack of wasps and hurt her back; but [she] is nearly well of it. The wasps being troublesome among the bushes this time of year.

I cannot have the satisfaction in this remote situation of hearing how it fares with near connections of Friends which would be especially agreeable today in this season perhaps and anxiety in the city;[55] but in about 8 days I expect by the coming [of] the remainder of our committee to have some intelligence. I shall be glad also if by the coming of them I can receive any account of Samuel whether he continues at Warner's or is got to boarding school.[56]

---

51. A town in the central Niagara region of Ontario, Canada, named by British governor John Graves Simcoe, and among those established by the British government to provide land for Revolutionary War Loyalists after the war.

52. In 1802, although land around Lakes Simcoe and Ontario remained wilderness, the region was inhabited and well traveled. See Johnson and Wilson, *Historical Essays on Upper Canada*.

53. Capital of Upper Canada, the town of York on the northwest (Canadian) shore of Lake Ontario was founded in 1793 by British governor John Graves Simcoe. In 1834, the British renamed it Toronto.

54. Timothy Rogers had led Vermont farmers to settle along the Yonge Street corridor. Before Anne and Hannah arrived, Friends from the Upper Susquehanna River region had also migrated to the area. Healey, *From Quaker to Upper Canadian*.

55. Far from home, Anne worried over another season of yellow fever infestation in Philadelphia that had tortured the city in 1793, 1797, and 1798.

56. Warner Mifflin Jr., Anne's stepson still living at Chestnut Grove in Kent County. She refers to Westtown, the school her son previously attended.

Dear Hannah unites with me in affectionate love to thee and Sister Howell and family. My love is also to Brother George's[57] family, other relatives and friendly inquirers and remain Thy loving daughter,

Anne Mifflin

ALS, EFP, box 2.

TO ANNE EMLEN SR.

Pelham, Upper Canaday [Canada]
10 Mo: 6th 1802
[October 6, 1802]

Following on her letter from Yonge Street, Anne continues to provide Mother Emlen with details of her travels within Upper Canada.

Beloved Mother,

Just after the rise of the Monthly/Yearly Meeting now in great haste, Peter Barker[58] of the Friends being just about to set out, I write. Tomorrow we expect also to set off; but they are able to travel faster than we and it would be too many to go in a company.

We have been favored to get through the difficulties of our journey in a more comfortable manner than we could have expected. But to enter into the particulars is more than I can at present from want of time; not knowing till now that our Friends were about going.

I have often been anxious about home; for my dear mother, children, connections and Friends but was some comforted in the account brought by Peter that there was not much of the sickness in the City when he left.[59]

This is a fine country for good land and very inviting to people in low circumstances, as each man who brings in a family to people the country on

---

57. Anne's older brother George Emlen IV, being the eldest son, had inherited much of the extensive Emlen estate in Philadelphia and its environs.

58. A Philadelphia Quaker merchant with the firm of Barker and Annesly. In 1795, Barker married Abigail Drinker, the niece of Henry and Elizabeth Drinker.

59. Yellow fever had abated with the first frost.

petitioning, is presented with 200 acres [of] good land, and many are greatly improving in their circumstances by coming here.[60]

I must take a few minutes to write to my little boys whilst Friends are eating their dinners before going. I have been concerned about them poor fellows. Particularly, Samuel not leaving him as well fixed as Lemuel. If there is any direction thee can take respecting him, [I] shall be obliged for thee to exercise thy judgement; with respect to where or how he should be. And if thee will please forward some lines will enclose them. Also to Lemuel which can go by some conveyances, letters for Sister Howell's children go.[61]

With near affection and a grateful sense of thy past and continued parental care and tenderness; I conclude with love to brothers, sisters, nephews, nieces, relations and friends.

Thy Affectionate Daughter, Anne Mifflin

ALS, EFP, box 2.

TO JOHN THOMAS, JOEL SWAYNE, AND COMPANY

Philadelphia 2 Mo: 25, 1804
[February 25, 1804]

This letter followed up on Anne's long 1803 journey to the Seneca reservations and shows her continued interest in "our native brethren." Her report of that mission is presented in chapter 9.

Esteemed Friends[62]

Adam Hoops having called to see if I had any commands for your parts, I set down to prepare the acknowledgement of my respectful remembrance

---

60. After the Revolutionary War, the federal government's treaties with the Iroquois League required tribes to cede their land to the United States. Though the government had provisioned that those millions of acres be allotted for war veterans' pensions, in many instances land speculators bought up these tracts to resell at a profit. Swatzler, *Friend Among the Senecas*, 110.

61. Margaret Emlen Howell, Anne's sister.

62. In 1798, John (Jonathan) Thomas and Joel Swayne accompanied Halliday Jackson on a mission to the Senecas. See note 17 above on page 272 as well as chapter 9, note 23, above.

of your characters and care in the laudable work of improving our brethren the natives.[63]

I have not heard of any females disposed to embrace the idea suggested of one or two going for a time for instructing the women and I heard also the Friends men's law: Should they increase sufficient for the purpose and a wife be taken out for one of the camp or two women the business might look more practicable. A Friend from England requesting a copy of my account respecting our visit and such sentiments and notes on the Indian subject as I might see proper to add; I have suggested the thought of a small manufacturing house[64] being established for instruction of the natives near their borders. If it takes, perhaps some supplies may be produced from thence; but not knowing the event it may be best not to say anything as they conceive, I am told, the color of an expectation given [is] as a kind of a promise.

Give my love to Corn Planter and [his] brother if you think of it.[65] [And] to Joesa and Wife, the one who made a speech to us at your habitation.[66] To the young man who interpreted for us at Coldspring and remembrance and good wishes to them generally.[67]

Mary Gilbert[68] has been afflicted in her own and family's health ever since our return. John Letchworth did not fully recover fatigue from a hard trotter, his wife told me, or effects of it until some weeks past.[69] Being favored with an easy, though not elegant creature, I bore the journey perhaps better than either. It is a matter of importance, having an easy hackney in traveling long journeys. We reached all the several places we set out with a view to and returned. I touch with the evidence of having been in such places. In company lately speaking of a Friend who had come from England, Ann Alexander, sister to Sarah Greeble,[70] and was travelling in New England, a lawyer present observed,

---

63. Adam Hoops (1760–1847) served as an officer in the Continental Army. In 1785, he surveyed land in western Pennsylvania representing Robert Morris in his title dispute with the Holland Land Company regarding previous Seneca lands.

64. The manufacturing house was a place for spinning and weaving.

65. Most likely Cornplanter's half brother Handsome Lake, the Seneca prophet.

66. Joesa acted as Anne's oarsman when she and companions traveled by canoe in this region.

67. A Seneca village on the Allegany Reservation that Anne and her party visited in 1803.

68. Anne's traveling partner.

69. For John Letchworth, see chapter 9, note 45, above. A hard trotter is a horse whose heavy footfall can render the rider a bone-jarring ride and a great deal of pain.

70. Ann Alexander, a Quaker minster, had arrived from Suffolk, England, several years before with her sisters, Quaker ministers Mary Alexander and Sarah Greeble.

"tell me of those who can encounter in the wilderness and so among the Indians where they will not have nice accommodations." I told him, I supposed he meant to put a feather in our caps.

May preservation and best peace accompany in your useful undertaking and cause the wilderness to appear as a fruitful field in the product of divine good, is the sincere wish of your sympathizing friend.

Anne Mifflin

I have freed up ½ of a hundred needles for such women as most need of the natives and 22 skeins[71] of thread with my case. It would not do to ask the bearer to take same I thought on horseback. They are to go by him if he can take them.

ALS, EFP, box 2.

TO DOROTHY RIPLEY

Philadelphia
5 mo. 31st [May 31] 1804

In this letter to the English Quaker traveling minister, Anne describes the admission requirements and regimen of the Westtown Boarding School and vents her frustration at the government's lingering animus against Quakers that had continued since the revolutionary years.

Dear Dorothy,

As from information received from thy sister Anna, who spent half an hour with me in her passage to the eastward, I find you are not well circumstanced for schools at Washington [DC] and that the most eligible one is an Amish institution: I thought friendship to thyself and the family claimed my attention in informing thee of a boarding school established by considerable expense to Society [of Friends], the benefit of which thou may avail thyself of from thy son's right in society; and if the object appears desirable by writing up here, thou may be furnished with a certificate bill of admission to be delivered to the Superintendent on his arrival there; as also a certificate of his

---

71. A skein of thread measures 8 yards or 288 inches in length.

health to be filled up and signed by some physician who must examine to see whether he is clear of any infectious disorders to prevent spreading of the Itch, etc. also signed by the parents. The price of board is paid at commencement of every quarter which is at present low, 16 dollars per quarter, board and tuition. His clothing should all be marked with the number on the bill, but as the form or fashion of the clothes worn there is most likely more divested of superfluity than thy son's may be, it would be best, should thee send him, to prepare no new clothes of any kind as the establishment is if they are not of the make worn there; the tailor alters them at expense of the parent; the shirts also should be plain without ruffling. There is a store there and every part of dress can be furnished.

No doubt thou hast heard of this establishment; many have visited it and Friends have been much pleased with the order and regularity that appears, superior to many public seminaries. A teacher from the city early visited it, formerly I believe a Parson who professed himself pleased and instructed, or mortified, drawing a comparison probably between the quiet regularity he there observed and his own sometimes other capable but passionate hurricane mode of teaching. I have been informed.

John Dickinson, former Governor here (his wife being a member and himself so far attached to the principle as to lead him into interested dispositions respectfully—the benefit of society and suitable education of its youth) professed to me years back that could he see a seminary for the instruction of young Friends under the care of the Philadelphia Yearly Meeting he would very freely hand forth to its promotion; and this arising in that time he and his wife made over a very handsome property.[72] It is as yet in debt, the building large enough to accommodate 100 of each sex (though it averages about 80 and they don't wish for full members) and other appurtenances, and the large valuable plantation purchased on which it is erected amounted to a considerable farm.[73] Nevertheless, to be accommodating to Friends who may have large families or are in rather straitened circumstances, the price is fixed as low as possible complemented by donations and bequests from members the more full reduction of the debt and Friends eventually also arising for the schooling

---

72. Anne refers to earlier letters with Dickinson regarding a charity school. See Anne Mifflin to Dickinson, December 21, 1787, above.

73. The PYM purchased the farm of James Gibbons, as detailed in Dewees and Dewees, *Centennial History of Westtown Boarding School*, 29–33.

[of] poor children of which has in measure commenced as a separate fund by some bequests.

I don't think our Assembly has shown us fair play, or equal measure; while schooling institutions of other societies are allowed to hold such large tracts of land exempt from tax, we have been refused such indulgence. No other society may be produced who bear all the burthen of their own poor and their schooling as well as their share in the general taxation for the purpose [of] principle bequests and in this city, property Friends bequeathed from members. I suppose from its beginning, thousands consisting of all societies as then in a constant succession of a number of free scholars; and their constant care and equitable agency of such an establishment without fee or reward is no small charge.

It just strikes me while I am writing, that although they did not yield to the grant of equal justice according to my ideas, from the brethren's representation a few years back, who knows but that might be in a frame of spirit disposed to listen to formal application. Was I more sure of success I should I think [to] improve this idea and join others in a petition. I was once a shower in something similar on the scene of the blacks in Annapolis when a member of the Maryland Quarterly Meeting; and though it did not succeed, yet it discharged our duty and they at best paid so much respect to our petitions as to read it before our brethren, perhaps from its novelty.[74]

And there is certainly ground to remonstrate were they limited though quantity of land allowed to hold by all such in situations as not taxable I should think well of it; but whilst others are unlimited and we are not all a foot free, I cannot but think it unjust. The debt and those circumstances prevent our liberty in enlarging some conveniences desirable. Yet there is endeavored for a generous care over their morals (and youth well taught, reading, writing, arithmetic, grammar, geography, mathematics, etc.). A French teacher has been sought but none yet obtained, as he must be a member though perhaps one of the strictest purity in morals might be admitted. Yet this lack can be supplied elsewhere. My eldest son, about 14 has mastered the French under Stephen M. Day, a young man of amicable manner, who once taught the language in the Academy at Burlington, joined Friends from convincement, and is now

---

74. The petition from Anne and Mary Berry is discussed in chapter 8, above.

a minister.[75] He teaches at a village 7 miles from this city, where my son boards at a worthy widow's whose two amicable daughters are a help to the manners of children. I part with both my children for their good to board elsewhere. My youngest when a scholar at Westtown drew a side view of the building which I enclose for thy son if you incline to hold up to his going there. It shows one of the back galleries and the belfry in the middle of the back part of the house and the front is considerably wider and it stands on a fine beautiful eminence. It is poorly done in the leisure moments of a lad of 12 years who occupied very little of his play time in that way for more active and health some diversions. The encircling ground and trees are properly represented.

The reason J. Dickinson assigned for wishing to see such an institution under care of the yearly meeting: he said public establishments were very liable to corruption and being predicated to private interests; and where it was an object of meeting care and subject to a succession of managers that danger would be removed. They are allowed to visit their connections (families) twice a year and spend 2 weeks with them or 3 if the parents choose, but I think it hurtful to keep them long from their studies and leads into dissipation. I don't know why I should be this particular; it was unexpected when I took up my pen. It may the better furnish with an opportunity of judging and choosing to subscribe by the year. I thought it might be the only chance thy son might have of being acquainted with Friends and then making his choice whether theirs should be his path in life: and it is also desirable thou should persevere in not sending him to the Roman (Catholic) School. We may respect the people but not their principles and attend in their religious leads into solicitude to make converts. Isaac Norris,[76] one of the hopes of a respectable family here, learnt French of a Roman tutor who instilled the principles at that early age, he embraced them but became a lapsed unsettled character and finally died to the grief of his connections an obscure lot.

With respect to thy husband and love to thy mother, if [she is] with thee, I conclude thy friend and well-wisher.

Anne Mifflin

75. Stephen Munson Day (1778–1812), a teacher at a Quaker school in Burlington, New Jersey, in about 1804 started his own school in Haddonfield, New Jersey, where he was a member of the Quaker meeting.

76. Isaac Norris (1760–1802), apparently the son of Charles Norris Sr. (1712–1765) and Mary Parker Norris (1731–1799). Little is known of his life.

I just received—I thought I heard thy mother had a certificate of membership but it was not delivered; if so she would do well to deliver it where sent, apologize for its neglect, and get an endorsement on it from Sandy (I believe it's called) Indian Spring Monthly Meeting[77] if she resides there the larger part of her time or a great deal with thee, it will be a means of excluding her from a right in Society [of Friends] which likely would not be desirable to her. Should thy son be sent, if you do not take a ride to bring him to Westtown, he might come by stage under care of some person to Wilmington and a request written to Samuel Canby[78] to have a conveyance to Westtown. Or come to James Todd's here who could send him on the Western stage.

ALS, Chicago History Museum.

TO ANNE EMLEN SR.

Baltimore
10 mo. 16th *1805*
[October 16, 1805]

In this letter sent as the Baltimore Yearly Meeting gathered, Anne writes of the perils of travel into the raw frontier, acknowledges the steady assistance of Friends, and expresses concern for her son Lemuel.

Our attendance of the Yearly Meeting[79] has been very satisfactory. Should our progress in the future part of the journey be equally so, [I] trust we [will] return home as with sheaves of peace. Diverse Friends have attended from different parts and James Cattle an amiable friend from Redstone[80] being here with part of his family is disposed to take us under his protection and guidance thitherward.

    77. Sandy Spring Monthly Meeting in Montgomery County, Maryland.
    78. Samuel Canby (1751–1832), a prosperous miller in Wilmington, was one of northern Delaware's notable Quaker leaders.
    79. This trip entailed many weeks; see chapter 5, above.
    80. A member of the Redstone Monthly Meeting. The Redstone Quarterly Meeting was established by the Maryland (Baltimore) Yearly Meeting for Quakers living west of the Allegheny Mountains and into the Ohio River Valley.

It seems indeed a weighty thing to go forth in this line and now the time is drawing nigh to proceed more single-handed and leave the collected body of Friends. (Its dispersion and evident loss of the strength of the Society is witnessed). The most finishing time to sensible feelings is like to be witnessed. Yet hope through Divine Aid we may experience preservation.

I wrote some lines informing of Lemuel's having been ill with the ague and so weakened he fainted when standing up to read and hurt his face much.[81]

I find the situation like to be very expensive as beside his board and schooling and two or three bills for clothing of various kinds, one for stationary matters, an amount to prove 30 dollars. But I have tried to convince him of the morality of frugality and he has promised to move carefully. If a letter was committed to Cook and Cresson's[82] care to be sent to their customers to Wheeling to the care of Aquilla Bolton, the course of this or the next month before the very better part of it should be likely to get it safe—or if given to Samuel Bolton, Aquila's brother.[83] As he talked of moving he might send or bring it; [I] wish Samuel to write [to] me fully in that way and can inquire for conveyances at those places.[84]

Mary Harper[85] is an agreeable companion and likely to improve in her health by the journey. I conclude with the salutation of regard to the family and tenderly so to thyself.

Thy affectionate Daughter Anne Mifflin

We lodge at John McKim's,[86] where also does Wm. Crotch, Nathan Hunt,[87] etc. As the horse our kind friend John Johnson has provided seems to have some propensity to run back, we have considered it very dangerous in traveling mountainous roads and our kind friend, J. McKim lets one of his carriage

---

81. Referring to an October 10, 1805, letter to her mother, which is not included in this selection of letters. What Anne describes as Lemuel's ague is likely a febrile condition; ague was associated with malaria.

82. Quaker merchants in Philadelphia.

83. The Bolton brothers, Philadelphia Quakers, had moved west a few years before and then onto Salem Ohio Meeting in 1813 with their mother Rachel.

84. The authors surmise that Anne is informing her mother that she will inquire where mail can be forwarded.

85. See chapter 5, page 115.

86. John McKim (1742–1819) flourished in Baltimore as a Quaker merchant. He is remembered for leaving money to build the city's first free, nondenominational public school, established by his sons in 1821.

87. These Friends could not be identified.

horses go and this horse to be left in its place. We drank tea at Benjamin James' and Brother William.[88]

Ann Emlen, Tawconey[89]

ALS, EFP, box 2.

TO ANNE EMLEN SR.

Allegany [Allegheny][90]
10th Mo: 28, 1805
[October 28, 1805]

Anne relates travels from meeting to meeting as her group journeyed westward from Baltimore across the Allegheny Mountains to Pittsburgh. The hazardous wintry conditions they encountered tested their dedication to go forth to minister to Friends in rural Quaker settlements.

Beloved Mother,

Meeting with [missing] at our present lodgings on the top of Allegany, thought I would embrace the opportunity of addressing thee in this way wishing it may meet thee in possession of like favorable health which I now enjoy. I had a very heavy cold but have been far roused to surmount it.

After leaving Baltimore we rode to New Market,[91] a town where 18 families of Friends reside and about as many of others. We attended this meeting next day and the morning following set off for Barkley[92] [Berkley] (near which meeting Lucy Pane Washington[93] resides) but was obliged to leave behind us

---

88. Not identified; perhaps Friends of the Gunpowder Meeting.

89. Tawconey (Tacony), a historic neighborhood in Northeast Philadelphia, about eight miles from City Center; in the late eighteenth century merely a rural area dotted with country seats. Anne's mother was at the country home of her son George Emlen IV.

90. A town in southwestern Pennsylvania, bounded by the Allegheny and Ohio Rivers, now part of incorporated Pittsburgh. Lots and land were laid out and sold by the state of Pennsylvania in 1788 or given as payment to Revolutionary War veterans.

91. A town in Frederick County, Maryland, forty-three miles west of Baltimore.

92. A rural crossroads near Frederick, Maryland.

93. The sister of Dolley Madison, Lucy Payne Washington (ca. 1769–1846) married George Steptoe Washington (1772–1809), nephew of George Washington. Widowed after her husband died at age thirty-seven, she married Supreme Court Justice Thomas Todd in March 1812 in the first White House wedding.

our very kind and accommodating Friend Brother John Johnson from a severe cold he had taken in Baltimore which brought on symptoms of his common complaint, the gout and made it seriously dangerous to move further lest he might be taken violent bad and indeed it seemed providential he was detained as it appears to me improbable he could have encountered the difficulties and exposure of those hazardous roads we have passed over which with all Nathaniel White's[94] skill in driving these roads from practice his strength and activity in getting in or out of the wagon and walking many miles, we could scarcely get along without oversetting. Wm. White is husband to Phebe Smedley that was of our meetings giving out on his return from Yearly Meeting he showed a willingness to take charge of us which has been very acceptable as he is so well qualified to drive. The Widow Poultney at whose house we left John has been skilled in nursing the gout as her husband had it for a length of years. From the circumstances we left him the more easy, knowing she was capable of nursing him with skill would he be worse. But we learn his gout got better and left there for Frederic to go by the stage homewards, from whence we shall be pleased to hear of his safe arrival and well-being.

We attended the Weekday Meeting at Berkley and the day after at Hopewell, the day following had a meeting at Back Creek and the day after at Bear Garden and the day succeeding which was yesterday being First Day not liking to travel all day, we called at a town called Frankfort[95] and with a short notice about 50 people were gathered in 20 minutes and after holding a meeting we came towards and performed a ride of about 30 miles that day. A good progress for such roads but the day has been greater though but 27 miles as it is on the Allegany Mountains a very bad road indeed—snow on it near 2 inches thick. Summer here lasts about 2 months and so cold they cannot raise corn I am told. We expect to get to Union Town[96] meeting on 5th day Redstone meeting the day following where lives our very kind Friend Jonas Cattle,[97] who has taken charge of us this journey and a young man also from Ohio stayed to help us along and indeed both were not too much. The young man who takes this resides at Union [Town] and Samuel must be sure to write

94. Possibly a member of Hopewell Monthly Meeting in Frederick County, Virginia.
95. Not identified.
96. A town about forty-six miles south of Pittsburgh, a few miles north of the Pennsylvania–West Virginia border.
97. Not identified; perhaps the brother of James Cattle of the Redstone Monthly Meeting who had led the Quaker party westward from Baltimore on the first part of this long journey.

largely to send by him not to neglect it, or I shall think much amiss of it. It should be directed to the care of Jonas Cattle near Brownsville.[98] Mary Harper is brave, sends her love to thee. Mine affectionate to Friends,

Anne Mifflin

ALS, EFP, box 2.

TO ANNE EMLEN SR.

Georgetown[99]
9th Mo. 19d. 1810
[September 19, 1810]

Leaving Philadelphia and journeying down the Delmarva Peninsula, Anne and her traveling companions crossed the Chesapeake Bay, reaching the nation's capital during the second year of James Madison's presidency. Lodging with Friends such as George Ellicott, Anne renewed her ties with the network of Quakers in the Upper South.

Beloved Mother,

Although I know of no opportunity for conveyance to thee, yet a little leisure this morning induces to put pen to paper. Since writing after attending one of the Monthly Meetings of Baltimore and tarrying a couple of days waiting for our men Friends, in which we paid a number of social visits and to James Casig's[100] at his country seat. We attended on First Day morning the other meeting of Baltimore and proceeded to Elk Ridge,[101] the settlement of the Ellicotts, where [we] attended at 4 o'clock at their meeting house a larger company than ever had been there, they said, from the circumstance of it being so accommodating to the people on a first day afternoon when at leisure from temporal engagements and the claims of other meetings. George

---

98. A rural village on the Monongahela River near Uniontown.

99. A neighborhood in Northwest Washington, DC, founded in 1751, it remained a separate municipality until 1871. The renowned Sidwell Friends School was established there in 1883.

100. Not identified.

101. An unincorporated city in Howard County, Maryland, where the Ellicott brothers built two-story stone houses on the bank of the Patapsco River.

Ellicott[102] said it was a satisfactory meeting. The next morning we went to view the great cotton factory establishment in that neighborhood, which is extensive and laudable, then rode to Samuel Snowden's and lodged, breakfasted next morning at the widow of Thomas Snowden,[103] who lives in great style; but this is tarnished by the reflection of its being supported by the labor of many slaves. She nevertheless seems sensible of the impropriety and seemed cordially to approve my suggestion of returning such of them as were disposed to go to the ancient bounds of their habitation by the settlement of a colony on the coast of Africa.[104] We then proceeded to Issachar Schofield's[105] to dine on our way to Washington [DC] and took coffee, lodged and breakfasted at John Teacle's[106] at Georgetown.

Alexandria 20th. From thence we attended the week day meeting at Washington returned to Georgetown and dined at Wm. Morgan's, a respectable Friend who dwells there. Then came to this place, lodged at John Ginney's,[107] and dined today at Edw. Stabler's,[108] a very sensible man and valuable minister who married Wm. Wartshorn's daughter; after attending this monthly meeting [we] are now about to set off for Occoquan, another small settlement of Friends.[109]

Thee can please let Hannah Pemberton see this. Sarah[110] not being prepared with a letter, and this opportunity I just heard of and concluded to hasten a conclusion before leaving this place.

102. George Ellicott (1760–1832), a Bucks County Quaker, moved with his brother to Maryland and founded the Ellicott Mills complex (today Ellicott City). A lifetime advocate for Africans and Native Americans, in 1801 he and brother Elias, along with a group of Native Americans, met with President Adams and the Congress in an effort to stop the distribution of whiskey to indigenous peoples. Morris, *Brief Account of the Settlement*, 60.

103. Samuel Thomas Snowden (1702–1780), a Quaker minister who resided in Montgomery County, Maryland.

104. Sierra Leone, the British-established colony where some of Baltimore's free black people resettled.

105. A Quaker resident of Montgomery County, just outside Washington, DC, and a member of the Sandy Spring meeting.

106. Not identified.

107. Not identified.

108. A member of the Alexandria Monthly Meeting, which met in Fairfax, Virginia. Edward Stabler, a Quaker minister, married Mary Hartshorn in July 1808.

109. Town in Prince William County, Virginia, about twenty miles south of Washington, DC, founded in 1804.

110. Sarah Zane, Anne's frequent traveling partner in these years.

We are comfortably banded together. Brother Jon overtook us on 6th day, having blacks' business to attend to on the 7th on which day John Paul[111] arrived. It appears very necessary to have his company and active assistance, Brother Jon being the weight of two common men, 240 lbs. and his baggage is very large—Sister Patience being very provident—and besides he is yet but delicate in health, prone to chills and by fatigue in the care of 2 horses, etc.—it might tend to bring on the bilious. Sarah is a kind and agreeable companion and we get along successfully beyond expectation. Sarah's love to thee and Sister Margaret, mine to sons, Sister Mary, relatives and friends with affection conclude, Thy, etc.

Anne Mifflin

ALS, EFP, box 2.

TO ANNE EMLEN SR.

Richmond
9th Mo: 30th 1810
[September 30, 1810]

Writing eleven days after her letter from Georgetown, Anne affirms her continued dedication to liberating enslaved Virginians.

Beloved Mother

I wrote from Alexandria, from whence we proceeded to Occoquan where we had a meeting with the families of Friends settled there and their neighbors who rode 16 miles from this meeting at Alexandria. Next day reached Fredericksburg and lodged at Joseph Carestie's,[112] one who inclines to Friends; where after being comfortably lodged and having an opportunity with him and his well-disposed wife we proceeded on to [North] Carolina and had a meeting at their meeting house the next day; the day after proceeded to Cedar Creek[113] and was the following day at this week day meeting. The next morning made to Genits[114] and was at their meeting—a settlement of the Pleasant family, a

111. Not identified.
112. Not identified.
113. A town in Cumberland County, North Carolina, near Fayetteville.
114. Not identified.

younger generation of hopeful young friends, where we dined and lodged: at Wm. And Tarton Pleasants.[115] And from thence the day following to this place: and yesterday was employed on calling on a few noted characters on the subject of a plan for the releasement of this country from the cloud of slavery that hangs over it.

The former governor of this state, General Wood[116] whom Sarah Zane[117] had some acquaintance with him, we called on in the morning. [He is] a benevolent character who had long set his blacks free and who with his worthy wife highly approved the plan and was very ready in offering what aid he could in the promotion of it. The present Governor Tyler was engaged in the morning in Council, but he let us know he would be glad to see us at 4 o'clock and that we would take tea with him. He well approved of the plan [and] said he had never thought of it and said the proposal felt grateful to him. We did not stay to tea being engaged at an acquaintance of Sarah's, a widow Harvey,[118] a daughter of her brother's Executor Gabriel Jones,[119] who lives in the high style of these who are encompassed with wealth and slaves; but being a sober-minded woman, on my opening to her the plan she much approved it and said it was a very benevolent plan, so had several slaveholders in our coming along to whom we have communicated the plan, in which brother Jon feels interested in and much united with and has been very helpful in obviating objections that were offered by some in Maryland whose minds have not been so awakened to fearful apprehensions as some of the Virginians and therefore not so prepared quite to join with what may prove a relief.

I queried with Sarah would she write, but she is engaged with some Friend and thee may please let W. Priad[120] this to see our progress instead of it Micajah Crew[121] have us company yesterday, one of the firmest pillars of this Yearly Meeting and who is much interested in the plan: having also thought of

---

115. A branch of the extensive Pleasants family, where at the home plantation, Curles, several hundred slaves were liberated. In 1803, Tarton W. Pleasants transferred his membership in the White Oak Swamp Monthly Meeting, near Richmond, to the Cedar Creek Monthly Meeting, where he was married in 1812.

116. See chapter 5, note 24, above.

117. See chapter 5, note 22, above.

118. Not identified.

119. Gabriel Jones Jr., whose father Gabriel Sr. was a Shenandoah Valley Anglican attorney, a prominent Virginia politician, and associate of George Washington. Gabriel Jr. inherited a sizeable estate from his father, which as Anne observed included slaves.

120. Not identified.

121. Micajah Crew (1750–1822), the son of Joseph (1715–1800) and Agnes (1722–1762) Crew and a Quaker resident of Cedar Creek, Virginia.

something a little in that way. It revived his spirit he said [of] the propositions and he wished it spread before as many who held slaves and others as may be. A melancholy report was spread in Philadelphia of Micajah having been greatly defrauded and of it having affected his finances but he wished it contradicted; there appears a mistake in the name and that it applied to a Friend in Carolina, Axam [Exum] Newby.[122]

Today we attend the 1st day meeting here and then expect to proceed on to Robert Evans' Cousin Thomas, Jane Cresson's[123] former husband, to lodge [there].

My love is affectionately to relatives and friends and particularly so to my sons whose well-being and care in their stepping along and that they may seek after best directions—attend meetings diligently and read sacred writings, and etc. is the earnest wish of their mother and thy affectionate daughter,

Anne Mifflin

ALS, EFP, box 2.

TO ANNE EMLEN SR.

Baltimore
10th Mo: 13th 1810
[October 13, 1810]

Continuing her ambitious sojourn through western Maryland, Anne offered her mother newsy tidbits about Friends she encountered and personal anecdotes on how she handled laundry and change of attire while traveling.

Beloved Mother,

We arrived here last evening a day or two sooner than expected in order to attend the Monthly Meeting which is to be held today as our kind and

---

122. Newby was among the North Carolina Quakers who had freed their slaves and worked from 1797 to 1798 to prevent the re-enslavement of four liberated males who had fled to Philadelphia. See Wood, "'Class of Citizens,'" 126n63.

123. Jane Coxe Evans Cresson (1754–1809), a Quaker minister and member of the PMM, Northern District. Her husband Caleb Cresson (1742–1816) was a leading figure in the PMM and PYM.

helping Friend John Cook[124] was given up in my mind to proceed as far as Washington or Alexandria with us; we lacked a Bible and proceeding forward some earlier than before John Paul and Brother Jonathan[125] should arrive here, but as he feels his mind turned homeward this morning and was not very well in the night we feel entirely satisfied to give him up, and perhaps it may be right not to travel quite as early from this place as we had some thought of and should we feel disposed to go forward to a meeting ahead on First Day there and Friends here who have carriages and can no doubt readily take us till our company overtakes.

After attending 5 monthly meetings of Chester County [and] the [London] Grove quarter, we proceeded over to the First Day at Fawn an obscure meeting in the Woods, which were all attended to satisfaction; we proceeded to Deer Creek[126] and spent one day in visiting Mother Mifflin at her son Joshua's[127] and two other friends we wished to visit there. We proceeded to Abington, a village on the road from Philadelphia to Baltimore accompanied by Elizabeth Cole,[128] who has not got out so far for a year; and by Hugh Judges' daughter Susanna Jewett, who is a Public Friend; and we had a meeting in their little meeting house at 3 o'clock on the 3rd day; and the next day we attended Little Falls Meeting[129] where Edward Churchman[130] lives and from thence came 21 miles to this place rather than have a fatiguing ride before meeting.

We feel very comfortable banded together. I believe it right the lot fell on Sarah to come and JC [John Cook] as far; whose company has been very acceptable to us and to those amongst whom our lot were cast. But now I can finally give him up.

After Nottingham Meeting we dined at Henry Physicks' whose wife is a fine and religious woman; her maiden name was Haines.[131] She herself has

---

124. Not identified.
125. Not identified.
126. An active meeting for worship in Darlington, Harford County, Maryland.
127. "Mother Mifflin" was Debby Howell Mifflin, who married Daniel Mifflin Jr., Warner's brother. Joshua Howell Mifflin (1786–?) was their fourth child.
128. Not identified.
129. Little Falls Meeting, an active meeting for worship, gathered at the historic meetinghouse in Fallston, Maryland.
130. Edward Churchman (1757–1834) was a resident of Thornbury Township, Delaware County, Pennsylvania, and an active member of the Nottingham Monthly Meeting.
131. Adriana Haynes, wife of Henry White Physick (1758–1821), the older brother to Dr. Phillip Syng Physick (1768–1837).

become rather skeptical since reading Paine's writing[132] and shows but a feeble mind to be overturned by such a flimsy opposer of Christianity. But the effects are very uncomfortable on his worthy wife who I have no doubt is often much tried under his disposition to darker "council by words without true knowledge." Yet he is kind and was very respectful to us.

I send an extra change, I brought on purpose to return dirty as it is sometimes difficult to get washing done where we may not long tarry at one place.

Hope my sons will endeavor so to work as to be a comfort to thee and bring on them the favor of heaven—and with love to them, Sister Mary and inquiring friends and relatives, I conclude with near affection and gratitude to thyself for all thy kindness, Thy affectionate

Anne Mifflin

As Lemuel said he would want trousers and there is lassamine[133] for the purpose and Samuel will look for cloth similar to that I left for him for a winter coat; as they charged me half a guinea for making a pair of trousers, I should be much obliged to thee to let a woman come in the house who with Mary's assistance which will be useful to her especially if sister Mary will help, may have them both completed in one day or a day and half at most. I forgot to leave out some coarse muslin for pockets and waist bands, but a yard suitable can be readily got at Joseph Clark's.[134] Sarah sends her endeared love to thee and Sister Mary.

ALS, EFP, box 2.

TO PAUL CUFFE

Philadelphia
2nd mo.: 8th 1811

In this letter to Paul Cuffe, the New Bedford Quaker merchant and sea captain, Anne revived her interest in supporting those black Americans who, despairing

132. Paine's *The Age of Reason* (1795) and perhaps his *The Rights of Man* (1792).
133. A textile finished with green synthetic dye.
134. Probably the Philadelphia merchant on Water Street; a friend of black Philadelphians, he had previously been appointed treasurer and secretary of their Free African Society.

that equality and social justice would never be possible for them in the new republic, desired to resettle in West Africa.

Dear Friend

I received thine of the 9th of 7th month last by the coming of our Friend Susanna Horne,[135] whose humble spirit and unassuming deportment is engaging and her gospel labors acceptable. It was forwarded to me at Baltimore when on my way to attend the yearly meeting of [North] Carolina, and other meetings in the course of going and returning. Previous to setting off on this journey, in looking towards the Southern Country and feeling concerned for the good of its inhabitants, it was forcibly renewed in my remembrance, the proposition of colonizing some of the blacks on the Coast of Africa provided a benevolent company in England would join hands in the measure and receive subjects for it from this country, whose expenses of conveyance and something toward their settlement should be paid by the people of this land: on which I wrote to thee a few years back, showing my letter first to our friends James Pemberton who approved and said thou would immediately open the matter to Granville Sharp. I also wrote to our cousin G[eorge] Logan in Congress respecting it, requesting his application to the President to consider of and promote the design.[136] And upon hearing sometime after of an able and influential society being established in England for promoting the civilization of the Africans, I was willing to hope this might possibly be one object that might come under thy notice, and if it had not already been the case, I concluded after this southern journey, if on inquiry there appeared a mutable disposition to promote the matter that perhaps through the medium of thy application or thy friend Granville Sharp, the Society might be stirred up to incline their attention and pursuit to such an object. To this end therefore I take up my pen. If no success attends, I have done but what appeared a duty; and if measurably successful, the reflection may afford consolation, should lengthened years prove my portion, when the active springs of life are slackened in their motions and looking towards a state of eternal rest—the experience of outward rest and exemption from busy undertakings is one of the desirable solaces of that day. Thou may please to refer to my letter on that subject and if any

---

135. A traveling minister from Tottenham Monthly Meeting in Middlesex County, England, Susanna arrived a few months before with approval from her monthly meeting and the London Yearly Meeting as a "Messenger of the Truth." Cuffe was in England, having sailed on his ship *The Traveler* just before that. We have not found his letter to Anne.

136. For Anne's involvement in this venture in 1806, see chapter 5, above.

improvement of the plan to promote its adoption may be formed, let it be brought into view. Sarah Zane, sister-in-law to John Pemberton, was my female companion, who had liberated about 30 blacks and was freely disposed to call with me on individuals in power to lay the plan before them and to stir them up to a consideration of the necessity of endeavoring to escape from the danger they are in and of bowing in mercy should a door of relief thus open for them rather than with hardened [blank] pursue former indulgences until judgement be poured forth without mercy.

Thomas Lynch, a very influential and valued Friend of Virginia Yearly Meeting, was relieved and comforted by the suggestion as affording a ray of hope on a subject that has very deeply engaged his attention and awakened his anxiety. He spent a day with us at Richmond (their Capital) in order to accompany us in a visit with the Governor; he was engaged in Council in the morning but would be glad to see us at the 4th hour and to take tea with him. The latter we could not accept it from another engagement but the proposition he said, "Felt grateful to him." We waited on the former Governor General Wood, who has freed his own blacks and met the idea most cordially as a relief he observed to tender consciences. Virginia having prohibited the freeing of blacks unless removed out of the state in one year; otherwise they are liable to be taken up and sold. This would open a door to their retreat to the original "bound of their habitation."

I proposed that associations might be instituted to raise subscriptions for carrying on the work in each state, provided there were those in Europe who would cooperate in the establishment; and that these might be called Returning Societies.[137] That inasmuch as (agreeable to apostolic declaration) the almighty "hath made of one blood all nations of men for to dwell on all the face of the earth" and hath [quotation mark missing somewhere in these words] determined the times before appointed and the bounds of their habitation."[138] And our predecessors and successors down to 1808[139] had forcibly removed them from the native bonds for mercenary purposes, but it is reasonable they should be returned to their bonds and not empty-handed—and I thought as England had been partaker in the unrighteous [blank] if they would unite in and carry on the work, I hope it might terminate in a benefit to that Nation. And it has

---

137. Anne's plan for "returning societies" would have provided reparations to freed people, paying them modest sums to finance their travel and resettlement to Africa.

138. Acts 17:26.

139. Federal law banned the importation of slaves from foreign countries, effective January 1, 1808.

been remarkable to me that [in] the first part of Africa, [where] Englishmen first violated the laws of universal liberty in forcing men into slavery who had not incurred it by any crime. Sierra Leone at that very place they erected a standard of liberty and mercy and are defending national restriction on that evil commerce, the slave trade by planting their great guns and floating batteries on the coast. [Blank] certainly if she continues to act on these principles, we may have cause to hope she will not be suffered to be devoured by her enemies.

We had an interview at Richmond with a Judge Tucker, who published a scheme for gradual emancipation;[140] he was not so cordial to embrace the view, as some others, being measurably riveted to his former train of ideas on that head, which I apprehend will never be realized. We conversed with some [blank] of note and fortune in high life, who much approved the proposition, one observed, "It is a benevolent plan" and with a look expressive of deep anxiety and apprehension we are so afraid of insurrections and one of her waiting men serving fruit round within a yard of her. Thus are they astonishingly off their guard from the abundance of the heart, the mouth speaking.

After being at a meeting near Williamsburg we devoted that afternoon to calling on some office there. Bishop Madison, president of the college in that place,[141] was from home but at his home we met with a [blank], an active member of the Congress who invited us to lodge saying he would be glad to show us some hospitality; and from him we first learned the plan was nothing new, that their legislatures had made a movement towards it some years back, etc.

We also called on Judge [John] Tyler, who appeared to treat the subject rather with indifference, saying there was a large new country to the westward which wanted cultivating, and they could get a good price for their blacks for that purpose. I replied, "I do not think it will be suffered to be so continued; if you will not live in mercy, you must in judgement" and many other things equally close. His wife, the governor's daughter and other young women present looked very serious. He was not offended at my freedom; perhaps my

---

140. Tucker, *Letter to a Member of the General Assembly*. Moved by the fear which Gabriel Prosser's rebellion of 1800 had spread among white Virginians, St. George Tucker (1775–1861) regarded slavery as a cancer on the body politic of a society based on universal freedom. He proposed gradually emancipating the state's enslaved people and relocating them to a colony west of the Mississippi River.

141. James Madison (1749–1812), bishop of the diocese of the Virginia Episcopal Church and the president of William and Mary College from 1788 to 1812.

sex was a protection against that effect. On the contrary, at parting he professed himself honored by our visit.

John Lynch, a worthy Friend and elder proprietor of Lynchburg, a growing commercial town on the James River, seemed much struck with the eligibility of the plan, and was desirous I should see his former schoolmate Thomas Jefferson on the occasion, which I was freely disposed to do to solicit his influence with the people in France from his acquaintance there, that in case such an establishment took place it should be free from injury from their arms in whatever state the nations might be as to war and might remain unmolested as an ensign sacred to benevolence. He was expected daily at a seat of his in the neighborhood but not arriving before our departure, at his request, I left a memorandum of the proposal who [Lynch] wrote and received a reply for the information and observations of which I have thought best to transcribe and forward.[142]

If there should be fears of their proving turbulent and ungovernable [blank], there might not be the same danger when they emigrate by smaller companies as there was with the Nova Scotia blacks, who were banded together before their departure.[143] It would tend to prevent that, from a proposition on the part of an English company that they would receive none of the blacks as could be recommended of tolerably good characters. This would create a kind of honorable distinction in the embracers from others and lead them to consider it a privilege to be admitted to go, for as Thos. Jefferson points out, it will require delicacy of management should the idea be taken up by them that it [is] a kind of transportation and that they are to be forced to go, they would at once feel repugnant to the plan.

T.J. [Thomas Jefferson] observes, "Nothing is more to be wished than that the United States would themselves undertake to make such an establishment on the coast of Africa. Exclusive of motives of humanity, the commercial advantages to be derived from it might repay all its expenses" and will, should

---

142. Lynch's December 15, 1810, letter to Jefferson, enclosing Anne's memorandum, is accessible at Founders Online, https://founders.archives.gov, as is Jefferson's reply to Lynch on January 21, 1811. Jefferson chose not to write Anne directly, but he did mention "Mrs. Mifflin" in his letter to Lynch and he responded to her proposals.

143. Anne refers here to the reverse diaspora of black Nova Scotians who sailed from Halifax in 1792 aboard British ships to join the Sierra Leone colony established by London's Sierra Leone Company in 1789. A detailed treatment of this repatriation of liberated Africans is provided by Schama, *Rough Crossings*.

this be the case with America, will it not more abundantly apply to Great Britain, to receive blacks from here acquainted with [the] culture of cotton, and transplant them there to raise cotton for their manufactures before our "National Mind" if prepared for it.[144]

It has been a strength to me in the prospect so clearly presented to view that is has been before contemplated by others, and that Captain Cuffe has now sailed to Sierra Leone with perhaps correspondent views. May the Lord prosper the work, if well pleasing in his sight and give peace in the exertion to those engaged therein.

I expected to have visited Pres. Madison (being acquainted with his wife)[145] and endeavored to obtain his attention to the object, but being entreated from Washington to their farm, it was too much out of our course to call, but as T. Jefferson observes "The National government can address themselves at once to those of Europe to obtain the desired security, and will unquestionably be ready to exert its influence with those nations for an object so benevolent in itself and so important to a great portion of its constituents."

Thy salutation of remembrance was offered to my dear aged parent now in her 91st year and whose mental faculties appear to me strong as ever but her bodily powers are much weakened. She is indisposed with the gout drawn into her feet by [blank] applications. Thy cousin P. Pemberton indisposed, other friends tolerably well I believe. The last account I heard respecting S. [blank] she was visiting families at Alexandria.

With affectionate remembrance to thy family I am
Thy assured Friend
Ann Mifflin

ALS, Miscellaneous Manuscript Collection, FHLSC.

144. Here and in the paragraph below Anne quotes from Jefferson's January 21, 1811, letter to Lynch.
145. Dolley Madison (1768–1849), a birthright Friend; after her father, John Payne, liberated his slaves in Virginia in 1783, the Paynes moved to Philadelphia. In 1790, Dolley married Philadelphia Quaker lawyer John Todd, who died in the 1793 of yellow fever; in 1794, she married future president James Madison.

TO ANNE EMLEN SR.

Lancaster
9th Mo 23rd 1813
[September 23, 1813]

In her last extended trip, Anne writes to her mother describing with relish her progress through meetings in Pennsylvania and Maryland and of her satisfaction over the hospitality of Friends along the way. Though she makes no mention of Lemuel, she is following the route he took when he left Philadelphia in 1812.

Dear Mother,

Although we talked of Columbia, yet I found on arrival here the fatigue of traveling over the Turnpike[146] was such that Sarah Zane seemed very willing and glad to rest. Anne seems in fine health and the family; that James is much better [and] Walter may be informed rested better.[147]

I told Jacob[148] to take the chair which was before at the hospital to have the leg put in; if done, he could take it there and I should be glad he would take some salt powdered fine to cleanse his mouth with. Poor dear Samuel under his injured state,[149] my mind was almost constantly with him in sympathy the day after setting out, thinking whether I did right to set out unless he could have come with me till at length I became more relieved.

Frederick Town: We proceeded to Columbia Meeting from Lancaster and dined there. Got to York to lodge and were hospitably accommodated at Friend Taylor's.[150] At Nathan Haines's[151] from York Town we proceeded to Hanover to dine and lodge at Tauney Town; dined [the] next day at Frederick and lodged at New Town. Dined [the] next day at Harper's Ferry and proceeded in the Evening here where we were kindly received and this Friend I find is either a 2nd and 3rd cousin to thee; [he] is a good, live and worthy Friend: has

---

146. The Philadelphia-Lancaster Turnpike in 1791 ran over sixty-two miles of muddy road before it was extended as the Pennsylvania Turnpike, which was completed in 1941.

147. This Anne may be her niece, daughter of Brother George Emlen. James—surname unknown—was probably Anne and Sarah's carriage driver on this long journey.

148. Likely a house servant.

149. Samuel's "injured state" was the onset of an emotional "derangement" described by a Mifflin cousin a few months later. See chapter 5, above, esp. notes 32 and 34.

150. Not identified.

151. Not identified.

some of his children settled comfortably round him: He married a McPherson whose brother married John Robert's daughter and since an Ellicott. We expect to attend meeting here being First Day and tomorrow reach Winchester.[152]

I began and resumed my letter at different places as thee may see. But interruptions, being many and the hurry of journeying prevented a procedure.

We found the Turnpike wearying from its roughness. I am in hopes Sarah has relinquished the idea of getting to part of the Yearly Meeting at Baltimore which she had looked toward if convenient as she wished to have seen some individual Friends who would probably be there. But as I have felt objections to attending large meetings, lest it should produce a crowd, unless some religious draft was felt; and I have not felt such attraction at present. I would prefer to take the more direct road home, as a means of getting there sooner. [In order] to expedite which I tell Sarah I am willing to be her secretary—to help her write or calculate if I can do anything so that she may be earlier released to return the period which I suppose will depend on the courts taking up her business to close it.

I will write some lines to Samuel which I wish cut off and directed and sent. But I fear from what I hear this morning that as the Post has just past here, I may not get an opportunity of conveying this my remembrances for some days, unless a private one offers: So [I] shall put this in a state of readiness to meet such and if none presents before post day, [I] may make an addition.

Although I felt very dull for a day or two after leaving home yet I have found my strength and appetite to improve and have been more released from the load of exercise attending my affairs at home. Sarah Zane is remarkably improved by her journey; she needed such an exertion to help reinstate her health, which had been much impaired.

We have been much favored with comfortable weather, no dust and no rain to incommode us. Sarah sends her love to thee, and wishes Prince[153] informed, [that] he need not open the house until further orders.

The stage is coming along, in haste thy, etc.
Anne Mifflin

ALS, EFP, box 2.

152. A town in northern Virginia and detention site of seventeen Philadelphia Quakers during the Revolutionary War. By this time Anne and her party had traveled about two hundred miles from Philadelphia.

153. Probably the black house servant employed by the spinster Sarah Zane.

TO ANNE EMLEN SR.

Salem, State of Ohio[154]
11th Mo. 12th [1813]
[November 12, 1813]

Hoping to find Lemuel, her twenty-one-year-old wayward son, Anne continued on a trip of nearly one thousand miles, reaching Ohio as winter set in. Despite suffering a respiratory infection, she visited numerous Quaker meetings, mostly those recently formed by Friends who, caught up in "Ohio Fever," had migrated west to Ohio.

Beloved Mother,

Since writing thee we proceeded to Redstone monthly meeting, then to Providence and Tweakley Meeting,[155] then on to Pittsburgh, where we were kindly entertained and lodged at Joseph Barker's, who thou may remember his wife and daughter drank tea at thy house. Then to Beaver where Friend Elizabeth Cadwallader[156] lives, who affectionately inquired after thee, stayed two days to rest our horses and be at their weekday meeting, then rode to Middleton, a large new settlement of Friends, and this day attended their Monthly Meeting; tomorrow expecting to attend a branch hereof called New Garden. It seems a fine landed country and were not the roads so new would be much better traveling in, even with our carriage, than the back part of Pennsylvania as the hills are not so trying. And though sometimes it is trying riding in a carriage, yet Nathaniel White is so excellent a driver we get along better than might be supposed. The carriage is gazed at in the woods as we pass along, one boy surveyed it round and round and said it was a very pretty cart. I suppose he never before saw one.

---

154. A town partly in north Columbiana County and a smaller section in Mahoning County, founded by Quakers in 1806. Salem became an active center for abolitionists and the Underground Railroad.

155. The Redstone Monthly Meeting comprised several preparative meetings on the east side of the Monongahela River; the Redstone Quarterly Meeting was the first established for Friends west of the Appalachian Mountains. The Providence Preparative Meeting had opened in 1790. What Anne called Tweakley was likely Sewickley, twelve miles northwest of Pittsburgh on the Ohio River.

156. Elizabeth Talbot Sharpless, widow of Isaac Sharpless, married Reese Cadwallader of Redstone Monthly Meeting in 1790. Beaver, seat of Beaver County, was thirty miles northwest of Pittsburgh.

I have had a very trying cold and stoppage in my head, but it seems recovering fast; Mary has been much favored with health. Friends are very kind and willing to do all they can for us in this newly cultivated wilderness: the more glad to see us because visitors are a rarity here as yet. This is but the third Monthly Meeting held since the opening of one here.

Jacob Vaugus[157] at the corner of Chestnut and Sixth Street promised to let me have the ground rent due before I came from the city, but as I hurried off sooner than expected rather, I neglected to call for it, or the time was not run out that he appointed to pay it in when I came away. I should be obliged to thee, if thee will please send for him, and tell him I request he would now pay the several quarters due. And if Samuel Bolton is not set off, please to send it to Wheeling[158] for me directed to the care of his Brother Aquilla. And if he is set off and no substantial opportunity occurs, I believe it may be safely put into one bill in a letter neatly folded up, and sent to Aquilla, whom I shall direct to open the letter and direct him how to apply for it. Robert [Anolse?] told me he had sent thousands of dollars by post, safely, and he thought there was no danger: and as it would be a matter of considerable convenience, for me to have it soon as may be, or to leave directions respecting it, I am willing to run the risk. I am sorry to put thee to this trouble, Samuel can do the errands and write out thy direction.

I hope to hear from you, on getting round towards Wheeling. I shall be comforted to hear of the preservation of thy health. Now the cold weather advances I feel anxieties on that score; but as it is moderate as yet hope thee may not have suffered on that ground.

I conclude with the salutation of affectionate regard to thyself and kind remembrance to family and Friends, hoping my son endeavors to be a steady and good boy and deserving of my regard and I conclude thy loving daughter,

Anne Mifflin

ALS, box 2, EFP.

---

157. Anne's Philadelphia neighbor who likely owned his house but paid ground rent to her.

158. Situated at the hub of the Ohio River and the National Road, Wheeling, part of Virginia, had originally been settled by yeoman farmers who did not own slaves. In the early nineteenth century, it became a center of abolitionist activity. When West Virginia was admitted into the Union as a state in 1863, Wheeling was subsumed into West Virginia.

Image Gallery

FIG. 1 | Watercolor of the Quaker meetinghouse at Second and Market Streets. Built in 1696 and replaced with a larger brick edifice in 1755, this is where Anne and her family worshipped until 1804. To the right is the city courthouse, where voters ascended the steps on the left, cast their ballots, and descended on the steps to the right. Courtesy of the Athenaeum of Philadelphia.

FIG. 2 | This portrait of Mary Emlen Beveridge, Anne's older sister, by Charles Willson Peale is the only known likeness of an Emlen family member. Mary's elaborate dress displays her abandonment of Quaker simplicity after she was dismissed from her monthly meeting for marrying David Beveridge; he had earlier been declared out of unity with Friends for various misdeeds. Quakers eschewed such portraits, deeming them presumptuous and vain. Courtesy of the Charles Coleman Sellers Papers, American Philosophical Society, Philadelphia.

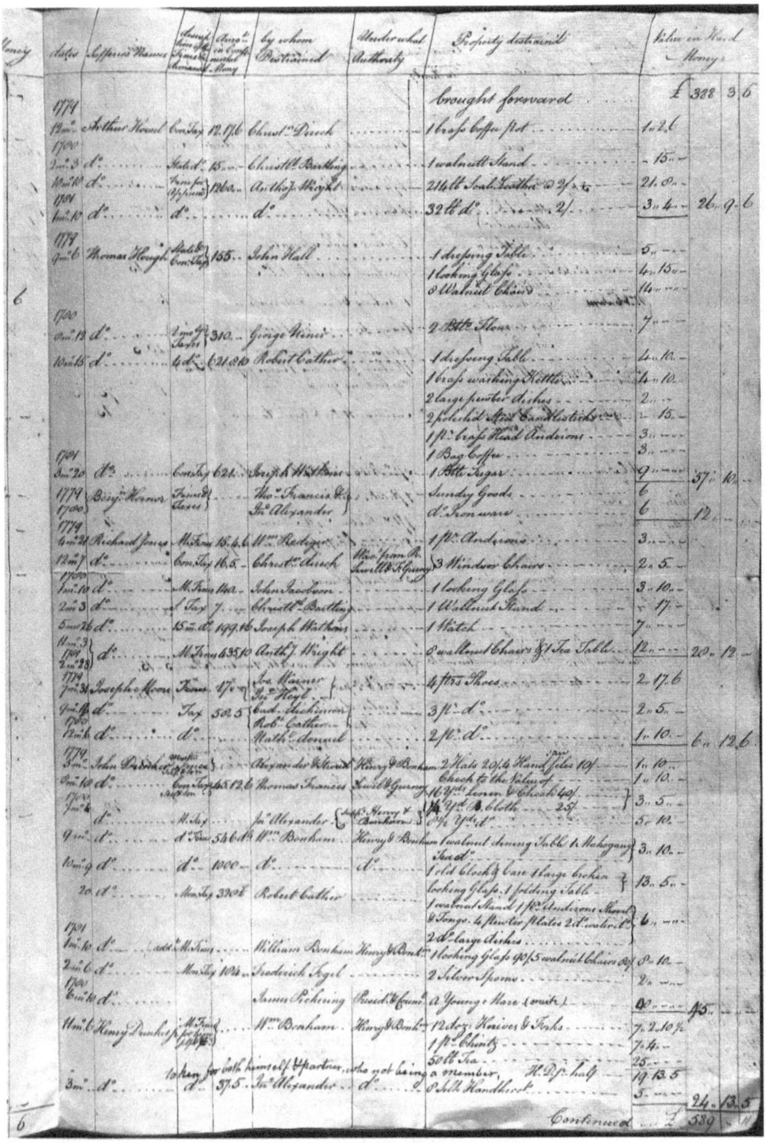

FIG. 3 | Seizure of property of John Drinker, in 1779 and 1781. John Drinker, like Anne, was a strict pacifist; hence he could expect annual visits from the sheriff to seize some of his movable property in lieu of war tax payments. Quaker monthly meetings recorded such distraints in detail as part of their venerable book of sufferings tracing back to seventeenth-century England. Philadelphia Yearly Meeting Minutes (1776–1792), May 1779.

FIG. 4 | Part of the series of views of Philadelphia by the English immigrant William Birch. This engraving shows the vibrant street life at the southeast corner of Second and Market Streets, where Anne often passed by on her way to the public market. At the center are men and women near a vendor of roasted chestnuts while a black Philadelphia woman and her child hurry by. Courtesy of the Library of Congress, Washington, DC, LCCN 2002718877.

FIG. 5 | A colored lithograph of Westtown School in 1858 by John Collins. A full day's carriage ride from Philadelphia, the school opened in May 1799 and since then has continued instruction. The building featured was replaced in 1870. Westtown was coeducational from the beginning, though girls and boys were taught in separate classes and entered the building from opposite ends by stairs to their second-story quarters, as shown here. Courtesy of the Westtown School Archives, West Chester, Pennsylvania.

QUAKER WOMEN PASSING: DEATHBED AS MINISTRY IN THE
MEMOIRS OF SUSANNA LIGHTFOOT AND MARTHA THOMAS

AN ACCOUNT of the RELIGIOUS EXPERIENCE AND SOME OF

THE TRIALS
of that faithful servant

and

MINISTER OF THE GOSPEL,
SUSANNA LIGHTFOOT

with

PARTICULARS OF HER LAST ILLNESS

and dying sayings,

compiled from the testimony given by friends in America, and from the minutes
kept by her husband, and an intimate friend, who attended upon her
She was born in Ireland, on the 10th of first Month, 1720, and died at Uwchlan,
in Pennsylvania, North America, 8th of 5th Month, 1781, aged 61, having been a

Minister about 44 years

Manchester, printed by John Harrison, Market Street
for the Manchester and Stockport tract depository and Association

FIG. 6 | The memorial to Susanna Lightfoot selected for inclusion in the Quakers' often-published commemoration of particularly venerable Friends. She was one of the few female members chosen for this recognition in Anne's lifetime. "The Testimony of Uwchlan Monthly Meeting concerning our Beloved friend Susanna Lightfoot," Philadelphia Yearly Meeting Minutes (1686–1850), 158.

FIG. 7 | Statehouse of the General Assembly, Annapolis, Maryland, where Anne Emlen Mifflin and Mary Berry witnessed, from the women's gallery of the chamber, their antislavery petition read and considered. The statehouse was constructed between 1769 and 1779, with the interior not completed until 1797. Courtesy of the Maryland State Archives, Annapolis, MSA SC 5916-6-128.

FIG. 8 | Coming to New York as an immigrant, Joseph F. Bartoli painted this portrait in oil of Cornplanter (ca. 1751–1835), after the Seneca war chief had visited New York City in 1786 to ask Congress whether they wanted to live in peace with the Senecas. Congress gave him the gorget and silver wrist bands pictured here; the nose ring and headdress are Seneca ornaments. Joseph F. Bartoli, portrait of Ki On Twog Ky (Cornplanter), 1796. Oil on canvas, 30 × 25 in. Gift of Thomas Jefferson Bryan. New-York Historical Society, 1867.314. Photo © New-York Historical Society.

Image Gallery | 317

FIG. 9 | Silhouette of Captain Paul Cuffe, dated 1812, based on a drawing by John Pole, MD, of Bristol, England. This print is the only known extant likeness of Cuffe. He was a well-known visitor to Philadelphia and had close contacts with Anne Mifflin and the city's antislavery leaders. He is pictured here with his ship, *The Traveler*, which was manned by an all-black crew. The background appears to be on the west coast of Africa, where Cuffe had transported black American emigrants. Courtesy of the New Bedford Whaling Museum, Massachusetts.

FIG. 10 | Replacing the "Great Meetinghouse" at Second and High Streets, this commodious, two-story New Quaker Meetinghouse opened in 1804 at Fourth and High Streets. This is the site where Anne Emlen Mifflin worshipped and was buried. The architect and builder, Owen Biddle, was not yet thirty when the Friends commissioned him to design the building. It was the largest meetinghouse at that time in the early republic. It remains today the vibrant center of Philadelphia Quakerism. Photographed at the northwest corner in 1974 by Jack E. Boucher. Courtesy of the Library of Congress, Washington, DC, HABS PA,51-PHILA,10-2.

APPENDIX

The following list includes letters and writings not included in parts 2 or 3.

LETTERS SENT BY ANNE EMLEN MIFFLIN

- 1776 May 18 to Hannah Pemberton, Pemberton Papers, 29/54, HSP
- 1777 September 13 to Thomas Burke, Thomas Burke Papers, box PC 55.1, State Archives of North Carolina, Raleigh
- 1779 March 8 to Hannah Pemberton, Pemberton Papers, 28/180, HSP
- 1781 June 12 to Sally Fisher, Corbitt, Higgins, Spruance Papers, DHS
- 1782 December 1 to John Pemberton, C-P-W, ser. 4, box 10, fol. 51
- 1789 April 23 to John Parrish, C-P-W, box 1, fol. 15
- 1798 April 1 to Henry Drinker, Vaux Collection, box 2, QCHC
- 1798 June 26 to Henry Drinker, Vaux Collection, box 2, QCHC (appended to Warner Mifflin to Henry Drinker)
- ca. 1799 [no date] to John Parrish, C-P-W, box 1, fol. 26
- 1799 May 5 to Ann Ridgeley, Ridgely Family Papers, Delaware Historical Society, Wilmington
- 1799 ca. December 12 to John Parrish, C-P-W, box 1, fol. 25
- 1800 March 17 to Thomas Fisher, Logan-Fisher-Fox Papers, HSP
- 1804 June [?] to Mother from Alloways Creek, New Jersey, EFP
- 1804 June 22 to Mother from Port Elizabeth, New Jersey, EFP
- 1804 December 11 to Ann Ridgely, Ridgely Collection, DPA
- 1805 October 10 to Mother from Trenton, New Jersey, EFP
- 1807 December 5 to Mother from Smyrna, Delaware, EFP
- 1813 March 23 to Mother Lancaster, EFP
- 1813 May 18 to Friend Holgate from Philadelphia, EFP
- 1814 June 18 to Mother, near Salem, Ohio, EFP
- 1814 July 8 to Mother from Burlington, Vermont, EFP
- n.d. to Lemuel Mifflin, EFP

LETTERS SENT TO ANNE EMLEN MIFFLIN

- 1777 June from Hannah Griffitts, Wharton Family Papers, HSP
- 1779 February 9 from Thomas Burke, in Smith, *Letters of Delegates to Congress*, 13:36
- 1779 ca. March 10 from Thomas Burke, EFP, box 2
- 1782 June 14 from Mary Berry, EFP
- 1788 June 14 from Mary Berry, Miscellaneous Collection, FHLSC
- 1788 August 12 from George Dillwyn, EFP
- 1796 March 1 from Joseph Galloway, EFP
- 1796 March 6 from Joseph Galloway, EFP
- 1796 April 28 from John Parrish, C-P-W, box 1, fol. 24
- ca. 1797 from Joseph Galloway, EFP

Note: Only a fraction of the letters to Anne Emlen Mifflin have survived.

ANNE'S COMMONPLACE BOOKS AND OTHER WRITINGS

- 1777 Colin and Chloe poems, Richard Walser, *Poems of Governor Thomas Burke*
- ca. 1778 "An Address to John Wesley on the History of the Quakers," EFP, box 1
- ca. 1778–82 "Notes on Religious Subjects" (five copybooks), EFP, box 1
- 1779–87 "Notes on Religion," EFP, box 1
- 1799 box 1, unpublished remarks on Brissot de Warville, C-P-W, box 1, fol. 25
- 1799 late December, testimonial for Ann Mifflin Raisin, Raisin Family Bible, FHLSC
- ca. 1799 "Defense of Warner Mifflin from 'An Observer,'" C-P-W, box 9, fol. 7
- n.d., "An Abridgment of the Life of Benjamin Ferris," EFP, box 1
- n.d., "Abstract from Minutes and Advices of the Yearly Meeting of Friends Held in London from Its First Institution," EFP, box 1
- n.d., "Extracts from Samuel Bownas Council [Counsel] to the Ministers and Elders," EFP, box 1

BIBLIOGRAPHY

ARCHIVAL COLLECTIONS

American Philosophical Society, Philadelphia
    Philadelphia Yearly Meeting, Indian Committee Minutes, microfilm edition
Cornell University Library, Division of Rare and Manuscript Collections, Ithaca, New York
    Indian Account
Delaware Historical Society, Wilmington
    Corbitt, Higgins, Spruance Papers
    Thomas Rodney Diary
Delaware Public Archives, Dover
    Cowgill-Mifflin Letters
    Kent County Orphans Court Records
    Kent County Tax Assessment Lists (1798–1801)
    Ridgeley Collection
Franklin and Marshall College Library, Special Collections, Lancaster, Pennsylvania
    Mifflin Family Papers
Haverford College, Quaker and Special Collections, Haverford, Pennsylvania
    Anne Emlen Diary
    George Churchman Diaries
    Miscellaneous Manuscripts
    Morris Wistar Wood Collection
    Richard J. Cadbury Collection
    Vaux Collection
Historical Society of Pennsylvania, Philadelphia
    Anne Rawle Diary
    Ann Warder Diary
    Cox-Parrish-Wharton Papers
    Duck Creek Monthly Meeting Minutes
    Emlen Family Papers
    Genealogical Society of Pennsylvania Collections
    Lemuel Mifflin Papers
    Logan-Fisher-Fox Papers
    Pemberton Papers
    Sarah Logan Fisher Diary
    Society Collection
    Wharton Family Papers
Library of Congress, Washington, DC
    Galloway Papers
    George Washington Papers (Founders Online)
    Thomas Jefferson Papers (Founders Online)

Massachusetts Historical Society, Boston
    John Adams Papers, microfilm edition
New-York Historical Society
    Gilder Lehrman Collection
Pennsylvania Archives, Harrisburg
Philadelphia City Archives
    Will of Anne Mifflin estate
Rhode Island Historical Society, Providence
    Moses Brown Papers
State Archives of North Carolina, Raleigh
    Thomas Burke Papers
Swarthmore College, Friends Historical Library, Swarthmore, Pennsylvania
    Emlen Family Papers (1796–1866)
    Henry Drinker Correspondence
    Hunt Family Papers
    Jackson-Conrad Family Papers (1748–1910)
    John Hunt Diary
    Lightfoot Manuscripts
    Miscellaneous Manuscript Collection
University of Pennsylvania, Van Pelt Library, Philadelphia
    1767 Tax Assessors Lists

PUBLISHED WORKS CITED

Abbot, Margery Post. *To Be Broken and Tender: A Quaker Theology for Today.* Palo Alto, CA: Friends Bulletin, 2010.

Abler, Thomas S. *Cornplanter: Chief Warrior of the Allegany Senecas.* Syracuse, NY: Syracuse University Press, 2007.

Account of the Religious Experience and Some of the Trials of That Faithful Servant and Minister of the Gospel Susanna Lightfoot, with Particulars of Her Last Illness and Dying Sayings. Manchester: John Harrison, 1844.

Adams, Charlotte. "The Belles of Old Philadelphia." *American Magazine* 8 (1888): 31–44.

Aiken, John R. "Benjamin Franklin, Karl Marx, and the Labor Theory of Value." *Pennsylvania Magazine of History and Biography* 90 (1966): 378–84.

Allen, James. "Diary of James Allen, Esq., of Philadelphia." *Pennsylvania Magazine of History and Biography* 9 (1885): 176–96, 278–96, 421–41.

Ancient Testimony and Principles of the People Called Quakers Renewed with Respect to the King and Government. Philadelphia, 1776.

Anderson, Matthew Smith. *The War of the Austrian Succession, 1740–1748.* London: Longman, 1995.

Andrews, Dee. *The Methodists and Revolutionary America, 1760–1800.* Princeton, NJ: Princeton University Press, 2000.

Anecdotes of Christian Missions. London: Religious Tract Society, 1799.

"Anecdotes of Warner Mifflin." *Friends Miscellany: Being a Collection of Essays and Fragments, Biographical, Religious, Epistolary, Narrative and Historical, Designed for the Promotion of Piety and Virtue* 5 (1834): 214–23.

Angell, Stephen W., and Pink Dandelion, eds. *The Oxford Handbook of Quaker Studies.* Oxford: Oxford University Press, 2013.

Bacon, Margaret Hope. *Mothers of Feminism: The Story of Quaker Women in America*. New York: Harper & Row, 1986.

———, ed. *"Wilt Thou Go on My Errand?": Journals of Three 18th Century Quaker Women Ministers*. Wallingford, PA: Pendle Hill, 1994.

Bauman, Richard. *For the Reputation of Truth: Politics, Religion, and Conflict Among the Pennsylvania Quakers, 1750–1800*. Baltimore: Johns Hopkins University Press, 1971.

Beaglehole, K. C. *The Life of Captain Cook*. Stanford, CA: Stanford University Press, 1992.

Bell, Whitfield J., Jr. *The College of Physicians of Philadelphia: A Centennial History*. Canton, MA: Science History Publications, 1987.

Benezet, Anthony. *Observations on the Inslaving, Importing, and Purchasing of Negroes with Some Advice Thereon*. Germantown, PA: Christopher Sower, 1759.

———. *A Short Account of That Part of Africa Inhabited by the Negroes, and the Manner by Which the Slave-Trade Is Carried On*. Philadelphia: W. Dunlap, 1768.

———. *Some Historical Observations of Guinea, Its Situation, Produce, and General Disposition of Its Inhabitants, with an Inquiry into the Rise and Progress of the Slave Trade, Its Nature, and Lamentable Effects*. Philadelphia: Printed and sold by Joseph Crukshank, 1784.

Berlin, Ira. *Slaves Without Masters: The Free Negro in the Antebellum South*. New York: Pantheon Books, 1975.

Berry, Mary. "Memoir of Mary Berry." *Friends' Miscellany* 1 (1831): 114–18.

Bezanson, Anne. *Price and Inflation During the American Revolution, Pennsylvania, 1770–1790*. Philadelphia: University of Pennsylvania Press, 1951.

Blecki, Catherine La Courreye, and Karin A. Wulf, eds. *Milcah Martha Moore's Book: A Commonplace Book from Revolutionary America*. University Park: Penn State University Press, 1997.

Bloch, Ruth. *Visionary Republic: Millennial Themes in American Thought, 1750–1899*. New York: Cambridge University Press, 1985.

Bogdan, Janet. "Care or Cure? Childbirth Practices in Nineteenth-Century America." *Feminist Studies* 4, no. 2 (1978): 92–99.

Bouldin, Elizabeth. "'The Days of Thy Youth': Eighteenth-Century Quaker Women and the Socialization of Children." In *New Critical Studies on Early Quaker Women, 1650–1800*, edited by Michele Lise Tarter and Catie Gill, 202–20. Oxford: Oxford University Press, 2018.

Bounds, Harvey Cochrane. *A Postal History of Delaware*. Newark, DE: Press of Kells, 1938.

Bownas, Samuel. *Account of the Life, Travel, and Christian Experiences of the Work of the Ministry of Samuel Bownas*. London and Philadelphia, 1759.

———. *A Description of the Qualifications Necessary to a Gospel Minister*. London: L. Hinde, 1750.

Branson, Susan. *Those Fiery, Frenchified Dames: Women and Political Culture in Early National Philadelphia*. Philadelphia: University of Pennsylvania Press, 2001.

Brekus, Catherine A., ed. *The Religious History of American Women: Reimagining the Past*. Chapel Hill: University of North Carolina Press, 2007.

Brewer, Mary Marshall, ed. *Kent County Guardian Accounts, McBride to Savin, 1739–1851*. Lewes, DE: Colonial Roots, 2003.

A Brief Account of the Proceedings of the Committee Appointed in the Year 1795 by the Yearly Meeting of Friends [. . .] for Improving and Gradual Civilization of the Indian Natives. Philadelphia: Kimber, Conrad, 1805.

Brinton, Howard H. *Friends for 300 Years: The History and Beliefs of the Society of Friends Since George Fox Started the Quaker Movement*. Wallingford, PA: Pendle Hill, 1994.

———. "The Quaker Contribution to Higher Education in Colonial America." *Pennsylvania History* 25 (1958): 234–50.

———. *Quaker Journals: Varieties of Religious Experience*. Wallingford, PA: Pendle Hill, 1972.

Brissot de Warville, J.-P. *New Travels in the United States of America, 1788*. Translated and edited by Mara Soceanu Vamos and Durand Echevarria. Cambridge, MA: Harvard University Press, 1964.

———. *Nouveau voyage dans les États-Unis de l'Amérique septentrionale, fait en 1788*. Paris, 1791.

Brock, Peter. *Pacifism in the United States: From the Colonial Era to the First World War*. Princeton, NJ: Princeton University Press, 1968.

Brookes, George S. *Friend Anthony Benezet*. Philadelphia: University of Pennsylvania Press, 1937.

Brown, Kathleen. *Good Wives, Nasty Wenches, and Anxious Patriarchs: Gender, Race, and Power in Colonial Virginia*. Chapel Hill: University of North Carolina Press, 2012.

Bruce, F. F. *The Canon of Scripture*. Westmont, IL: InterVarsity Press, 1988.

Burkett, William. *The New Testament with the Original Greek and illustrated with critical and explanatory notes*. London: R. Penny, 1736.

Burnell, S. Jocelyn. *Broken for Life: The Swarthmore Lecture*. London: Quaker Home Service, 1989.

Cadbury, Henry J. "Negro Membership in the Society of Friends." *Journal of Negro History* 21 (1936): 151–213.

Calvert, Jane E. *Quaker Constitutionalism and the Political Thought of John Dickinson*. New York: Cambridge University Press, 2009.

———. "Thomas Paine, Quakerism, and the Limits of Religious Liberty During the American Revolution." In *Selected Writing of Thomas Paine*, edited by Jane E. Calvert, 602–29. New Haven, CT: Yale University Press, 2014.

Campisi, Jack. "The Oneida Treaty Period, 1783–1838." In *The Oneida Experience: Two Perspectives*, edited by Jack Campisi and Laurence M. Huptman, 293–94. Syracuse, NY: Syracuse University Press, 1988.

Carey, Mathew. *Plumb Pudding for the Humane, Chaste, Valiant, Enlightened Peter Porcupine*. Philadelphia: M. Carey, 1799.

Carroll, Kenneth Lane. "Another Look at the Nicholites." *Southern Friend* 5 (1983): 3–26.

———. *Joseph Nichols and the Nicholites: A Look at the "New Quakers" of Maryland, Delaware, North and South Carolina*. Easton, MD: Easton, 1962.

———. *Quakerism on the Eastern Shore*. Baltimore: Maryland Historical Society, 1970.

Carson, Cary, Ronald Hoffman, and Peter J. Albert, eds. *Of Consuming Interest: The Style of Life in Eighteenth-Century America*. Charlottesville: University Press of Virginia, 1994.

Caton, Mary Anne. "The Aesthetics of Absence: Quaker Women's Plain Dress in the Delaware Valley, 1790–1900." In *Quaker Aesthetics: Reflections on a Quaker Ethic in American Design and Consumption*, edited by Emma Jones Lapsansky and Anne A. Verplanck, 246–71. Philadelphia: University of Pennsylvania Press, 2003.

Chambers-Shiller, Virginia. *Liberty, a Better Husband: Single Women in America, the Generation of 1780–1840*. New Haven, CT: Yale University Press, 1984.

The Christian Observer Conducted by Members of the Established Church for the Year 1806. London: C. Whittingham, 1806.

The Church or the State of the Church under the Gospel where it may appear. Glenside, PA: Quaker Heritage Press, n.d.

Clark, Joseph. "Account of a Journey to Indian Country." *Friends Miscellany* 1 (1837): 367–80.

Cobbett, William. *A Bone to Gnaw for the Democrats; or Observations on a Pamphlet, Entitled, "The Political Progress of Britain."* Philadelphia: Thomas Bradford, 1795.

Condie, Thomas, and Richard Folwell. *History of the Pestilence Commonly Called Yellow Fever, Which Almost Desolated Philadelphia in the Months of August, September and October 1798.* Philadelphia: R. Folwell, 1799.

Coogan, Michael David, et al., eds. *The New Oxford Annotated Bible.* 4th ed. New York: Oxford University Press, 2010.

Cooperman, Emily T., ed. *The Country Seats of the United States,* by William Russell Birch. Philadelphia: University of Pennsylvania Press, 2009.

Cox, Robert S. "Supper and Celibacy: Quaker-Seneca Reflexive Missions." In *The Sixty Years' War for the Great Lakes, 1754–1814,* edited by David Curtis Skaggs and Larry L. Nelson, 243–74. East Lansing: Michigan State University Press, 2001.

Crabtree, Sarah. *Holy Nation: The Transatlantic Quaker Ministry in an Age of Revolution.* Chicago: University of Chicago Press, 2015.

———. "In the Light and on the Road: Patience Brayton and the Quaker Itinerant Ministry." In *New Critical Studies on Early Quaker Women, 1650–1800,* 128–45. Oxford: Oxford University Press, 2018.

Crane, Elaine Forman, ed. *The Diary of Elizabeth Drinker.* 3 vols. Boston: Northeastern University Press, 1991.

Croft, Herbert. *A Brother's Advice to His Sisters.* London: Printed for J. Ridley, 1776.

Crothers, A. Glenn. *Quakers Living in the Lion's Mouth: The Society of Friends in Northern Virginia, 1730–1865.* Gainesville: University Press of Florida, 2012.

Cruden, Alexander. *A Complete Concordance to the Holy Scripture of the Old and New Testament.* London: J. Buckland, 1769.

Davidson, Robert L. D. *War Comes to Quaker Pennsylvania, 1682–1756.* New York: Columbia University Press, 1957.

Demanche, Robert. *The New Bedford–Fairhaven Bridge.* New Bedford, MA: Spinner Publications, 1986.

Dennis, Matthew. *Cultivating a Landscape of Peace: Iroquois-European Encounters in Seventeenth-Century America.* Ithaca, NY: Cornell University Press, 1993.

———. *Seneca Possessed: Indians, Witchcraft, and Power in the Early American Republic.* Philadelphia: University of Pennsylvania Press, 2010.

Densmore, Christopher. "New York Quakers Among the Brothertown, Stockbridge, and Oneida, and Onondaga, 1795–1834." *Northeast Anthropology* 44 (1992): 83–93.

De Pauw, Linda Grant, et al., eds. *Documentary History of the First Federal Congress of the United States of America: 4 March 1789–3 March 1791.* 21 vols. Baltimore: Johns Hopkins University Press, 1972–2017.

Dewees, Watson W., and Sarah Dewees. *Centennial History of Westtown Boarding School, 1799–1899.* Philadelphia: Sherman, 1899.

Deyle, Steven. *Carry Me Back: The Domestic Slave Trade in American Life.* New York: Oxford University Press, 2005.

Di Giacomantonio, William C. "'For the Gratification of a Volunteering Society': Antislavery and Pressure Group Politics in the First Federal Congress." *Journal of the Early Republic* 15, no. 2 (1995): 169–97.

Discipline of the Religious Society of Friends of London Yearly Meeting, 1682–1811. London: London Yearly Meeting, 1911.

Dorland, Arthur G. *The History of the Society of Friends (Quakers) in Canada*. Toronto: Macmillan of Canada, 1927.

"Dorothy Ripley: Unaccredited Missionary." *Journal of the Friends Historical Society* 22 (1925): 33–51, 77–79.

Dorsey, Bruce. *Reforming Men and Women: Gender in the Antebellum City*. Ithaca, NY: Cornell University Press, 2001.

Drake, Thomas E. "Joseph Drinker's Plea for the Admission of Colored People to the Society of Friends, 1795." *Journal of Negro History* 32 (1947): 110–12.

Drinker, John. *Observations of the Late Popular Measures*. Philadelphia, 1774.

Dunn, Mary Maples. "Saints and Sisters: Congregational and Quaker Women in the Early Colonial Period." *American Quarterly* 30 (1978): 582–601.

Edelson, S. N. *Plantation Enterprise in Colonial South Carolina*. Cambridge, MA: Harvard University Press, 2006.

Edgerton, Robert B., and Craig MacAndrew. *Drunken Comportment: A Social Explanation*. Chicago: Aldine Publications, 1969.

Egerton, Douglas R. "Averting a Crisis: The Proslavery Critique of the American Colonization Society." *Civil War History* 43 (1997): 142–56.

Elwood, Thomas. *The History of Thomas Ellwood Written by His Own Hand*. London: Morley's Universal Library, 1714.

Emlen, James. "Memoir of James Emlen, Late of Delaware and Pennsylvania." *The Friend: A Religious and Literary Journal* 54 (1881): 161–62.

Epistles from the Yearly Meeting of Friends, Held in London to the Quarterly and Monthly Meetings in Great Britain, Ireland, and Elsewhere. 2 vols. London: Edward Marsh, 1858.

Erben, Patrick M. *A Harmony of the Spirits: Translation and the Language of Community in Early Pennsylvania*. Chapel Hill: University of North Carolina Press, 2012.

Estep, William Roscoe. *The Anabaptist Story: An Introduction to Sixteenth-Century Anabaptism*. Grand Rapids, MI: William B. Eerdmans, 1996.

Ethridge, Robbie F. *Creek Country: The Creek Indians and Their World*. Chapel Hill: University of North Carolina Press, 2003.

Evans, Elisabeth. *Weathering the Storm: Women of the American Revolution*. New York: Charles Scribner's Sons, 1975.

Everson, Elisa Ann. "'A Little Labor of Love': The Extraordinary Career of Dorothy Ripley, Female Evangelist in Early America." PhD diss., Georgia State University, 2007.

The Famous and Memorable works of Josephus, a man of much honour and learning among the Levis. London: Thomas Adams, 1620.

Fatherly, Sarah. *Gentlewomen and Learned Ladies: Women and Elite Formation in Eighteenth-Century Philadelphia*. Bethlehem, PA: Lehigh University Press, 2008.

Feeser, Andrea. *Red, White, and Black Make Blue: Indigo in the Fabric of Colonial South Carolina*. Athens: University of Georgia Press, 2013.

Fenton, William N., ed. "The Journal of James Emlen Kept on a Trip to Canandaigua, New York." *Ethnohistory* 12, no. 4 (1965): 279–342.

"The First Tax List for Philadelphia County, AD 1693." Introductory note by William Brooke Rawle. *Pennsylvania Magazine of History and Biography* 8 (1884): 82–105.

Fisher, Samuel Rowland. "Journal of Samuel Rowland Fisher, 1779–1781." *Pennsylvania Magazine of History and Biography* 41 (1917): 145–97, 274–333, 399–457.

Fisher, Sarah Logan. "A Diary of Trifling Occurrences, Philadelphia, 1776–1778." Edited by Nicholas Wainwright. *Pennsylvania Magazine of History and Biography* 82 (1958): 311–65.
Florette, Henri. *The Southern Indians and Benjamin Hawkins, 1796–1816*. Norman: University of Oklahoma Press, 1986.
Flower, Milton. *John Dickinson: Conservative Revolutionary*. Charlottesville: University of Virginia Press, 1983.
Folwell, Richard. *Short History of the Yellow Fever that Broke Out in the City of Philadelphia in July 1797 with a List of the Dead* [. . .]. Philadelphia: Richard Folwell, 1797.
Fox, George. "The Woman Learning in Silence, or the Mystery of the Woman's Subjection to Her Husband." In *The Works of George Fox*, vol. 4, *Doctrinal Book 1*. Philadelphia: M. T. C. Gould, 1831. https://www.hallvworthington.com/PDFs/Doctrine1.pdf.
[Fox, William]. *An Address to the People of Great Britain on the Utility of Refraining from the Use of West India Sugar and Rum*. London: I. Phillips, 1791.
Friends Miscellany; Being a Collection of Essays and Fragments, Biographical, Religious, Epistolary, Narrative and Historical [. . .]. 12 vols. Byberry, PA, 1831–39.
Frost, J. William. *The Quaker Family in Colonial America: A Portrait of the Society of Friends*. New York: St. Martin's Press, 1973.
Furstenberg, François. *When the United States Spoke French: Five Refugees Who Shaped a Nation*. New York: Penguin, 2014.
Galloway, Grace Growden. "The Diary of Grace Growden Galloway." Edited by Raymond C. Werner. *Pennsylvania Magazine of History and Biography* 55 (1931): 32–94; 58 (1934): 152–89.
Gannett, Cinthia. *Gender and the Journal: Diaries and Academic Discourse*. Albany: State University of New York Press, 1992.
Gerona, Carla. "Ann Moore's Secrets: Dream Production in the Late Eighteenth-Century Quaker Culture." *Journal of Feminist Studies* 16 (2000): 43–70.
———. *Night Journeys: The Power of Dreams in Transatlantic Quaker Culture*. Charlottesville: University of Virginia Press, 2004.
Gibson, Campbell. *The Population of the 100 Largest Cities and Other Urban Places in the United States, 1790–1990*. Washington, DC: US Bureau of the Census, 1998.
[Gilpin, Thomas]. *Exiles in Virginia with Observations on the Conduct of the Society of Friends During the Revolutionary War*. Philadelphia: C. Sherman, 1848.
Godbeer, Richard. *World of Trouble: A Philadelphia Quaker's Family's Journey Through the American Revolution*. New Haven, CT: Yale University Press, 2019.
Gragg, Larry D. *The Quaker Community in Barbados: Challenging the Culture of the Planter Class*. Columbia: University of Missouri Press, 2009.
Gregory, John. *A Father's Legacy to His Daughters*. London: Ludlow, 1801.
Gross, David M. *American Quaker War Tax Resistance*. 2nd ed. Charleston, SC: CreateSpace, 2011.
Gudmestad, Robert. *A Troublesome Commerce: The Transformation of the Interstate Slave Trade*. Baton Rouge: Louisiana State University Press, 2003.
Guenther, Karen. *"Rememb'ring Our Time and Work Is the Lord's": The Experiences of Quakers on the Eighteenth-Century Pennsylvania Frontier*. Selinsgrove, PA: Susquehanna University Press, 2005.
Gummere, Amelia Mott. *The Quaker: A Study in Costume*. Philadelphia: Ferris & Leach, 1901.

Harrison, Eliza Cope, ed. *Philadelphia Merchant: The Diary of Thomas P. Cope, 1800–1851*. South Bend, IN: Gateway Editions, 1978.

Harrison, Richard A. *Princetonians, 1769–1775*. Princeton, NJ: Princeton University Press, 1980.

Harrison, Sarah. "Memoirs of the Life and Travels of Sarah Harrison." *Friends Miscellany* 11 (1838): 97–216.

Hauptman, Laurence. *Tonawanda Senecas' Heroic Battle Against Removal*. Albany: State University of New York Press, 2011.

Haviland, Margaret M. "Beyond Women's Sphere: Young Quaker Women of Charity in Philadelphia." *William and Mary Quarterly*, 3rd ser., 54 (1994): 419–46.

Hayes, Derek. *First Crossing: Alexander Mackenzie, His Expedition Across North America, and the Opening of the Continent*. Seattle: Sasquatch Books, 2001.

Hazard, Caroline. *The Narragansett Friends' Meeting in the XVIII Century with a Chapter on Quaker Beginnings in Rhode Island*. Boston: Houghton Mifflin, 1899.

Healey, Robynne Rogers. *From Quaker to Upper Canadian: Faith and Community Among Younge Street Friends, 1801–1850*. Toronto: McGill-Queen's University Press, 2012.

Henderson, Desiree. "'The Impudent Fellow Came in Swareing': Constructing and Defending the Quaker Community of Elizabeth Drinker's Diary." In *New Critical Studies on Early Quaker Women, 1650–1800*, edited by Lise Tarter and Catie Gill, 146–63. Oxford: Oxford University Press, 2018.

Herbert, Amanda E. "Companions in Preaching and Suffering: Itinerant Female Quakers in the Seventeenth- and Eighteenth-Century British Atlantic World." *Early American Studies* 9 (2011): 73–113.

Hinshaw, William Wade, et al., eds. *Encyclopedia of American Quaker Genealogy, 1607–1943*. 6 vols. Ann Arbor, MI: Edwards Brothers, 1936. Reprinted, Baltimore: Genealogical Publishing, 1991–94.

Historical Sketches of the Formation and Founders of the Philadelphia Hose Company. Philadelphia: Crissey and Markley, 1891.

Hodgson, W. H., ed. *The Life and Travels of John Pemberton, a Minister of the Gospel of Christ*. London: W. H. Hodgson, 1844.

Holcomb, Julie L. *Moral Commerce: Quakers and the Transatlantic Boycott of the Slave Labor Economy*. Ithaca, NY: Cornell University Press, 2016.

Hole, Helen. *Westtown Through the Years*. Westtown, PA: Westtown Alumni Association, 1942.

Holmes, Jack D. L. "Indigo in Colonial Louisiana." *Louisiana History* 8 (1967): 329–49.

Hood, Adrienne. "Cloth and Color: Fabrics in Chester County Quilts." In *Layers: Unfolding the Stories of Chester County Quilts*, edited by Catherine E. Hutchins, 79–103. West Chester, PA: Chester County Historical Society, 2009.

Horle, Craig, et al. *Lawmaking and Legislators in Pennsylvania: A Biographical Dictionary*. 3 vols. Philadelphia: University of Pennsylvania Press, 1991–2005.

Horsman, Reginald. *Expansion and American Indian Policy*. East Lansing: Michigan University Press, 1968.

Hunt, Alan. *The Governance of the Consuming Passions: A History of Sumptuary Law*. New York: St. Martin's Press, 1996.

[Hunt, John]. "John Hunt's Journal." *Friends' Miscellany* 10 (1837): 213–416.

Ingrams, Richard. *The Life and Adventures of William Cobbett*. New York: HarperCollins, 2005.

Ireland, Owen S. *Sentiments of a British-American Woman: Esther Deberdt Reed and the American Revolution*. University Park: Penn State University Press, 2017.

Jackson, Halliday. *Civilization of the Indian Natives* [. . .]. Philadelphia: Marcus F. C. Gould, 1930.

Jackson, Maurice. *Let This Voice Be Heard: Anthony Benezet, Father of Atlantic Abolitionism*. Philadelphia: University of Pennsylvania Press, 2009.

James, Sydney V. "The Impact of the American Revolution on Quakers' Ideas About Their Sect." *William and Mary Quarterly*, 3rd ser., 19 (1962): 360–82.

———. *A People Among Peoples: Quaker Benevolence in Eighteenth-Century America*. Cambridge, MA: Harvard University Press, 1963.

Jarvis, Brad E. *The Brothertown Nation of Indians: Land Ownership and Nationalism in Early America, 1740–1840*. Lincoln: University of Nebraska Press, 2010.

Jelinek, Estelle C., ed. *Woman's Autobiography*. Bloomington: Indiana University Press, 1980.

Jimenez, Mary Ann. *Changing Faces of Madness: Early American Attitudes and Treatment of the Insane*. Hanover, NH: University Press of New England, 1987.

Johnson, James K., and Bruce G. Wilson. *Historical Essays on Upper Canada: New Perspectives*. Toronto: McGill-Queens University Press, 1989.

Jones, Rufus M. *A Dynamic Faith*. London: Headley Bros., 1920.

———. *The Faith and Practice of the Quakers*. London: Methuen, 1927.

Jordan, John W., ed. *Colonial and Revolutionary Families of Pennsylvania*. 3 vols. New York: Lewis Historical Publishing, 1911.

Jordan, Richard. *A Journal of the Life and Religious Labours of Richard Jordan*. Philadelphia: T. Kite, 1829.

Judge, Hugh. *Memoirs and Journal of Hugh Judge, A Member of the Society of Friends and Minister of the Gospel*. Byberry, PA: John and Isaac Comly, 1841.

Justice, Hilda. *The Life and Ancestry of Warner Mifflin: Friend, Philanthropist, Patriot*. Philadelphia: Ferris and Leach, 1905.

Keller, Rosemary Skinner, and Rosemary Radford Skinner, eds. *Encyclopedia of Women and Religion in North America*. 3 vols. Bloomington: Indian University Press, 2006.

Kellogg, Louise Phelps. "Portage Trails in Minnesota, 1630s–1870s." US Department of the Interior, 1992. https://mn.gov.

Kelsey, Rayner W. *Friends and Indians, 1655–1917*. Philadelphia: Associated Executive Committee of Friends of Indian Affairs, 1917.

Kerber, Linda. *Women of the Republic: Intellect and Ideology in Revolutionary America*. Chapel Hill: University of North Carolina Press, 2000.

King James Bible. New York: American Bible Society, 1962.

Klepp, Susan. *Revolutionary Conceptions: Women, Fertility, and Family Limitation in America, 1760–1820*. Chapel Hill: University of North Carolina Press, 2009.

Klepp, Susan, and Karin Wulf, eds. *The Diary of Hannah Callender Sansom: Sense and Sensibility in the Age of the American Revolution*. Ithaca, NY: Cornell University Press, 2010.

Knott, Susan. *Sensibility and the American Revolution*. Chapel Hill: University of North Carolina Press, 2009.

Kokomoor, Kevin. *Of One Mind and One Government: The Rise and Fall of the Creek Nation*. Lincoln: University of Nebraska Press, 2018.

Kriebel, David W. *Powwowing Among the Pennsylvania Dutch: A Traditional Medical Practice in the Modern World*. University Park: Penn State University Press, 2016.

Labouchere, Rachel. *Deborah Darby of Coalbrookdale, 1754–1810: Her Visits to America, Ireland, Scotland, Wales, England, and the Channel Islands*. York: William Sessions, 1993.

Lapsansky, Emma J. "Plainness and Simplicity." In *The Oxford Handbook of Quaker Studies*, edited by Stephen W. Angell and Pink Dandelion, 335–46. Oxford: Oxford University Press, 2013.

Larson, Rebecca. *Daughters of Light: Quaker Women Preaching and Prophesying in the Colonies and Abroad, 1700–1775*. New York: Alfred A. Knopf, 1999.

Lawson, Carlton W. W. "The Revolutionary American Jury: A Case Study of the 1778–1789 Philadelphia Treason Trials." *SMU Law Review* 61 (2008): 1441–1524.

Leach, Robert E., and Peter Gow. *Quaker Nantucket: The Religious Community Behind the Whaling Empire*. Nantucket, MA: Mill Hill Press, 1999.

Lengel, Edward G., ed. *The Papers of George Washington: The Revolutionary Series (1775–1783)*. 28 vols. Charlottesville: University of Virginia Press, 1985–2021.

Levy, Barry. *Quakers and the American Family: British Settlement in the Delaware Valley*. New York: Oxford University Press, 1988.

Lindman, Janet. "Beyond the Meetinghouse: Women and Protestant Spirituality in Early America." In *The Religious History of American Women: Reimagining the Past*, edited by Catherine A. Brekus, 142–60. Chapel Hill: University of North Carolina Press, 2007.

———. "'To Have a Gradual Weaning and Be Ready and Willing to Resign All': Piety and Pain Among Quaker Women of the Early Mid-Atlantic." *Early American Studies* 17 (2019): 498–518.

Lindsey, Jack L., and Richard S. Dunn. *Worldly Goods: The Arts of Early Pennsylvania, 1680–1758*. Philadelphia: Philadelphia Museum of Art, 1999.

Locke, Mary. *Anti-Slavery in America: From the Introduction of African Slaves to the Prohibition of the Slave Trade (1619–1808)*. New York: Johnson Reprint Company, 1968.

[London Yearly Meeting]. *Commons of Great-Britain, in Parliament Assembled: The Petition of the People called Quakers*. Philadelphia, 1784.

Lossing, Benson J. *Field-Book of the War of 1812*. New York: Harper & Brothers, 1868.

———. *Pictorial Field-Book of the Revolution*. 2 vols. New York: Harper & Brothers, 1851–52.

Luff, Nathaniel. *Journal of the Life of Nathaniel Luff, M.D. of the State of Delaware*. New York: Clark & Sickels, 1848.

MacKenzie, Alexander. *Voyages from Montreal Through the Continent of North America on the River St. Lawrence to the Frozen and Pacific Oceans, in 1789 and 1793*. 2 vols. London: T. Cadell Jr. and W. Davies, 1801.

Maier, Pauline. "A New Englander as Revolutionary: Samuel Adams." In *The Old Revolutionaries: Political Lives in the Age of Samuel Adams*, 1–7. New York: W. W. Norton, 1980.

Mancall, Peter. *Deadly Medicine: Indians and Alcohol in Early America, 1659–1770*. Ithaca, NY: Cornell University Press, 1995.

Manion, Jen. *Liberty's Prisoners: Carceral Culture in Early America*. Philadelphia: University of Pennsylvania Press, 2015.

Manskar, Steven. *Accountable Discipleship: Living in God's Household*. Nashville: Discipleship Resources, 2000.

Marietta, Jack. *The Reformation of American Quakerism, 1748–1783*. Philadelphia: University of Pennsylvania Press, 1984.

Maxey, David W. *A Portrait of Elizabeth Willing Powel (1743–1830)*. Philadelphia: American Philosophical Society, 2006.
———. "Treason on Trial in Revolutionary Pennsylvania." *Transactions of the American Philosophical Society*, n.s., 101, no. 2 (2011): 1–204.
McGuire, Thomas J. *The Philadelphia Campaign: Germantown and the Road to Valley Forge*. Mechanicsburg, PA: Stackpole Books, 2007.
Mekeel, Arthur J. *Relation of the Quakers to the American Revolution*. Washington, DC: University Press of America, 1979.
Memorials Concerning Deceased Friends: Being a Selection from the Records of the Yearly Meeting for Pennsylvania &c from 1788 to 1819. Philadelphia: S. W. Conrad, 1821. 3rd ed., Philadelphia: Joseph Rakestraw, 1850.
Meranze, Michael. *Laboratories of Virtue: Punishment, Revolution, and Authority in Philadelphia, 1760–1835*. Chapel Hill: University of North Carolina Press, 1996.
Merrell, James H., *Into the American Woods: Negotiators on the Pennsylvania Frontier*. New York: W. W. Norton, 1999.
Michener, Ezra. *Retrospect of Early Quakerism: Being Extracts from the Records of Philadelphia Yearly Meeting and the Meetings Composing It*. Philadelphia: T. Ellwood Zell, 1860.
Mifflin, Warner. *The Defence of Warner Mifflin Against Aspersions cast on him on Account of his Endeavors To promote Righteousness, Mercy, and Peace*. Philadelphia: Samuel Sansom Jr., 1796.
———. *A Serious Expostulation with the Members of the House of Representatives of the United States*. Philadelphia, 1793.
Millar, Peter. *Dissertation on Man's Fall*. Ephrata, PA: n.p., 1765.
Miller, John. *Triumph of Freedom, 1775–1783*. Boston: Little, Brown, 1948.
Miller, Marla R. *Betsy Ross and the Making of America*. New York: Henry Holt, 2012.
Moore, Christopher. *The Loyalists: Revolution, Exile, Settlement*. Toronto: Macmillan, 1984.
Morgan, Philip D. *Counterpoint: Black Culture in the Eighteenth-Century Chesapeake and Lowcountry*. Chapel Hill: University of North Carolina Press, 1998.
Morris, John Gottlieb. *A Brief Account of the Settlement of Ellicott's Mills*. N.p.: n.p., 1871.
Morton, Robert. "The Diary of Robert Morton Kept in Philadelphia While the City Was Occupied by the British Army." *Pennsylvania Magazine of History and Biography* 1 (1877): 867.
Nash, Gary B. *First City: Philadelphia and the Forging of Historical Memory*. Philadelphia: University of Pennsylvania Press, 2002.
———. *Forging Freedom: The Formation of Philadelphia's Free Black Community*. Cambridge, MA: Harvard University Press, 1988.
———. "Philadelphia's Radical Caucus that Propelled Pennsylvania to Independence and Democracy." In *Revolutionary Founders: Rebels, Radicals, and Reformers in the Making of the Nation*, edited by Alfred F. Young, Gary B. Nash, and Ray Raphael, 3–14. New York: Alfred A. Knopf, 2011.
———. "Slaves and Slaveowners in Colonial Philadelphia." *William and Mary Quarterly* 30 (1973): 223–56.
———. *Warner Mifflin: Unflinching Quaker Abolitionist*. Philadelphia: University of Pennsylvania Press, 2017.
Nash, Gary B., and Michael McDowell, eds. *The Writings of Warner Mifflin: Forgotten Quaker Abolitionist of the Revolutionary Era*. Newark: University of Delaware Press, 2021.

Nash, Gary B., and Jean R. Soderlund. *Freedom by Degrees: Emancipation in Pennsylvania and Its Aftermath*. New York: Oxford University Press, 1991.

Nash, R. C. "South Carolina Indigo, European Textiles, and the British Atlantic Economy in the Eighteenth Century." *Economic History Review* 63 (2010): 362–92.

Naylor, James. *The Lamb's War: Against the Man of Sin*. London: Thomas Simmons, 1657.

Neale, Mary. *Some Account of the Life and Religious Exercises of Mary Neale, Formerly Mary Peisley, Principally Compiled from Her Own Writing*. Philadelphia: Friends Bookstore, 1845.

Neale, Samuel, Mary Neale, and Abram Rawlinson Barclay. *Some Account of the Life and Religious Labours of Samuel Neale*. Dublin: J. Gough, 1805.

Norton, Mary Beth. *The British Americans: The Loyalist Exiles in England*. Boston: Little, Brown, 1972.

———. *Liberty's Daughters: The Revolutionary Experience of American Women, 1750–1800*. Boston: Little, Brown, 1980.

Oaks, Robert. "Big Wheels in Philadelphia: Du Simitiere's List of Carriage Owners." *Pennsylvania Magazine of History and Biography* 101 (1972): 351–62.

Ousterhout, Anne M. "Controlling the Opposition in Pennsylvania During the Revolution." *Pennsylvania Magazine of History and Biography* 105 (1981): 3–34.

———. *The Most Learned Woman in America: A Life of Elizabeth Graeme Fergusson*. University Park: Penn State University Press, 2004.

———. "Pennsylvania Land Confiscations During the Revolution." *Pennsylvania Magazine of History and Biography* 102 (1978): 328–43.

———. *A State Divided: Opposition in Pennsylvania to the American Revolution*. New York: Greenwood Press, 1987.

Paine, Thomas. *Age of Reason, Being an Investigation of Truth and of Fabulous Theology*. Paris: Printed for Barrois, 1794.

———. *Common Sense*. Philadelphia, 1776.

Painter, Levinus K. "The Rise and Decline of Quakerism in the Monongahela Valley." *Bulletin of Friends Historical Society* 45 (1956): 24–28.

Pargas, Damian Alan. *Slavery and Forced Migration in the Antebellum South*. New York: Cambridge University Press, 2015.

Parker, Peter. "Rich and Poor in Philadelphia, 1709." *Pennsylvania Magazine of History and Biography* 99 (1975): 3–19.

Parrish, John. *Remarks on the Slavery of the Black People*. Philadelphia: Kimser and Conrad, 1806.

Pemberton, John. *The Diary of John Pemberton for the Years 1777 and 1778*. Philadelphia: Henry B. Ashmead, 1867.

Penington, Isaac. *The Church or the State of the Church Under the Gospel Where It May Appear*. Glenside, PA: Quaker Heritage Press, 1666. http://www.qhpress.org/texts/penington/church.html.

———. *The Jew outward, being a glass for the professors of this age*. London: G. D. Lodowych Lloyd, 1659.

Penn, William. *No cross, no crown*. London: Andrew Sowle, 1669.

Pilkington, Walter, ed. *Journals of Samuel Kirkland: 18th-Century Missionary, Government Agent, Father of Hamilton College*. Clinton, NY: Hamilton College, 1760.

Plank, Geoffrey. *John Woolman's Path to the Peaceable Kingdom: A Quaker in the British Empire*. Philadelphia: University of Pennsylvania Press, 2012.

Premo, Terri L. *Winter Friends, Women Growing Old in the New Republic, 1785–1835.* Urbana: University of Illinois Press, 1990.

Proceedings Relative to Calling the Conventions of 1776 and 1790. Harrisburg, PA: John S. Wiestling, 1825.

Pybus, Cassandra. *Epic Journeys of Freedom: Runaway Slaves of the American Revolution and Their Quest for Liberty.* Boston: Beacon Press, 2006.

Rappleye, Charles. *Sons of Providence: The Brown Brothers, the Slave Trade, and the American Revolution.* New York: Simon & Schuster, 2006.

Rediker, Marcus. *The Fearless Benjamin Lay: The Quaker Dwarf Who Became the First Revolutionary Abolitionist.* Boston: Beacon Press, 2017.

Reinberger, Mark L., and Elizabeth McLean. *The Philadelphia Country House.* Baltimore: Johns Hopkins University Press, 2015.

"Relics of the Past, No. 13." *The Friend: A Religious and Literary Journal* 18 (1844): 236.

Richardson, John. *An Account of the Life of that Ancient servant of Jesus Christ, John Richardson, giving a relation of many of his Trials [. . .].* London: Luke Hinde, 1757.

Richter, Daniel. "'Believing That Many of the Red People Suffer Much for the Want of Food': Hunting, Agriculture, and a Quaker Construction of Indianness in the Early Republic." *Journal of the Early Republic* 19 (1999): 601–28.

———. *Ordeal of the Longhouse: The People of the Iroquois League in the Era of European Civilization.* Chapel Hill: University of North Carolina Press, 1992.

[Ripley, Dorothy]. *The Extraordinary Conversion and Religious Experience of Dorothy Ripley [. . .] with Her First Voyage and Travels in America.* New York: G. and R. Waite, 1810.

Roberts, James. *The Narrative of James Roberts, a Soldier in the Revolutionary War and at the Battle of New Orleans.* Hattiesburg, MS, 1858.

Rossignol, Marie-Jeanne. "Jacques-Pierre Brissot and the Fate of Atlantic Antislavery During the Age of Revolutionary Wars." In *War, Empire and Slavery, 1770–1830*, edited by Richard Bessel, Nicholas Guyatt, and Jane Rendall, 139–56. London: Palgrave Macmillan, 2010.

Rossman, Kenneth R. *Thomas Mifflin and the Politics of the American Revolution.* Chapel Hill: University of North Carolina Press, 1952.

Rosswurm, Steven. *Arms, Country, and Class: The Philadelphia Militia and the "Lower Sort" During the American Revolution.* New Brunswick, NJ: Rutgers University Press, 1987.

Rothenberg, Diane. "The Mothers of the Nation: Seneca Resistance to Quaker Intervention." In *Women and Colonization: Anthropological Perspective*, edited by Mona Etienne and Eleanor Leacock, 63–87. New York: Praeger, 1960.

Rothman, Adam. *Slave Country: American Expansion and the Origins of the Deep South.* Cambridge, MA: Harvard University Press, 2005.

Routh, Martha. *Memoir of the Life, Travels, and Religious Experiences of Martha Routh.* London: W. Alexander and Son, 1822.

Rowe, G. S. *Thomas McKean: The Shaping of an American Republicanism.* Boulder: Colorado Associated University Press, 1978.

Rush, Benjamin. *An Account of the Origins, Progress, and Present Condition of the Philadelphia Society for the Establishment and Support of Charity Schools.* In *The Account of the Life and Character of Christopher Ludwick by Benjamin Rush.* Philadelphia: Printed for the Society by Garden and Thompson, 1831.

———. *Account of the Yellow Fever Epidemic of 1798.* Philadelphia: Thomas Dobson, 1798.

[Rush, Benjamin]. *An Address to the Inhabitants of the British Settlements in America, on the Slavery of the Negroes in America: To which is added, a vindication of the address, in answer to a pamphlet entitled, "Slavery not forbidden in Scripture; or, A Defence of the West India planters by a Pennsylvanian."* Philadelphia: Printed and sold by John Dunlap, 1773.

———. *Considerations upon the Present Test-Law of Pennsylvania: Addressed to the Legislature and Freemen of the State.* Philadelphia: Hall and Sellars, 1784.

Rutherford, Anne. *Quaker Women Passing: Deathbed as Pulpit in the Memoirs of Susanna Lightfoot.* Cambridge, MA: Rhywmbooks, 1999.

Salinger, Sharon V. *"To Serve Well and Faithfully": Labor and Indentured Servants in Pennsylvania, 1682–1800.* New York: Cambridge University Press, 1987.

Sands, David. *Journal of the Life and Gospel Labours of David Sands.* London: Charles Gilpin, 1848.

Savage, Carlton J. "In Search of a Benevolent Despot: John Thompson Emlen and the Establishment of the First Colored Boys Club, 1903–1930." *Peabody Journal of Education* 88 (2013): 421–48.

Savery, William. *The Life, Travels, and Religious Labours of William Savery.* London: Charles Gilpin, 1844.

Schama, Simon. *Rough Crossings: Britain, the Slaves, and the American Revolution.* New York: HarperCollins, 2006.

Scholten, Catherine. "On the Importance of the Obstetrick Art: Changing Customs of Childbirth in America, 1760–1825." *William and Mary Quarterly* 34 (1977): 426–45.

[Scott, Job]. *Journal of the Life, Travel, and Gospel Labors of that Faithful Servant and Minister of Christ, Job Scott.* New York: Isaac Collins, 1797.

Seebohm, Benjamin. *Memoirs of the Life and Gospel Labours of Stephen Grellet.* Philadelphia: Longstreth, 1850.

Sellers, Charles Coleman. *Portraits and Miniatures by Charles Willson Peale.* Philadelphia: American Philosophical Society, 1952.

Sergeant, Thomas, and William Rawle, eds. *Reports of Cases Adjudged in the Supreme Court of Pennsylvania*, vol. 6. Philadelphia, 1872.

Sharpless, Isaac. *The Quakers in the Revolution.* Vol. 2 of *A History of Quaker Government in Pennsylvania.* Philadelphia: T. S. Leach, 1899.

Sharrer, G. Terry. "The Indigo Bonanza in South Carolina, 1740–1790." *Technology and Culture* 12 (1971): 447–55.

Shea, William N. *The Lion and the Lamb: Evangelicals and Catholics in America.* Oxford: Oxford University Press, 2004.

Shields, David S., and Fredrika J. Teute. "The Meschianza: Sum of All Fêtes." *Journal of the Early Republic* 35 (2015): 185–214.

Showman, Richard K., et al., eds. *The Papers of Nathanael Greene.* 13 vols. Chapel Hill: University of North Carolina Press, 1976–2015.

Silverman, David J. *Red Brethren: The Brothertown and Stockbridge Indians and the Problem of Race in Early America.* Ithaca, NY: Cornell University Press, 2010.

Sinha, Manisha. *The Slave's Cause: A History of Abolition.* New Haven, CT: Yale University Press, 2018.

Slaughter, Thomas P. *The Beautiful Soul of John Woolman, Apostle of Abolition.* New York: Hill and Wang, 2009.

Smith, Adam. *The Wealth of Nations.* London: W. Strahan and T. Cadell, 1776.

Smith, Billy G. *Ship of Death: A Voyage That Changed the Atlantic World*. New Haven, CT: Yale University Press, 2013.
Smith, Paul H., ed. *Letters of Delegates to Congress, 1774–1789*. 26 vols. Washington, DC: Government Printing Office, 1976–2000.
Snyder, Martin P. *City of Independence: Views of Philadelphia Before 1800*. New York: Praeger, 1975.
Soderlund, Jean R. *Lenape Country: Delaware Valley Society Before William Penn*. Philadelphia: University of Pennsylvania Press, 2015.
———. *Quakers and Slavery: A Divided Spirit*. Princeton, NJ: Princeton University Press, 1985.
———. "Women's Authority in Pennsylvania and New Jersey Quaker Meetings." *William and Mary Quarterly* 44 (1987): 722–49.
Stackhouse, Thomas. *A New History of the Holy Bible*. 2 vols. London: J. Huggonsons, 1733.
Sullivan, Aaron. *The Disaffected: Britain's Occupation of Philadelphia During the American Revolution*. Philadelphia: University of Pennsylvania Press, 2019.
Swatzler, David. *A Friend Among the Senecas: The Quaker Mission to Cornplanter's People*. Mechanicsburg, PA: Stackpole Books, 2000.
Sweeney, John A. H., ed. "The Norris-Fisher Correspondence: A Circle of Friends, 1779–82." *Delaware History* 6 (1955): 187–232.
Tarter, Michele Lise. "Reading a Quaker's Book: Elizabeth Ashbridge's Testimony of a Quaker Literary Theory." *Quaker Studies* 9, no. 2 (2005): 176–90.
———. "Written from the Body of Sisterhood: Quaker Women's Prophesying and the Creation of a New World." In *New Critical Studies on Early Quaker Women, 1650–1800*, ed. Michele Lise Tarter and Catie Gill, 69–90. New York: Oxford University Press, 2018.
Taylor, Francis R. *The Life of William Savery of Philadelphia, 1750–1804*. New York: Macmillan, 1925.
Taylor, Jeremy. *The Great Exemplar or, the Life of Our Ever-Blessed Jesus Christ*. London: Roger Norton, 1694.
Thomas, Lamont. *Rise to Be a People: A Biography of Paul Cuffe*. Urbana: University of Illinois Press, 1986.
Thompson, Mack. *Moses Brown: Reluctant Reformer*. Chapel Hill: University of North Carolina Press, 1962.
Thompson, Peter. *Rum, Punch, Revolution: Tavern Going and Public Life in Eighteenth-Century Philadelphia*. Philadelphia: University of Pennsylvania Press, 1999.
Tiro, Karim M. *The People of the Standing Stone: The Oneida Nation from the Revolution Through the Era of Removal*. Amherst: University of Massachusetts Press, 2011.
———. "'We Wish to Do You Good': The Quaker Mission to the Oneida Nation, 1790–1840." *Journal of the Early Republic* 26 (2006): 353–76.
Tolles, Frederick B. *Meeting House and Counting House: The Quaker Merchants of Colonial Philadelphia, 1782–1763*. Chapel Hill: University of North Carolina Press, 1948.
———. *Quakers and the Atlantic Culture*. New York: Macmillan, 1960.
Toogood, Anna Coxe. *Historic Resource Study: Independence Mall, the 18th Century Development, Block One, Chestnut to Market, Fifth to Sixth Streets*. Philadelphia: Independence National Historic Park, 2001.
Townsend, William P., ed. *A Brief Narrative of the Life of Jacob Lindley [. . .]*. Philadelphia: Friend's Book Store, 1893.

Tucker, St. George. *A Letter to a Member of the General Assembly of Virginia, on the Subject of the Late Conspiracy of the Slaves; with a Proposal for Colonization.* Baltimore: Bonsal & Niles, 1801.

Turges, C. Dickinson. "Friends in Barbados." *Journal of the Friends Historical Society* 5 (1908): 43–46.

Tyson, John S., and John W. McGrain. *The Founders of Ellicott's Mills.* Baltimore: Maryland Historical Society, 1994.

Ulrich, Laurel Thatcher. *Good Wives: Image and Reality in the Lives of Women in Northern New England, 1650–1750.* New York: Vintage Books, 1991.

Vann, Richard, and David Eversley. *Friends in Life and Death, the British and Irish Quakers in the Demographic Transition, 1650–1900.* Cambridge: Cambridge University Press, 1992.

Voltaire, François-Marie Arouet. *The History of Charles XII of Sweden.* Oxford: Voltaire Foundation, 1996.

Waldstreicher, David. *In the Midst of Perpetual Fêtes: The Making of American Nationalism, 1776–1820.* Chapel Hill: University of North Carolina Press, 1997.

———. *Slavery's Constitution: From Revolution to Ratification.* New York: Hill and Wang, 2009.

Wallace, Anthony F. C. *The Death and Rebirth of the Seneca.* New York: Alfred K. Knopf, 1970.

Wallace, Paul A. W. *Indians in Pennsylvania.* Harrisburg: Pennsylvania Historical and Museum Commission, 1961.

Walser, Richard, ed. *The Poems of Governor Thomas Burke of North Carolina.* Raleigh: State Department of Archives and History, 1961.

Warder, Ann. "The Diary of Ann Warder." *Pennsylvania Magazine of History and Biography* 17 (1893): 444–61; 18 (1894): 51–63.

Watterson, John Sayle. *Thomas Burke: Restless Revolutionary.* Washington, DC: University Press of America, 1980.

Wayland, John W., ed. *Hopewell Friends History, 1734–1934, Frederick County, Virginia.* Strasburg, VA: Shenandoah, 1936. Reprinted, Baltimore: Genealogical Publishing, 1975.

Wells, Robert V. "Family Size and Fertility Control in Eighteenth-Century America: A Study of Quaker History." *Population Studies* 26 (1971): 73–82.

Wharton, Susanna Parrish, and Dillwyn Parrish, eds. *The Parrish Family, Philadelphia, Pennsylvania, Including the Related Families of Cox, Dillwyn, Roberts, Chandler, Painter, Pusey by Dillwyn Parrish (1809–1886, with Special Reference to Joseph Parker, M.D., 1779–1840)* [. . .]. Philadelphia: George H. Buchanan, 1925.

Whitby, Daniel. *A Paraphrase and Commentary on the New Testament.* 2 vols. London: W. Bowyer, 1703.

White, Richard. *The Middle Ground: Indians, Empires, and Republics in the Great Lakes Region, 1650–1815.* Cambridge: Cambridge University Press, 1991.

Wilbur, Henry W. *The Life and Labors of Elias Hicks.* Philadelphia: Friends General Conference, 1910.

Williamson, Jane W. *Annapolis, City on the Severn: A History.* Baltimore: Johns Hopkins University Press, 2011.

Wilson, Lisa. *A History of Stepfamilies in Early America.* Chapel Hill: University of North Carolina Press, 2014.

———. *Life After Death: Widows in Pennsylvania, 1750–1850*. Philadelphia: Temple University Press, 1992.

Winch, Julie. *A Gentleman of Color: The Life of James Forten*. New York: Oxford University Press, 2002.

Wolf, Edwin. *Book Culture of an American City*. New York: Oxford University Press, 1988.

Wolf, Edwin, and Marie Elena Korey, eds. *Quarter of a Millennium: The Library Company of Philadelphia, 1731–1989*. Philadelphia: Library Company of Philadelphia, 1981.

Wolfe, John. "A Comparative Historical Categorization of Anti-Catholicism." *Journal of Religious History* 39 (2015): 182–292.

Wood, Nicholas P. "A 'Class of Citizens': The Earliest Black Petitioners to Congress and Their Quaker Allies." *William and Mary Quarterly*, 3rd ser., 74 (2017): 109–44.

———. "Considerations of Humanity and Expediency: The Slave Trades and African Colonization in the Early National Antislavery Movement." PhD diss., University of Virginia, 2014.

Woolman, John. *An Account of the Life, Gospel Labours, and Christian Experiences of a Faithful Minister of Jesus Christ, John Woolman*. Philadelphia: Joseph Crukshank, 1774.

Woolman, John. *The Journal and Major Essays of John Woolman*. Edited by Phillips P. Moulton. New York: Oxford University Press, 1971.

Worrall, Jay, Jr. *The Friendly Virginians: America's First Quakers*. Athens, GA: Iberian Publishing, 1994.

Wright, James Martin. *The Free Negro in Maryland, 1634–1860*. New York: Columbia University Press, 1921.

Wulf, Karin, *Not All Wives: Women of Colonial Philadelphia*. Ithaca, NY: Cornell University Press, 2000.

Younger, Karen. "Africa Stretches Forth Her Hands unto You: Female Colonization Supporters in the Antebellum U.S." PhD diss., Penn State University, 2006.

Zuckerman, Michael, ed. *Friends and Neighbors: Group Life in America's First Plural Society*. Philadelphia: Temple University Press, 1982.

BIOGRAPHICAL NOTE: GARY B. NASH, 1933–2021

Gary grew up in the 1930s and '40s in the upper-middle-class suburb of Philadelphia's Main Line. Graduating from Merion High School in 1951, he was elated to be accepted into Princeton, which he afforded through an ROTC scholarship and a steady job. Upon graduation, Gary owed three years of military service to the navy. In 1958, Lieutenant Nash walked down the gangway of his destroyer for the last time, headed for what he described as "an uncertain career." Princeton took him on as an assistant to the graduate dean, but with the immediacy of the civil rights movement, Gary knew it was time to find his life's work.

He chose to study history, and Princeton allowed him to enroll as an "incidental" graduate student (incidental due to a spotty undergraduate record). Gary found inspiring mentors such as Richard S. Dunn and worked quickly through the doctoral program, compelled by the need to support a growing family. By 1964 he had his PhD in hand and an assistant professorship appointment at his alma mater. His dissertation, *Quakers and Politics*, already displayed his egalitarian sympathies in the writing of history and the shift away from the main focus of historical interpretation.

In 1966, UCLA offered—and Gary accepted—a position in the department of history. Deeply affected by the movement for racial equality, he immediately began to create what would be an impressive "life's work" of activism, scholarship, and teaching. He worked at ground level to integrate local banks, stores, and housing in west Los Angeles, where he lived with his family. At UCLA Gary poured himself into instructing undergraduates and graduate students and designing a curriculum that introduced the topic of race and racial attitudes in America. By the end of the 1970s, Gary had made his mark as a prolific scholar, culminating the decade with the publication of his magnum opus, *The Urban Crucible*.

In the early 1990s, Gary turned his and UCLA's attention to the teaching of history in the schools. As founding codirector of the National Center for History in the Schools, he led teachers from around the country in an enlightened revamping of how history was taught from kindergarten through twelfth grade. He served his profession well as president of the Organization of

American Historians (1994–95) and proudly represented educators on the National Parks Second Century Commission (2008–9).

I was a graduate student at UCLA in 1977 when I met Gary. When we married in 1981, he had already published perhaps the two most influential books of his career. *Red, White, and Black: The Peoples of Early America* (1974) confronted head-on the conventional interpretation of race relations in America's early history, demonstrating how the interaction and engagement of Native Americans, Europeans, and Africans shaped the story of the period. *The Urban Crucible: Social Change, Political Consciousness, and the Origins of the American Revolution* (1979) was a pathbreaking work in American social history, giving agency and voice to the ordinary people who brought the American Revolution to fruition. Gary published dozens more books after *Urban Crucible*, which was no surprise to me: I observed firsthand, over forty years, what an extremely disciplined writer he was. Gary had many passions within a life filled with purpose and joy, but he was truly driven by a passion for the research and telling of history.

By the time Gary stopped writing (just three weeks before his death), he had authored or coauthored more than thirty books, most of them influential, many groundbreaking. His scholarly output concluded where he had started—on Quakers and Quakerism in the colonial period. In coming full circle, he also came back to one of the things he loved most about his career: collaborating with other scholars to write history. On July 5, 2021, a day before leaving for a weeklong family vacation, Gary could be found at the desk in his home office corresponding with various collaborators and putting the finishing touches on *Our Beloved Friend: The Life and Writings of Anne Emlen Mifflin*. Gary died on July 29, two days after his eighty-eighth birthday.

—Cynthia Shelton

INDEX

Page numbers in italics refer to illustrations and maps. Anne Emlen Mifflin is indicated by "AEM" in index subentries. Correspondence with Anne Emlen Mifflin is indexed by the name of the correspondent.

Abbott, Jennifer, 199n18
Abeel, Henry, 213, 213n49
Abington Monthly Meeting, 245n50
abolitionism, 4–5, 194–99
    AEM and Berry letter to General Assembly of Maryland, 73–75, 197–99
    AEM and Lay letter to New Garden Monthly Meeting, 70, 194–97
    Back to Africa initiative, 117–19, 300–304
    in Britain, 83n18
    in France, 255, 255n81
    in Philadelphia, 191, 191n13
    Quaker women and, 14n28
Abraham (biblical), 220
"Account of a Visit to Some of the Seneca Nation . . ." (AEM and others), 212–25
"Account of My Religious Progress" (AEM), 12, 35, 58, 141–85
    July 3, 1779, 148–49
    July 7, 1779, 149
    July 14, 1779, 150
    November 1779, 150–51
    January 1780, 151–52
    February 1780, 152
    March 1780, 152–53
    May 1780, 153
    March 1781, 153, 154
    April 13, 1781, 154–55
    April 20, 1781, 155–56
    April 27, 1781, 156–57
    May 2, 1781, 157–59
    May 20, 1781, 159
    May 26, 1781, 160–63
    August 1781, 163
    September 1781, 163–64
    October 1781, 164–65
    November 1781, 165
    December 1781, 165–66
    March 1782, 166–68
    September 1782, 169
    December 1782, 169–70
    January 14, 1783, 170
    March 2, 1783, 170–71
    March 16, 1783, 171–73
    March 21, 1783, 173
    March 23, 1783, 173
    June 1783, 173–74
    July 3, 1783, 174
    July 5, 1783, 174
    July 6, 1783, 174
    September 1783, 174–75
    January 18, 1785, 175
    March 9, 1785, 175–76
    April 30, 1785, 176
    May 1, 1785, 176–77
    June 28, 1785, 177–78
    December 1786, 178–81
    October 1788, 181–82
    April 5, 1790, 183–84
    July 1791, 182–83
    March 23, 1792, 184–85
    April 13, 1792, 183
Ackworth School, 248n60
ACS (American Colonization Society), 118, 119
Adams, Abigail, 10
Adams, Charlotte, 40n27
Adams, John, 35, 80–81, 86n63, 90–91, 252n69, 253n74
Addison, Joseph, 27
African Institution, 117
Aimwell School for the Free Instruction of Females, 5, 95
alcohol
    Lemuel Mifflin and, 126–27
    Native peoples and, 202, 202n7, 206n23, 210n36, 215
    Quakers and, 56

Alexander, Ann, 284, 284n70
Alexander, Mary, 284n70
Alexandria Monthly Meeting, 294n108
Allegheny region, 103, 104, 116, 121
Allen, Eleanor. *See* Emlen, Eleanor Allen
Allen, James, 26, 41n35
Allen, Nathaniel, 18
Allen, Richard, 58
American Colonization Society (ACS), 118, 119
Anglican Church, 234n13
Anthony, Susan B., 135
Arch Street Meetinghouse, 13–14n22, 125

Bacon, Margaret Hope, 14n26
  Mothers of Feminism, 13n12
Baltimore Yearly Meeting (BYM), 115, 116, 127n3, 289–90
Bank Street Meetinghouse, 62n25
Baptists, 201, 201n2
Barbados, 79, 93
Barker, Joseph, 307
Barker, Peter, 282, 282n58
Barney, Elizabeth, 109n33
Bartoli, Joseph F., *317*
Battle of Brandywine, 31–32
Battle of Detroit, 122
Battle of Germantown, 42n60, 58
Battle of Whitemarsh, 37
Bauman, Richard: *For the Reputation of Truth*, 111n53
Bell, John, 212n45
Bell, Mary, 104, 112n68
  "Account of a Visit to Some of the Seneca Nation . . ." (AEM and others), 212–25
Benezet, Anthony, 21–22, 23, 25, 39n16, 47, 61n20, 89, 192n18, 194, 254n76
Berry, Joseph, 51, 85n32
Berry, Mary, 4, 74, 79, 84n30, 85n32, 93, 197–99, 251–52, 251n67
Beveridge, David, 24, 40n26
Beveridge, Mary Emlen, 24, 40n27, 125, *311*
Biddle, Owen, *319*
Birch, William, 40n28, *313*
Blecki, Catherine La Courreye: *Milcah Martha Moore's Book* (ed.), 10
Blue Eyes (Seneca chief), 215, 215n53
Blue Sky (Seneca chief), 203, 203n13
Boehm, Jacob, 26

Bolton, Aquila, 290, 290n83, 308
Bolton, Samuel, 290, 290n83, 308
Boudinot, Elias, 224n73
Bownas, Samuel
  Account of the Life, Travel, and Christian Experiences of the Work of the Ministry of Samuel Bownas, 35
  A Description of the Qualifications Necessary to a Gospel Minister, 57
Bradford Monthly Meeting, 244n47
Brandywine, Battle of, 31–32
Branson, Susan: *Those Fiery, Frenchified Dames*, 9
Brayton, Isaac, 277n38
Brayton, Mary, 277n38
Brayton, Patience, 60n3, 84n28, 277, 277n38
Bringhurst, Israel, 23
Brinton, Howard, 40n30
  Friends for 300 Years, 13n7, 60n5
Brissot de Warville, Jacques-Pierre, 57, 65n79, 89, 254, 254nn76–78
  New Travels to the United States of America, 90, 254n78
Brookes, Elizabeth, 40n30, 59, 65n93
Brothertown people, 102
Brown, Kathleen: *Goodwives, Nasty Wenches, and Anxious Patriarchs*, 13n16
Brown, Moses, 12, 95, 107n9, 109n32, 254, 254n76, 277
  AEM letter to (October 3, 1801), 278–80
Bunting, Josiah, 251n65
Burke, Thomas, 12, 30–32, 41n49, 46–48, 125, 142
  AEM letter to (March 3, 1779), 61n17, 232–37
Burkett, William, 187
BYM. *See* Baltimore Yearly Meeting

Cadbury, Henry J.: "Negro Membership," 85n45
Cadwallader, Elizabeth Talbot Sharpless, 307, 307n156
Cadwallader, Reese, 307n156
Calvert, Jane, 28
Canandaigua, 94
Canby, Samuel, 272, 272n18, 289, 289n78
Caresties, Joseph, 295
Carey, Mathew, 254n76
Carlisle, Abraham, 45, 144

Carpenter, Joshua, 20
Casig, James, 293
Catawissa, 103, 106
Catawissa Monthly Meeting, 94
Catherall, Hannah, 25
Catholics, 243n43
Cattle, James, 115, 289, 292n97
Cattle, Jonas, 292–93, 292n97
Cayuga people, 212n45
Cecil Monthly Meeting, 266n107, 279n44
Cedard Creek Monthly Meeting, 296n115
Ceres-town, 103
Chester Monthly Meeting, 79
Chestnut Grove plantation, 51, 60, 66, 76, 88, 107n1
Chestnut Street house, 20, 22–23, 27, 39n18, 87, 92, 125, 135
Chippewa people, 221n66
Churchman, Edward, 298, 298n130
Churchman, George, 34, 90–91, 253n74, 260n90, 260n92
Churchman, John, 192
  An Account of the Gospel Labors and Christian Experiences of a Faithfull Minister of Christ, 186
Clark, Joseph, 224n71, 299
Clark, Samuel, 252, 252n71
Clarkson, Thomas, 65n79
Clinton, Henry, 37
Cobbett, William ("Peter Porcupine"), 89–90, 107n8
  AEM letter to (April 1799), 253–55
Cold Spring Meeting, 83n14
Collins, John, *314*
Collins, Rachel Budd, 196n11
Comfort, Stephen, 279n47
Comly, John & Isaac: *Friends Miscellany*, 134
Committee of Observation and Inspection, 29, 34
Concord Monthly Meeting, 54, 127n8
Continental Congress, 27, 29, 32, 38, 41n40, 41n47, 43, 46
Continental currency, 33–34, 48–54, 145–46, 145n20, 151n46, 163n72, 165n77, 190n12
convincement, 12n3
Cook, James, 218, 218n57
Cook, John, 298
Cooper, David, 260n92

Cope, Benjamin, 113n78
Cope, Rachel, 113n78
Cope, Thomas, 60, 97, 110n42
Cornplanter (Seneca chief), 4, 104, 211–12, 211n41, 213, 284, *317*
Cornwallis, Charles, 33
Cowgill, Clayton, 75, 93
Cowgill, John, 75, 266n106, 267, 267n114
Cow Marsh plantation, 88
Crabtree, Sarah, 2, 11, 108n18, 108n23
  "In the Light and on the Road," 60n3
Cram, Jacob, 217n56
Creek people, 224, 224n72
Cresson, Caleb, 297n123
Cresson, Jane Coxe Evans, 297, 297n123
Cresson, Sarah, 106, 108n27, 137n2
Cresson, Sarah, Jr., 126, 128n13
Crew, Agnes, 296n121
Crew, Joseph, 296n121
Crew, Micajah, 296, 296n121
Croft, Herbert, 231n7
Crotch, William, 290
Crudence, Alexander, 187
Cuffe, Paul, 12, 117–18, 128n17, *318*
  AEM letter to (February 8, 1811), 299–304

Daniel (biblical), 152
Darby, Deborah, 96, 271n12
David (biblical), 263–64
Davis, Timothy, 273, 273n27
Dawes, Ann, 270, 270n9
Day, Stephen M., 129n31, 287–88, 288n75
Deberdt, Esther, 10
Declaration of Independence, 29
Dennis, Matthew: *Seneca Possessed*, 202n6, 206n23, 207n26, 210n36, 217n56
Detroit, Battle of, 122
Dickinson, John, 12, 286, 288
  AEM letter to (December 21, 1787), 247–49
Dickinson, Mary Norris, 247n58
Dickinson, Philemon, 247, 247n57
Dillwyn, George, 144, 144n18
Dillwyn, William, 117
Dorsey, Bruce: *Reforming Men and Women*, 9, 14n28, 65n79, 109n35
Drinker, Abigail, 282n58
Drinker, Elizabeth, 10, 38, 45, 56, 61n9, 62n25, 125, 134, 143n12

Index | 343

Drinker, Henry, 56, 59, 77, 125, 134, 155n56
Drinker, John, 29, 77, *312*
  Observations on the Late Popular Measures, 41n44
Drinker, Joseph, 77
Dryden, John, 27
Duck Creek Monthly Meeting, 67, 82n3
Dunkers, 26
Dunn, Mary Maples, 8, 10, 14n24

Eastern Shore of Maryland Meetings, 14n23, 51
Eddy, Thomas, 201n4, 202n9, 269–70n1
Edward, Christiana, 23
Ellicott, Elias, 294n102
Ellicott, George, 128n23, 293–94, 294n102
Emlen, Anne (niece), 270, 270n10, 272, 272n17, 273, 274, 275
Emlen, Anne Reckless (mother), 2, 17, 21, 29, 34, 45, 46, 48, 50, 89, 92, 93, 103, 114–15, 119–20, 122–23, 126, 132
  AEM letter to (June 3, 1801), 269–71
  AEM letter to (June 8, 1801), 271–73
  AEM letter to (June 26, 1801), 274–75
  AEM letter to (June 30, 1801), 275–76
  AEM letter to (July 21, 1801), 277–78
  AEM letter to (September 1802), 280–82
  AEM letter to (October 6, 1802), 282–83
  AEM letter to (October 16, 1805), 289–91
  AEM letter to (October 28, 1805), 291–93
  AEM letter to (September 19, 1810), 293–95
  AEM letter to (September 30, 1810), 295–97
  AEM letter to (October 13, 1810), 297–99
  AEM letter to (September 23, 1813), 305–6
  AEM letter to (November 12, 1813), 307–8
Emlen, Caleb (brother), 23, 32, 49–50, 62n30
Emlen, Caleb (great uncle), 20
Emlen, Eleanor Allen (great grandmother), 18
Emlen, George, II (grandfather), 19–20
Emlen, George, III (father), 17, 21, 24, 26–28
Emlen, George, IV (brother), 23, 49–50, 270n10, 272, 272n17, 282, 282n57
Emlen, George (great grandfather), 18–19
Emlen, Hannah Garrett (step great grandmother), 18
Emlen, James, Jr. (nephew), 135, 138n12
Emlen, James (brother), 2, 19, 23, 81, 86n64, 88, 94, 97, 110n46, 110n48, 132, 135
Emlen, John Thompson, 135, 138n11
Emlen, Joseph (brother), 49, 50, 62n33, 132
Emlen, Joshua (great uncle), 19, 20
Emlen, Margaret. *See* Howell, Margaret Emlen
Emlen, Mary Heath (grandmother), 20–22, 24, 28, 39n12, 137n2
Emlen, Mary (sister). *See* Beveridge, Mary Emlen
Emlen, Mary Warder (sister in-law), 62n30
Emlen, Samuel (brother), 69, 132
Emlen, Samuel (cousin), 51, 81, 153n51
Emlen, Samuel (great uncle), 19
Emlen, Samuel (nephew), 126
Emlen, Samuel, Jr. (cousin of George Emlen, III), 32
Emlen, Sarah Foulke Farquhar, 138n12
English Civil War (1642–51), 152n47
Evans, Robert, 297
Ezekiel (biblical), 191, 191n14

Fairer, David, 231n7
Falls Monthly Meeting, 56
Fatherly, Sarah: *Gentlewomen and Learned Ladies*, 9
Feast of the Tabernacles, 206, 206n21, 220
Female Society for the Relief and Employment of the Poor, 5, 95
Fergusson, Elisabeth Graeme, 9–10
First Continental Congress, 33
Fishbourne, Thomas, 230, 230n3
Fishbourne, William and Mary, 230n3
Fisher, Sally, 42n66, 49
Fisher, Samuel Rowland, 29, 60n7
Fisher, Sarah Logan, 33, 36, 62n27, 125–26
Fisher, Thomas, 29
Fisher, William, 270
Forman, Elaine Crane: *Diary of Elizabeth Drinker* (ed.), 10
Forten, James, 130n49
Fort Stanwix, Second Treaty of (1784), 211, 211n40

Fothergill, John, 248, 248n60
Fox, George, 6, 7, 63n52, 92, 127n3
Fox, William, 83nn17–18
Franklin, Benjamin, 19, 68, 235n16
  "Nature and Necessity of a Paper Currency," 149n38
Free African Society, 58
free blacks
  Back to Africa initiative and, 117–19, 300–304
  in Maryland, 85n38
  in Philadelphia, 58, 65n84
Free Instruction of African Females, 5
Free Produce Movement, 4, 70, 136, 196n10
Free Quakers, 29, 41n45
Friends Burying Ground, 45
Friends Miscellany, 134
Frost, J. William, 133, 175n106
  Quaker Family, 13n8, 137n4

Gainsborough tract, 88
Galloway, Elizabeth, 246, 246n52
Galloway, Grace Growden, 38, 45–46, 61nn12–13, 246, 246nn52–53
Galloway, Joseph, 33, 45–46, 121, 129n36, 246, 246nn52–53
Gannet, Cinthia, 3
Garrett, Hannah. *See* Emlen, Hannah Garrett
Garvin, James, 23
Genesinguhta (Old Town), 4, 104
Gérard de Rayneval, Alexandre, 61nn15–16
Germantown, Battle of, 42n60, 58
Gerona, Carla: *Night Journeys*, 150n41
Gibbons, James, 286n73
Gideon (biblical), 63n52
Gilbert, John, 109n31
Gilbert, Mary, 95, 103, 106, 109n31, 112n68, 212, 271, 275, 277, 279–80, 280n48, 284
Gilbert, Robert, 280, 280n48
Gill, Joseph, 253n73
Ginney, John, 294
Godbeer, Richard, 41n48
  World of Trouble, 10
Goshen Monthly Meeting, 62n34, 245n49
Great Meetinghouse (Philadelphia), 13n22, 22, 62n25, *310*
Greeble, Sarah, 284, 284n70
Gregory, John, 231n7

Gregory, Susanna, 100–101, 111n54, 214n51
Grellet, Stephen, 271, 271n12
Griffitts, Hannah, 27, 38, 230n5
Grimke, Angelina, 199n18
Gross, David M.: *American Quaker War Tax Resistance*, 186n1

Haines, Reuben, 130n38
Half-Moon Valley, 103
Hall, John, 270, 271, 279
Hampton Institute for Industrial Arts, 138n11
Handsome Lake (Seneca prophet), 4, 104, 203n13, 284n65
Harper, Mary, 115, 290, 293
Harris, Martha, 49, 62nn25–26, 143–45, 145n22, 168, 172, 172n96, 244–45, 245n49
Harrison, Sarah, 108n27
Hartshorn, Mary, 294n108
Harvey, Widow, 296
Hassell, William, 23
Haviland, Margaret, 109n36
Hawkins, Benjamin, 211, 211n38
Heath, Mary. *See* Emlen, Mary Heath
Heath, Robert, 20
Heath, Susanna, 20
Henderson, Desiree: "Impudent Fellow Came in Swareing," 141n3
Herbert, Amanda: "Companions in Preaching and Suffering," 14n29
Heyrick, Elisabeth, 85n33
Historical Society of Pennsylvania, 2, 135
Hobbes, Thomas, 5
Holcomb, Julie L., 83n17
Holgate, Jacob, 129n35
Holland Land Company, 112n72, 222n70, 284n63
Holliday, Robert, 110n48
Hoopes, Joshua, 244, 244n47
Hoops, Adam, 283–84, 284n63
Hopewell Monthly Meeting, 127n11
Hopkins, Samuel, 265n105
Horne, Susanna, 300, 300n135
Howe, William, 32, 34–35, 37
Howell, Ann, 109n30, 181n115
Howell, Arthur, 94
Howell, Joseph, 279
Howell, Margaret Emlen (sister), 125, 171, 270n8, 273, 275, 283

Howell, Samuel, 107n2, 270, 270n8
Hudson Monthly Meeting, 102
Hughes, Job, 52
Hunn, Jonathan, 107n2
Hunt, John, 77, 86n47, 125, 130n41, 130n53, 133, 192n18
Hunt, Nathan, 290
Hunt, Rachel, 62n34

Illinois Confederacy, 221n66
Independence Hall, 20, 97
indigo dye, 4, 70, 83n18, 196, 196nn10–12
Ingram, Richard: *The Life and Adventures of William Cobbett*, 107n8
Ireland, Owen S.: *Sentiments of a British-American Woman*, 10
Iroquois people, 12, 97, 98, 104, 110n46, 207n27, 283n60
Isaiah (biblical), 189

Jackson, Halliday, 213n47, 220n65, 283n62
Jackson, Hannah, 100–102, 111n54, 113n78, 214n51
Jackson, William, 92, 121, 122, 129n37, 266, 266n108, 272, 272n115
James, Benjamin, 291
James, Sydney, 56
James, William, 291
Jay, John, 201n4
Jefferson, Thomas, 117, 118, 121, 303–4
Jenuchshadago (Burnt House), 104
Jeremiah (biblical), 63n52
Jewett, Susanna, 298
Johns, Elizabeth, 256, 256n83
Johnson, John, 290, 292
Jonah (biblical), 264
Jonathan (biblical), 264
Jones, Absalom, 58
Jones, Gabriel, 296, 296n119
Jones, James, 270
Jones, Rebecca, 25
Jones, Richard, 270, 270n7
Jones, Robert, 274
Jones, Rufus, 11
Jordan, Richard, 109n38
Josephus, Titus Flavius, 187
Judge, Hugh, 279, 279n47, 298

Kerber, Linda, 10
King William's War (1689–97), 192n16

Kirkbride, Hannah, 98–99, 100, 111n49
  "Relation of a Visit Made to the Indians in 1802" (with AEM), 200–212
Kirkland, Samuel, 101, 201n2, 207n24
Klepp, Susan
  The Diary of Hannah Callender Sansom (ed.), 10
  Revolutionary Conceptions, 9
Knott, Sarah: *Sensibility and the American Revolution*, 9
Knyphausen, Wilhelm, 33

Lapham, Abraham, 204–5, 204n16
Larson, Rebecca, 108n16, 119
  Daughters of Light, 13n12, 13n15, 108n23, 129n27
Lauden, E., 160
Lay, Baptist, 83n14
Lay, Benjamin, 61n20, 194, 244–45, 244n48, 245n50
Lay, Philena, 70, 72, 73, 82n6, 194–97, 194nn1–3
Lermon, Richard, 270, 270n3
Letchworth, John, 112n68, 212n45, 284
  "Account of a Visit to Some of the Seneca Nation . . ." (AEM and others), 212–25
Lewis, Samuel, 130n38
Library Company, 19–20
Lightfoot, Susanna, 7–8, 50–54, 62n34, 137n2, 146, 154, 154n54, 157–59, 240, 240n37, 315
Lightfoot, Thomas, 50–51, 54, 62n34, 145–46, 145n24, 150n42, 159, 160, 172, 239
Lindley, Jacob, 55, 90–91, 97, 253n74
Lindman, Janet
  "Beyond the Meetinghouse," 14n28, 137n3
  "To Have a Gradual Weaning," 14n29
Logan, George, 118, 300
Logan, James, 118
London Yearly Meeting, 9, 67
Lossing, Benson J.: *Pictorial Field-Book of the Revolution*, 42n68
Lowry, Robert Wadsworth, 161n63
Loyalists, 28, 34, 38, 45
Luff, Nathaniel, 81
Lynch, John, 118, 128n15, 303, 303n142
Lynch, Thomas, 301
Lyon, Patrick, 130n38

Mackenzie, Alexander, 218, 218n58, 220
Madison, Dolley, 291n93, 304, 304n145
Madison, James, 128n24, 302, 302n141, 304, 304n145
Malcolm, James Peller, 40n28
manumission of enslaved persons, 23–24, 40n22, 85n32, 260n93, 301–2
See also free blacks
maps
    Journey from Philadelphia to Lake Simcoe, Canada (August-September 1802), *99*
    Journey to the Seneca villages along the Allegheny River (October-November 1803), *99*
Marietta, Jack: *Reformation of American Quakerism*, 39n16, 137n3
Marshall, Christopher, 36
Marsh Plantation, 107n4
Martens, John, 270–71, 270n11
Maryland General Meeting, 63n42, 287
Maryland State Assembly, 4, 73–75, 136, *316*
    AEM and Berry antislavery letter to, 197–99
Maryland Yearly Meeting, 127n3
Mason, George, 149, 149n37
Massey, Isaac, 172, 172n97
Maxey, David: *A Portrait of Elizabeth Willing Powel*, 10
McDonald, Archibald, 219n60
McGuire, Thomas, 42n60
McKim, John, 115, 252, 290–91, 290n86
Mekeel, Arthur, 41n45
Memorials Concerning Deceased Friends (1786), 21, 137n2
Mennonites, 26, 170, 170n93
Merrell, James H.: *Into the American Woods*, 202n6
Meschianza festivity, 37–38, 47
Methodists, 148, 148n35, 160–61, 160n62, 161n63
Micah (biblical), 189
Miers, Cynthia, 77
Mifflin, Ann (stepdaughter). *See* Raisin, Ann Mifflin
Mifflin, Anne (cousin), 96
Mifflin, Anne Emlen
    adolescence of, 24–27
    biographical overview, 17–138; (1775–1778), 17–42; (1778–1788), 43–65; (1788–1798), 66–86; (1798–1804), 87–113; (1805–1816), 114–31
    births of children, 69–70, 71–72, 73, 84n28
    childhood of, 21–24
    Continental currency and, 48–54
    death of, 125
    education of, 25
    estate of, 126
    family history, 18–21
    legacy of, 132–37
    marriage to Warner, 58–60
    ministry work of, 54–55, 66–75, 84n25, 115–27
    Native American ministry trips by, 97–107
    poetry of, 30–32
    property holdings in Ohio, 130n40
    property holdings in Philadelphia, 144, 144n16, 152n48, 308, 308n157
    Revolutionary War and, 27–38, 44–48
Mifflin, Anne Emlen, writings of
    "Account of My Religious Progress" (MRP), 12, 35, 58, 141–85
    "Notes on Quaker Doctrine," 35
    "Notes on the Bible," 35
    "Some Notes on the Payment of Taxes Appropriated for Military Purposes," 36, 186–93
Mifflin, Daniel (brother-in-law), 107n2, 265, 267, 298n127
Mifflin, Daniel (father-in-law), 59, 75, 83n14, 181n115
Mifflin, Debby Howell (Warner's sister in-law), 298, 298n127
Mifflin, Elizabeth (stepdaughter), 75, 93
Mifflin, Elizabeth (Warner's first wife), 51
Mifflin, John R. (cousin), 124
Mifflin, Joseph, Jr. (cousin), 121
Mifflin, Joshua Howell (nephew), 298, 298n127
Mifflin, Lemuel (son), 71–72, 81–82, 84n28, 87–89, 91–93, 115, 120–25, 133–34, 273, 290, 290n81, 299, 307–8
    AEM letter to (October 25, 1799), 256–65
    AEM on birth of, 184–85
    death of, 126–27, 131n57
Mifflin, Lloyd (cousin), 121
Mifflin, Mary Ann (daughter), 73, 75, 84n28

Mifflin, Mary Pusey (Warner's stepmother), 77, 82n6
Mifflin, Samuel Emlen (son), 69–70, 81, 87–89, 91–93, 115, 120–23, 126, 129n36, 133–34, 271–73, 271n14, 283, 299, 305
  AEM letter to (October 25, 1799), 256–65
  AEM on birth of, 183–84
Mifflin, Sarah (stepdaughter). *See* Neall, Sarah Mifflin (stepdaughter)
Mifflin, Susanna (stepdaughter), 75, 79, 81, 82, 266, 266n106, 267, 267n114
  AEM letter to (August 4, 1788), 249–51
Mifflin, Thomas (cousin), 121
Mifflin, Warner
  AEM letter to sons on life of (October 25, 1799), 91, 256–65
  AEM's defense of legacy of, 12
  AEM's first meeting of, 145n24
  antislavery movement and, 194, 198n15
  Brissot and, 57
  courting of AEM, 58–60, 180, 180n111, 181n115
  death of, 81–82, 134, 263
  estate of, 88–89, 107nn1–2, 261–62, 261n95
  health of, 78–81, 86n57
  marriage to AEM, 4, 58–60
  marriage to Elizabeth, 51
  Native American ministry work and, 110n46, 110n48
  Revolutionary War and, 34
  scholarship on, 134–35
  travels of, 67–68, 74, 75–76, 96
Mifflin, Warner, writings of
  The Defence of Warner Mifflin Against Aspersions cast on him on Account of his Endeavors To promote Righteousness, Mercy, and Peace, 78, 259
  A Serious Expostulation with the Members of the House of Representatives of the United States, 72, 84n23
Mifflin, Warner, Jr., 81–82, 88, 93, 125–26, 250, 250n64, 267n111, 281, 281n56
Millar, Peter: *Dissertation on Man's Fall*, 41n35
Miller, Marla R.: *Betsy Ross and the Making of America*, 10
Moore, Ann Herbert, 164, 164n76
Moore, Milcah Martha, 10

Moravians, 26
Morgan, John, 52
Morgan, William, 294
Morris, Abigail Dorsey, 172n101
Morris, Deborah, 61n13
Morris, John, 171n101, 172
Morris, Robert, 23, 284n63
Morris, Sarah, 230n5
Morton, Robert, 230n2
Moses (biblical), 63n52, 142, 204, 259
Moss, Philena, 83n14
Mott, Dr., 246
Mott, Lucretia, 85n33, 135
Mott, Richard, 279, 279n47
MRP. *See* "Account of My Religious Progress"
Muhlenberg, Frederick, 36
Muncy Monthly meeting, 94
Munsey, 103
Munsy-Catawissa Monthly Meeting, 123
Murderkill Monthly Meeting, 129n29, 252n72, 267, 267n114
Murderkill Women's Monthly Meeting, 67, 70, 73, 82n3, 86n48, 279n44
Murray, William Vans, 252n69

Native peoples, 4, 36, 87, 94, 97–107, *99–100*, 115, 200–225
  "Account of a Visit to Some of the Seneca Nation . . ." (AEM and others), 212–25
  "Relation of a Visit Made to the Indians in 1802" (AEM and Kirkbride), 200–212
  See also specific groups
Neale, Samuel, 158n60, 246, 246n55
Neall, Daniel, 120, 125, 129nn28–29, 138n10
Neall, Sarah Mifflin (stepdaughter), 81, 89, 92, 120, 125, 126, 129nn28–29, 138n10
neutrality, 28–30
Newby, Axam/Exum, 297, 297n122
New Garden Monthly Meeting, 12, 70
Newgate State Prison, 269, 269n1
New Quaker Meetinghouse, *319*
New York Yearly Meeting, 128n13
Nicholites, 77–78, 79, 86n50
Nichols, Joseph, 86n50
Nine Partners Boarding School, 275n33
Nine Partners Meeting, 102, 275, 275n33
Norris, Charles, Sr., 288n76
Norris, Isaac, 288, 288n76

Norris, Mary Parker, 288n76
Norris, Sarah Logan, 196n11
North Carolina Yearly Meeting, 118, 128n22
North Wales Meeting, 49
Northwest Territory, 116, 127n9, 307–8
   See also Ohio
Norton, Mary Beth, 10
   Liberty's Daughters, 137n3

Occum, Samson, 201n2
O'Connell, Pat, 224n71
Ohio
   AEM property in, 126, 130n40
   AEM trip to, 122–24, 127n6, 292, 307–8
   Lemuel Mifflin in, 122–23
   Native Americans in, 172n98, 211n38
   Quaker migration to, 115–16, 307
Oneida people, 97, 98–102, 111n55, 111n61, 113n78, 200–212, 214n51, 222, 222n67
Oriske village, 101, 102
Ottawa people, 221n66
Ousterhout, Anne: *The Most Learned Woman in America*, 9

pacifism, 28–30, 186–93
   See also war taxes
Paine, Thomas, 127n2, 254n76, 299, 299n132
   Common Sense, 29
Parrish, Anne, Jr., 95
Parrish, John, 12, 85n36, 97, 107n9, 110n48, 199n19, 260n91
   AEM letter to (March 1799), 251–53
   AEM letter to (November 16, 1799), 265–66
   AEM letter to (December 6, 1799), 266–68
   Remarks on the Slavery of Black People, 128n17
Parsons, James, 270
Parsons, Samuel, 275, 275n32
Paul (biblical), 63n52, 148, 151
Payne, John, 304n145
Payton, Catharine, 158, 158n60
Peale, Charles Willson, 24, 40n27, 46, 209n33, *311*
Peisley, Mary, 158, 158n60, 246n55
Pelham, 102
Pemberton, Hannah, 26, 27, 48, 97, 237n28, 294
   AEM letter to (March 6, 1776), 229–31

Pemberton, Hannah Lloyd, 229n1
Pemberton, Israel, Sr., 237n28
Pemberton, Israel, Jr., 238n28
Pemberton, James, 59–60, 64n75, 77, 97, 229n1, 238n28, 300
Pemberton, John, 12, 54, 55, 237n28, 246n51
   AEM letter to (June 12, 1781), 239–41
   letter to AEM (June 6, 1781), 237–39
   letter to AEM (January 15, 1785), 242–46
Pemberton, Phoebe, 97
Pemberton, Rachel Read, 237n28
Penet, Pierre, 203n14
Penington, Isaac: *The Jew outward, being a glass for the professors of this age*, 149n36
Penn, William, 6, 61n19, 146, 151, 173
   Address to Protestants upon the present conjuncture, 19
Pennsylvania Abolition Society (PAS), 58, 68, 118
"Peter Porcupine." *See* Cobbett, William
Pharisees, 187, 187n7
Pharsalia, 96
Philadelphia Armstrong Association, 138n11
Philadelphia Hose Company, 121, 130n38
Philadelphia Meeting for Elders and Ministers, 5, 67, 71, 93–94
Philadelphia Meeting for Sufferings, 5, 28, 73
Philadelphia Monthly Meeting (PMM), 8, 24, 41n45, 62n33, 65n90, 93–94, 114, 124
Philadelphia Museum, 209, 209n33
Philadelphia National Bank, 129n35
Philadelphia Quarterly Meeting (PQM), 9, 123
   Committee to Inquire into the Conditions of Freed Slaves, 65n84
Philadelphia Society for Free Instruction of Indigent Boys, 120
Philadelphia Women's Monthly Meeting (PWMM), 8, 20, 57–58, 62n30, 64n68, 113n80, 126
Philadelphia Yearly Meeting (PYM), 5, 9, 13n19, 22, 23, 28, 34, 48, 62n30, 76–77, 78, 80–81, 106, 286
   Indian Committee for Promoting the Improvement and Gradual Civilization of the Indian Natives, 97–98, 100, 101, 103, 110n47, 112n63
Phillips, William, 158n60

Index | 349

Physick, Adriana Haynes, 298, 298n131
Physick, Henry, 298, 298n131
Physick, Phillip Syng, 298n131
Pierce, John, 213n47
Pine Street Meetinghouse, 62n25
Pitcher, Molly, 10
Pleasant, Tarton W., 296, 296n115
Pleasant, William, 296
poetry, 30–32, 232n8
Pole, John, *318*
Pope, Alexander, 27
Potowatomy people, 221, 221n66
Poulson, Zachariah, 132
Poulson's Daily Advertiser, 132, 134
Poultney, Widow, 292
Powel, Elizabeth Willing, 10
Premo, Terri L.: *Winter Friends*, 129n27
Priad, William, 296
Prior, Edmund, 201n4, 202n9
Providence Preparative Meeting, 307n155
Purchase Monthly Meeting, 279n47
Puritans, 5

Queen, Ann, 23
Queen Anne's War (1701–13), 192n17

Raisin, Abraham, 267, 267n112
Raisin, Ann Mifflin (stepdaughter), 75, 266, 266n107, 279, 279n44
Raisin, Warner, 266n107, 267, 267n111, 279n44
Rawle, Anna "Peggy," 54
Reckless, Anne. *See* Emlen, Anne Reckless
Rediker, Marcus, 61n20
Redman, Samuel, 278
Redstone Quarterly Meeting, 116, 127n4, 289n80, 307n155
"Relation of a Visit Made to the Indians in 1802" (AEM and Kirkbride), 200–212
Richardson, John, 192
Richardson, Joseph, 109n28
Richardson, Ruth, 94, 109n28, 109n30
Ridgely, Ann, 89
Ridgely, Nicholas, 89
Ripley, Dorothy, 96–97, 110nn41–42, 129n31
  AEM letter to (May 31, 1804), 285–89
Roaring Creek Monthly Meeting, 123–24
Roberts, John, 45, 144
Roberts, Moses, 52

Rodney, Caesar, 81
Rodney, Thomas, 81
Rogers, Elisabeth, 181n115
Rogers, Timothy, 281n54
Ross, Betsy, 10
Ross, John Gray, 277n38
Rotch/Roacks/Resch, Sylvia, 277n40, 278
Rotch/Roacks/Resch, Thomas, 277, 277n40
Rotch/Roacks/Resch, William, 64n75, 95, 109n33, 273, 273n23, 275n31, 276
Routh, Martha, 86n48
Rowland, Rachael, 128n13
Rush, Benjamin, 86n60, 92, 254n76
Rutledge, Edward, 29, 85n40

Salem settlement, 123
Sands, David, 155, 155n56, 164, 168
Sandy Spring Meeting, 59, 289, 289n77
Sansom, Hannah Callender, 10
Savery, Thomas, 172, 172n99, 221
Savery, William, 97, 110n45
Savery, William, Jr., 172, 172n98
Schofield, Issachar, 294, 294n105
Schwenkfelders, 26
Scott, Job, 13n7, 85n35
Scriptural citations
  Genesis 37–49, 167
  Exodus 12–24, 219n62
  Exodus 14:15, 257
  Leviticus 21:19–21, 63n53
  Numbers 22, 191, 191n15
  Deuteronomy 27:16, 150
  2 Samuel 1–2, 183n121
  2 Samuel 1:21, 195
  2 Samuel 1:26, 264
  2 Samuel 2:30, 196
  Job 17:9, 63n40
  Job 29:13–17, 259
  Psalms 2:12, 236
  Psalms 27:10, 263
  Proverbs 1:26, 196
  Proverbs 19:14, 179
  Proverbs 30:9, 262
  Ecclesiastes 12:12, 129n32, 230n4
  Isaiah 1:27, 165
  Isaiah 5:4, 195
  Isaiah 5:26, 236
  Isaiah 9:16, 243, 243n44
  Isaiah 33:16, 242n41
  Isaiah 49:5, 155

Isaiah 49:23, 236
Isaiah 65:8, 243
Jeremiah 6:16, 184
Ezekiel 14:4, 191
Daniel 2:36–44, 152
Joel 2:17, 195
Jonah 2:7, 264
Micah 4:4, 237
Haggai 1:4, 193
Malachi 1:9, 189
2 Esdras 13:29–45, 218–19, 218n59
Matthew 5:34, 60n5
Matthew 13:31–32, 151n45
Matthew 18:20, 162
Matthew 22:15–22, 186n1
Matthew 24:6, 190
Matthew 25:30, 221
Matthew 25:35–36, 146
Mark 4:30–32, 151n45
Mark 12:13–17, 186n1
Luke 2:4, 258
Luke 6:34, 235
Luke 9:23, 233
Luke 11:47, 189
Luke 13:18–19, 151n45
Luke 20:20–26, 186n1
Luke 21:9, 190
John 1:33, 180
John 4:10, 274
John 14:27, 236, 258
John 14:27–28, 264
John 15:5, 215
John 16:2, 189
John 16:13, 236
Acts 2:44–45, 200n1
Acts 4:32, 200n1
Acts 13:41, 148
Acts 13:46, 161
Acts 16:27, 148
Acts 17:26, 301
Acts 21:8, 162
Acts 21:9, 162
Romans 8:2, 257
Romans 13:1–7, 151n46
1 Corinthians 14:34, 162
2 Corinthians 12:9, 181n113
Ephesians 4, 240n35
Philippians 2:4–5, 262
1 Thessalonians 5:17, 161
1 Timothy 2:2, 187

1 Timothy 4:8, 145
Philemon 4:6, 183
Hebrews 11:23, 142
Hebrews 12:25, 257
James 4:17, 146
1 Peter 2:13, 187n8
Revelations 13:8, 169
Revelations 13:12, 151
Revelations 17:14, 64n70
Revelations 18:7, 236
Second Treaty of Fort Stanwix (1784), 211, 211n40
Sellers, Charles Coleman, 40n27
Seneca people, 97, 103–6, 110n48, 211
  "Account of a Visit to Some of the Seneca Nation . . ." (AEM and others), 212–25
Sergeant, John, Jr., 201n2, 202n8, 220n63
Seven Years' War (1756–63), 17, 111n53, 192n18, 237n28
Sharp, Granville, 65n79, 117, 300
Sharpless, Joshua, 213n47
Shenandoah (chief), 101
Shippen, Joseph, 23
Shrewsbury Monthly Meeting, 113n80
Sidwell Friends School, 293n99
Sierra Leone colony, 117, 118, 294, 294n104, 302, 303–4, 303n143
Simcoe, John Graves, 281n51
Simmons, Henry, 201n3, 205n18, 213n47
simplicity, Quaker commitment to, 6, 20–21, 40n27, 56–57, 70, 164n74, 192n18, 233, 242n39, 272n21
Six [Iroquois] Nations, 104
  See also Iroquois people
slavery. *See* abolitionism; manumission of enslaved persons
Smith, Benjamin, 172, 172n100
Smith, Deborah Morris, 172n97
Smith, I. A., 187
Smith, Robert
  The Friend: A Religious and Literary Journal, 135
  "Relics of the Past," 135
Smith, William Loughton, 85n40
Snowden, Samuel Thomas, 294, 294n103
Société des Amis des Noirs (Society of Friends of the Blacks), 57
Society for Effecting the Abolition of the Slave Trade, 65n79, 83n18

Society for the Free Instruction of African Females, 95
Society for the Free Instruction of Females of Color, 5, 95
Society for the Propagation of Christian Knowledge, 201n2
Soderlund, Jean, 10, 82n4
Quakers and Slavery, 14n28
"Some Notes on the Payment of Taxes Appropriated for Military Purposes" (AEM), 36, 186–93
Southern Quarterly Meeting (SQM), 67, 70, 73, 78, 82n5, 84n24, 110n47, 251n66
Spenser, Edmund, 30
Stabler, Edward, 294, 294n108
Stackhouse, Thomas: *New History of the Holy Bible*, 186
Stamford Quarterly Meeting, 102
Stanton, Elizabeth Cady, 135
Stephen Munson Day School, 93
Stevenson, Sarah, 279, 279n47
Stewardson, Thomas, 272, 272n20
Stockbridge people, 102
Strahan, William, 246n56
sugar boycotts, 83n18, 196n10
sumptuary laws, 48, 234n14, 235n16
Swatzler, David, 222n69
Friend Among the Senecas, 217n56
Swayne, Joel, 213n47, 283n62
AEM letter to (February 25, 1804), 283–85

Tarter, Michele Lise: "Reading a Quaker's Book," 13n9
taxes. *See* war taxes
Taylor, Bishop: *Great Exemplar*, 187
Teacle, John, 294
Third Haven General Meeting, 51
Thomas, John, 283n62
AEM letter to (February 25, 1804), 283–85
Thomas, Lamont: *Rise to Be a People*, 128n17
Thompson, Susan Trotter, 135
Thornton, James, 176–77, 176n108, 260n92
Three Tuns Tavern, 18–19
Tiro, Karim, 111n55, 111n61, 203n11
Todd, John, 304n145
Todd, Thomas, 291n93

Tolles, Frederick, 7
Meeting House and Counting House, 14n23, 170n93
Quakers and Atlantic Culture, 13n14
Tonawanda reservation, 102
Toogood, Anna Coxey, 23
Toronto (York), 102
Treaty of Vincennes (1803), 220n64
Tucker, St. George, 302, 302n140
Tunesassa, 104
Tuscarora reservation, 102, 207n27
Tuscarora War (1711–13), 207n27
Tyler, John, Sr., 119, 128n24, 302
Tyler, John, Jr., 128n24

Ulrich, Laurel Thatcher: *Good Wives*, 84n29
Upper Canada, 12
usury, 235, 235n17
Uwchlan Meeting, 62n34

Valentine, Rachel Edge, 156n58
Valentine, Robert, 136, 156–57, 156n58, 164–65
Valiant Sixty, 234n13
Vaugus, Jacob, 308, 308n157
Vaux, Roberts, 130n38
Vincennes Treaty (1803), 220n64
Virginia Yearly Meeting, 301

Wallace, Anthony F. C.: *Death and Rebirth*, 213n49, 221n66
Waln, Nicholas, 270, 270n4
Walnut Street Jail (Philadelphia), 270n1
Warder, Ann, 56
war taxes
Continental currency and, 37
PYM on, 164n75
refusal to pay, 34–35, 37, 48–49, 146n26, 152, 170, 190n11
Seven Years' War and, 192nn17–18
"Some Notes on the Payment of Taxes Appropriated for Military Purposes" (AEM), 36, 186–93
Wartshorn, William, 294
Washington, George, 34–36, 68, 97, 211–12
Washington, George Steptoe, 291n93
Washington, Lucy Payne, 291, 291n93
Wells, Robert: "Family Size and Fertility Control," 84n29

Wesley, Charles, 160n62
Wesley, John, 160n62
Western Quarterly Meeting (WQM), 5, 50, 67, 128n22, 145, 145n24, 265
West River Meeting, 63n42
Westtown Friends School, 5, 92–93, 95, 108n18, 108n25, 138n12, 272, 281, 281n56, 285–88, *314*
Wharton, Joseph, 37
Wheelock, Eleazar, 201n2
Whitby, Daniel, 187
White, Nathaniel, 116, 127n6, 292, 307
White, Phebe Smedley, 292
White, William, 127n6, 292
White Dog ceremony (Senecas), 217, 217n56
Whitemarsh, Battle of, 37
Whitemarsh home, 26, 36–37
White Oak Swamp Monthly Meeting, 296n115
Wiley, Penrose, 112n68, 225
William and Mary College, 302, 302n141
Wilmington Monthly Meeting, 272n18, 279n47
Wilmington Packet (boat), 272, 272n16

Wilson, Lisa
  History of Stepfamilies in Early America, 182n116, 250n63
  Life After Death, 137n3
Wilson, Samuel and Rebecca, 111n49
Wissahickon Boys Club, 138n11
Wood, James, 119, 128n24
Wood, Nicholas P., 85n36, 199n19
Woolman, John, 13n7, 39n16, 47, 61n20, 127n11, 143n11, 192, 194, 232n8
Wright, Susanna, 27
Wulf, Karin
  The Diary of Hannah Callender Sansom (ed.), 10
  Milcah Martha Moore's Book (ed.), 10
  Not All Wives, 9

yellow fever, 78, 79–81, 84n24, 90, 252n70, 281n55, 282, 282n59
York (Toronto), 102
Young, Rebecca, 96
Younger, Karen, 128n17

Zane, Sarah, 118, 123, 126, 128n22, 294–95, 301, 305–6

www.ingramcontent.com/pod-product-compliance
Lightning Source LLC
Chambersburg PA
CBHW022027290426
44109CB00014B/781